SUPERMAN BATMAN

PUBLIC ENEMIES

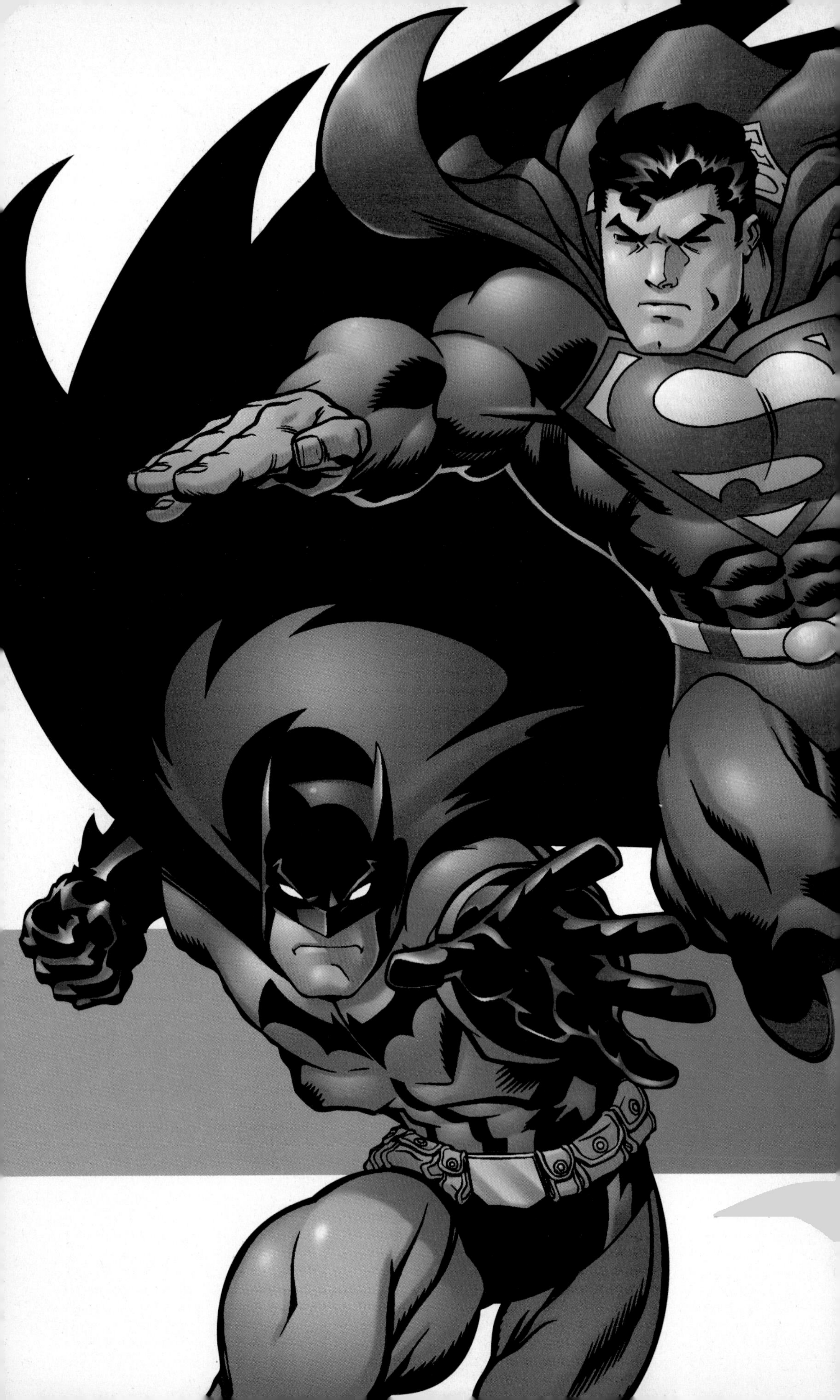

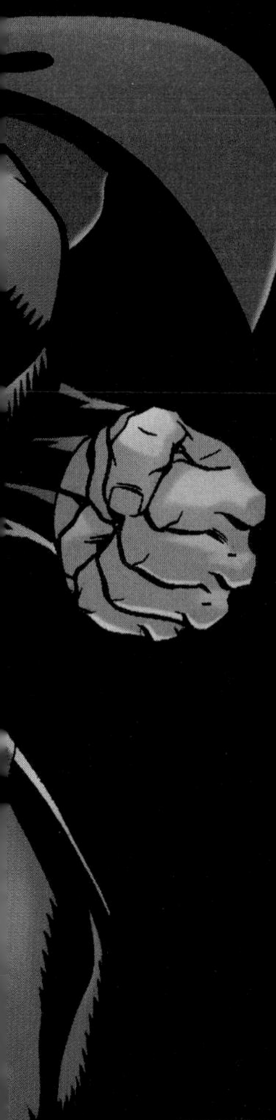

Jeph Loeb
Writes

Ed McGuinness
Pencils

Dexter Vines
Inks

Dave Stewart
Colors

Richard Starkings
Letters

Tim Sale with Mark Chiarello
Art and colors on pages 4 and 5

Ed McGuinness & Dexter Vines
Original Series Covers

Batman created by Bob Kane

Superman created by Jerry Siegel and Joe Shuster

SUPERMAN BATMAN

PUBLIC ENEMIES

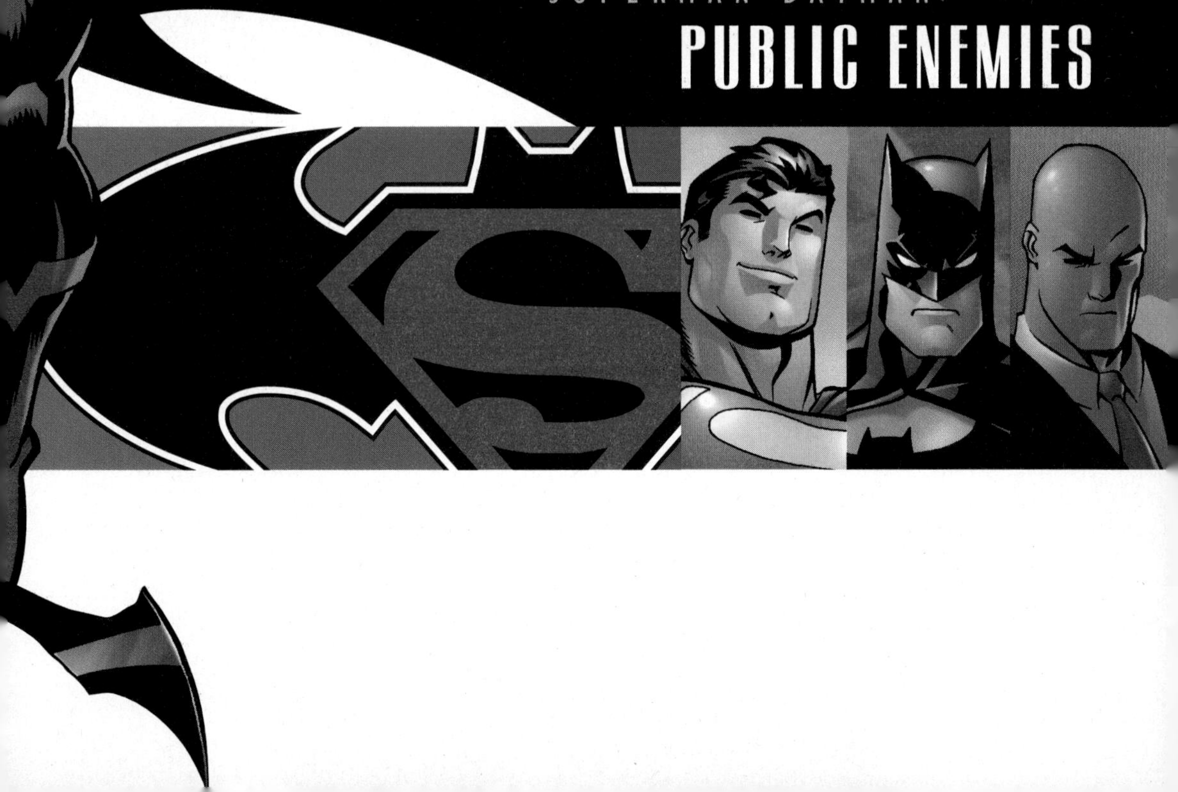

When Clark met Bruce
A TALE FROM THE DAYS OF SMALLVILLE

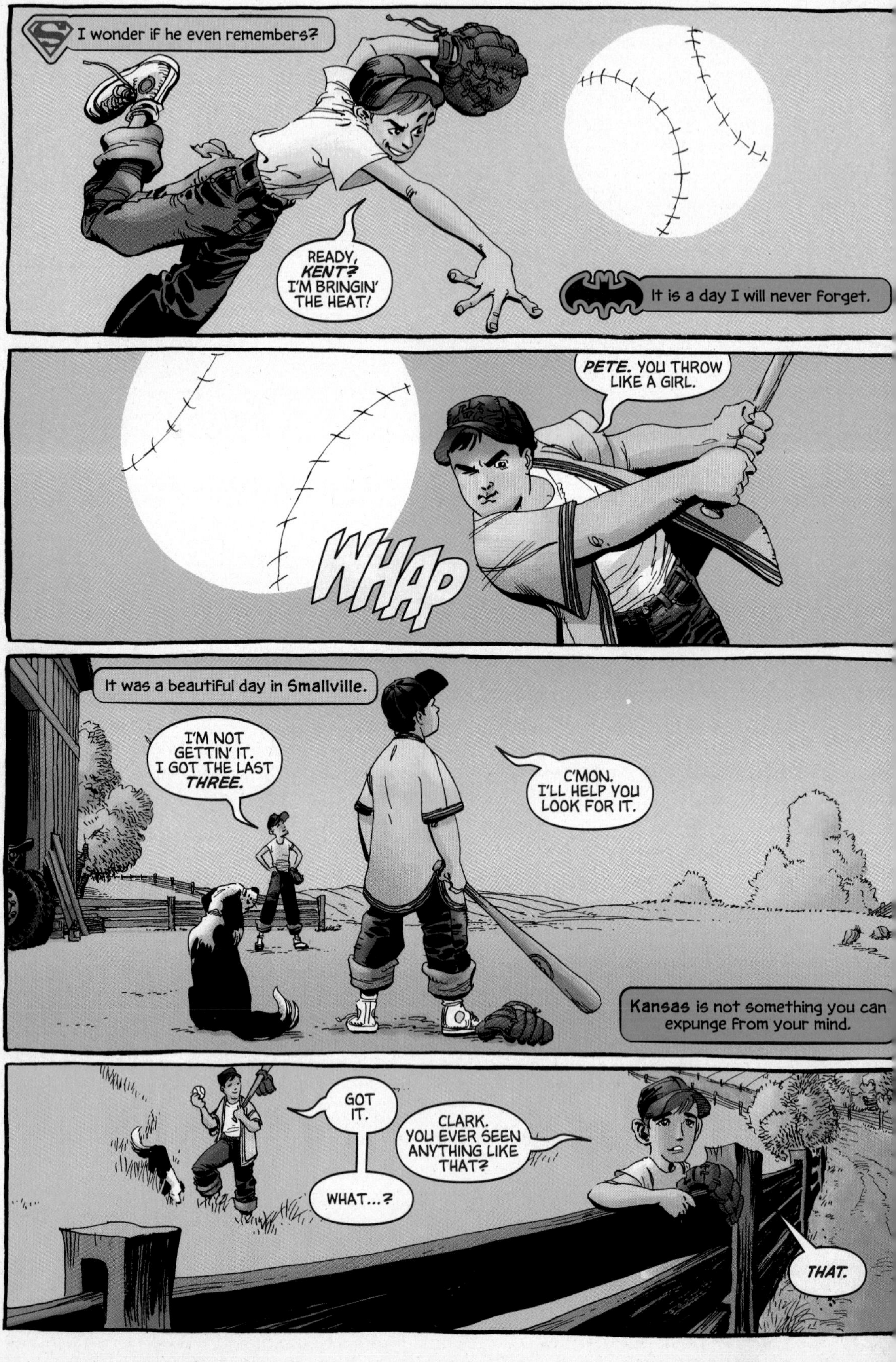
I wonder if he even remembers?
READY, KENT? I'M BRINGIN' THE HEAT!
It is a day I will never forget.
PETE. YOU THROW LIKE A GIRL.
WHAP
It was a beautiful day in Smallville.
I'M NOT GETTIN' IT. I GOT THE LAST THREE.
C'MON. I'LL HELP YOU LOOK FOR IT.
Kansas is not something you can expunge from your mind.
GOT IT.
WHAT...?
CLARK. YOU EVER SEEN ANYTHING LIKE THAT?
THAT.

Pete was right. No one in Smallville had that kind of wealth.

After my parents died, Alfred thought that I needed to get out of Gotham City. We drove to California.

THINK WE SHOULD ASK THAT KID TO PLAY BALL?

CLARK. LOOK AT HIM. THAT KID HAS NEVER PLAYED *ANYTHING.*

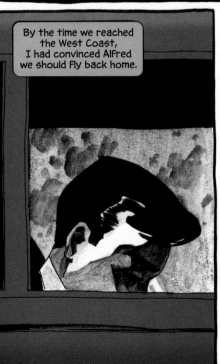

By the time we reached the West Coast, I had convinced Alfred we should fly back home.

WONDER WHO THAT WAS...?

WHO CARES? RACE YA.

LAST ONE IN HAS TO KISS *LANA!*

I still wonder if we should've asked him to play. If it would've made a difference.

Sometimes, I wish they had asked me to play. But, by then, my life had changed. I had no time for games.

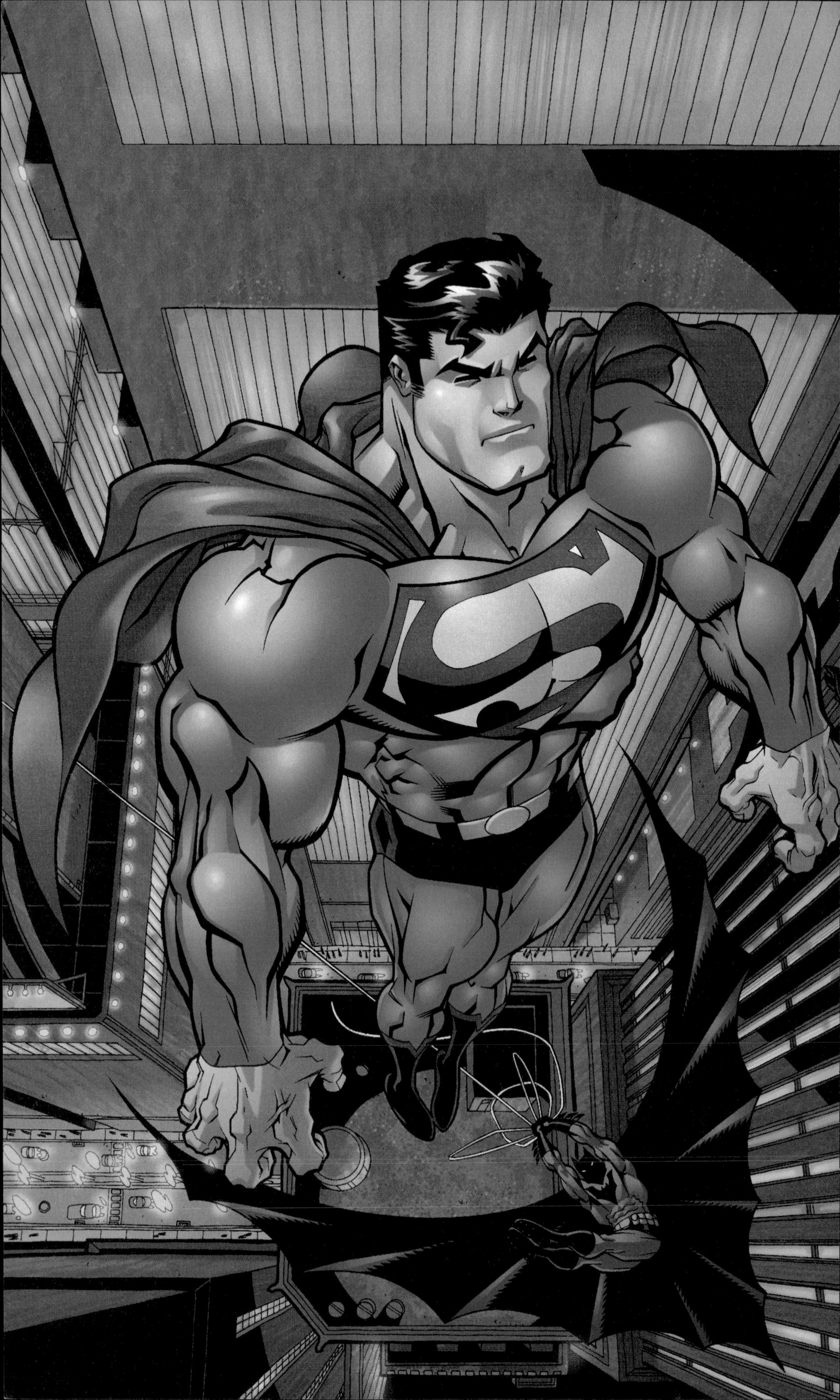

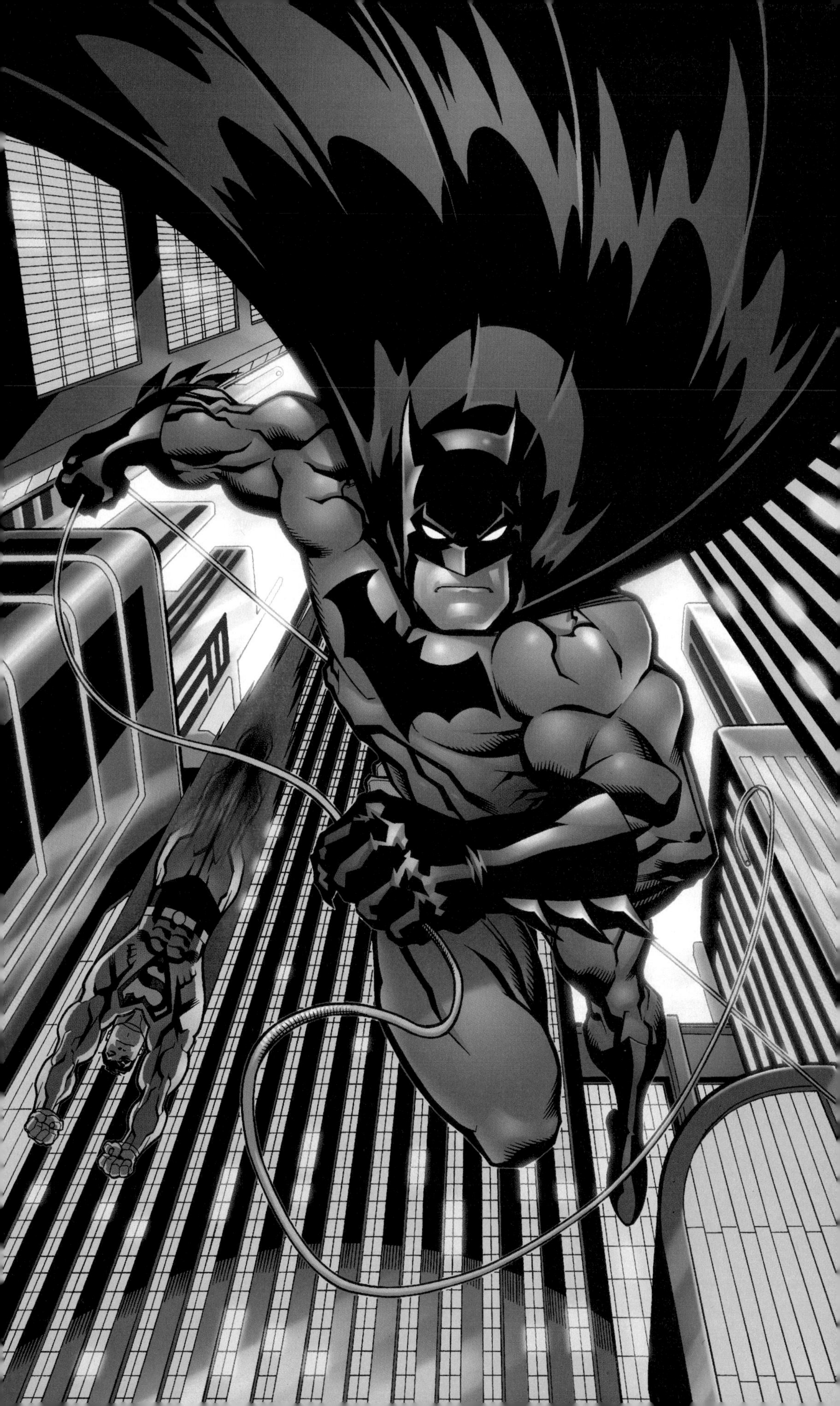

"Clark, sometimes you can be a fool."

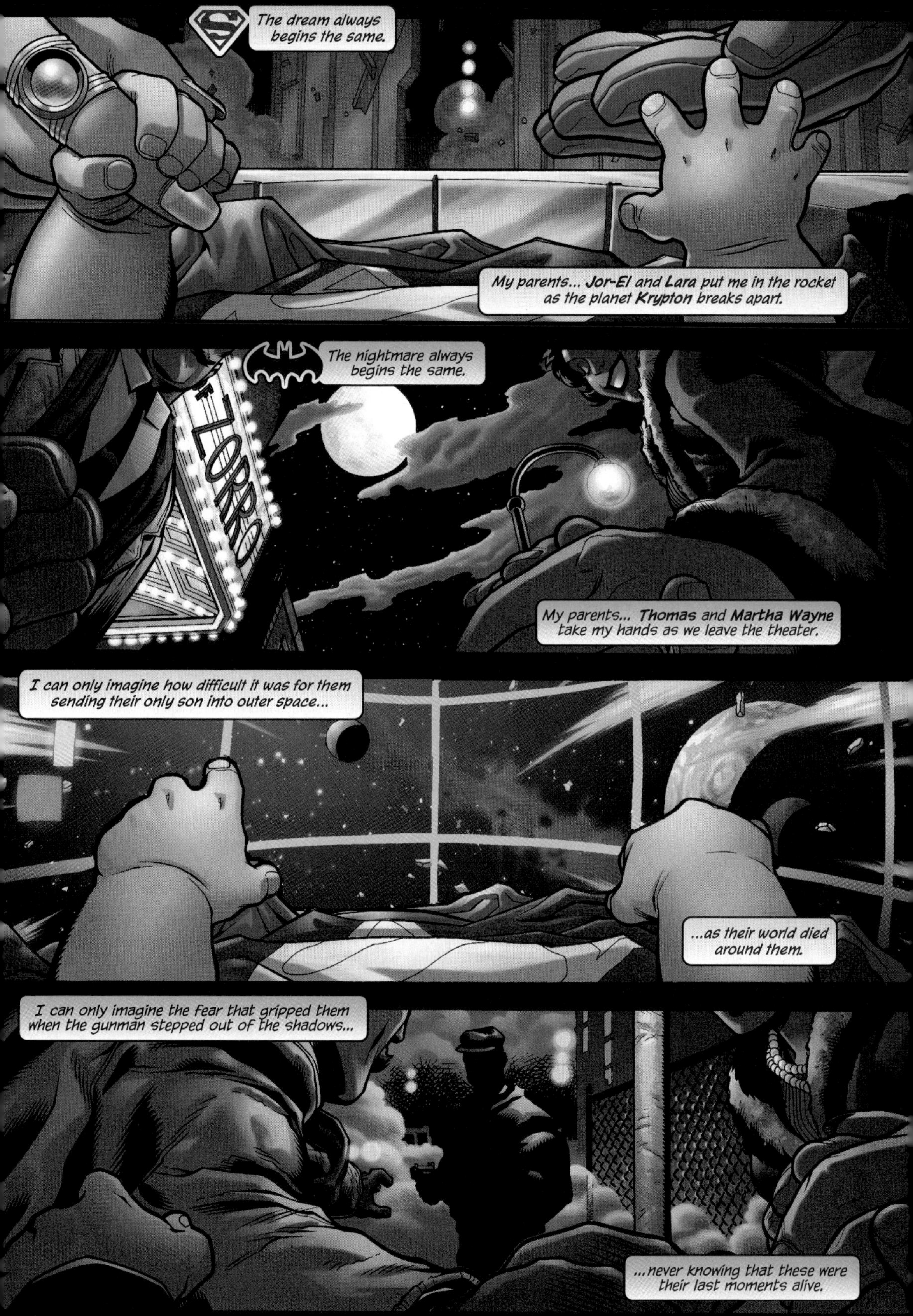
The dream always begins the same.
My parents... Jor-El and Lara put me in the rocket as the planet Krypton breaks apart.
The nightmare always begins the same.
ZORRO
My parents... Thomas and Martha Wayne take my hands as we leave the theater.
I can only imagine how difficult it was for them sending their only son into outer space...
...as their world died around them.
I can only imagine the fear that gripped them when the gunman stepped out of the shadows...
...never knowing that these were their last moments alive.

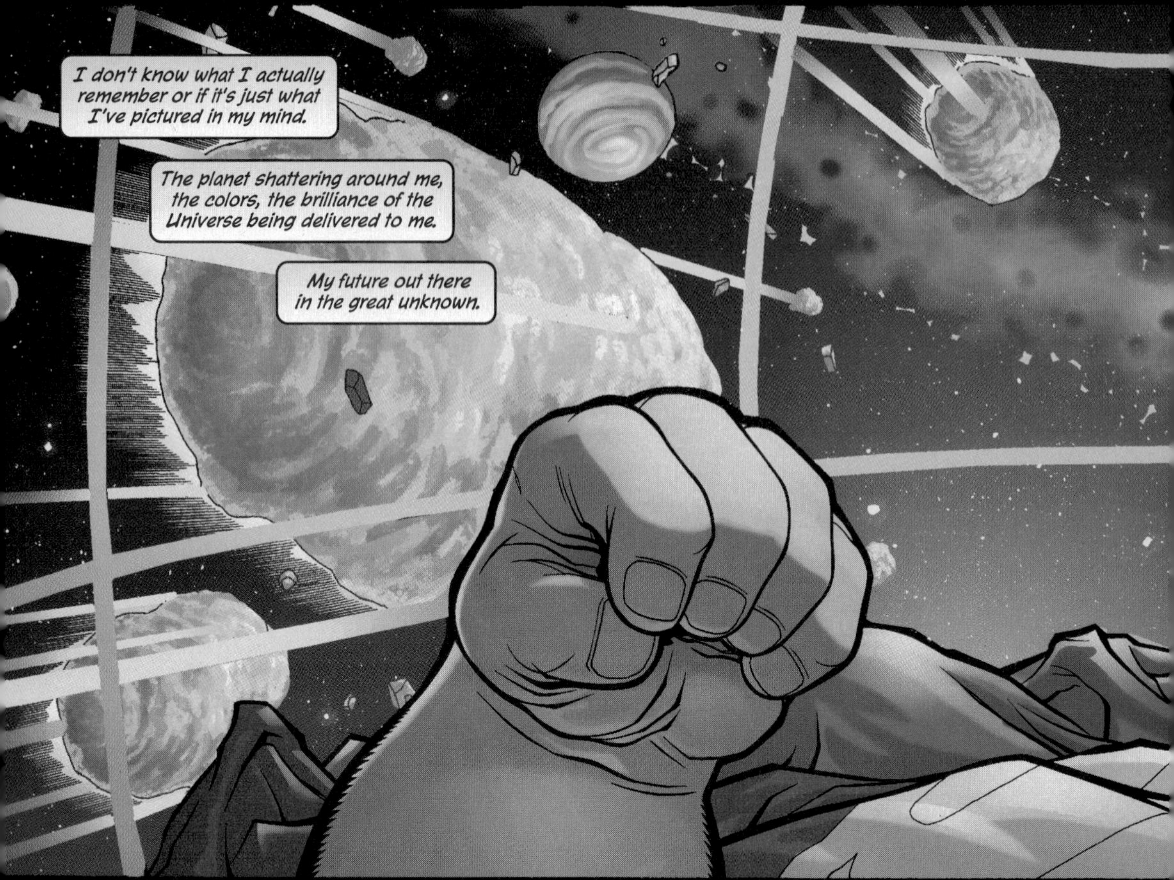
I don't know what I actually remember or if it's just what I've pictured in my mind.
The planet shattering around me, the colors, the brilliance of the Universe being delivered to me.
My future out there in the great unknown.

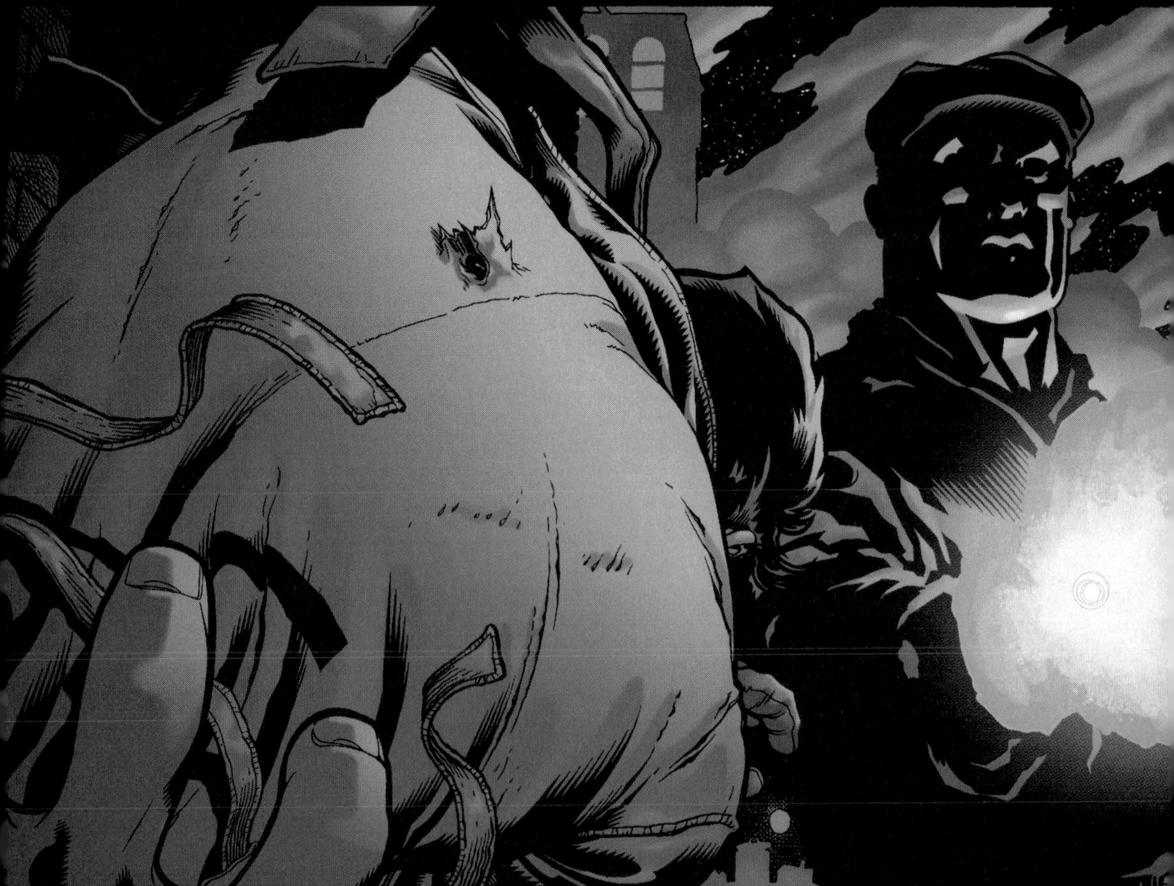

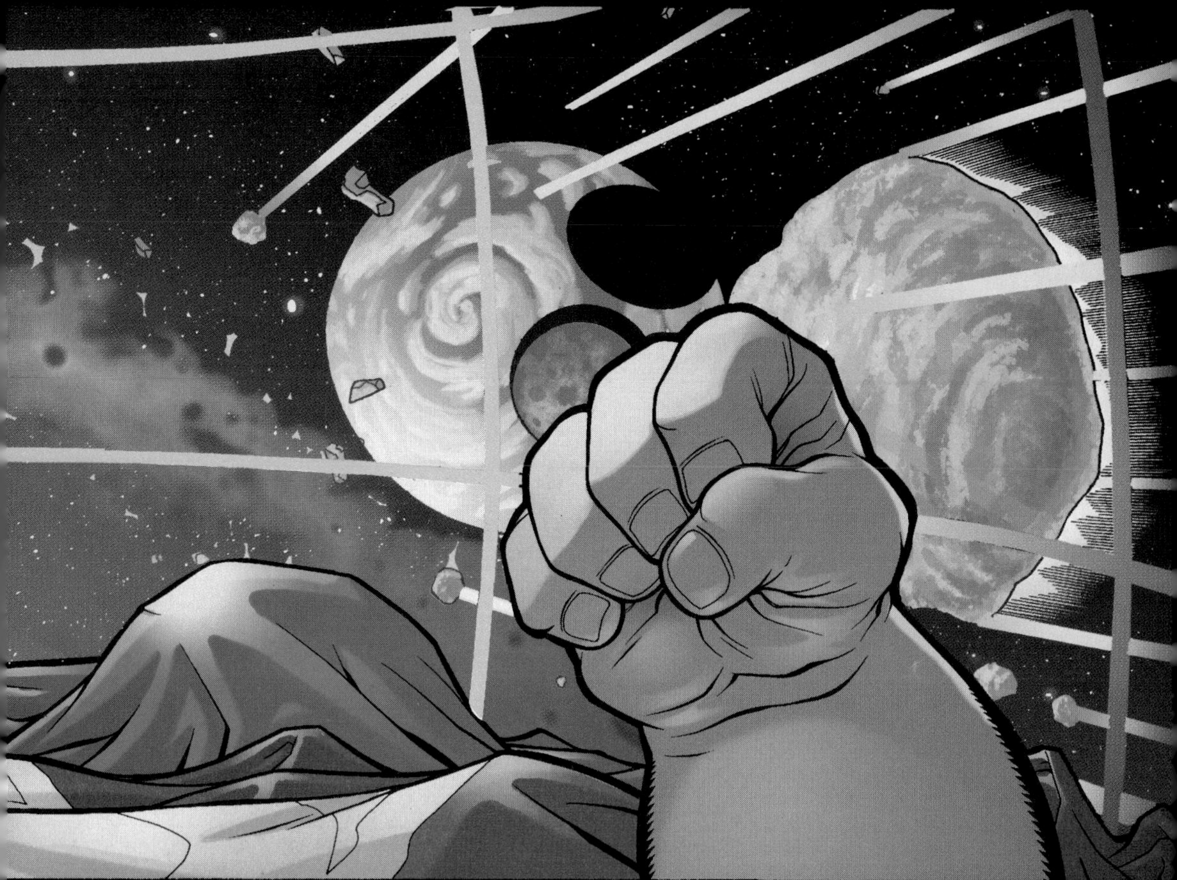

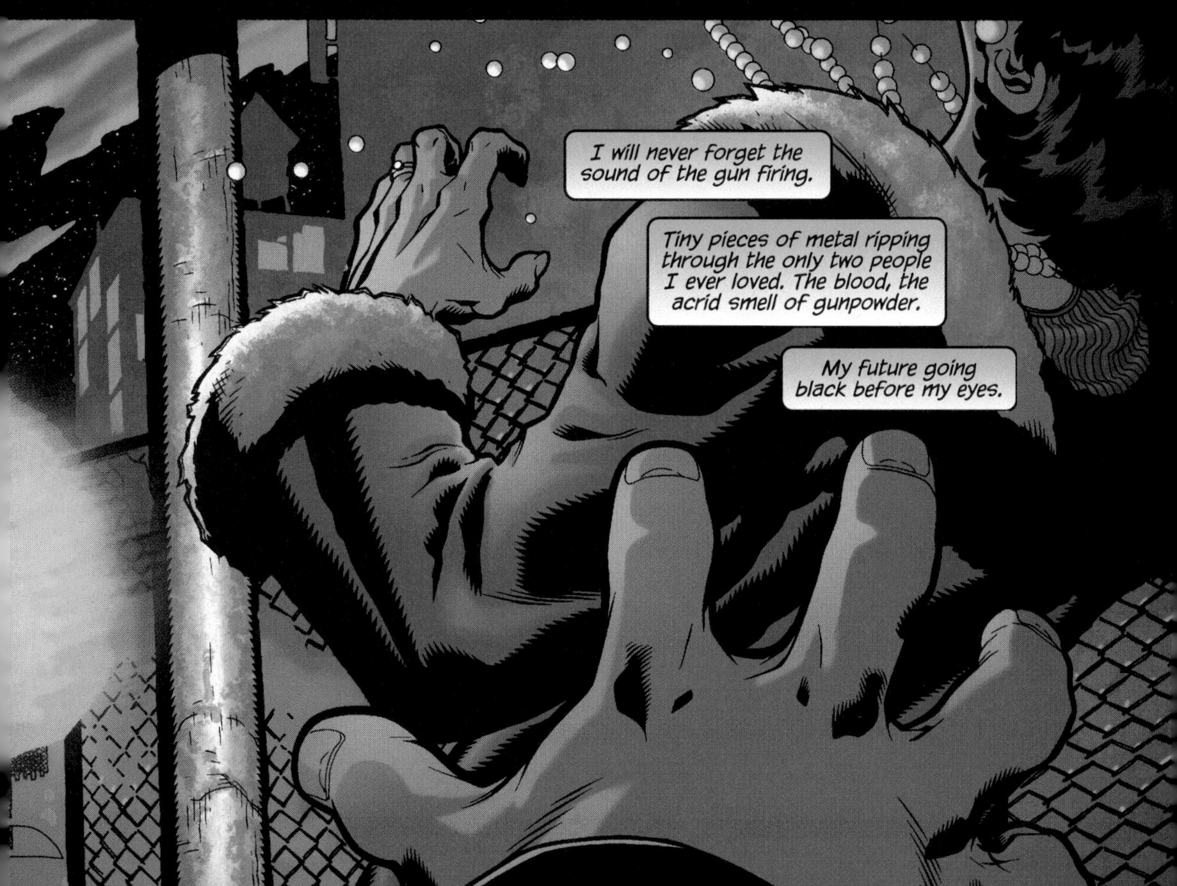
I will never forget the sound of the gun firing.
Tiny pieces of metal ripping through the only two people I ever loved. The blood, the acrid smell of gunpowder.
My future going black before my eyes.

The rocket landed in a cornfield on *Jonathan* and *Martha Kent's* farm.

This was *Smallville, Kansas* on the planet Earth.

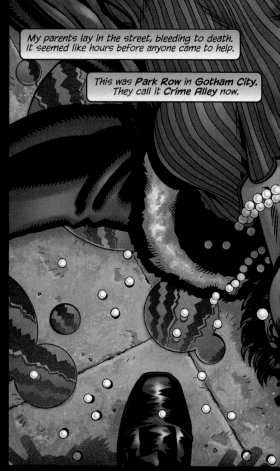

My parents lay in the street, bleeding to death. It seemed like hours before anyone came to help.

This was *Park Row* in *Gotham City.* They call it *Crime Alley* now.

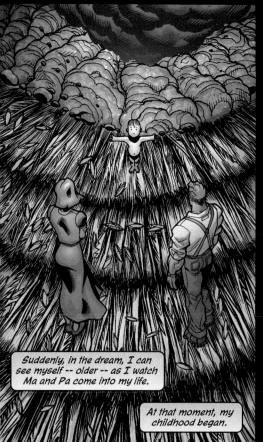

Suddenly, in the dream, I can see myself -- older -- as I watch Ma and Pa come into my life.

At that moment, my childhood began.

Unexpectedly, in the nightmare, I can see myself -- alone -- as I watch my Mother and Father leave me forever.

At that moment, my childhood ended.

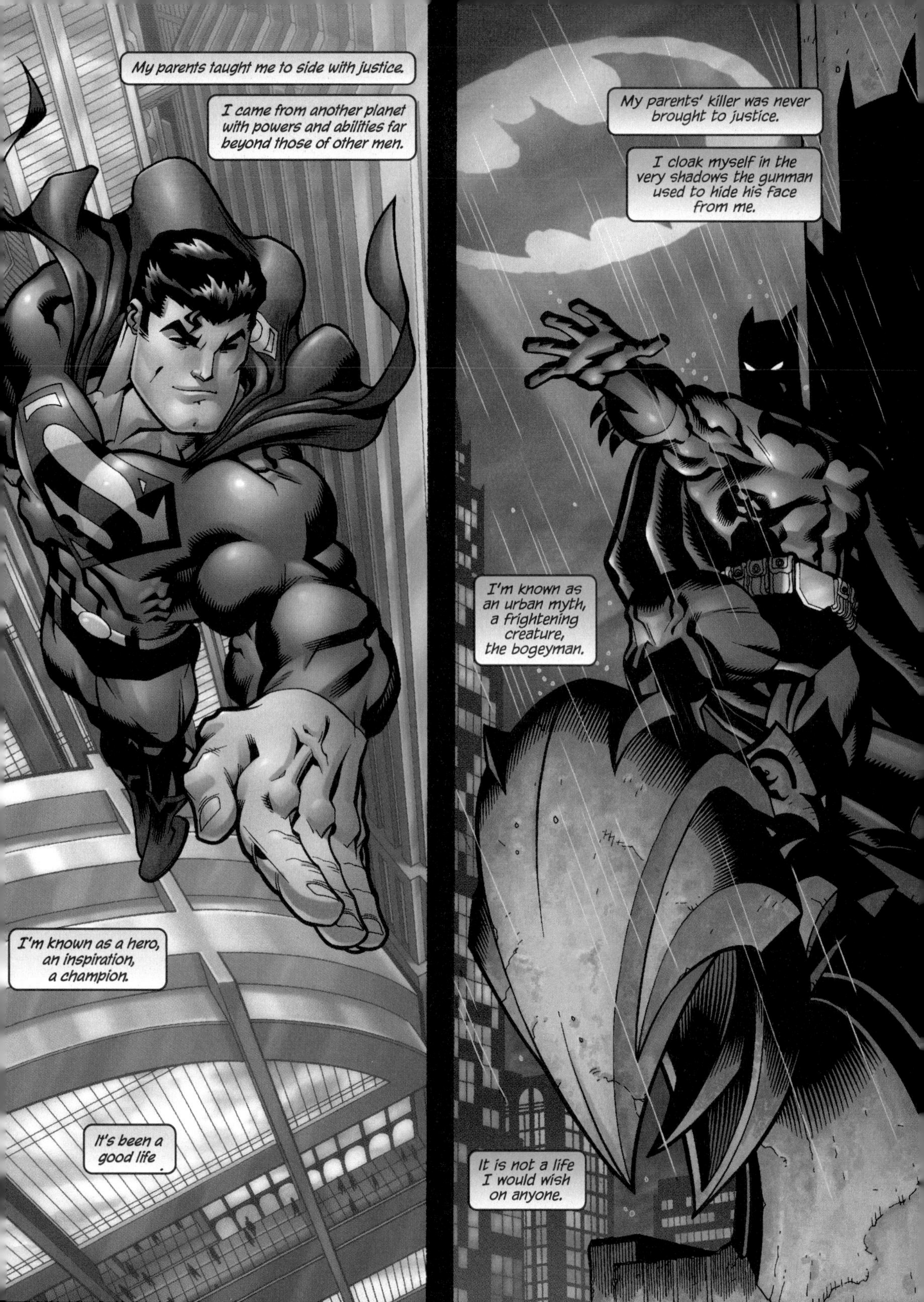
My parents taught me to side with justice.
I came from another planet with powers and abilities far beyond those of other men.
I'm known as a hero, an inspiration, a champion.
It's been a good life.
My parents' killer was never brought to justice.
I cloak myself in the very shadows the gunman used to hide his face from me.
I'm known as an urban myth, a frightening creature, the bogeyman.
It is not a life I would wish on anyone.

PART ONE : WORLD'S FINEST

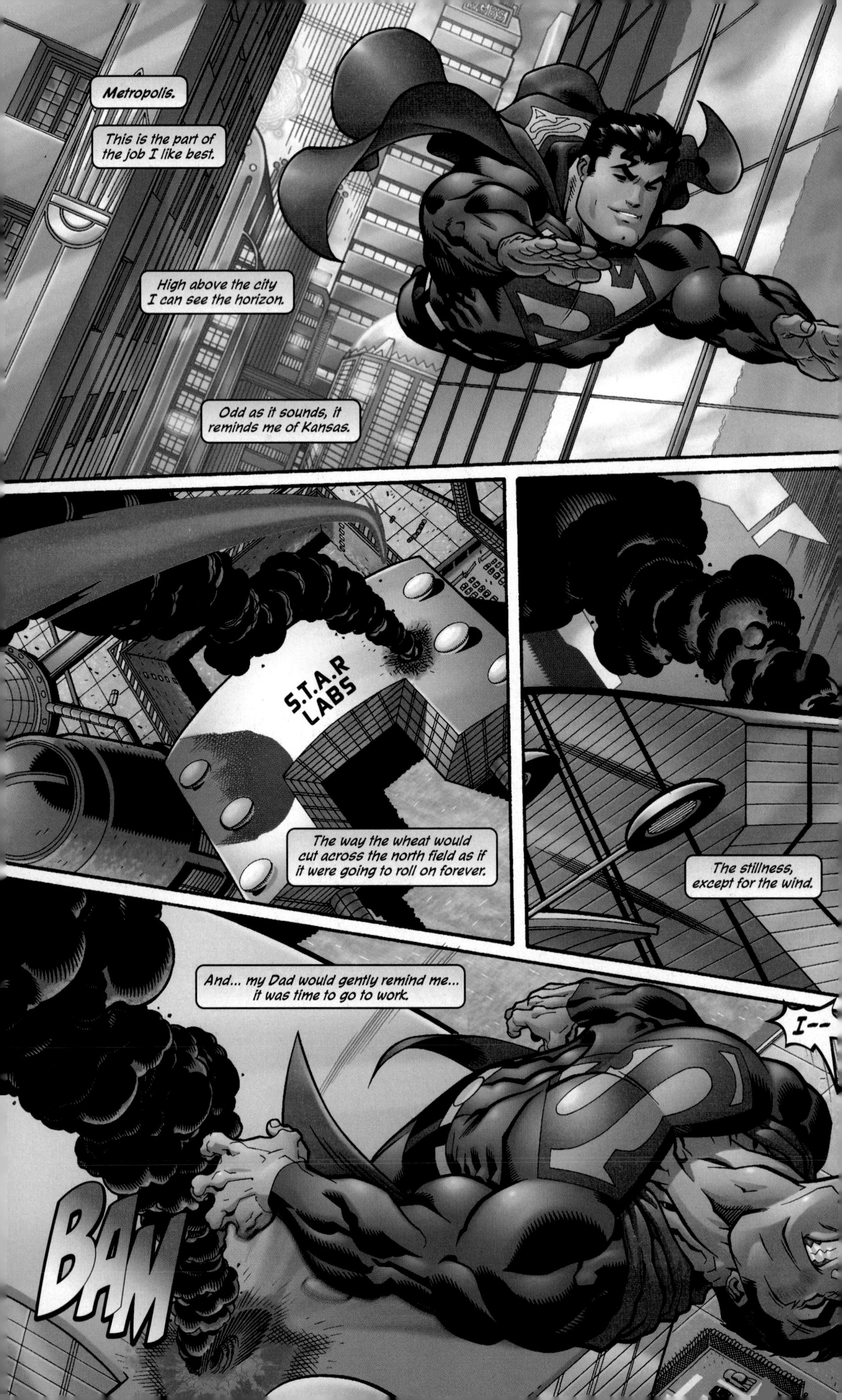
Metropolis.
This is the part of the job I like best.
High above the city I can see the horizon.
Odd as it sounds, it reminds me of Kansas.
S.T.A.R LABS
The way the wheat would cut across the north field as if it were going to roll on forever.
The stillness, except for the wind.
And... my Dad would gently remind me... it was time to go to work.
I--
BAM

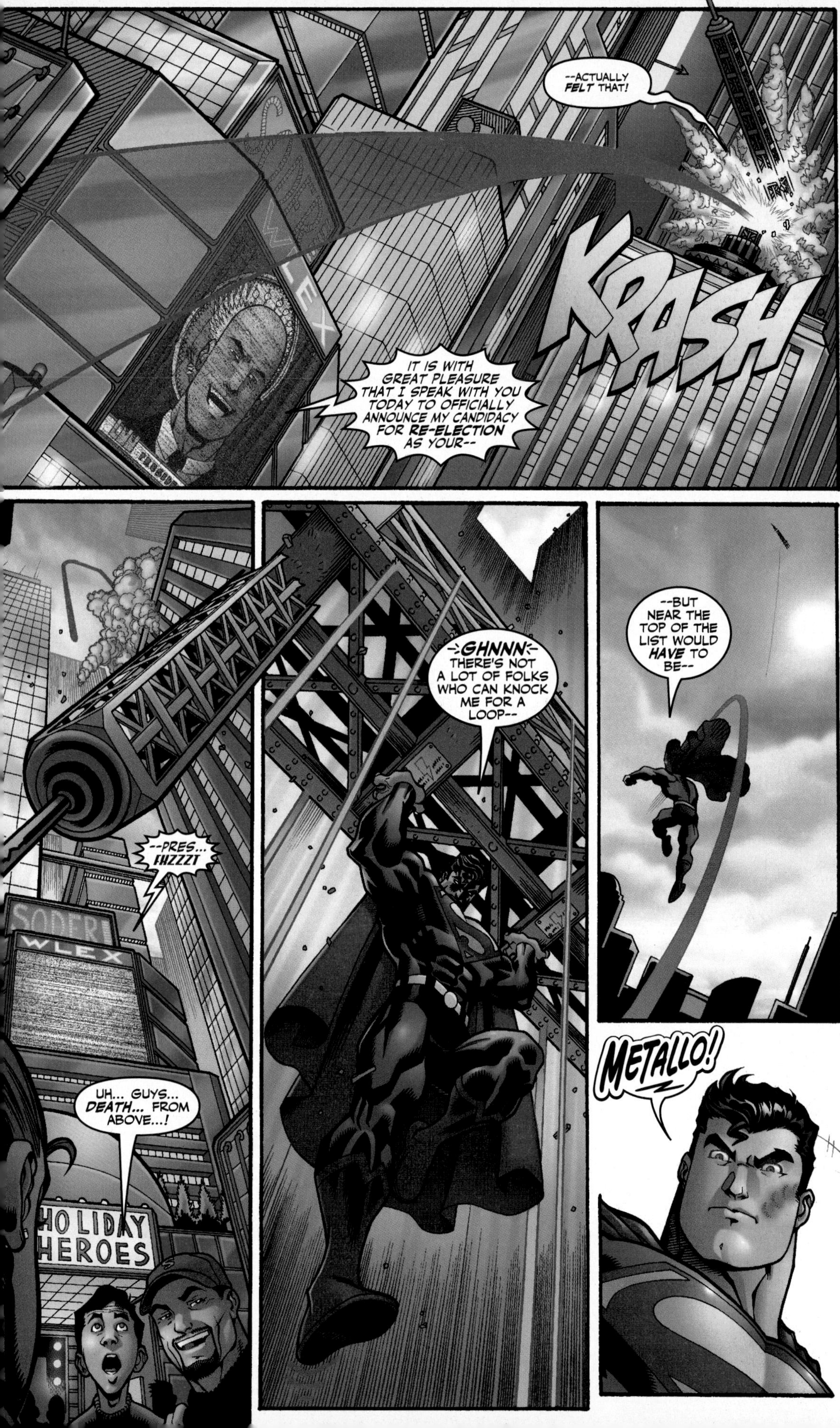
--ACTUALLY FELT THAT!
KRASH
IT IS WITH GREAT PLEASURE THAT I SPEAK WITH YOU TODAY TO OFFICIALLY ANNOUNCE MY CANDIDACY FOR RE-ELECTION AS YOUR--
WLEX
--PRES... FHZZZT
WLEX
HOLIDAY HEROES
UH... GUYS... DEATH... FROM ABOVE...!
-GHNNN- THERE'S NOT A LOT OF FOLKS WHO CAN KNOCK ME FOR A LOOP--
--BUT NEAR THE TOP OF THE LIST WOULD HAVE TO BE--
METALLO!

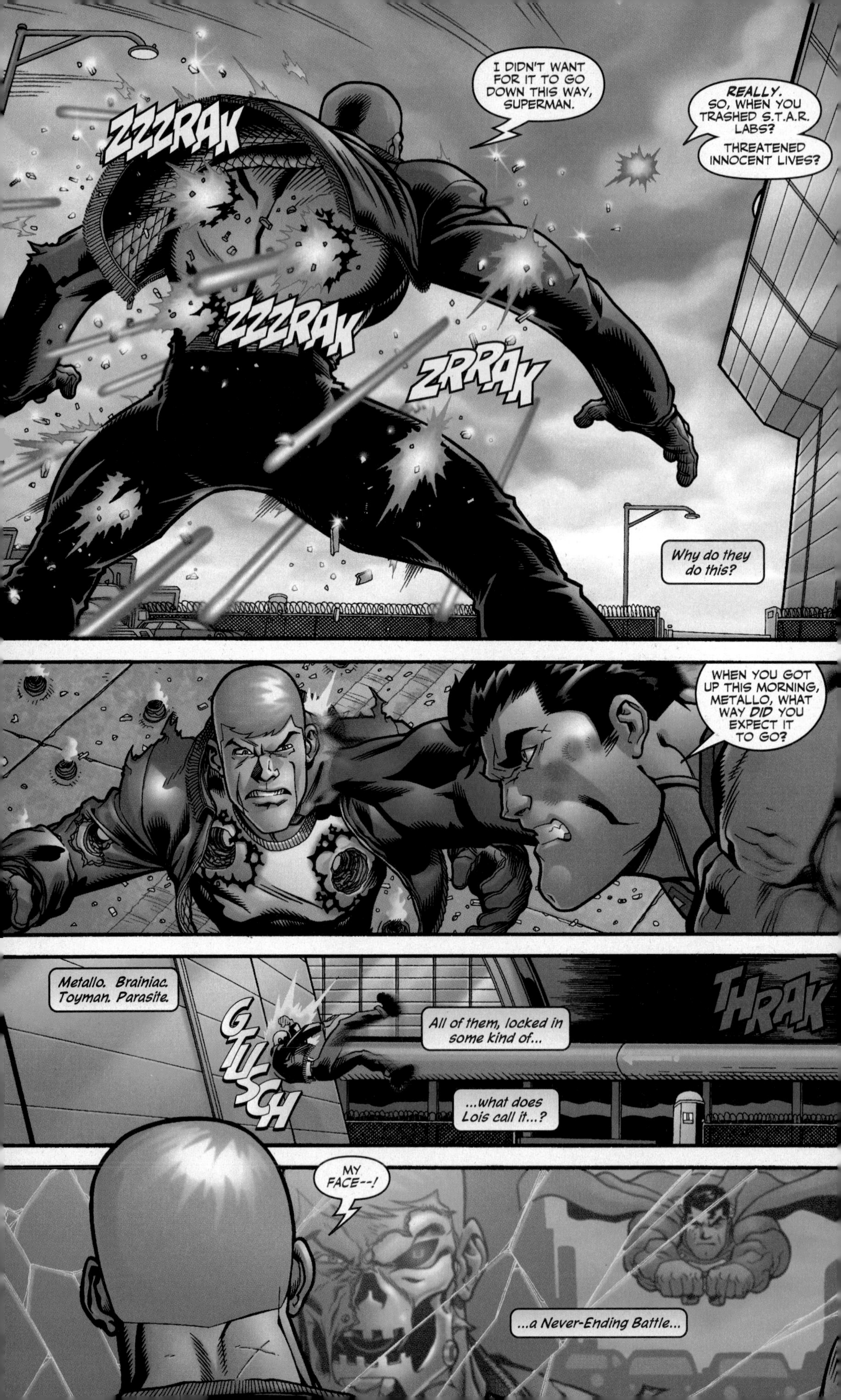
ZZZRAK
I DIDN'T WANT FOR IT TO GO DOWN THIS WAY, SUPERMAN.
REALLY. SO, WHEN YOU TRASHED S.T.A.R. LABS?
THREATENED INNOCENT LIVES?
ZZZRAK
ZRRAK
Why do they do this?
WHEN YOU GOT UP THIS MORNING, METALLO, WHAT WAY DID YOU EXPECT IT TO GO?
Metallo. Brainiac. Toyman. Parasite.
THRAK
GTUSCH
All of them, locked in some kind of...
...what does Lois call it...?
MY FACE--!
...a Never-Ending Battle...

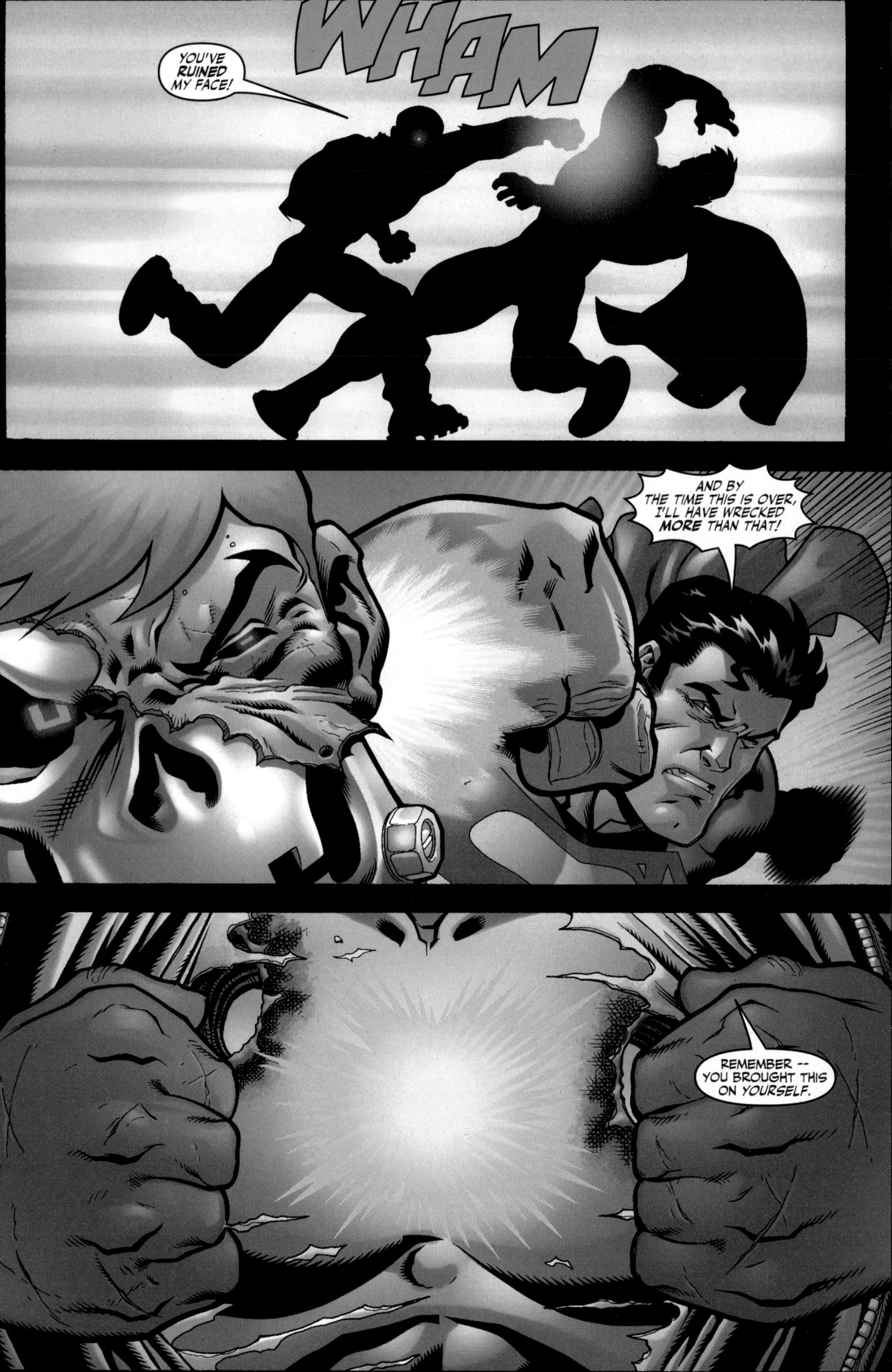
WHAM
YOU'VE RUINED MY FACE!
AND BY THE TIME THIS IS OVER, I'LL HAVE WRECKED MORE THAN THAT!
REMEMBER -- YOU BROUGHT THIS ON YOURSELF.

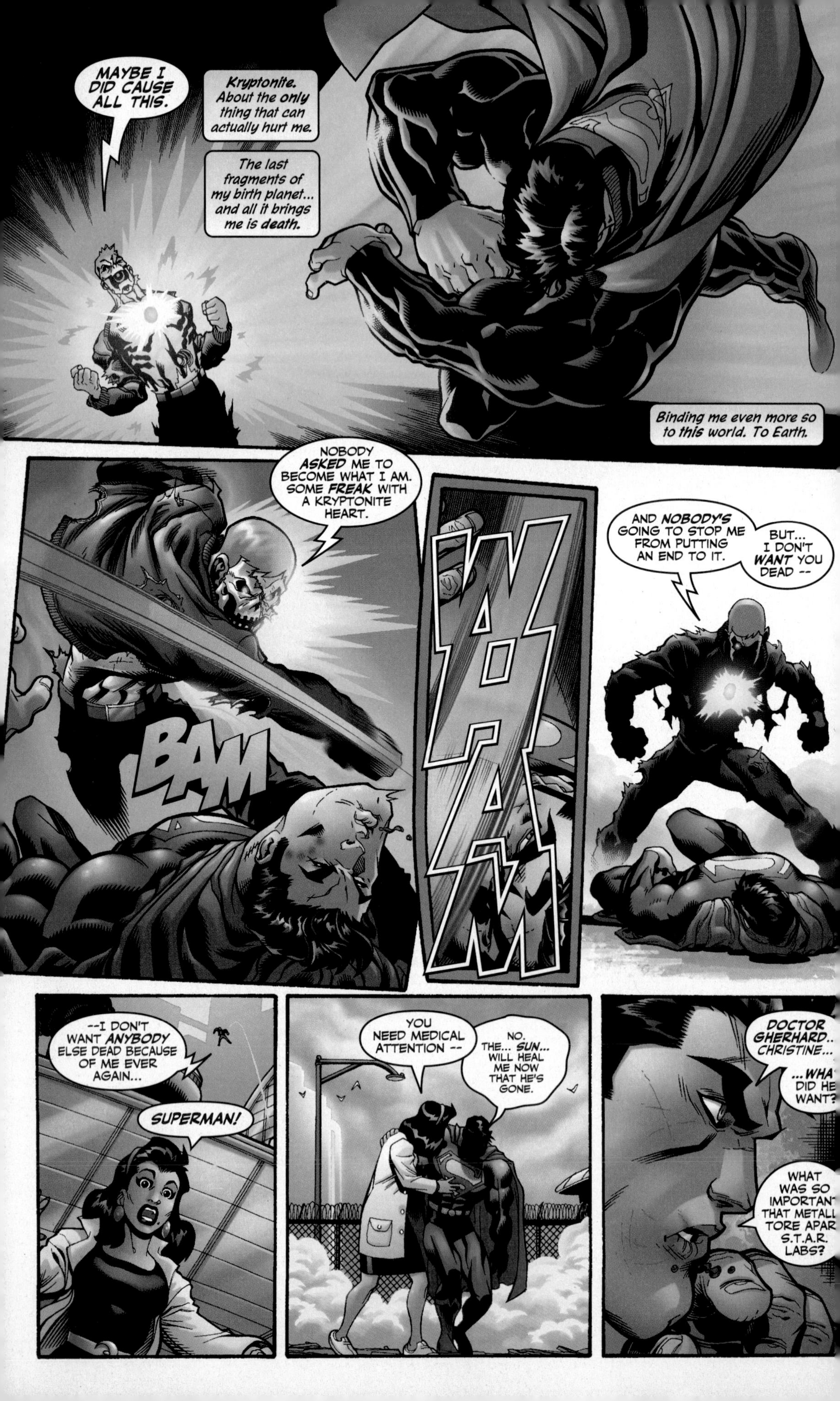
MAYBE I DID CAUSE ALL THIS.
Kryptonite. About the only thing that can actually hurt me.
The last fragments of my birth planet... and all it brings me is death.
Binding me even more so to this world. To Earth.
NOBODY ASKED ME TO BECOME WHAT I AM. SOME FREAK WITH A KRYPTONITE HEART.
BAM
WHAM
AND NOBODY'S GOING TO STOP ME FROM PUTTING AN END TO IT.
BUT... I DON'T WANT YOU DEAD --
--I DON'T WANT ANYBODY ELSE DEAD BECAUSE OF ME EVER AGAIN...
SUPERMAN!
YOU NEED MEDICAL ATTENTION --
NO. THE... SUN... WILL HEAL ME NOW THAT HE'S GONE.
DOCTOR GHERHARD... CHRISTINE...
...WHA DID HE WANT?
WHAT WAS SO IMPORTAN THAT METALL TORE APAR S.T.A.R. LABS?

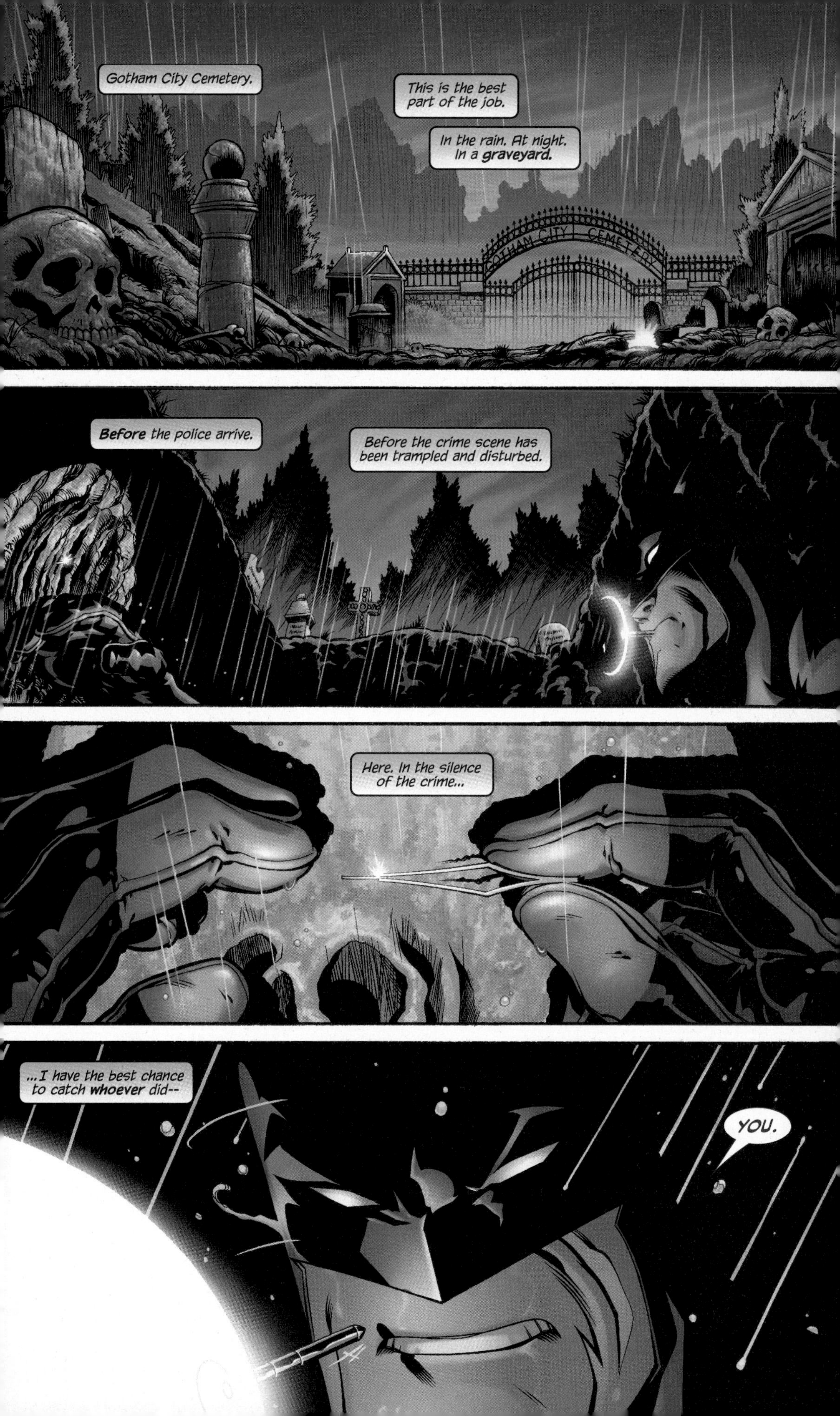
Gotham City Cemetery.
This is the best part of the job.
In the rain. At night. In a graveyard.
GOTHAM CITY CEMETERY
Before the police arrive.
Before the crime scene has been trampled and disturbed.
Here. In the silence of the crime...
...I have the best chance to catch whoever did--
YOU.

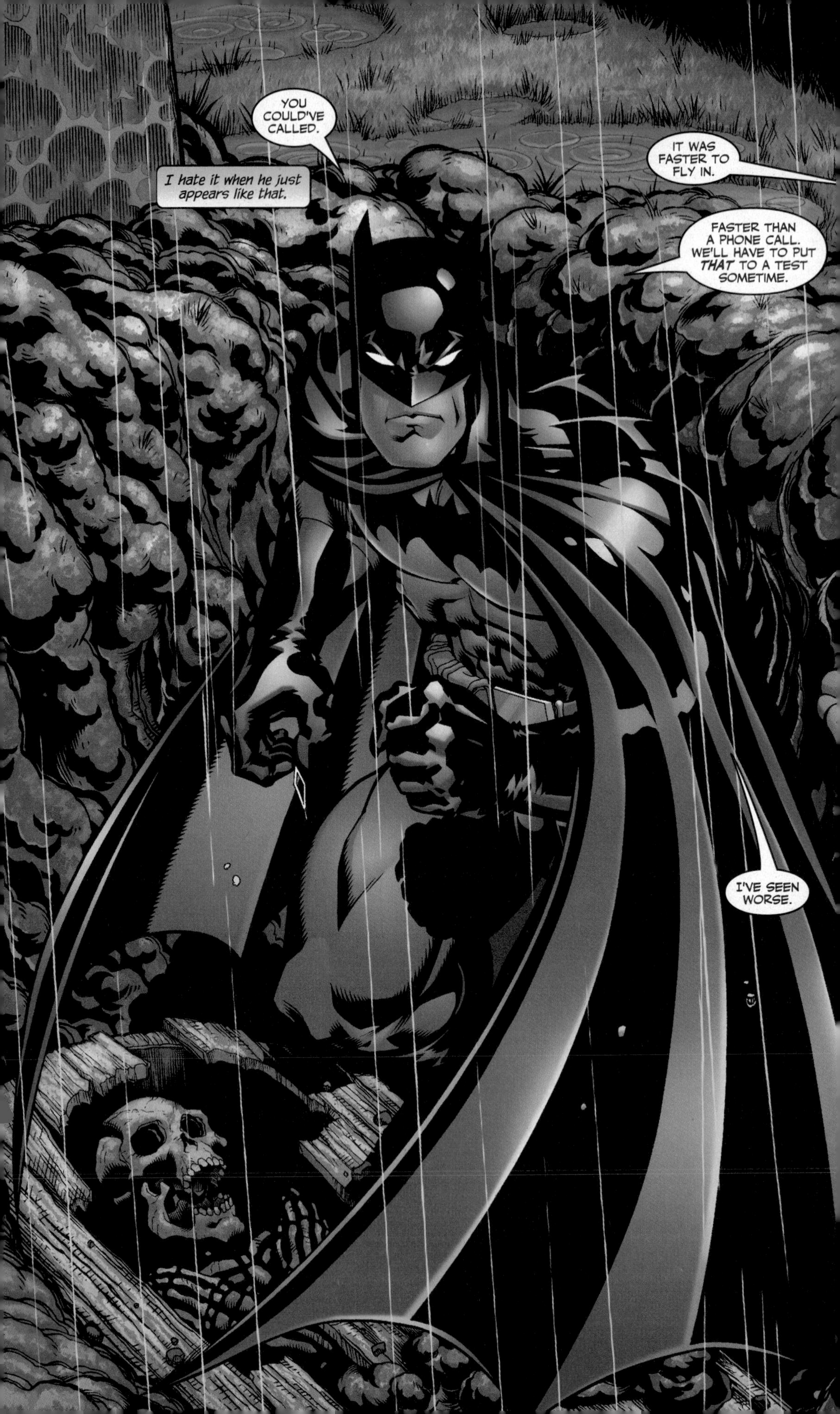
YOU COULD'VE CALLED.
I hate it when he just appears like that.
IT WAS FASTER TO FLY IN.
FASTER THAN A PHONE CALL. WE'LL HAVE TO PUT THAT TO A TEST SOMETIME.
I'VE SEEN WORSE.

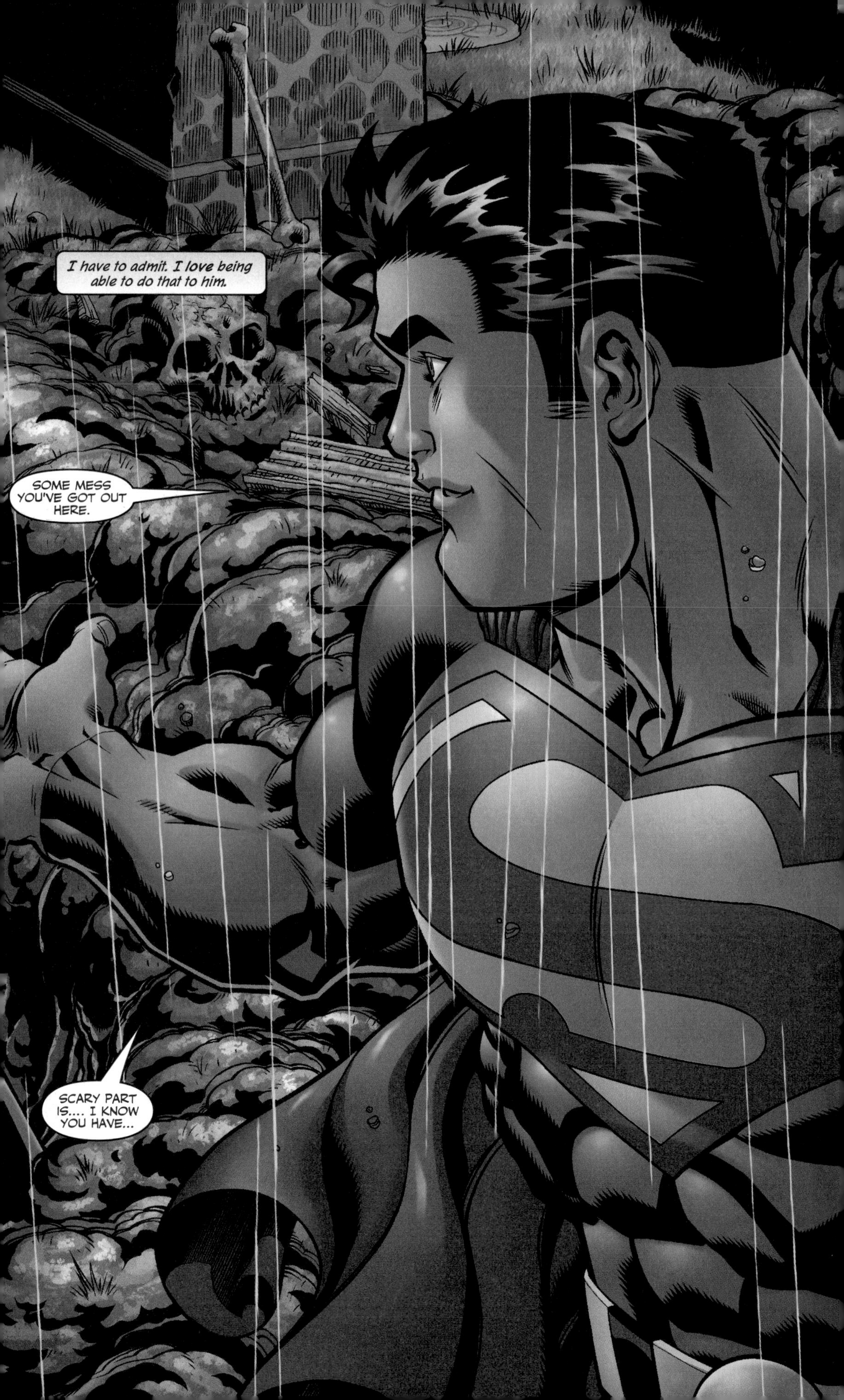
I have to admit. I love being able to do that to him.
SOME MESS YOU'VE GOT OUT HERE.
SCARY PART IS.... I KNOW YOU HAVE...

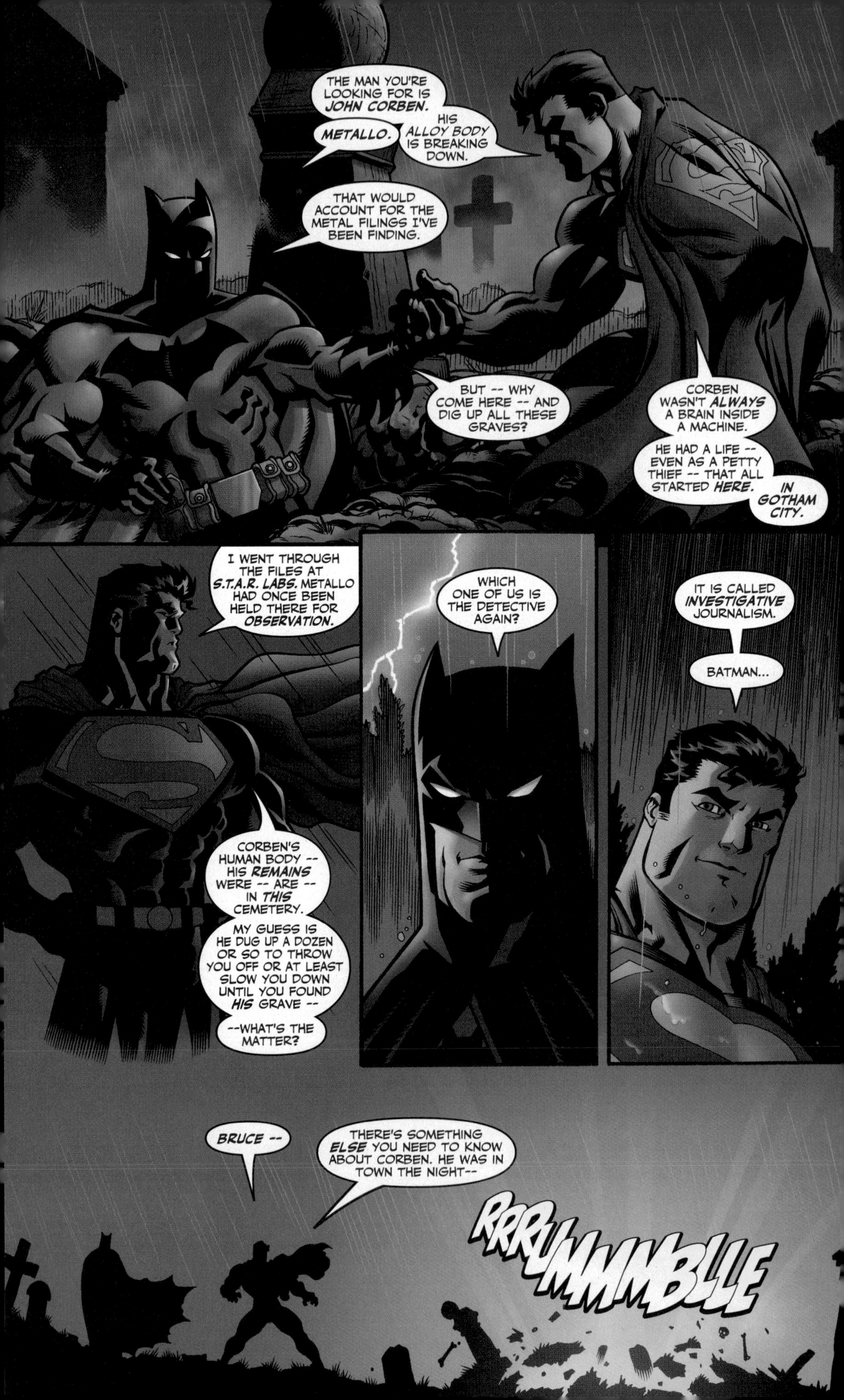
THE MAN YOU'RE LOOKING FOR IS JOHN CORBEN.
METALLO.
HIS ALLOY BODY IS BREAKING DOWN.
THAT WOULD ACCOUNT FOR THE METAL FILINGS I'VE BEEN FINDING.
BUT -- WHY COME HERE -- AND DIG UP ALL THESE GRAVES?
CORBEN WASN'T ALWAYS A BRAIN INSIDE A MACHINE.
HE HAD A LIFE -- EVEN AS A PETTY THIEF -- THAT ALL STARTED HERE.
IN GOTHAM CITY.
I WENT THROUGH THE FILES AT S.T.A.R. LABS. METALLO HAD ONCE BEEN HELD THERE FOR OBSERVATION.
CORBEN'S HUMAN BODY -- HIS REMAINS WERE -- ARE -- IN THIS CEMETERY.
MY GUESS IS HE DUG UP A DOZEN OR SO TO THROW YOU OFF OR AT LEAST SLOW YOU DOWN UNTIL YOU FOUND HIS GRAVE --
--WHAT'S THE MATTER?
WHICH ONE OF US IS THE DETECTIVE AGAIN?
IT IS CALLED INVESTIGATIVE JOURNALISM.
BATMAN...
BRUCE --
THERE'S SOMETHING ELSE YOU NEED TO KNOW ABOUT CORBEN. HE WAS IN TOWN THE NIGHT--
RRRUMMMBLLE

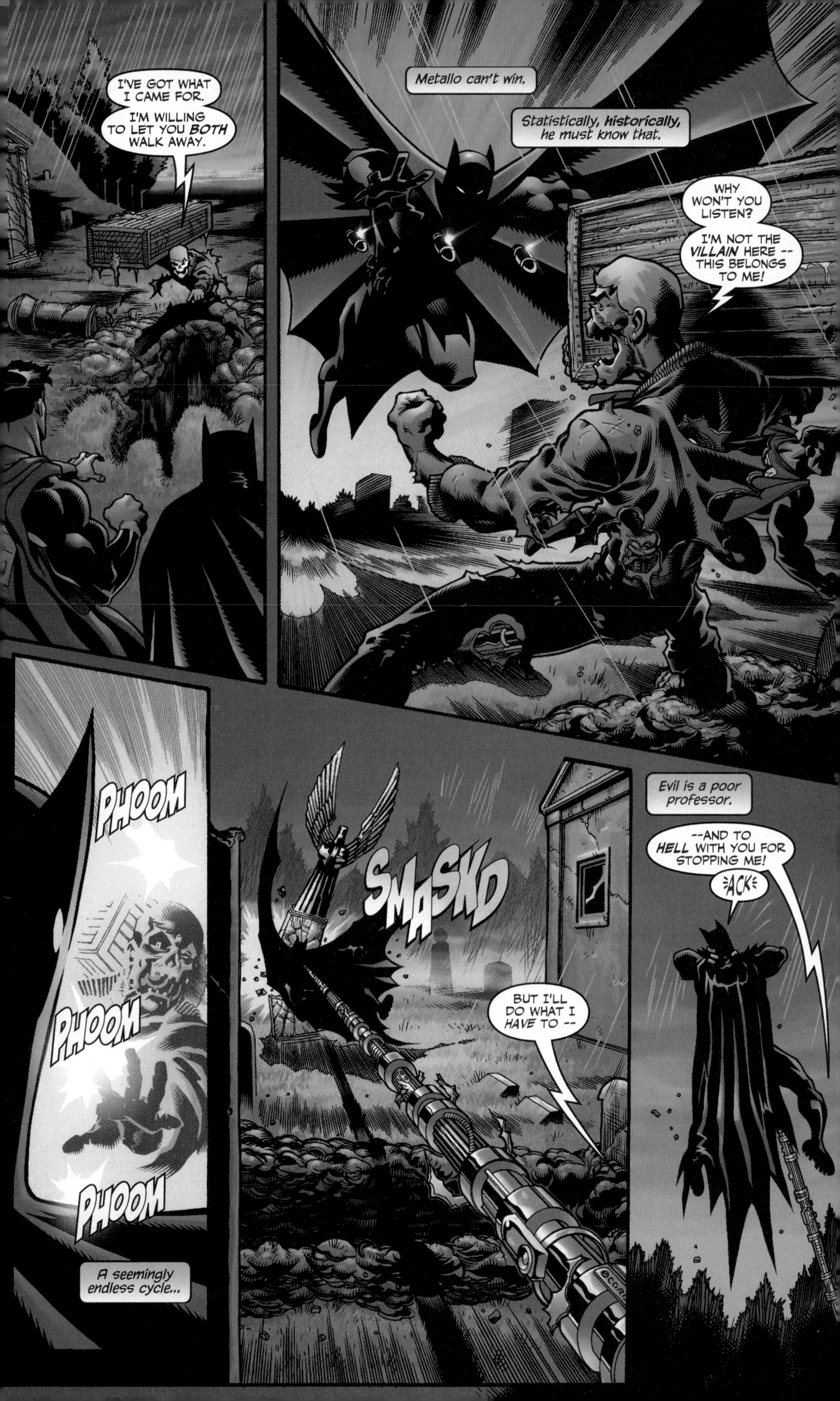

I'VE GOT WHAT I CAME FOR.
I'M WILLING TO LET YOU BOTH WALK AWAY.
Metallo can't win.
Statistically, historically, he must know that.
WHY WON'T YOU LISTEN?
I'M NOT THE VILLAIN HERE -- THIS BELONGS TO ME!
PHOOM
PHOOM
PHOOM
A seemingly endless cycle...
SMASKD
BUT I'LL DO WHAT I HAVE TO --
Evil is a poor professor.
--AND TO HELL WITH YOU FOR STOPPING ME!
ACK

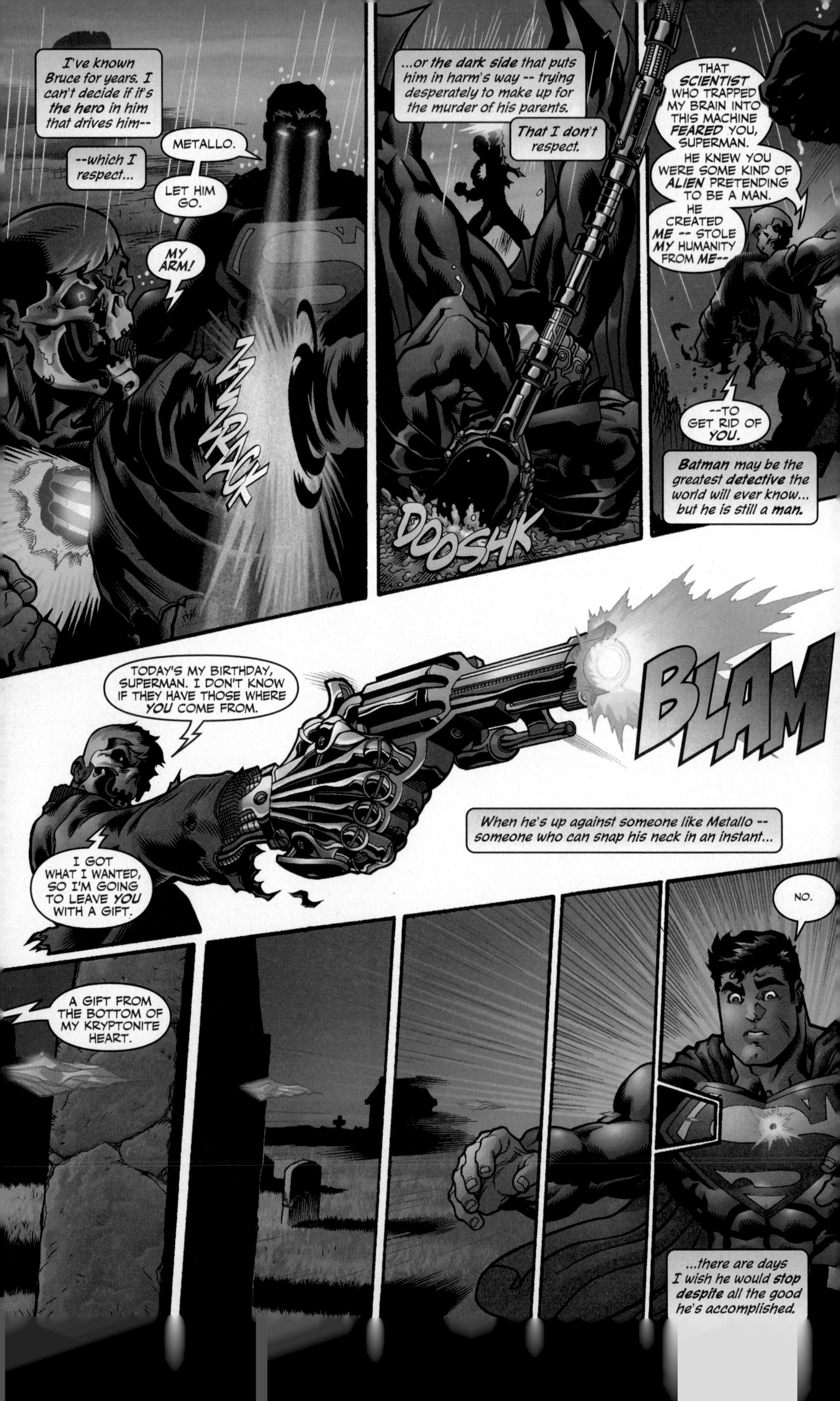
I've known Bruce for years. I can't decide if it's the hero in him that drives him--
--which I respect...
METALLO.
LET HIM GO.
MY ARM!
ZZZKRACK
...or the dark side that puts him in harm's way -- trying desperately to make up for the murder of his parents.
That I don't respect.
DOOSHK
THAT SCIENTIST WHO TRAPPED MY BRAIN INTO THIS MACHINE FEARED YOU, SUPERMAN.
HE KNEW YOU WERE SOME KIND OF ALIEN PRETENDING TO BE A MAN.
HE CREATED ME -- STOLE MY HUMANITY FROM ME--
--TO GET RID OF YOU.
Batman may be the greatest detective the world will ever know... but he is still a man.
TODAY'S MY BIRTHDAY, SUPERMAN. I DON'T KNOW IF THEY HAVE THOSE WHERE YOU COME FROM.
BLAM
I GOT WHAT I WANTED, SO I'M GOING TO LEAVE YOU WITH A GIFT.
When he's up against someone like Metallo -- someone who can snap his neck in an instant...
NO.
A GIFT FROM THE BOTTOM OF MY KRYPTONITE HEART.
...there are days I wish he would stop despite all the good he's accomplished.

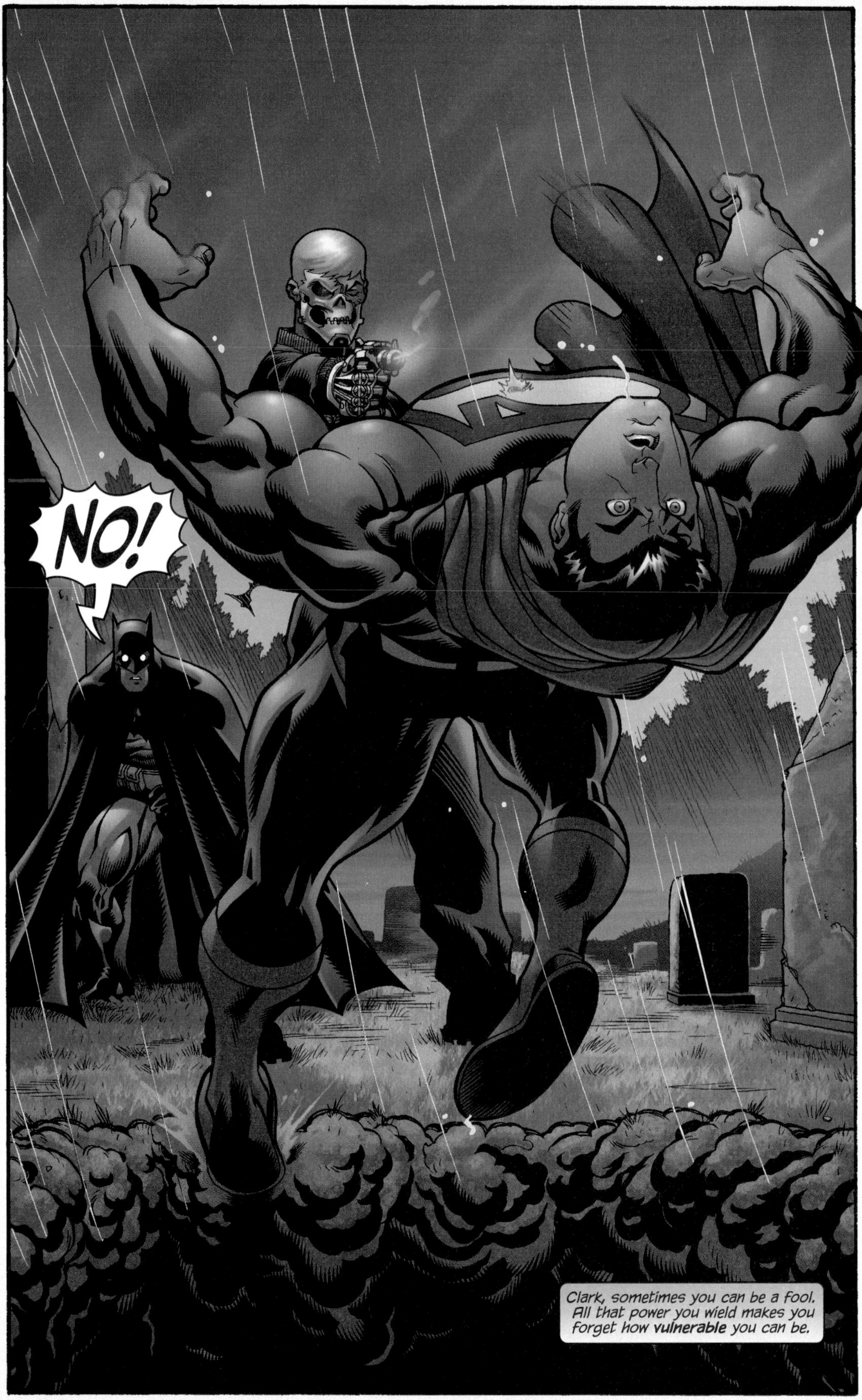
NO!
Clark, sometimes you can be a fool. All that power you wield makes you forget how **vulnerable** you can be.

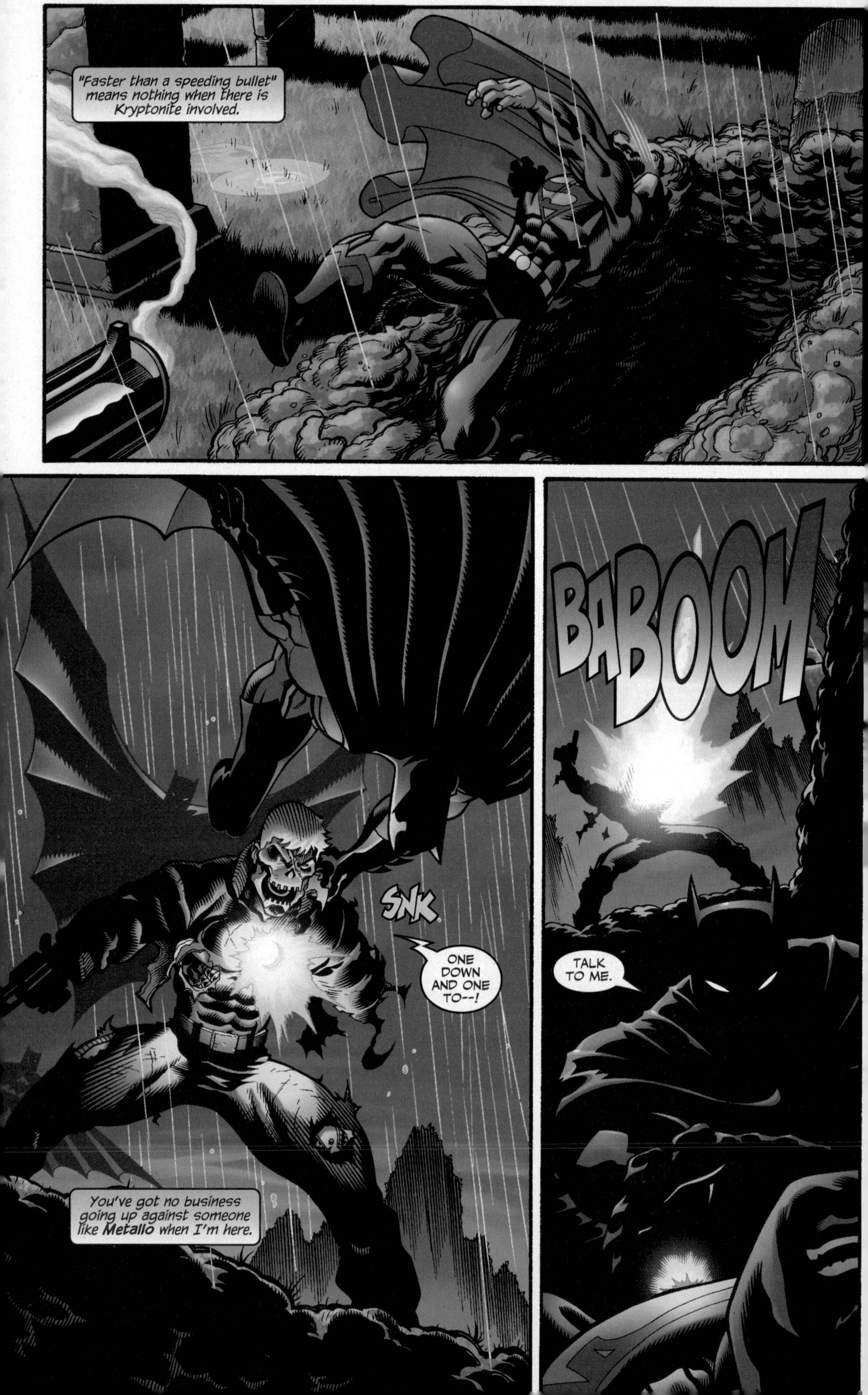
"Faster than a speeding bullet" means nothing when there is Kryptonite involved.
SNK
ONE DOWN AND ONE TO--!
You've got no business going up against someone like **Metallo** when I'm here.
BABOOM
TALK TO ME.

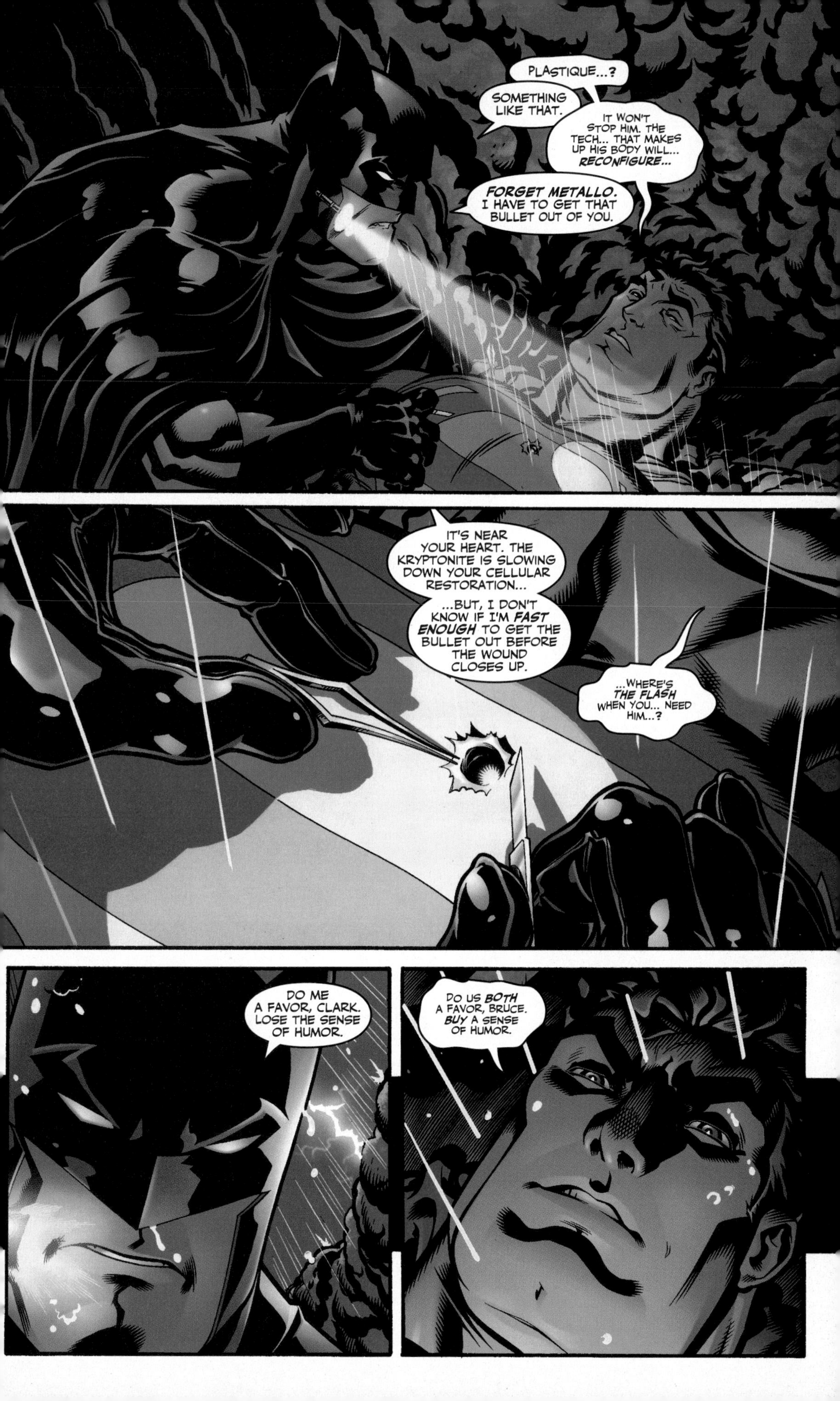
PLASTIQUE...?
SOMETHING LIKE THAT.
IT WON'T STOP HIM. THE TECH... THAT MAKES UP HIS BODY WILL... RECONFIGURE...
FORGET METALLO. I HAVE TO GET THAT BULLET OUT OF YOU.
IT'S NEAR YOUR HEART. THE KRYPTONITE IS SLOWING DOWN YOUR CELLULAR RESTORATION...
...BUT, I DON'T KNOW IF I'M FAST ENOUGH TO GET THE BULLET OUT BEFORE THE WOUND CLOSES UP.
...WHERE'S THE FLASH WHEN YOU... NEED HIM...?
DO ME A FAVOR, CLARK. LOSE THE SENSE OF HUMOR.
DO US BOTH A FAVOR, BRUCE. BUY A SENSE OF HUMOR.

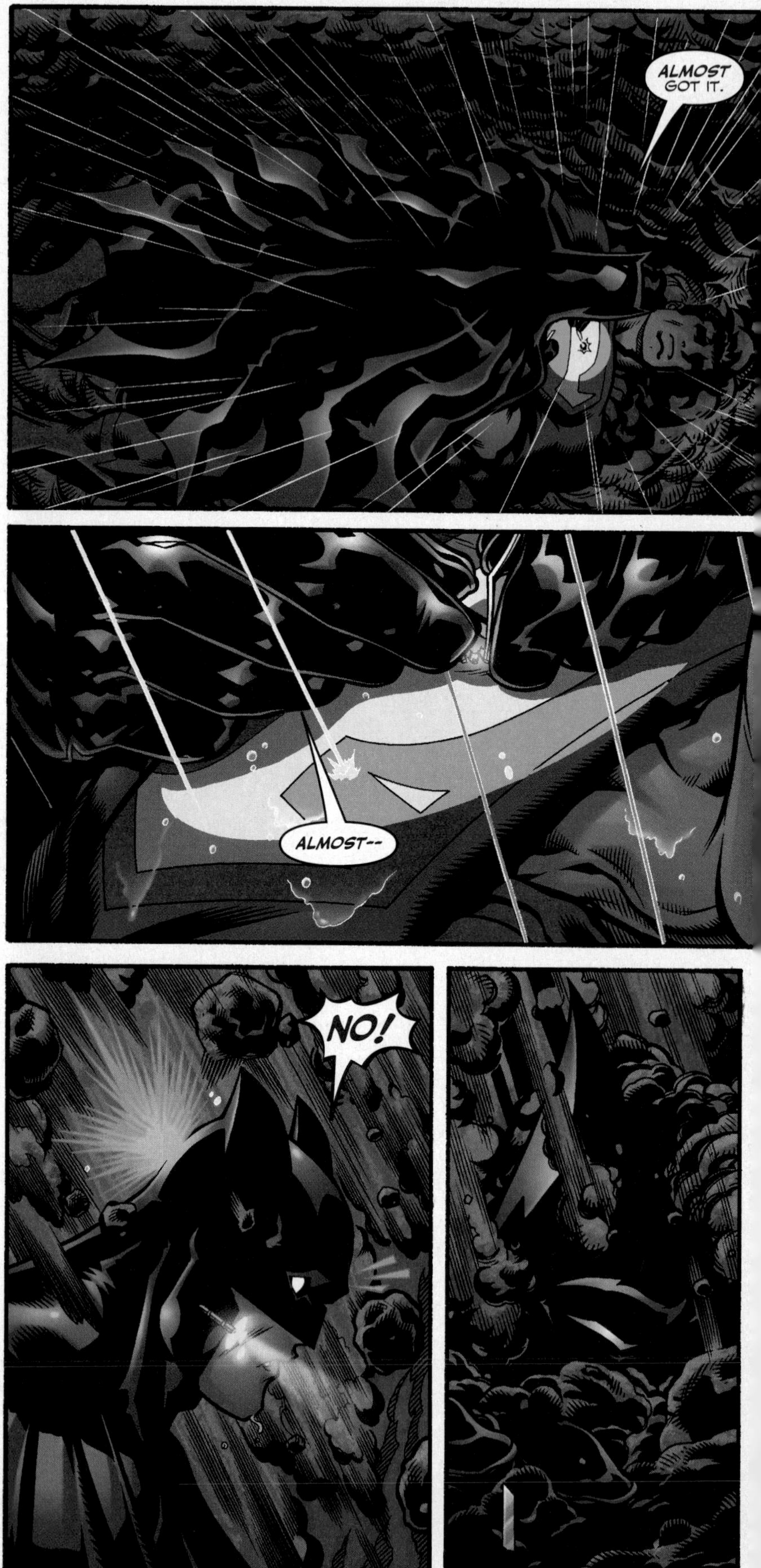
ALMOST GOT IT.
ALMOST--
NO!

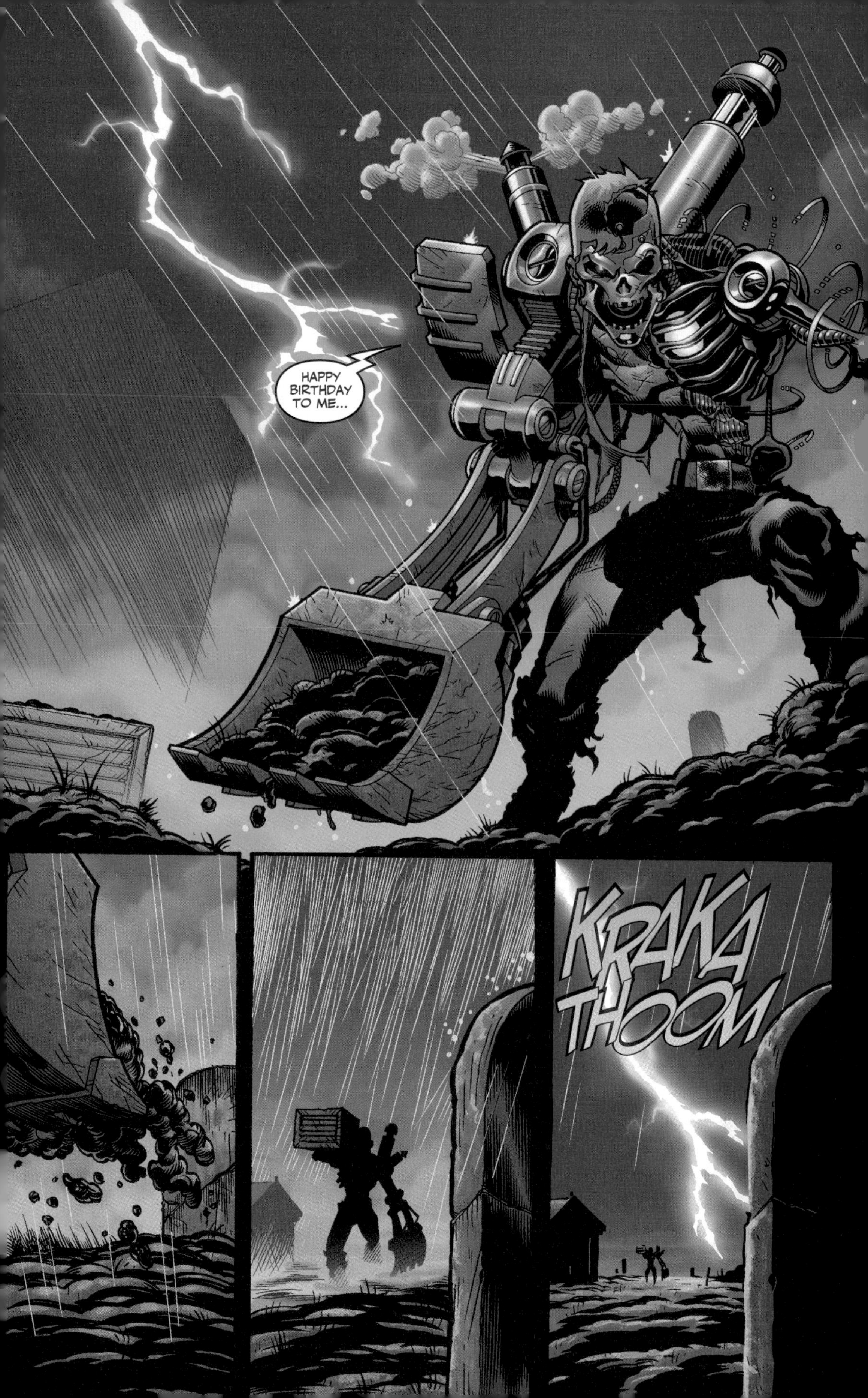
HAPPY BIRTHDAY TO ME...
KRAKA THOOM

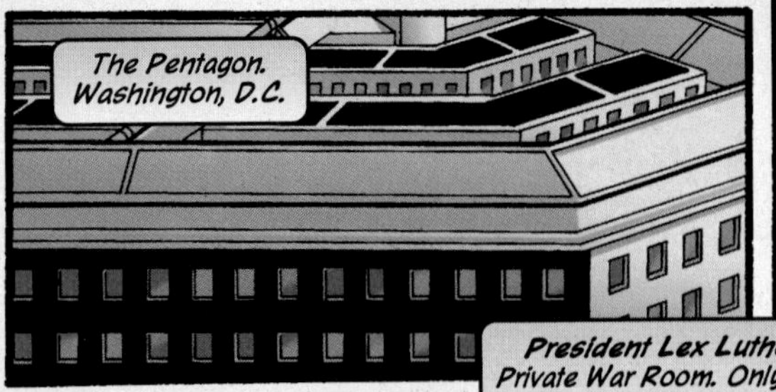
The Pentagon. Washington, D.C.

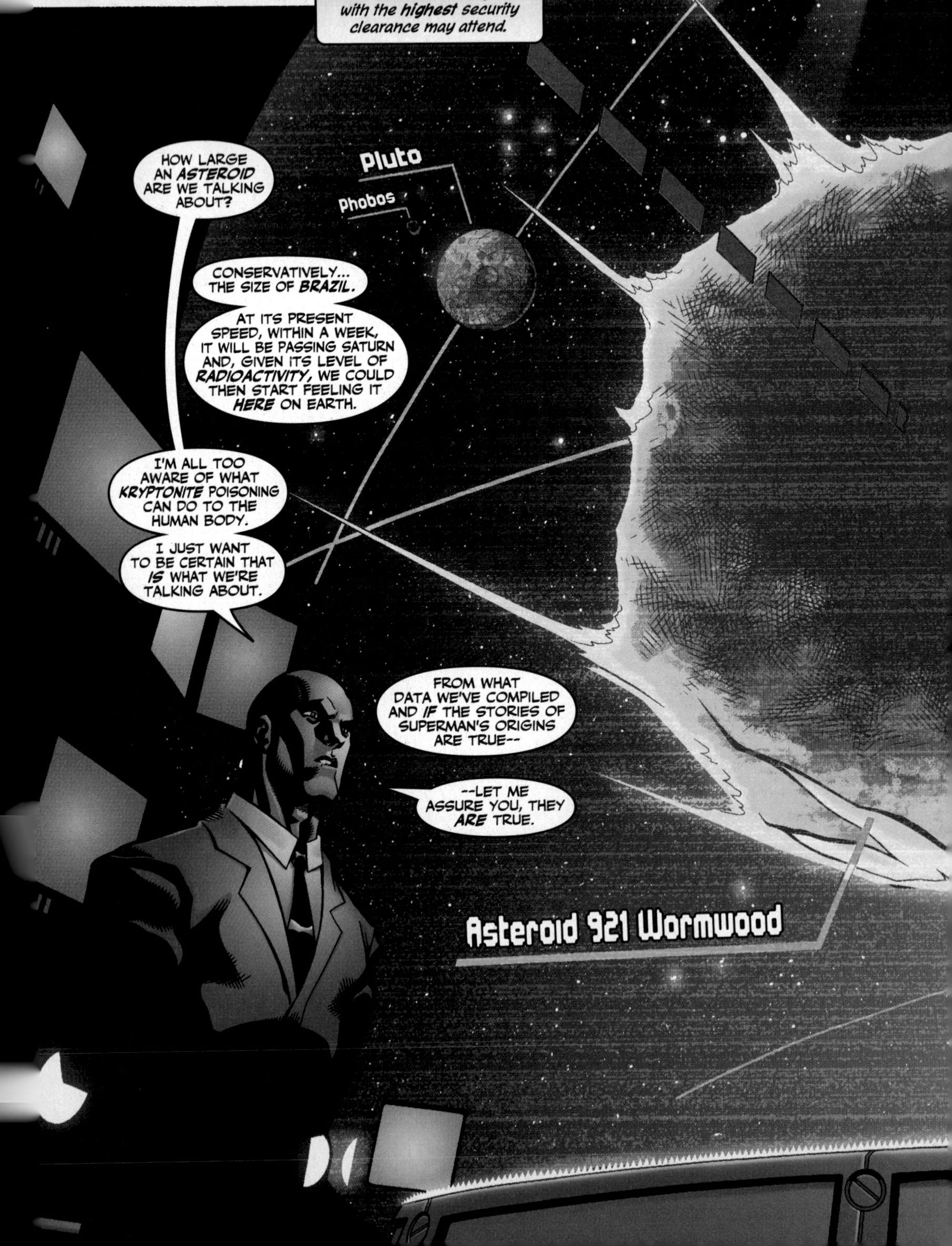
President Lex Luthor's Private War Room. Only those with the highest security clearance may attend.
HOW LARGE AN ASTEROID ARE WE TALKING ABOUT?
Pluto
Phobos
CONSERVATIVELY... THE SIZE OF BRAZIL.
AT ITS PRESENT SPEED, WITHIN A WEEK, IT WILL BE PASSING SATURN AND, GIVEN ITS LEVEL OF RADIOACTIVITY, WE COULD THEN START FEELING IT HERE ON EARTH.
I'M ALL TOO AWARE OF WHAT KRYPTONITE POISONING CAN DO TO THE HUMAN BODY.
I JUST WANT TO BE CERTAIN THAT IS WHAT WE'RE TALKING ABOUT.
FROM WHAT DATA WE'VE COMPILED AND IF THE STORIES OF SUPERMAN'S ORIGINS ARE TRUE--
--LET ME ASSURE YOU, THEY ARE TRUE.
Asteroid 921 Wormwood

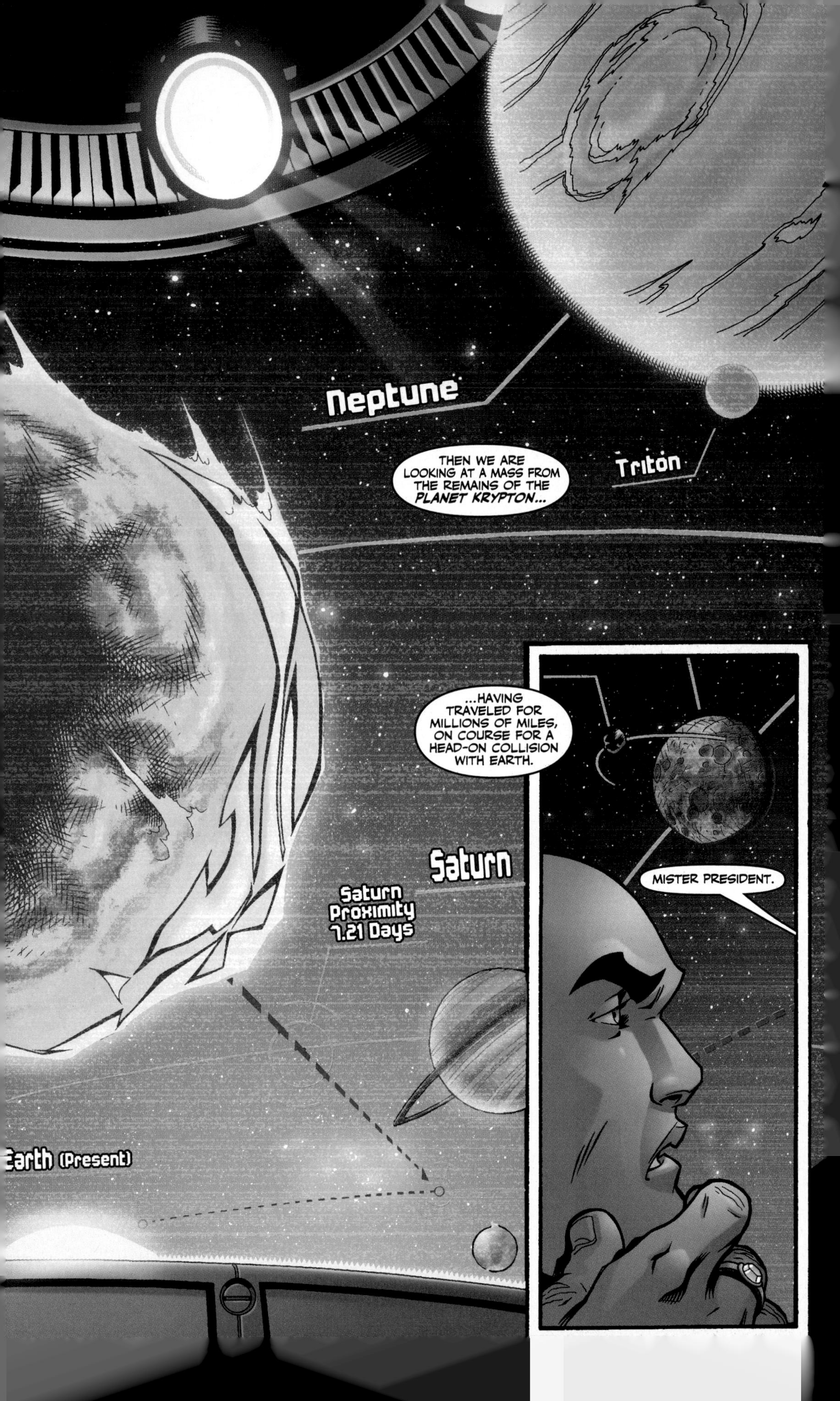
Neptune
Triton
THEN WE ARE LOOKING AT A MASS FROM THE REMAINS OF THE *PLANET KRYPTON*...
...HAVING TRAVELED FOR MILLIONS OF MILES, ON COURSE FOR A HEAD-ON COLLISION WITH EARTH.
Saturn
Saturn Proximity 7.21 Days
MISTER PRESIDENT.
Earth (Present)

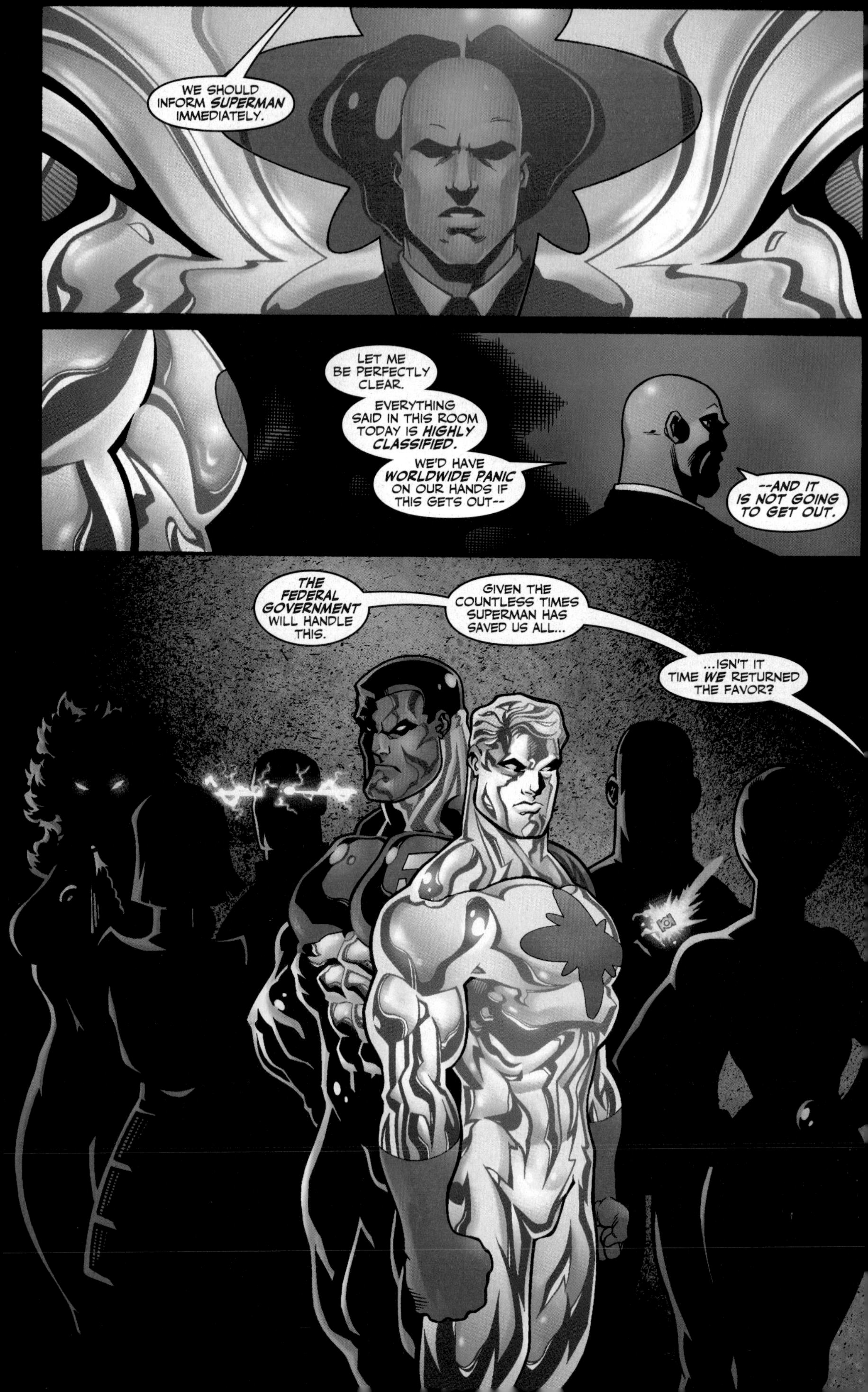
WE SHOULD INFORM SUPERMAN IMMEDIATELY.
LET ME BE PERFECTLY CLEAR.
EVERYTHING SAID IN THIS ROOM TODAY IS HIGHLY CLASSIFIED.
WE'D HAVE WORLDWIDE PANIC ON OUR HANDS IF THIS GETS OUT--
--AND IT IS NOT GOING TO GET OUT.
THE FEDERAL GOVERNMENT WILL HANDLE THIS.
GIVEN THE COUNTLESS TIMES SUPERMAN HAS SAVED US ALL...
...ISN'T IT TIME WE RETURNED THE FAVOR?

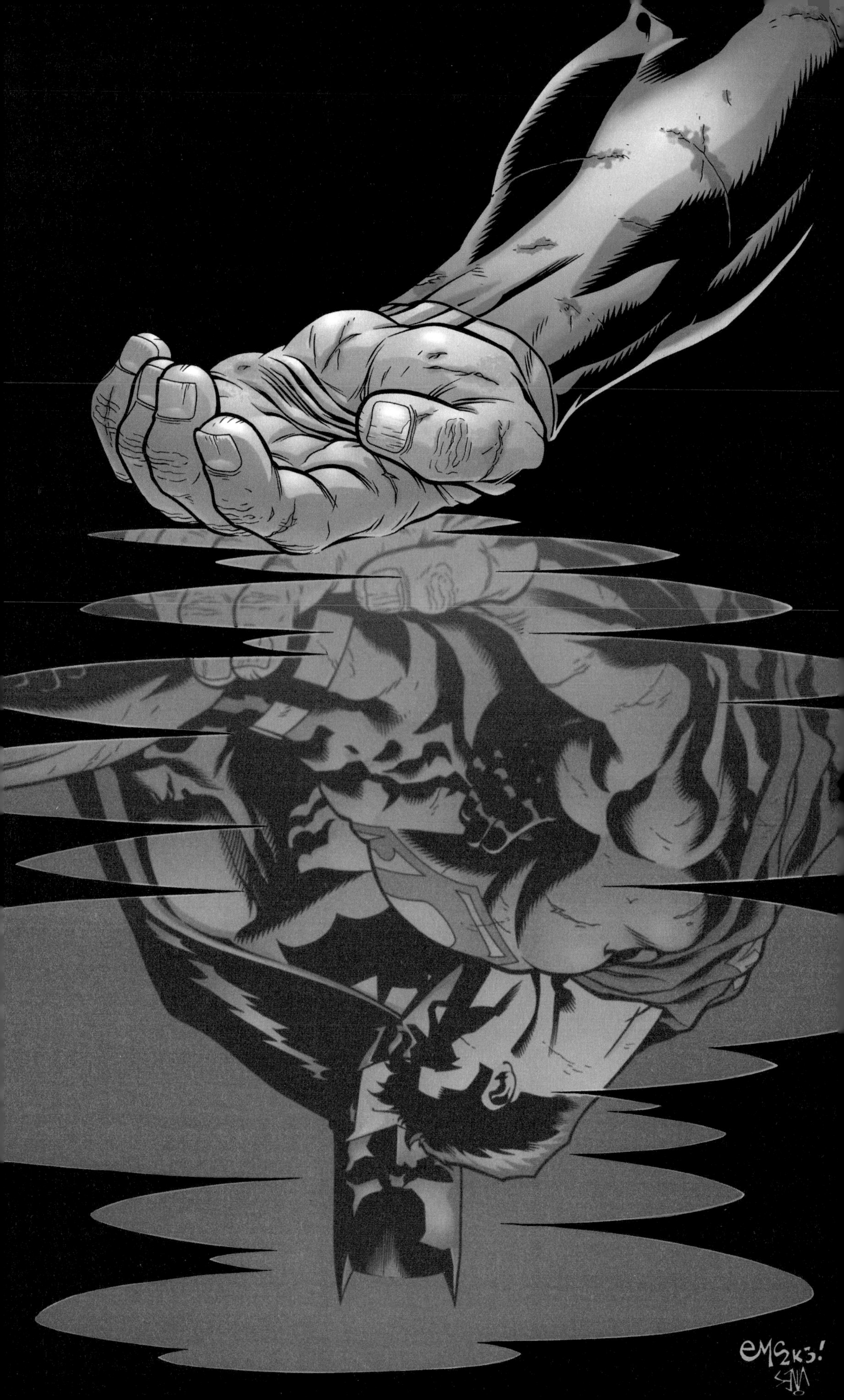

"I'm you. Years from now. I've come to stop you."

It's... odd what goes through your head when... it seems like the worst of times.

No more air.

We were kids, **Pete Ross** and I. We had gone camping in this horrible storm back in Smallville.

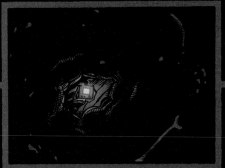

003

The **Kryptonite bullet** lodged in Clark's chest has immobilized him.

The ground had softened and I fell into an old well. It was maybe a hundred feet down. And all around me were these green rocks. **Meteor rocks.**

002

We can't go up. **Metallo** may still be there, and neither of us is in any shape to take him on.

I'd never felt anything like it before. My head was spinning. My stomach going upside-down. I didn't know then it was **Kryptonite.** I only knew I was hurt.

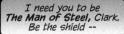

I need you to be **The Man of Steel,** Clark. Be the shield --

001

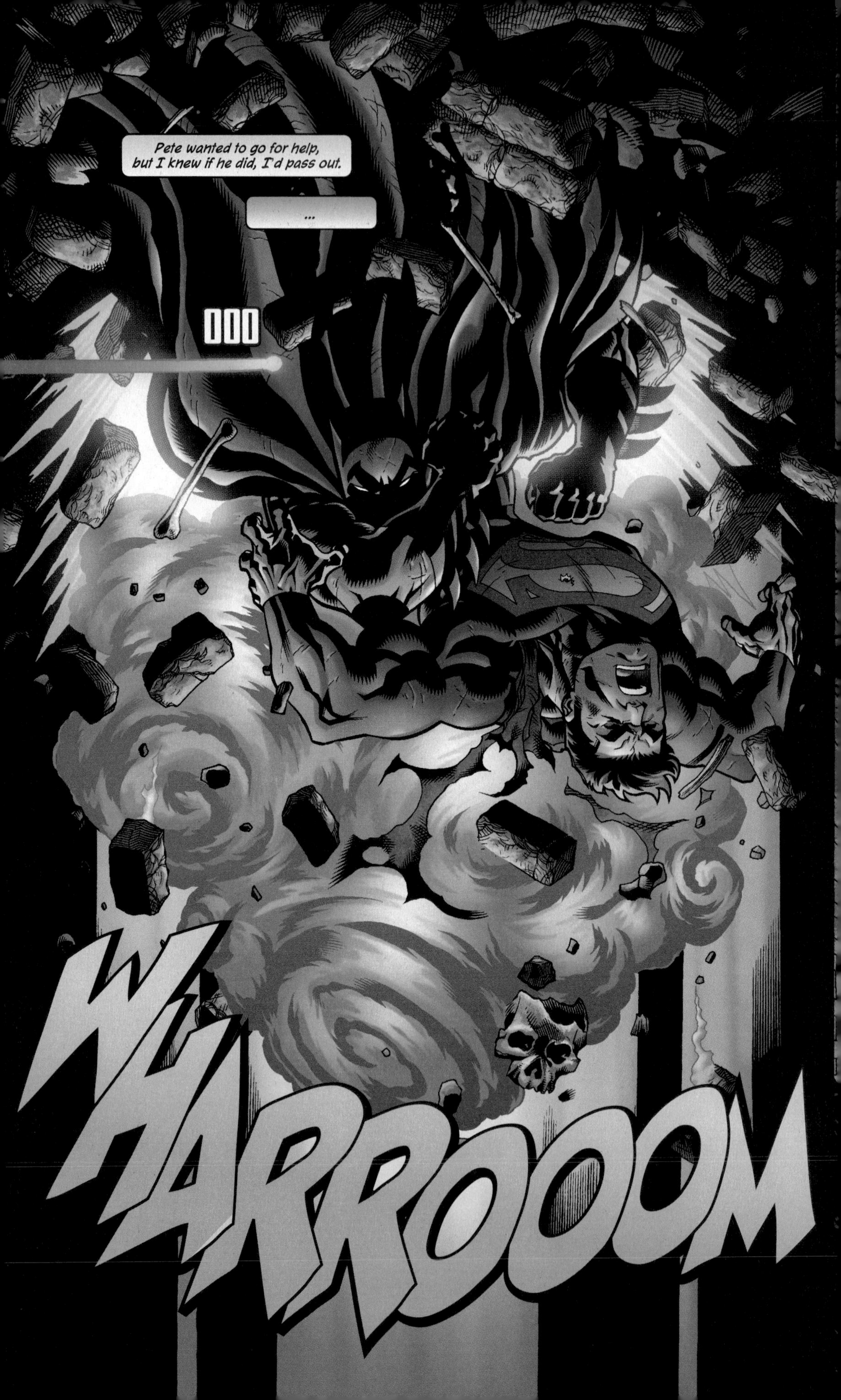
Pete wanted to go for help, but I knew if he did, I'd pass out.
...
OOO
WHARROOOM

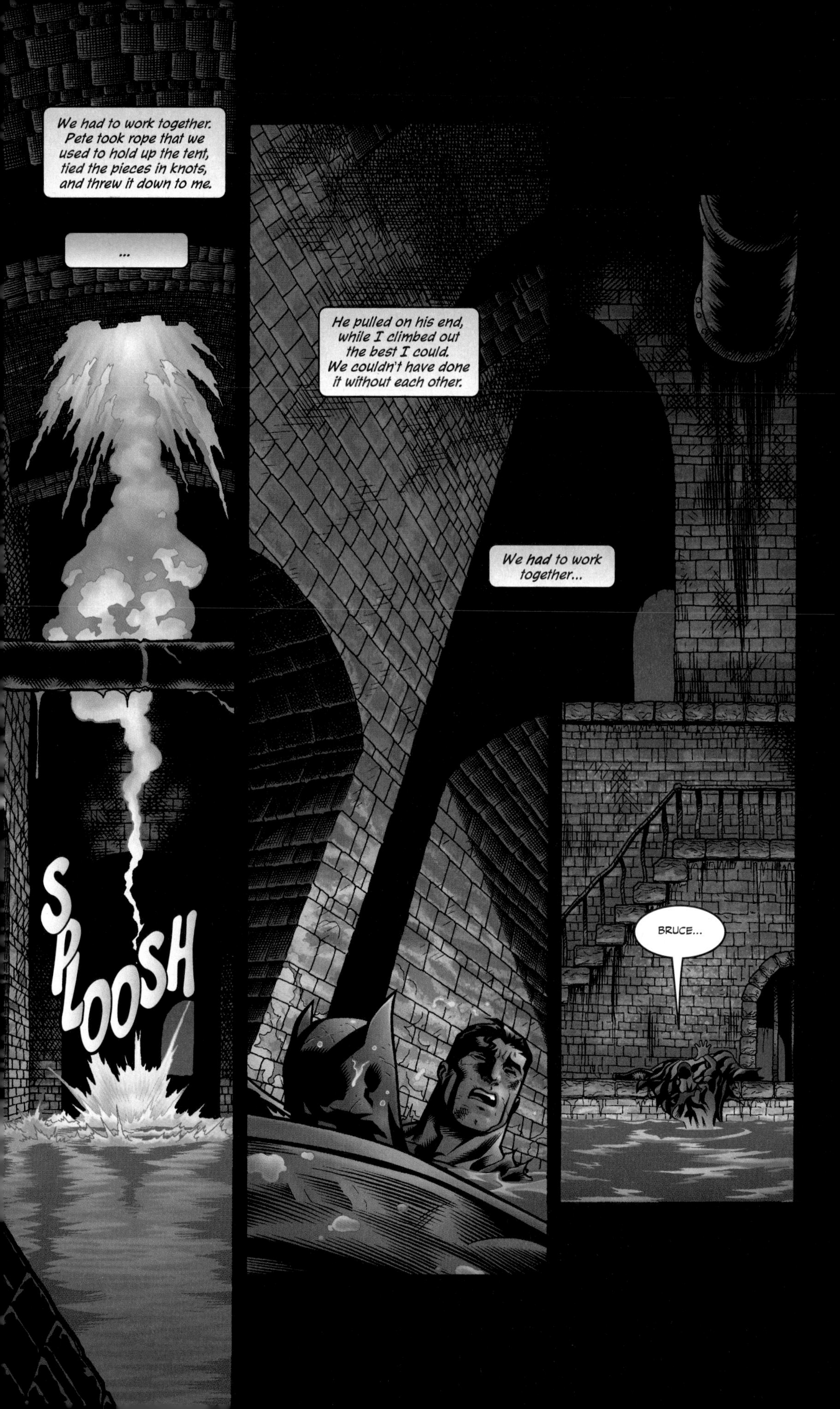
We had to work together. Pete took rope that we used to hold up the tent, tied the pieces in knots, and threw it down to me.
...
SPLOOSH
He pulled on his end, while I climbed out the best I could. We couldn't have done it without each other.
We had to work together...
BRUCE...

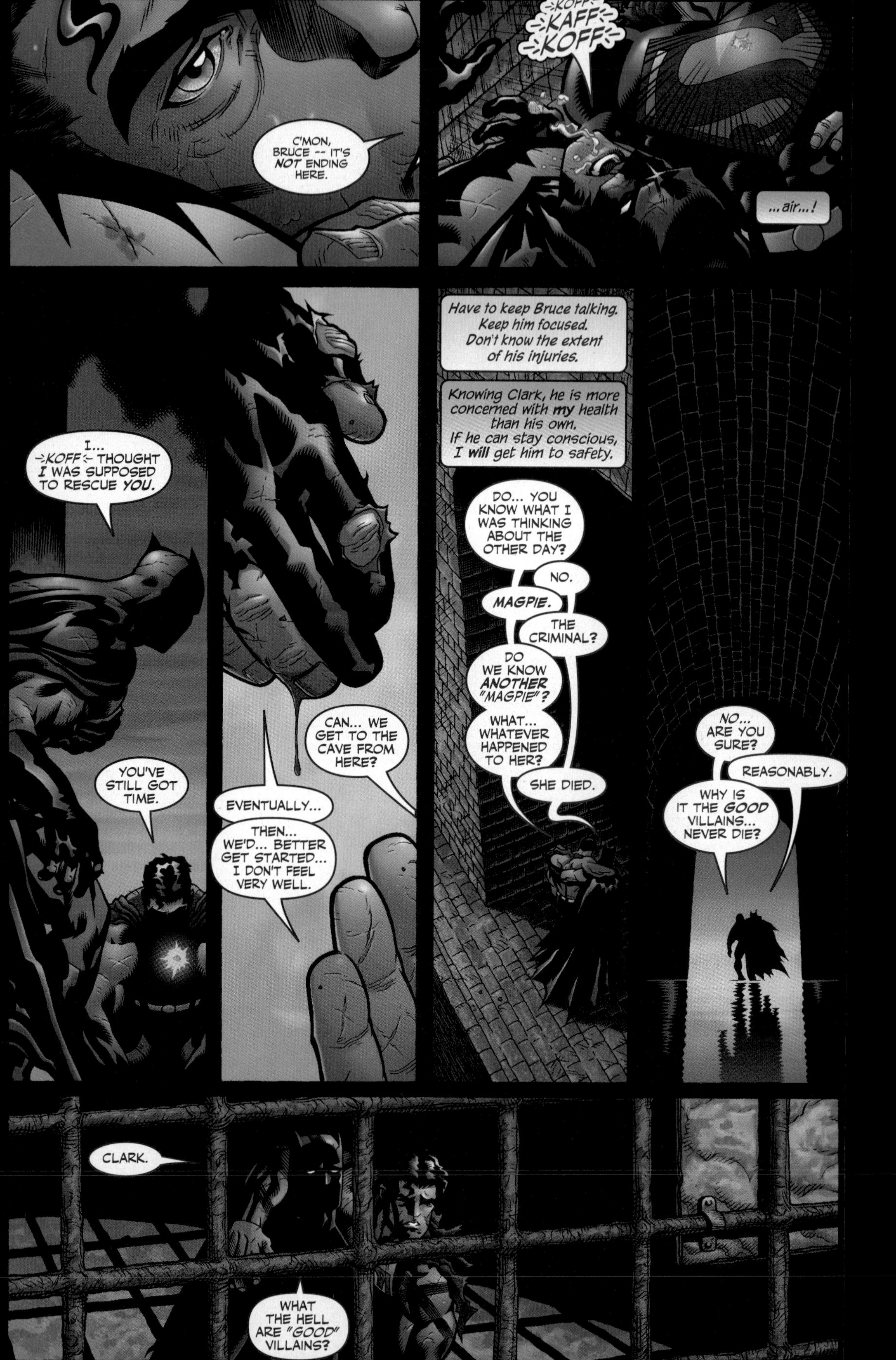
C'MON, BRUCE -- IT'S NOT ENDING HERE.
-KOFF- KAFF KOFF
...air...!
I... -KOFF- THOUGHT I WAS SUPPOSED TO RESCUE YOU.
YOU'VE STILL GOT TIME.
CAN... WE GET TO THE CAVE FROM HERE?
EVENTUALLY...
THEN... WE'D... BETTER GET STARTED... I DON'T FEEL VERY WELL.
Have to keep Bruce talking. Keep him focused. Don't know the extent of his injuries.
Knowing Clark, he is more concerned with my health than his own. If he can stay conscious, I will get him to safety.
DO... YOU KNOW WHAT I WAS THINKING ABOUT THE OTHER DAY?
NO.
MAGPIE.
THE CRIMINAL?
DO WE KNOW ANOTHER "MAGPIE"?
WHAT... WHATEVER HAPPENED TO HER?
SHE DIED.
NO... ARE YOU SURE?
REASONABLY.
WHY IS IT THE GOOD VILLAINS... NEVER DIE?
CLARK.
WHAT THE HELL ARE "GOOD" VILLAINS?

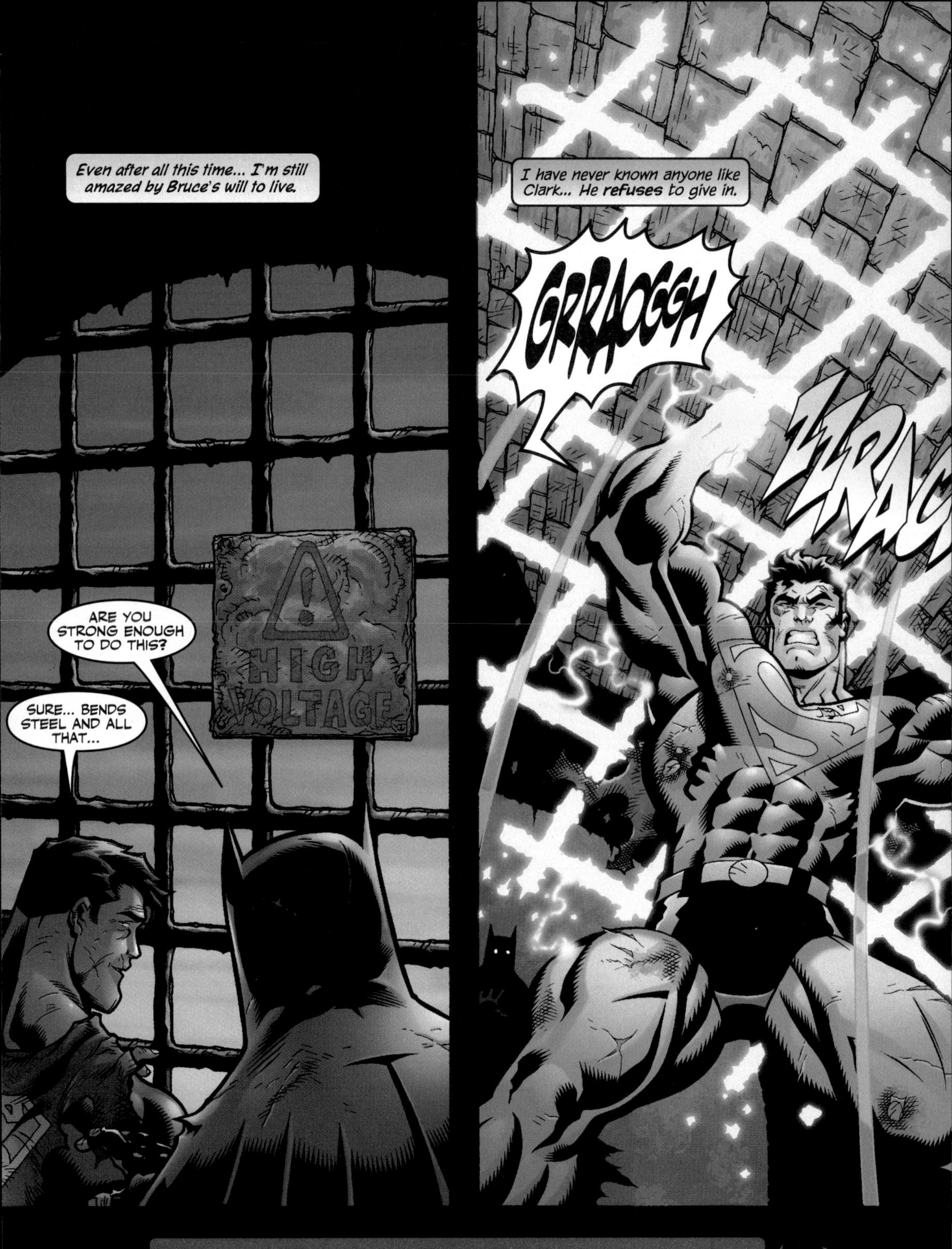
Even after all this time... I'm still amazed by Bruce's will to live.
ARE YOU STRONG ENOUGH TO DO THIS?
SURE... BENDS STEEL AND ALL THAT...
HIGH VOLTAGE
I have never known anyone like Clark... He refuses to give in.
GRRAOGGH

PART TWO: EARLY WARNING

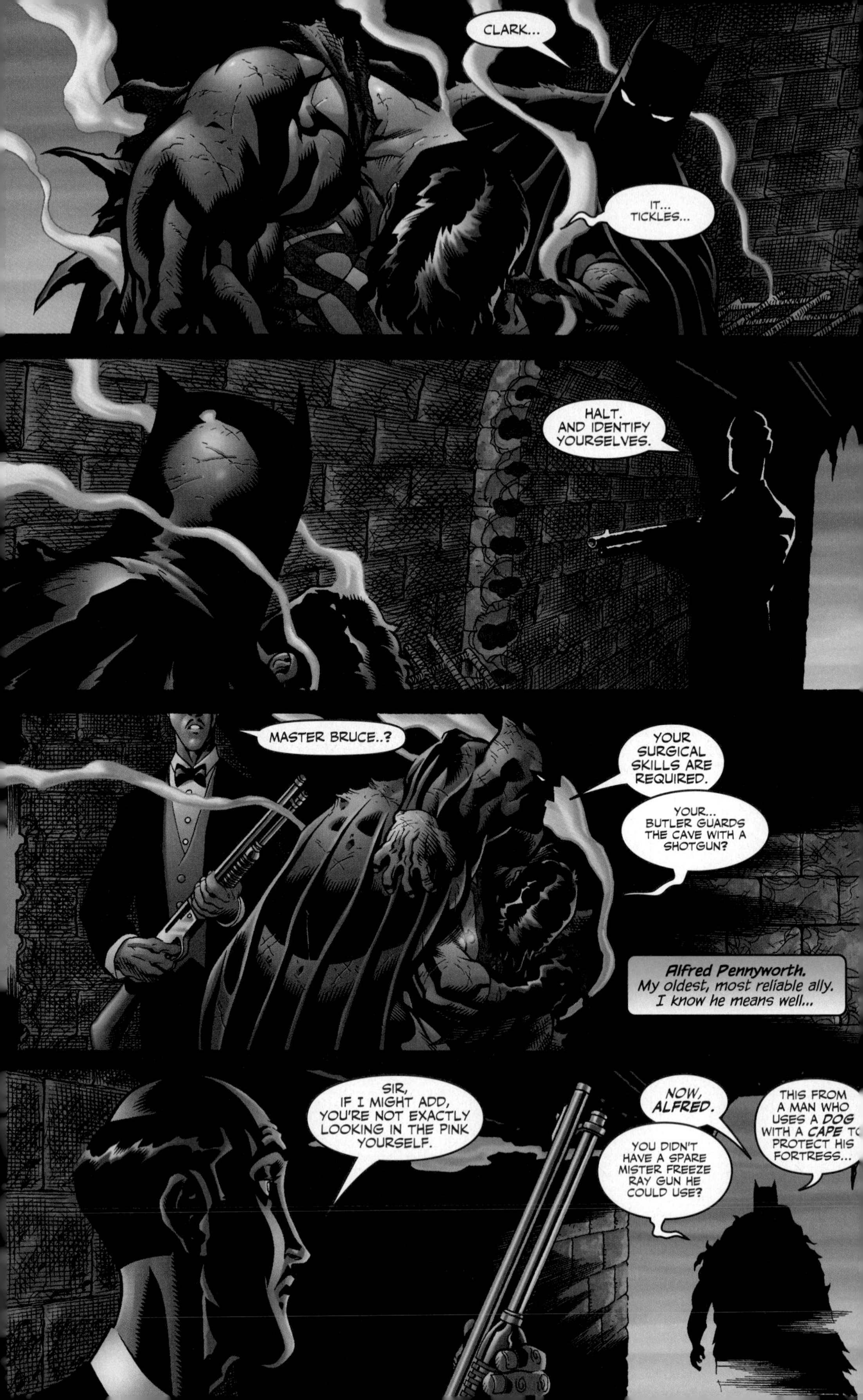
CLARK...
IT... TICKLES...
HALT. AND IDENTIFY YOURSELVES.
MASTER BRUCE..?
YOUR SURGICAL SKILLS ARE REQUIRED.
YOUR... BUTLER GUARDS THE CAVE WITH A SHOTGUN?
Alfred Pennyworth. My oldest, most reliable ally. I know he means well...
SIR, IF I MIGHT ADD, YOU'RE NOT EXACTLY LOOKING IN THE PINK YOURSELF.
NOW, ALFRED.
YOU DIDN'T HAVE A SPARE MISTER FREEZE RAY GUN HE COULD USE?
THIS FROM A MAN WHO USES A DOG WITH A CAPE TO PROTECT HIS FORTRESS...

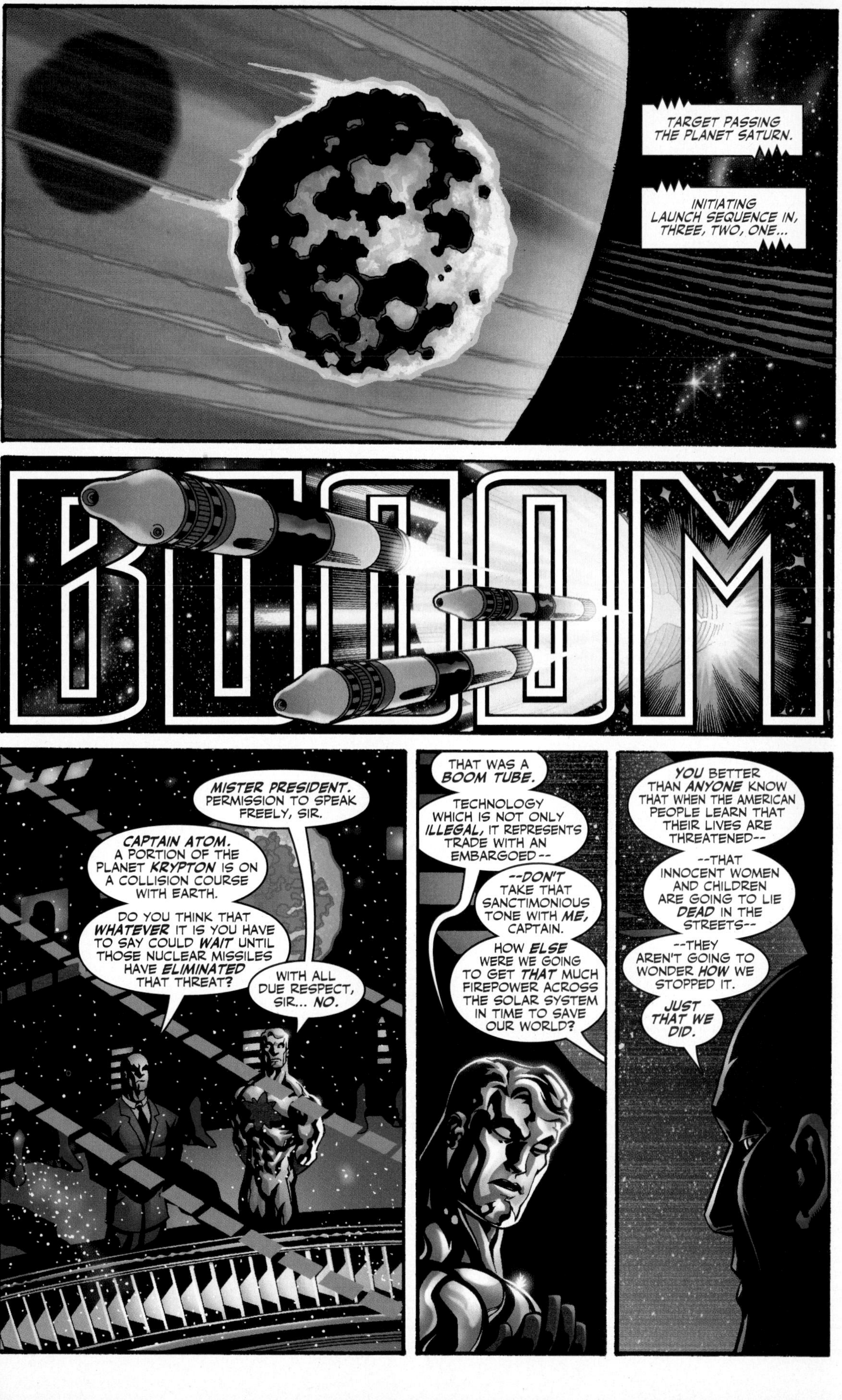
TARGET PASSING THE PLANET SATURN.
INITIATING LAUNCH SEQUENCE IN, THREE, TWO, ONE...
BOOOOM
MISTER PRESIDENT. PERMISSION TO SPEAK FREELY, SIR.
CAPTAIN ATOM. A PORTION OF THE PLANET KRYPTON IS ON A COLLISION COURSE WITH EARTH.
DO YOU THINK THAT WHATEVER IT IS YOU HAVE TO SAY COULD WAIT UNTIL THOSE NUCLEAR MISSILES HAVE ELIMINATED THAT THREAT?
WITH ALL DUE RESPECT, SIR... NO.
THAT WAS A BOOM TUBE.
TECHNOLOGY WHICH IS NOT ONLY ILLEGAL, IT REPRESENTS TRADE WITH AN EMBARGOED--
--DON'T TAKE THAT SANCTIMONIOUS TONE WITH ME, CAPTAIN.
HOW ELSE WERE WE GOING TO GET THAT MUCH FIREPOWER ACROSS THE SOLAR SYSTEM IN TIME TO SAVE OUR WORLD?
YOU BETTER THAN ANYONE KNOW THAT WHEN THE AMERICAN PEOPLE LEARN THAT THEIR LIVES ARE THREATENED--
--THAT INNOCENT WOMEN AND CHILDREN ARE GOING TO LIE DEAD IN THE STREETS--
--THEY AREN'T GOING TO WONDER HOW WE STOPPED IT.
JUST THAT WE DID.

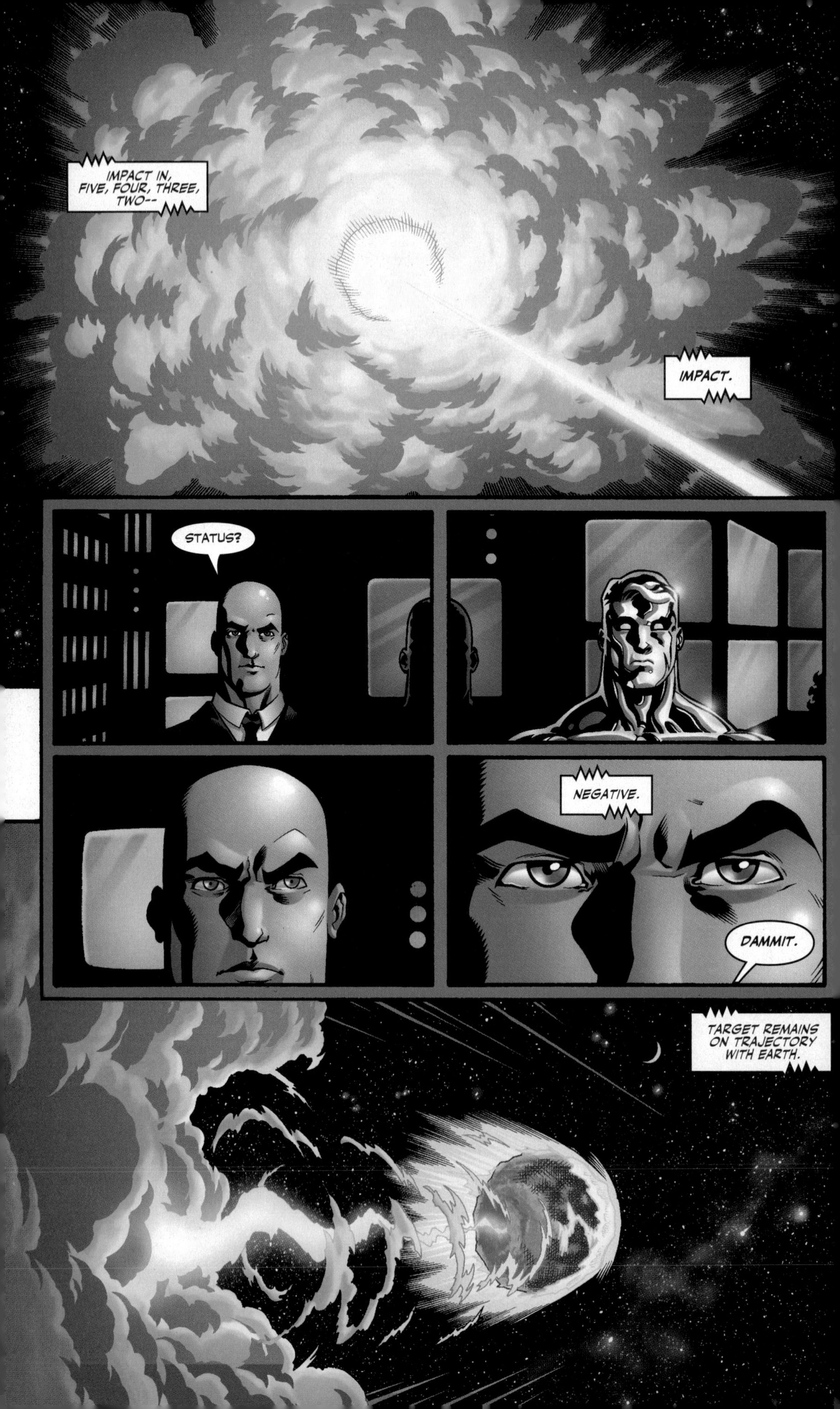
IMPACT IN, FIVE, FOUR, THREE, TWO--
IMPACT.
STATUS?
NEGATIVE.
DAMMIT.
TARGET REMAINS ON TRAJECTORY WITH EARTH.

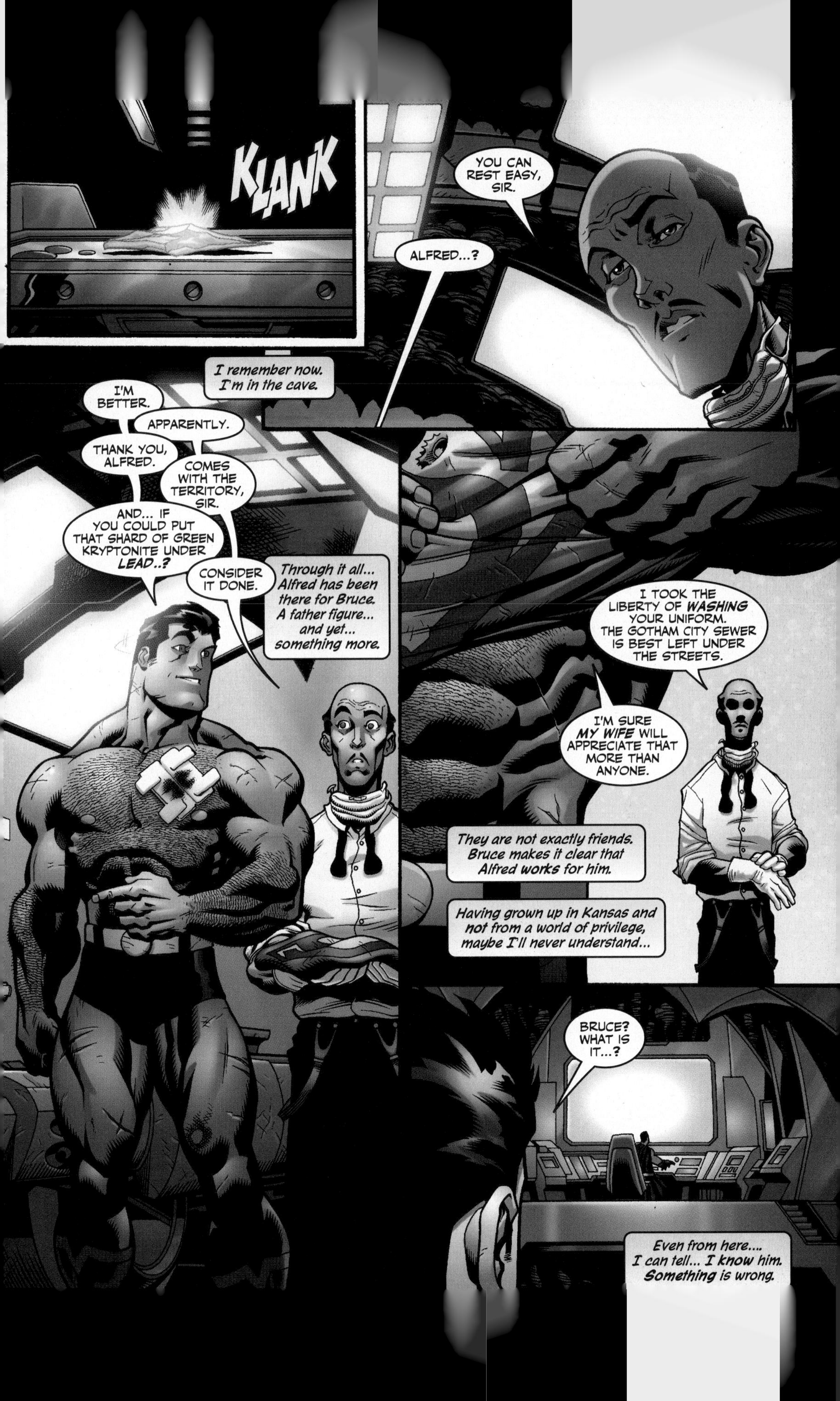
KLANK
YOU CAN REST EASY, SIR.
ALFRED...?
I remember now. I'm in the cave.
I'M BETTER.
APPARENTLY.
THANK YOU, ALFRED.
COMES WITH THE TERRITORY, SIR.
AND... IF YOU COULD PUT THAT SHARD OF GREEN KRYPTONITE UNDER LEAD..?
CONSIDER IT DONE.
Through it all... Alfred has been there for Bruce. A father figure... and yet... something more.
I TOOK THE LIBERTY OF WASHING YOUR UNIFORM. THE GOTHAM CITY SEWER IS BEST LEFT UNDER THE STREETS.
I'M SURE MY WIFE WILL APPRECIATE THAT MORE THAN ANYONE.
They are not exactly friends. Bruce makes it clear that Alfred works for him.
Having grown up in Kansas and not from a world of privilege, maybe I'll never understand...
BRUCE? WHAT IS IT...?
Even from here.... I can tell... I know him. Something is wrong.

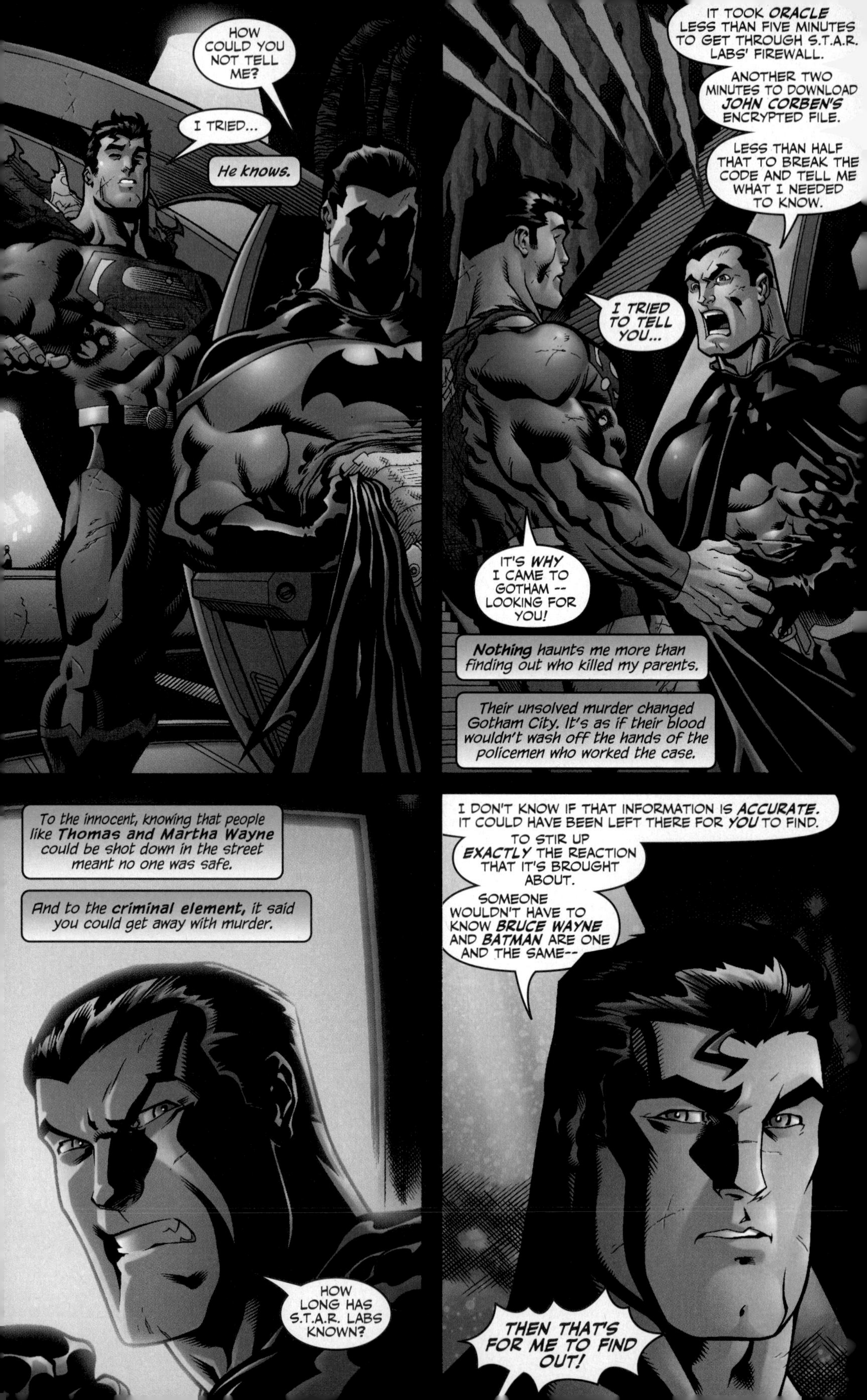

HOW COULD YOU NOT TELL ME?
I TRIED...
He knows.
IT TOOK ORACLE LESS THAN FIVE MINUTES TO GET THROUGH S.T.A.R. LABS' FIREWALL.
ANOTHER TWO MINUTES TO DOWNLOAD JOHN CORBEN'S ENCRYPTED FILE.
LESS THAN HALF THAT TO BREAK THE CODE AND TELL ME WHAT I NEEDED TO KNOW.
I TRIED TO TELL YOU...
IT'S WHY I CAME TO GOTHAM -- LOOKING FOR YOU!
Nothing haunts me more than finding out who killed my parents.
Their unsolved murder changed Gotham City. It's as if their blood wouldn't wash off the hands of the policemen who worked the case.
To the innocent, knowing that people like Thomas and Martha Wayne could be shot down in the street meant no one was safe.
And to the criminal element, it said you could get away with murder.
HOW LONG HAS S.T.A.R. LABS KNOWN?
I DON'T KNOW IF THAT INFORMATION IS ACCURATE. IT COULD HAVE BEEN LEFT THERE FOR YOU TO FIND.
TO STIR UP EXACTLY THE REACTION THAT IT'S BROUGHT ABOUT.
SOMEONE WOULDN'T HAVE TO KNOW BRUCE WAYNE AND BATMAN ARE ONE AND THE SAME--
THEN THAT'S FOR ME TO FIND OUT!

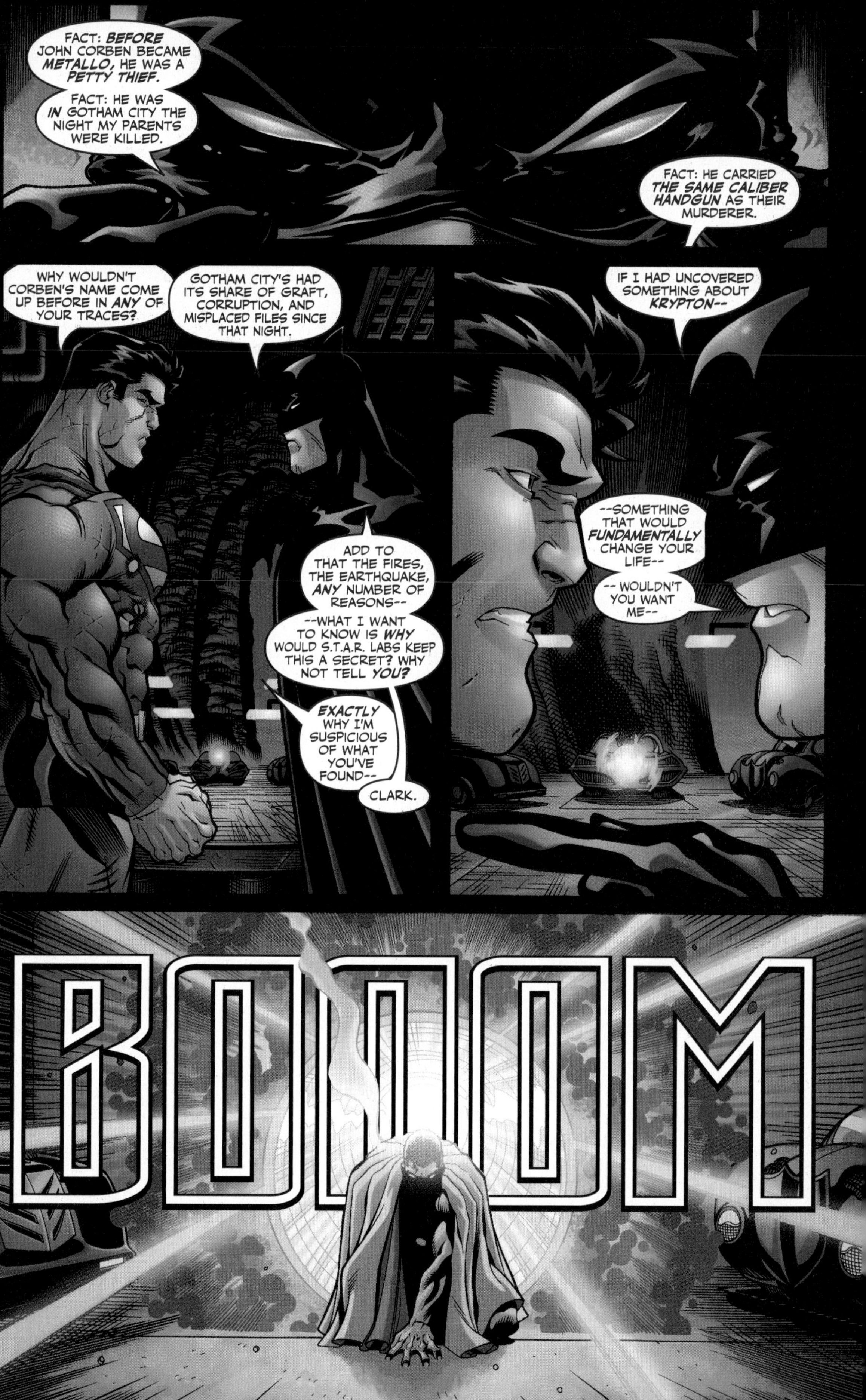
FACT: BEFORE JOHN CORBEN BECAME METALLO, HE WAS A PETTY THIEF.
FACT: HE WAS IN GOTHAM CITY THE NIGHT MY PARENTS WERE KILLED.
FACT: HE CARRIED THE SAME CALIBER HANDGUN AS THEIR MURDERER.
WHY WOULDN'T CORBEN'S NAME COME UP BEFORE IN ANY OF YOUR TRACES?
GOTHAM CITY'S HAD ITS SHARE OF GRAFT, CORRUPTION, AND MISPLACED FILES SINCE THAT NIGHT.
ADD TO THAT THE FIRES, THE EARTHQUAKE, ANY NUMBER OF REASONS--
--WHAT I WANT TO KNOW IS WHY WOULD S.T.A.R. LABS KEEP THIS A SECRET? WHY NOT TELL YOU?
EXACTLY WHY I'M SUSPICIOUS OF WHAT YOU'VE FOUND--
CLARK.
IF I HAD UNCOVERED SOMETHING ABOUT KRYPTON--
--SOMETHING THAT WOULD FUNDAMENTALLY CHANGE YOUR LIFE--
-- WOULDN'T YOU WANT ME--
BOOOM

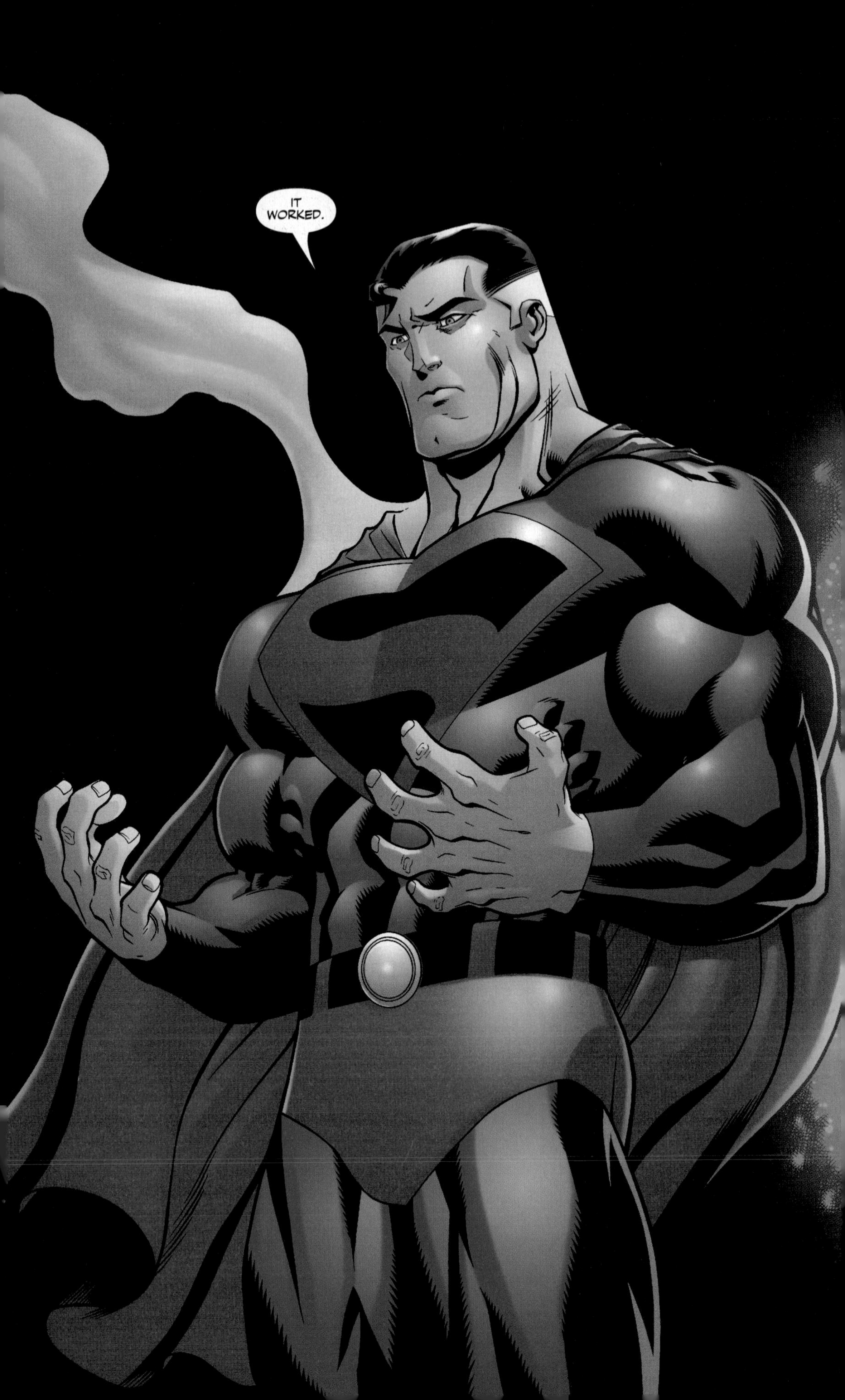
IT WORKED.

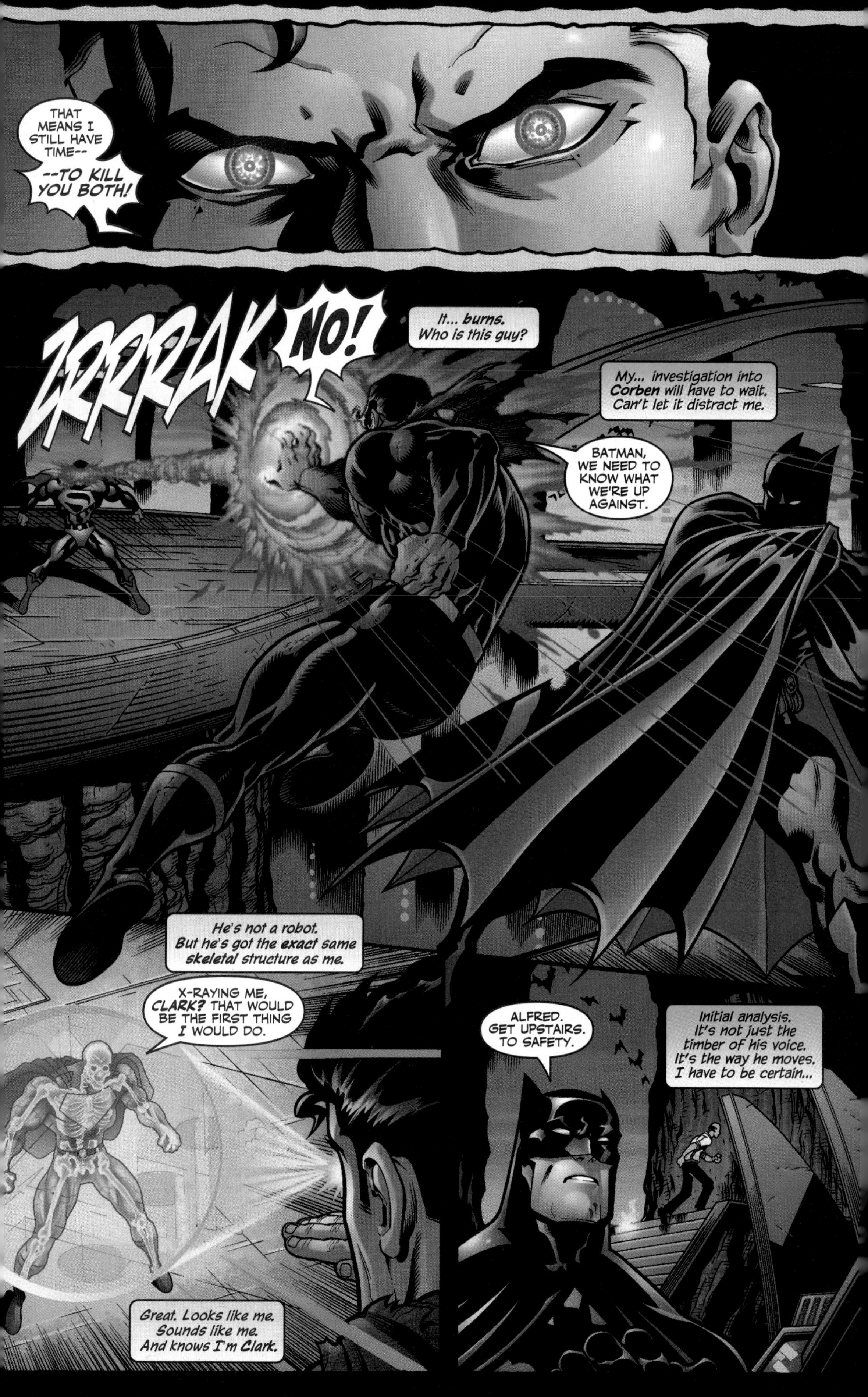
THAT MEANS I STILL HAVE TIME--
--TO KILL YOU BOTH!
ZZRRRAK
NO!
It... burns. Who is this guy?
My... investigation into Corben will have to wait. Can't let it distract me.
BATMAN, WE NEED TO KNOW WHAT WE'RE UP AGAINST.
He's not a robot. But he's got the exact same skeletal structure as me.
X-RAYING ME, CLARK? THAT WOULD BE THE FIRST THING I WOULD DO.
Great. Looks like me. Sounds like me. And knows I'm Clark.
ALFRED. GET UPSTAIRS. TO SAFETY.
Initial analysis. It's not just the timber of his voice. It's the way he moves. I have to be certain...

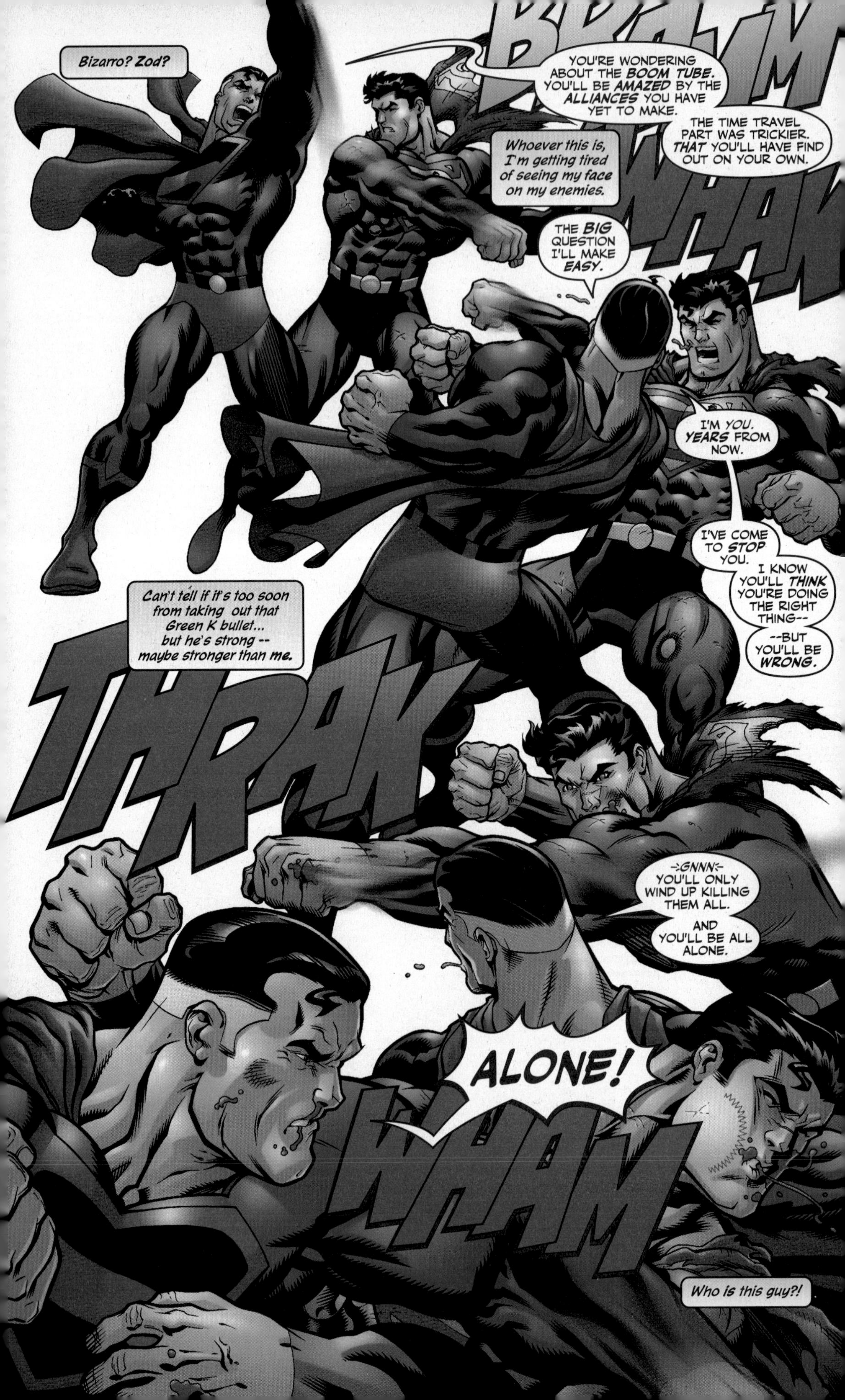
Bizarro? Zod?
BRAAM
YOU'RE WONDERING ABOUT THE BOOM TUBE. YOU'LL BE AMAZED BY THE ALLIANCES YOU HAVE YET TO MAKE.
THE TIME TRAVEL PART WAS TRICKIER. THAT YOU'LL HAVE FIND OUT ON YOUR OWN.
Whoever this is, I'm getting tired of seeing my face on my enemies.
WHAK
THE BIG QUESTION I'LL MAKE EASY.
I'M YOU. YEARS FROM NOW.
I'VE COME TO STOP YOU.
I KNOW YOU'LL THINK YOU'RE DOING THE RIGHT THING--
--BUT YOU'LL BE WRONG.
Can't tell if it's too soon from taking out that Green K bullet... but he's strong -- maybe stronger than me.
THRAK
-GNNN- YOU'LL ONLY WIND UP KILLING THEM ALL.
AND YOU'LL BE ALL ALONE.
ALONE!
WHAM
Who is this guy?!

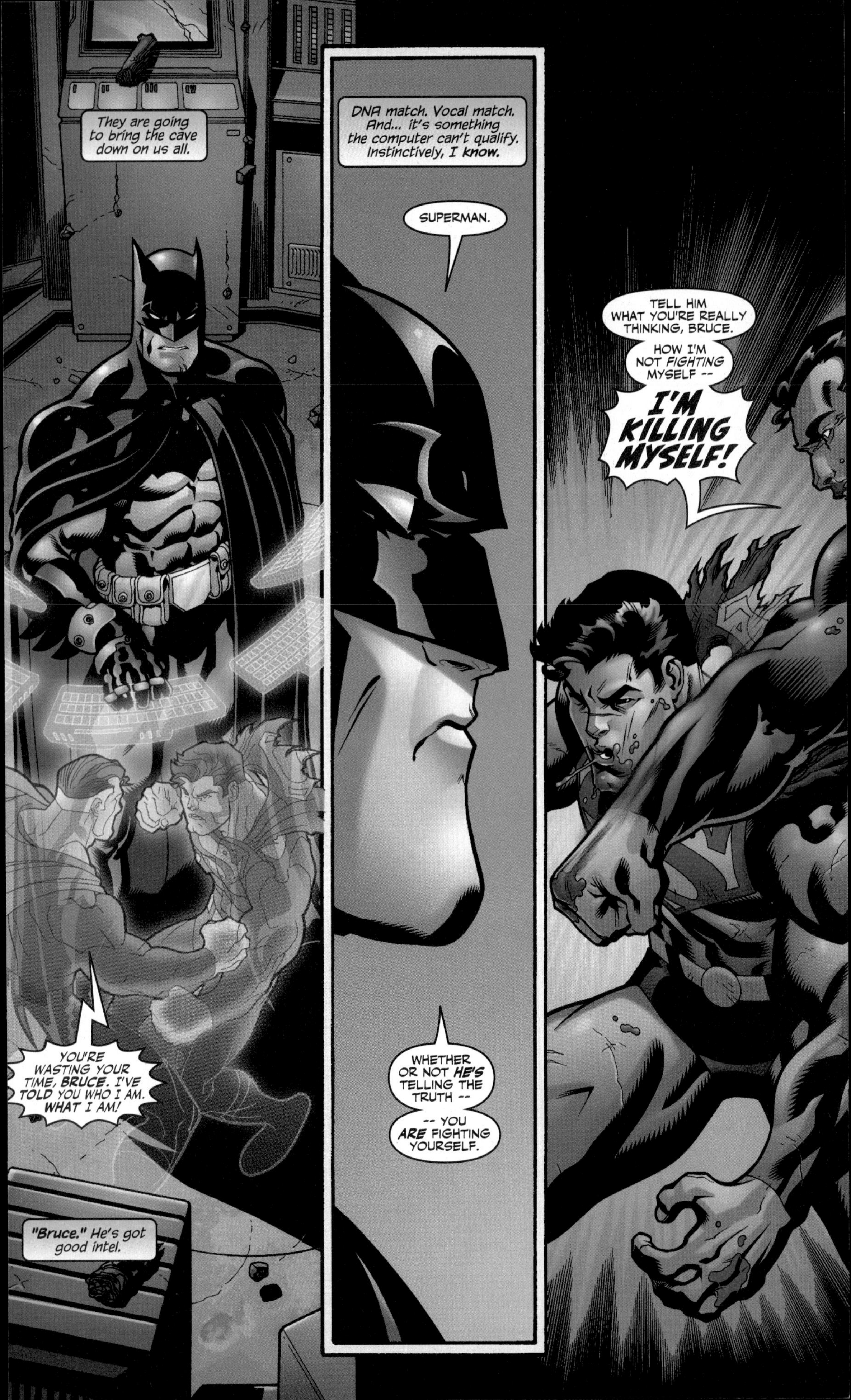
They are going to bring the cave down on us all.
DNA match. Vocal match. And... it's something the computer can't qualify. Instinctively, I know.
SUPERMAN.
TELL HIM WHAT YOU'RE REALLY THINKING, BRUCE.
HOW I'M NOT FIGHTING MYSELF --
I'M KILLING MYSELF!
YOU'RE WASTING YOUR TIME, BRUCE. I'VE TOLD YOU WHO I AM. WHAT I AM!
WHETHER OR NOT HE'S TELLING THE TRUTH --
-- YOU ARE FIGHTING YOURSELF.
"Bruce." He's got good intel.

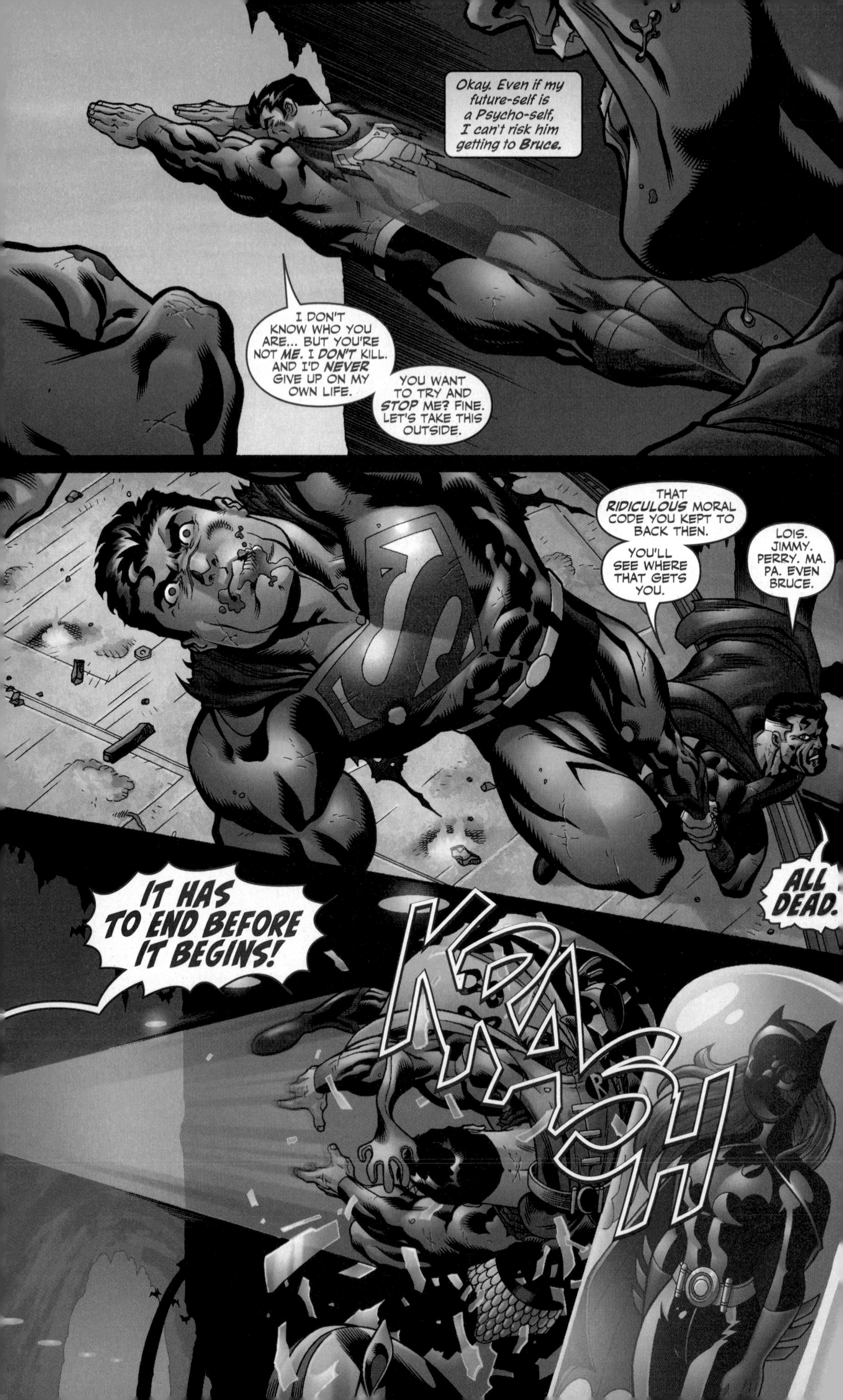
Okay. Even if my future-self is a Psycho-self, I can't risk him getting to Bruce.
I DON'T KNOW WHO YOU ARE... BUT YOU'RE NOT ME. I DON'T KILL. AND I'D NEVER GIVE UP ON MY OWN LIFE.
YOU WANT TO TRY AND STOP ME? FINE. LET'S TAKE THIS OUTSIDE.
THAT RIDICULOUS MORAL CODE YOU KEPT TO BACK THEN.
YOU'LL SEE WHERE THAT GETS YOU.
LOIS. JIMMY. PERRY. MA. PA. EVEN BRUCE.
ALL DEAD.
IT HAS TO END BEFORE IT BEGINS!
KRASH

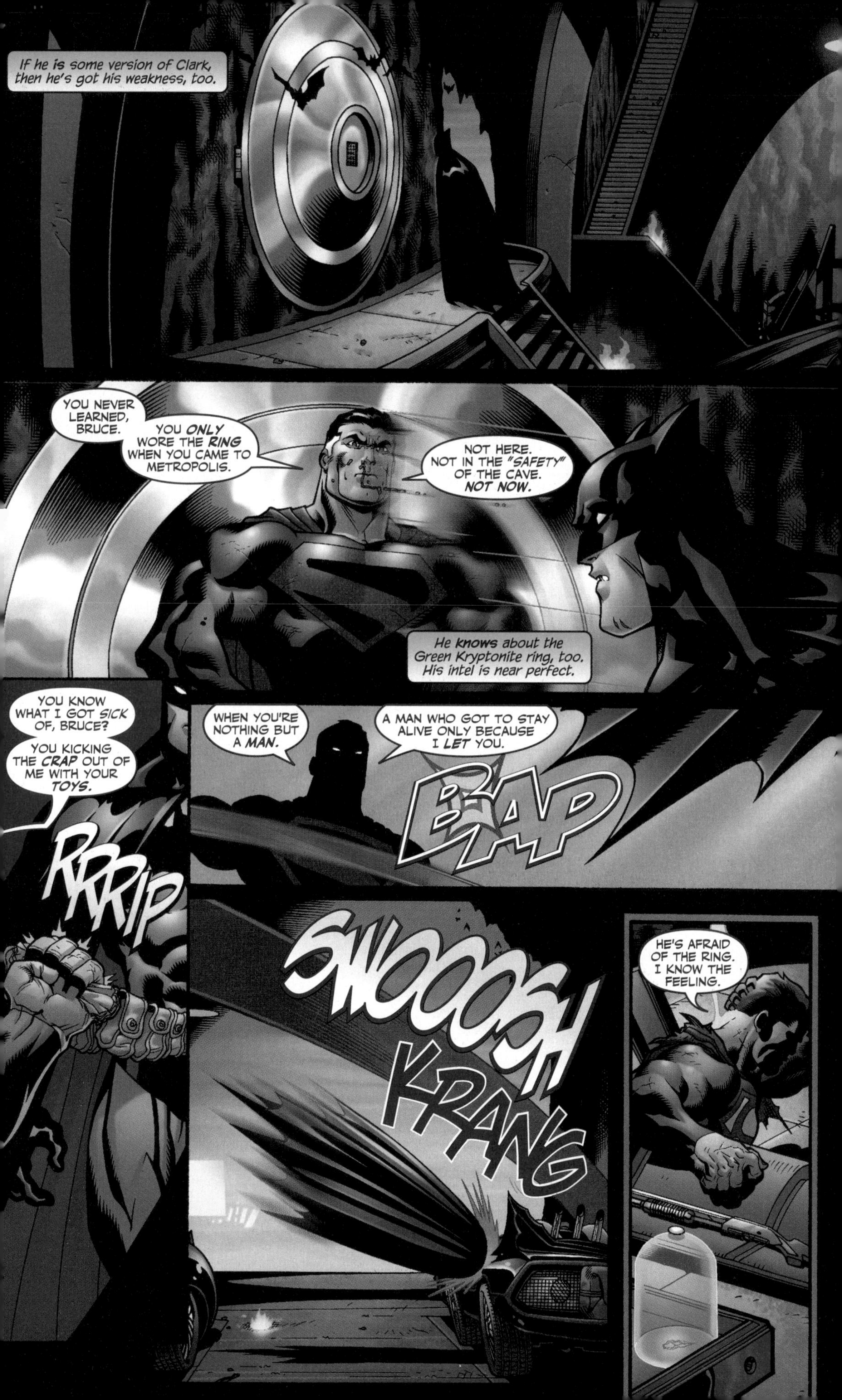
If he is some version of Clark, then he's got his weakness, too.
YOU NEVER LEARNED, BRUCE.
YOU ONLY WORE THE RING WHEN YOU CAME TO METROPOLIS.
NOT HERE. NOT IN THE "SAFETY" OF THE CAVE. NOT NOW.
He knows about the Green Kryptonite ring, too. His intel is near perfect.
YOU KNOW WHAT I GOT SICK OF, BRUCE?
YOU KICKING THE CRAP OUT OF ME WITH YOUR TOYS.
RRRIP
WHEN YOU'RE NOTHING BUT A MAN.
A MAN WHO GOT TO STAY ALIVE ONLY BECAUSE I LET YOU.
BRAP
SWOOOSH
KRANG
HE'S AFRAID OF THE RING. I KNOW THE FEELING.

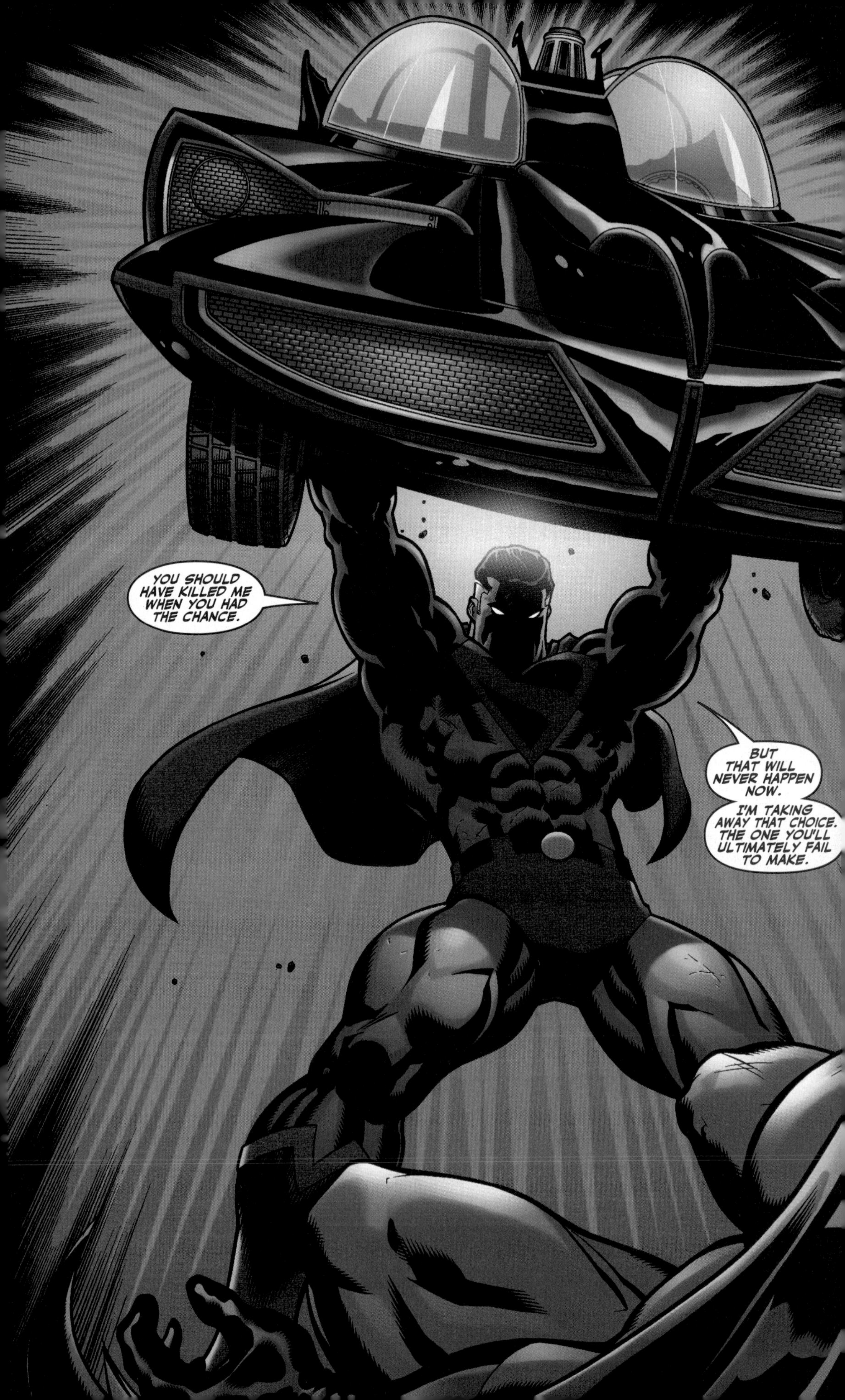
YOU SHOULD HAVE KILLED ME WHEN YOU HAD THE CHANCE.
BUT THAT WILL NEVER HAPPEN NOW.
I'M TAKING AWAY THAT CHOICE. THE ONE YOU'LL ULTIMATELY FAIL TO MAKE.

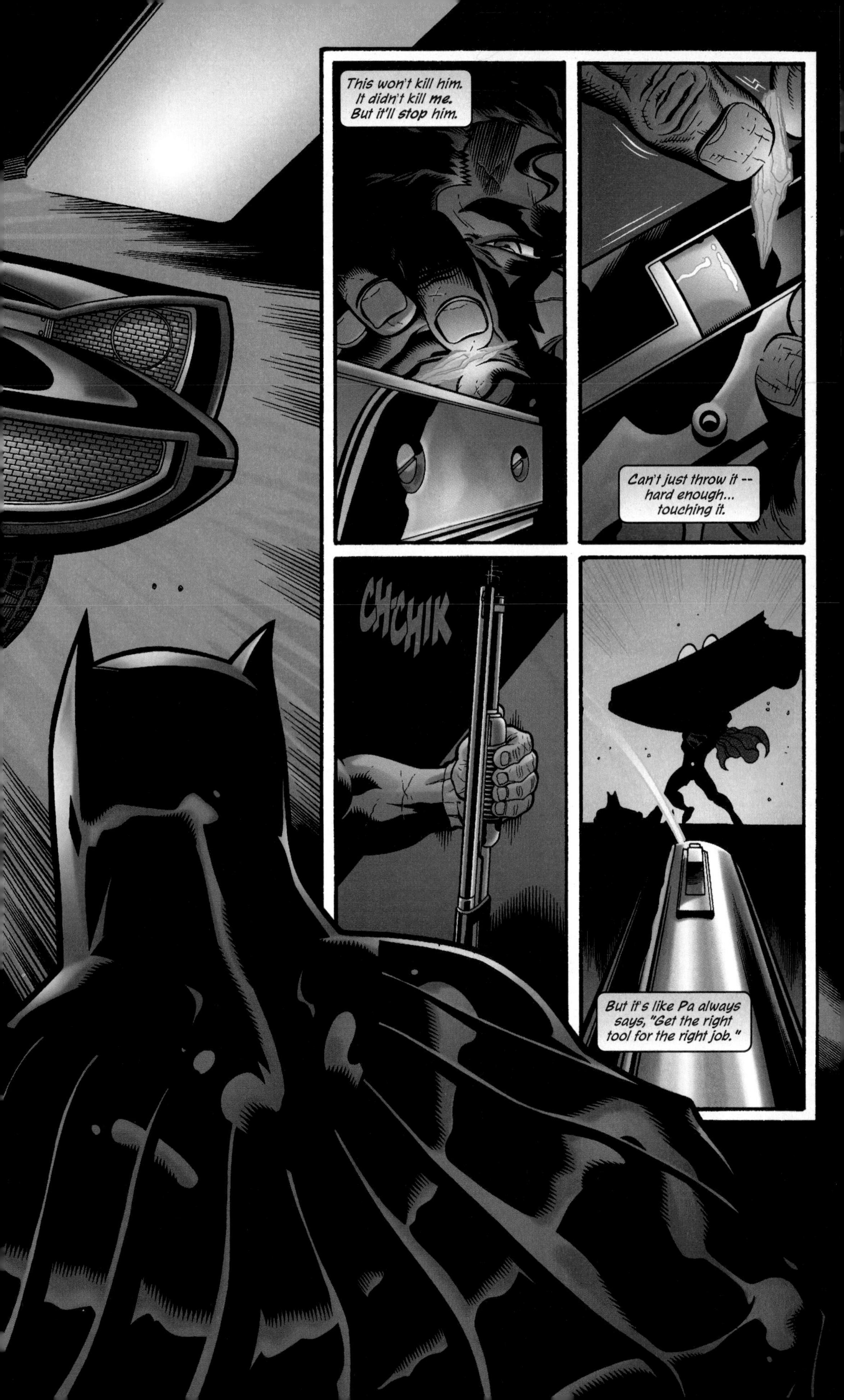
This won't kill him.
It didn't kill me.
But it'll stop him.
Can't just throw it --
hard enough...
touching it.
CH'CHIK
But it's like Pa always
says, "Get the right
tool for the right job."

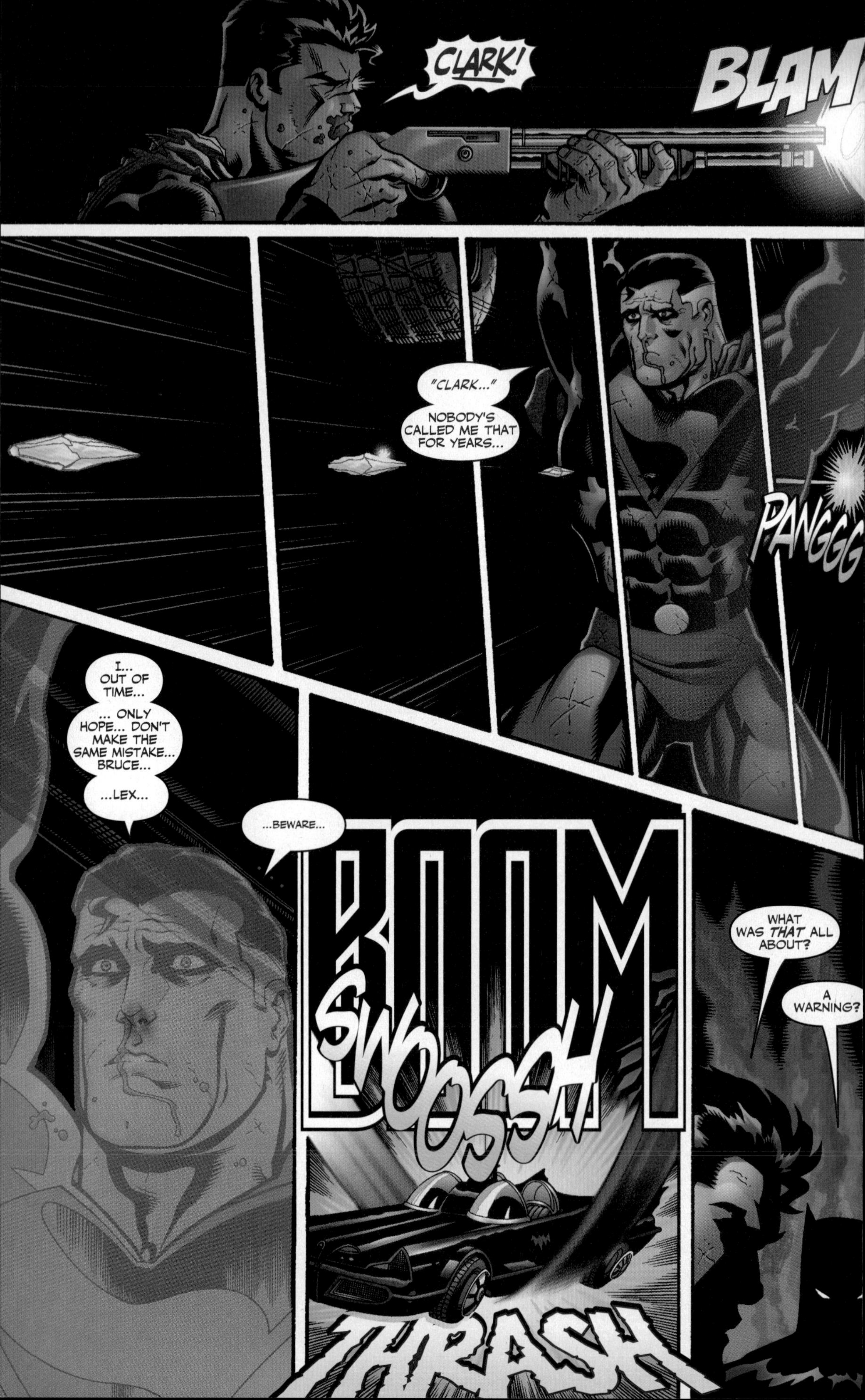
CLARK!
BLAM
"CLARK..."
NOBODY'S CALLED ME THAT FOR YEARS...
PANGGG
I... OUT OF TIME...
... ONLY HOPE... DON'T MAKE THE SAME MISTAKE... BRUCE...
...LEX...
...BEWARE...
BOOM
SWOOSSH
WHAT WAS *THAT* ALL ABOUT?
A WARNING?
THRASH

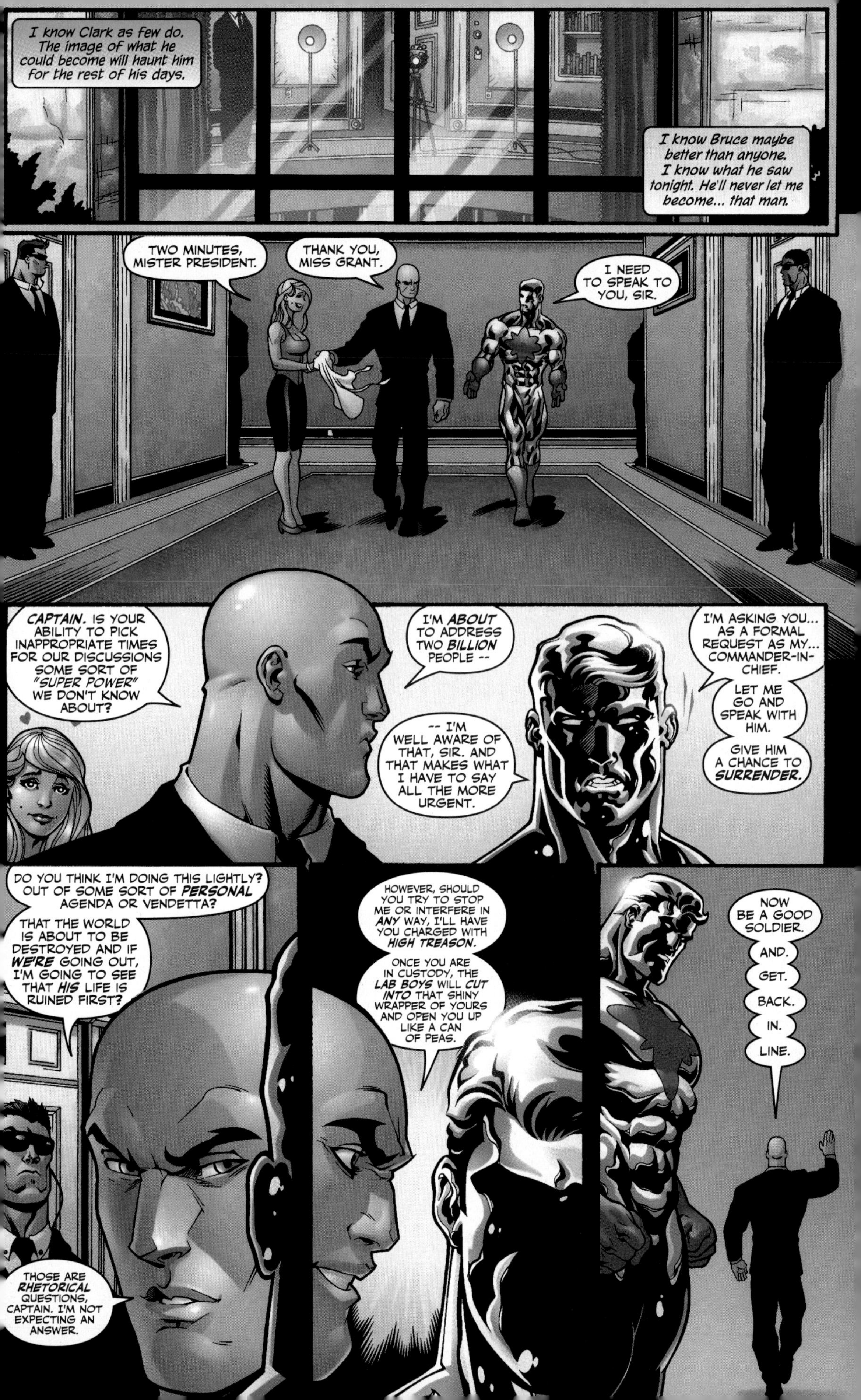
I know Clark as few do. The image of what he could become will haunt him for the rest of his days.
I know Bruce maybe better than anyone. I know what he saw tonight. He'll never let me become... that man.
TWO MINUTES, MISTER PRESIDENT.
THANK YOU, MISS GRANT.
I NEED TO SPEAK TO YOU, SIR.
CAPTAIN. IS YOUR ABILITY TO PICK INAPPROPRIATE TIMES FOR OUR DISCUSSIONS SOME SORT OF "SUPER POWER" WE DON'T KNOW ABOUT?
I'M ABOUT TO ADDRESS TWO BILLION PEOPLE --
-- I'M WELL AWARE OF THAT, SIR. AND THAT MAKES WHAT I HAVE TO SAY ALL THE MORE URGENT.
I'M ASKING YOU... AS A FORMAL REQUEST AS MY... COMMANDER-IN-CHIEF.
LET ME GO AND SPEAK WITH HIM.
GIVE HIM A CHANCE TO SURRENDER.
DO YOU THINK I'M DOING THIS LIGHTLY? OUT OF SOME SORT OF PERSONAL AGENDA OR VENDETTA?
THAT THE WORLD IS ABOUT TO BE DESTROYED AND IF WE'RE GOING OUT, I'M GOING TO SEE THAT HIS LIFE IS RUINED FIRST?
THOSE ARE RHETORICAL QUESTIONS, CAPTAIN. I'M NOT EXPECTING AN ANSWER.
HOWEVER, SHOULD YOU TRY TO STOP ME OR INTERFERE IN ANY WAY, I'LL HAVE YOU CHARGED WITH HIGH TREASON.
ONCE YOU ARE IN CUSTODY, THE LAB BOYS WILL CUT INTO THAT SHINY WRAPPER OF YOURS AND OPEN YOU UP LIKE A CAN OF PEAS.
NOW BE A GOOD SOLDIER.
AND.
GET.
BACK.
IN.
LINE.

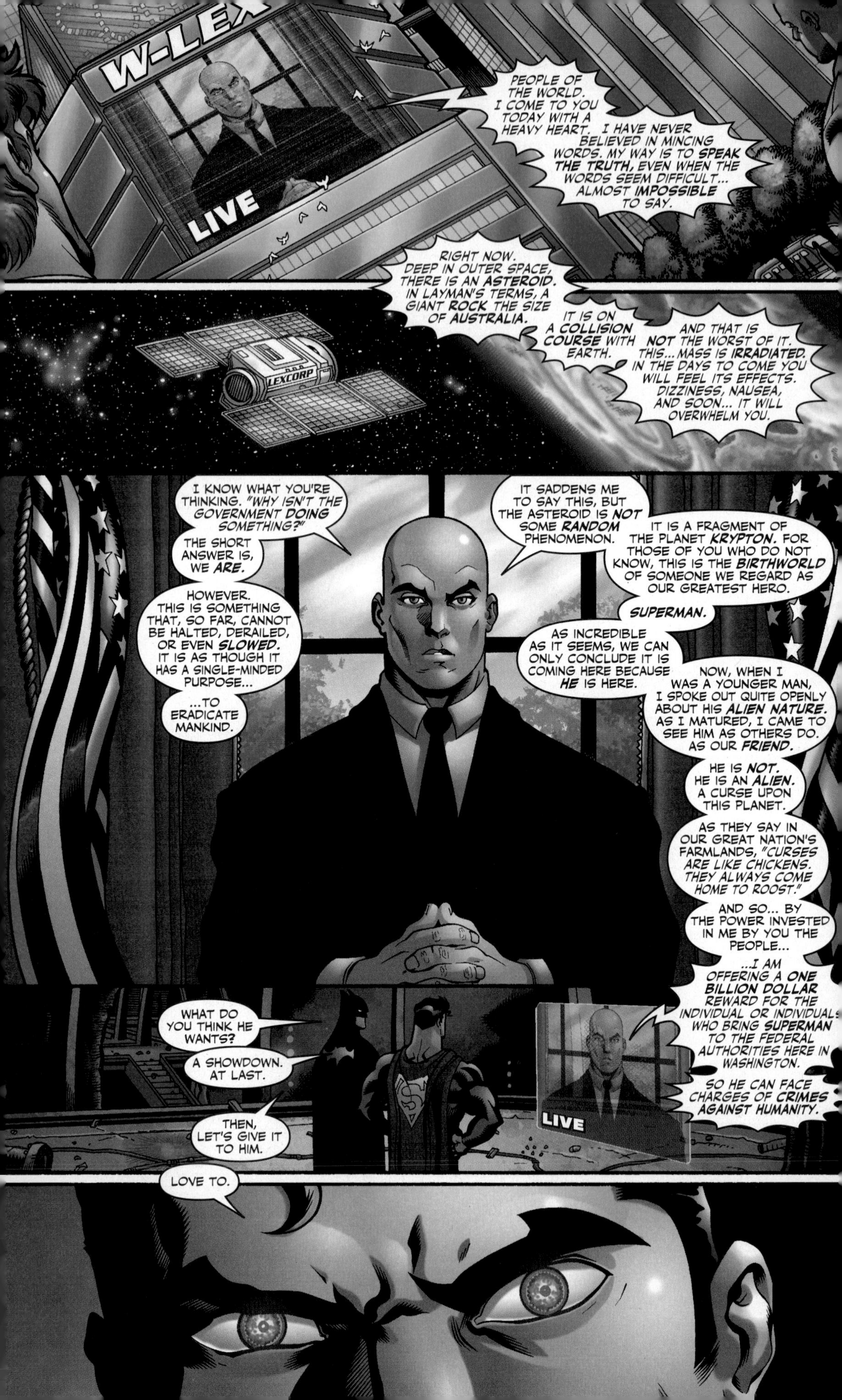
W-LEX
LIVE
PEOPLE OF THE WORLD. I COME TO YOU TODAY WITH A HEAVY HEART. I HAVE NEVER BELIEVED IN MINCING WORDS. MY WAY IS TO SPEAK THE TRUTH, EVEN WHEN THE WORDS SEEM DIFFICULT... ALMOST IMPOSSIBLE TO SAY.
RIGHT NOW. DEEP IN OUTER SPACE, THERE IS AN ASTEROID. IN LAYMAN'S TERMS, A GIANT ROCK THE SIZE OF AUSTRALIA.
LEXCORP
IT IS ON A COLLISION COURSE WITH EARTH.
AND THAT IS NOT THE WORST OF IT. THIS... MASS IS IRRADIATED. IN THE DAYS TO COME YOU WILL FEEL ITS EFFECTS. DIZZINESS, NAUSEA, AND SOON... IT WILL OVERWHELM YOU.
I KNOW WHAT YOU'RE THINKING. "WHY ISN'T THE GOVERNMENT DOING SOMETHING?"
THE SHORT ANSWER IS, WE ARE.
HOWEVER. THIS IS SOMETHING THAT, SO FAR, CANNOT BE HALTED, DERAILED, OR EVEN SLOWED. IT IS AS THOUGH IT HAS A SINGLE-MINDED PURPOSE...
...TO ERADICATE MANKIND.
IT SADDENS ME TO SAY THIS, BUT THE ASTEROID IS NOT SOME RANDOM PHENOMENON.
IT IS A FRAGMENT OF THE PLANET KRYPTON. FOR THOSE OF YOU WHO DO NOT KNOW, THIS IS THE BIRTHWORLD OF SOMEONE WE REGARD AS OUR GREATEST HERO.
SUPERMAN.
AS INCREDIBLE AS IT SEEMS, WE CAN ONLY CONCLUDE IT IS COMING HERE BECAUSE HE IS HERE.
NOW, WHEN I WAS A YOUNGER MAN, I SPOKE OUT QUITE OPENLY ABOUT HIS ALIEN NATURE. AS I MATURED, I CAME TO SEE HIM AS OTHERS DO. AS OUR FRIEND.
HE IS NOT. HE IS AN ALIEN. A CURSE UPON THIS PLANET.
AS THEY SAY IN OUR GREAT NATION'S FARMLANDS, "CURSES ARE LIKE CHICKENS. THEY ALWAYS COME HOME TO ROOST."
AND SO... BY THE POWER INVESTED IN ME BY YOU THE PEOPLE...
...I AM OFFERING A ONE BILLION DOLLAR REWARD FOR THE INDIVIDUAL OR INDIVIDUALS WHO BRING SUPERMAN TO THE FEDERAL AUTHORITIES HERE IN WASHINGTON.
SO HE CAN FACE CHARGES OF CRIMES AGAINST HUMANITY.
WHAT DO YOU THINK HE WANTS?
A SHOWDOWN. AT LAST.
THEN, LET'S GIVE IT TO HIM.
LIVE
LOVE TO.

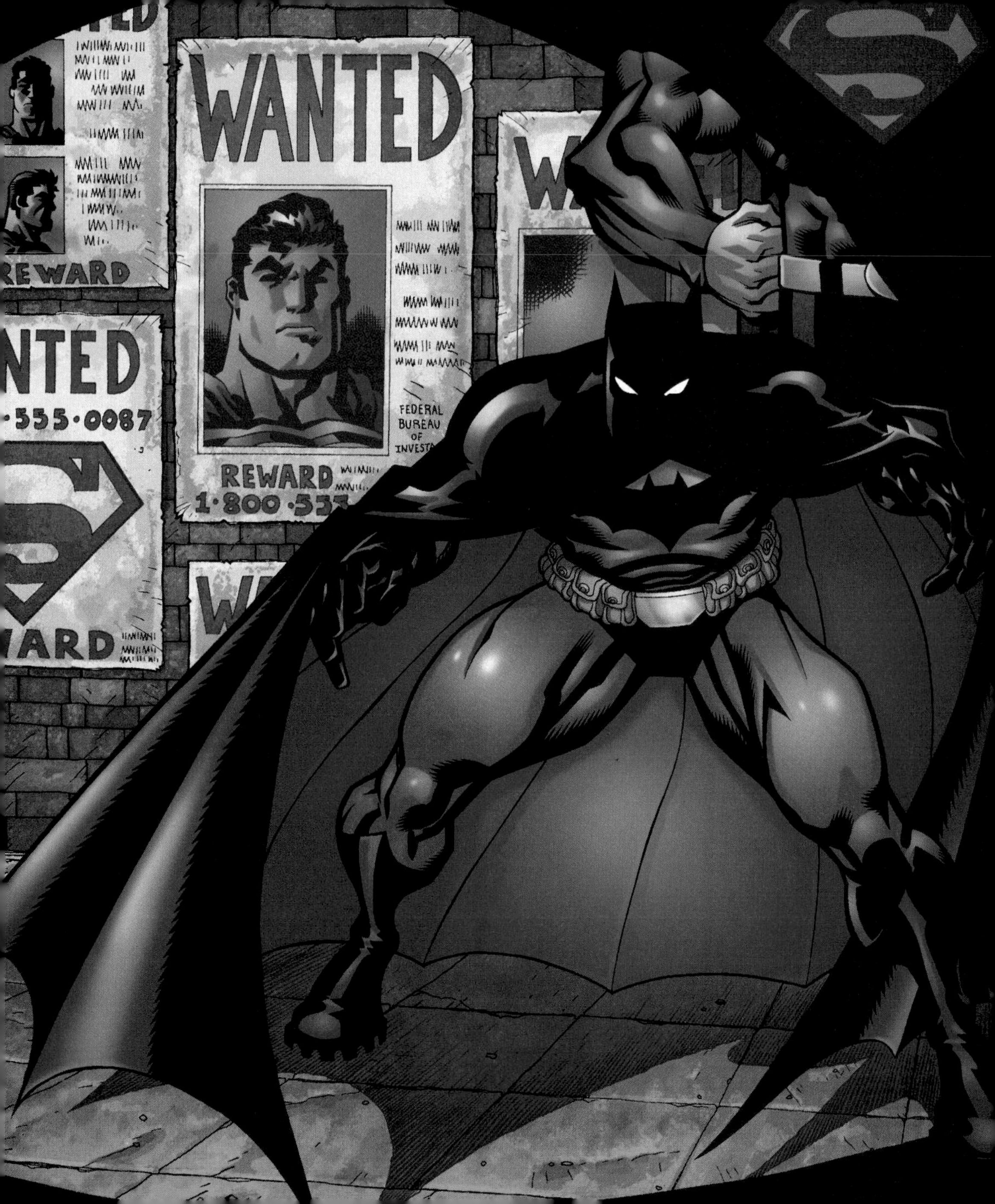
WANTED
FEDERAL
BUREAU
OF
REWARD
-555-0087

"I told you Luthor wouldn't go quietly..."

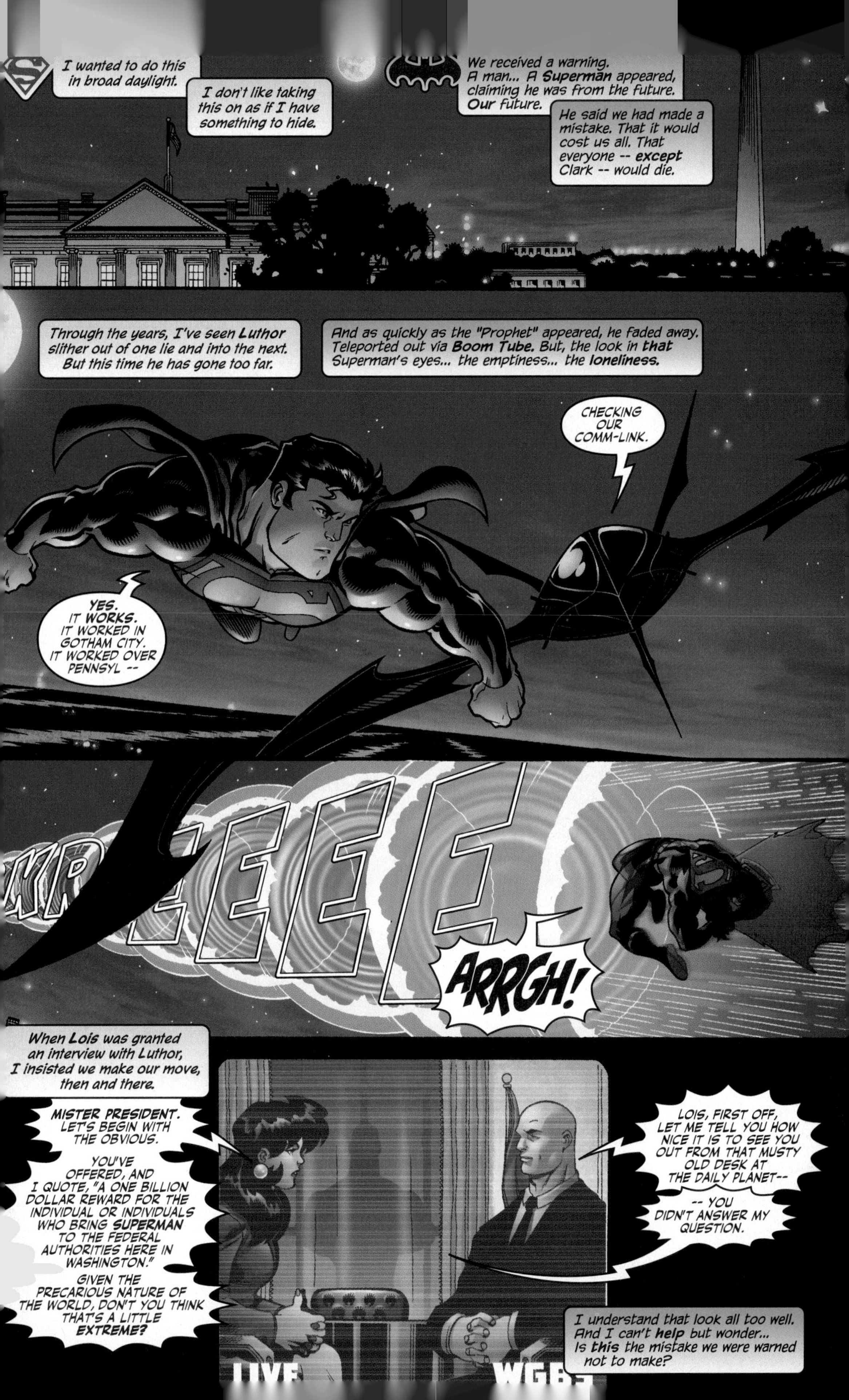

I wanted to do this in broad daylight.
I don't like taking this on as if I have something to hide.
We received a warning. A man... A Superman appeared, claiming he was from the future. Our future.
He said we had made a mistake. That it would cost us all. That everyone -- except Clark -- would die.
Through the years, I've seen Luthor slither out of one lie and into the next. But this time he has gone too far.
And as quickly as the "Prophet" appeared, he faded away. Teleported out via Boom Tube. But, the look in that Superman's eyes... the emptiness... the loneliness.
CHECKING OUR COMM-LINK.
YES. IT WORKS. IT WORKED IN GOTHAM CITY. IT WORKED OVER PENNSYL --
KREEEE
ARRGH!
When Lois was granted an interview with Luthor, I insisted we make our move, then and there.
MISTER PRESIDENT. LET'S BEGIN WITH THE OBVIOUS.
YOU'VE OFFERED, AND I QUOTE, "A ONE BILLION DOLLAR REWARD FOR THE INDIVIDUAL OR INDIVIDUALS WHO BRING SUPERMAN TO THE FEDERAL AUTHORITIES HERE IN WASHINGTON."
GIVEN THE PRECARIOUS NATURE OF THE WORLD, DON'T YOU THINK THAT'S A LITTLE EXTREME?
LOIS, FIRST OFF, LET ME TELL YOU HOW NICE IT IS TO SEE YOU OUT FROM THAT MUSTY OLD DESK AT THE DAILY PLANET--
-- YOU DIDN'T ANSWER MY QUESTION.
I understand that look all too well. And I can't help but wonder... Is this the mistake we were warned not to make?
LIVE
WGBS

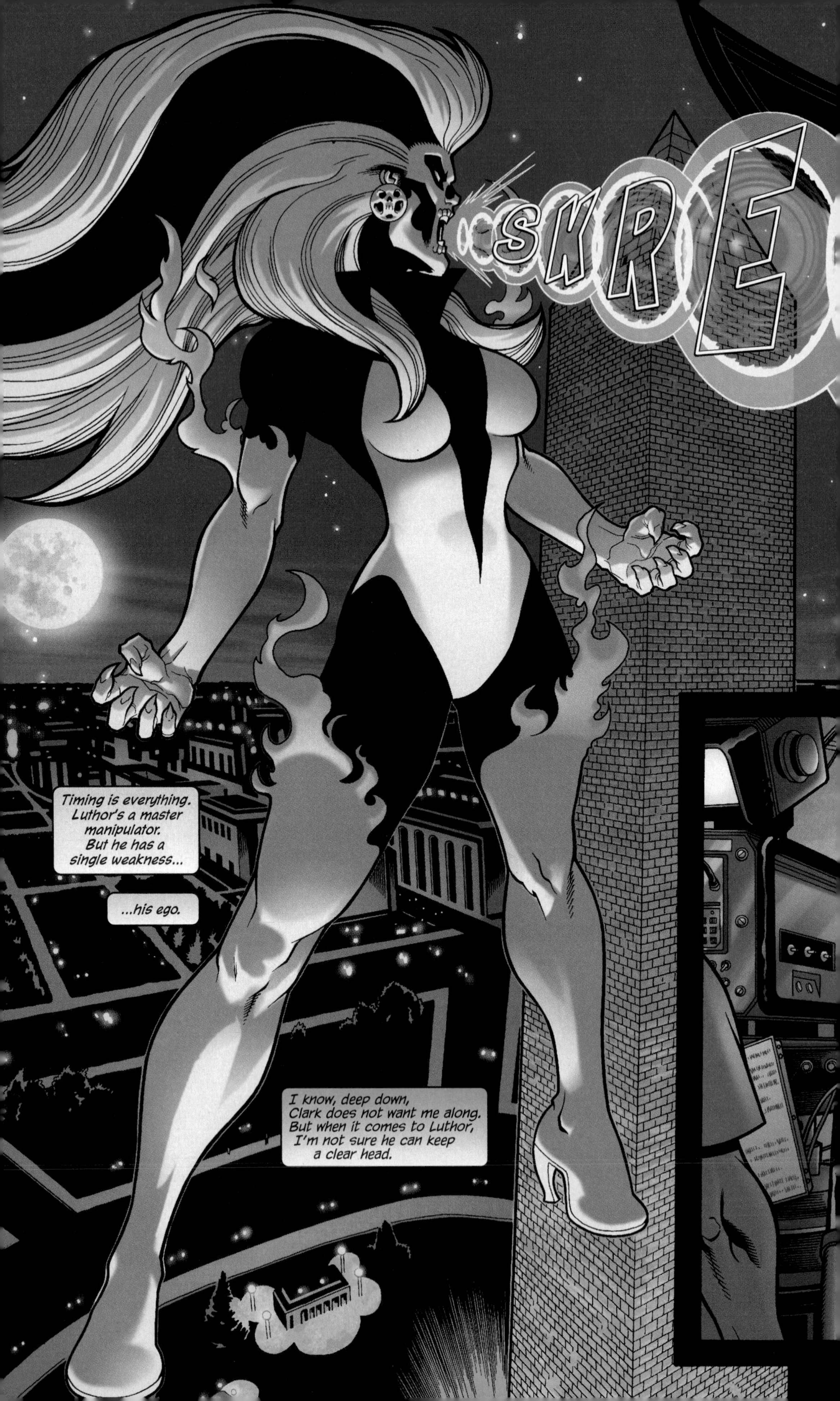
SKRE
Timing is everything. Luthor's a master manipulator. But he has a single weakness...
...his ego.
I know, deep down, Clark does not want me along. But when it comes to Luthor, I'm not sure he can keep a clear head.

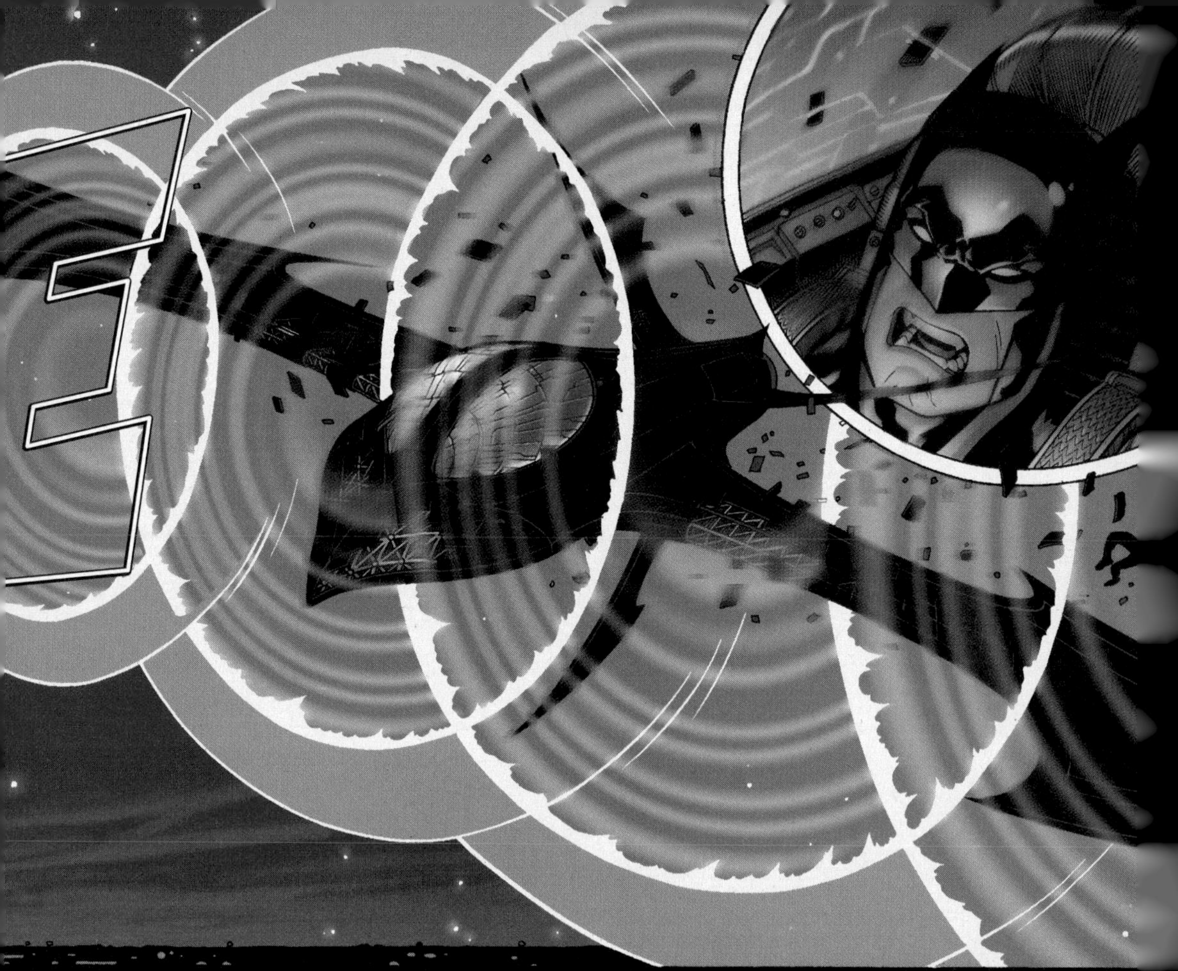

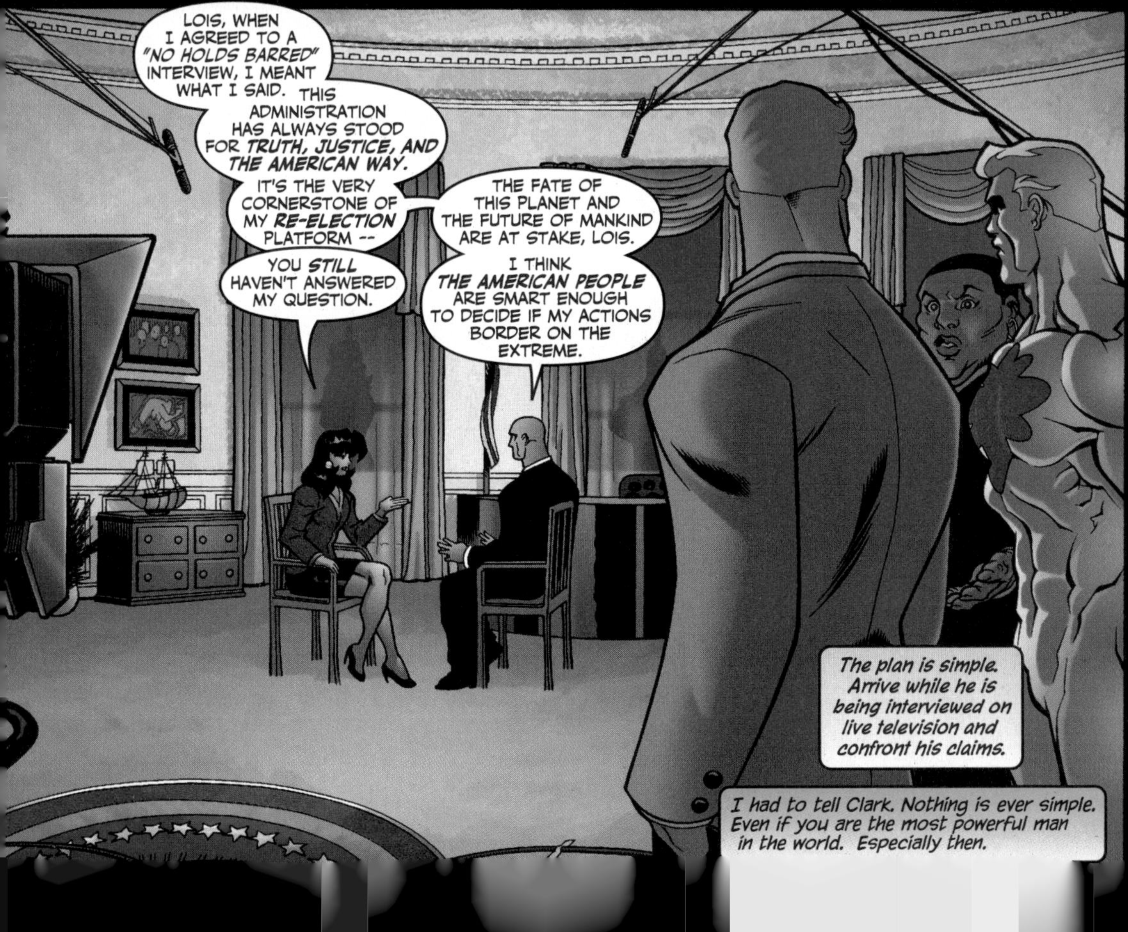
LOIS, WHEN I AGREED TO A "NO HOLDS BARRED" INTERVIEW, I MEANT WHAT I SAID.
THIS ADMINISTRATION HAS ALWAYS STOOD FOR TRUTH, JUSTICE, AND THE AMERICAN WAY.
IT'S THE VERY CORNERSTONE OF MY RE-ELECTION PLATFORM --
YOU STILL HAVEN'T ANSWERED MY QUESTION.
THE FATE OF THIS PLANET AND THE FUTURE OF MANKIND ARE AT STAKE, LOIS.
I THINK THE AMERICAN PEOPLE ARE SMART ENOUGH TO DECIDE IF MY ACTIONS BORDER ON THE EXTREME.
The plan is simple. Arrive while he is being interviewed on live television and confront his claims.
I had to tell Clark. Nothing is ever simple. Even if you are the most powerful man in the world. Especially then.

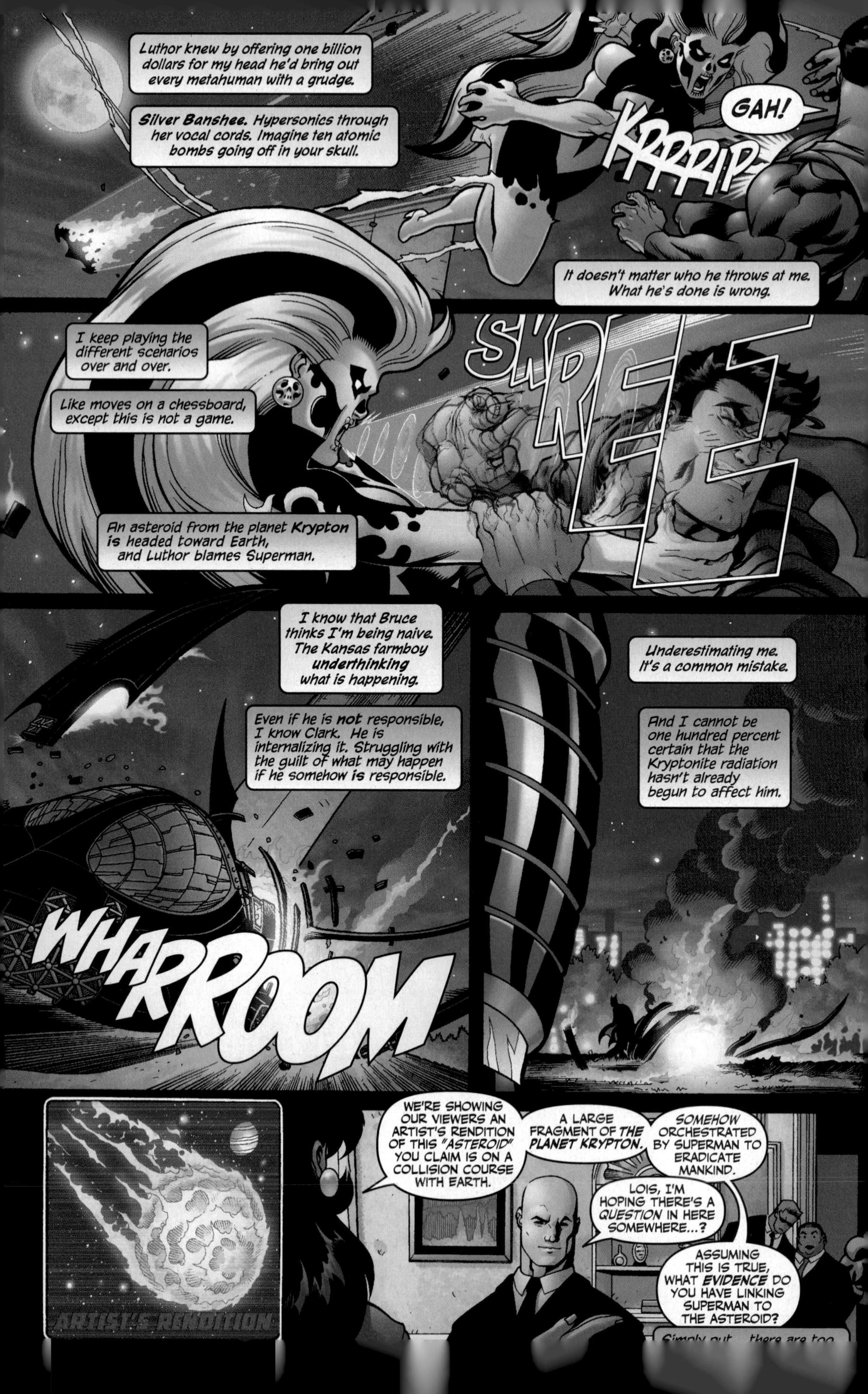
Luthor knew by offering one billion dollars for my head he'd bring out every metahuman with a grudge.
Silver Banshee. Hypersonics through her vocal cords. Imagine ten atomic bombs going off in your skull.
GAH!
KRRRRIP
It doesn't matter who he throws at me. What he's done is wrong.
I keep playing the different scenarios over and over.
Like moves on a chessboard, except this is not a game.
SKREEE
An asteroid from the planet Krypton is headed toward Earth, and Luthor blames Superman.
I know that Bruce thinks I'm being naive. The Kansas farmboy underthinking what is happening.
Even if he is not responsible, I know Clark. He is internalizing it. Struggling with the guilt of what may happen if he somehow is responsible.
WHARROOM
Underestimating me. It's a common mistake.
And I cannot be one hundred percent certain that the Kryptonite radiation hasn't already begun to affect him.
ARTIST'S RENDITION
WE'RE SHOWING OUR VIEWERS AN ARTIST'S RENDITION OF THIS "ASTEROID" YOU CLAIM IS ON A COLLISION COURSE WITH EARTH.
A LARGE FRAGMENT OF THE PLANET KRYPTON.
SOMEHOW ORCHESTRATED BY SUPERMAN TO ERADICATE MANKIND.
LOIS, I'M HOPING THERE'S A QUESTION IN HERE SOMEWHERE...?
ASSUMING THIS IS TRUE, WHAT EVIDENCE DO YOU HAVE LINKING SUPERMAN TO THE ASTEROID?
Simply put... there are too

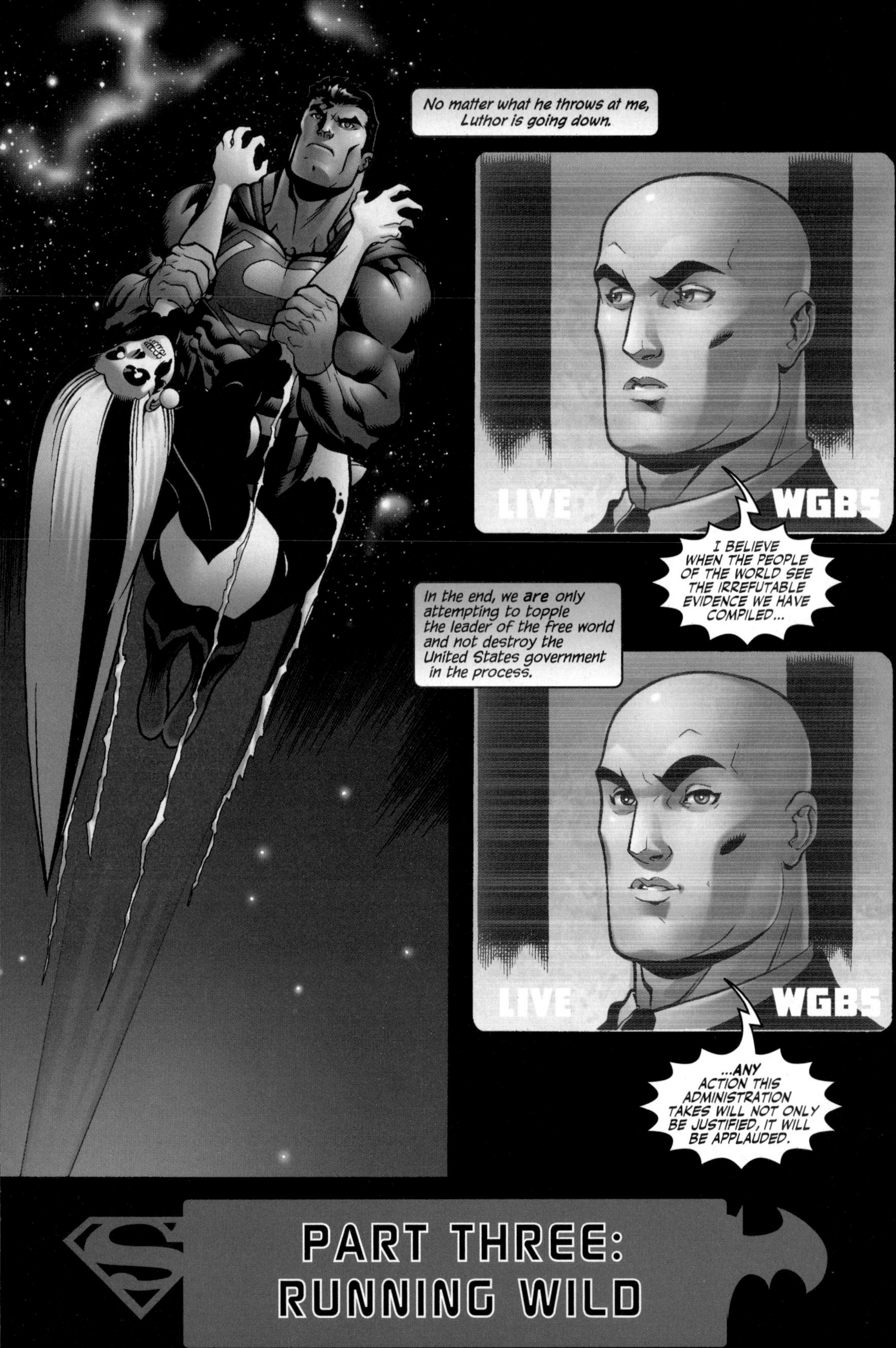
No matter what he throws at me, Luthor is going down.
LIVE
WGBS
I BELIEVE WHEN THE PEOPLE OF THE WORLD SEE THE IRREFUTABLE EVIDENCE WE HAVE COMPILED...
In the end, we are only attempting to topple the leader of the free world and not destroy the United States government in the process.
LIVE
WGBS
...ANY ACTION THIS ADMINISTRATION TAKES WILL NOT ONLY BE JUSTIFIED, IT WILL BE APPLAUDED.
PART THREE: RUNNING WILD

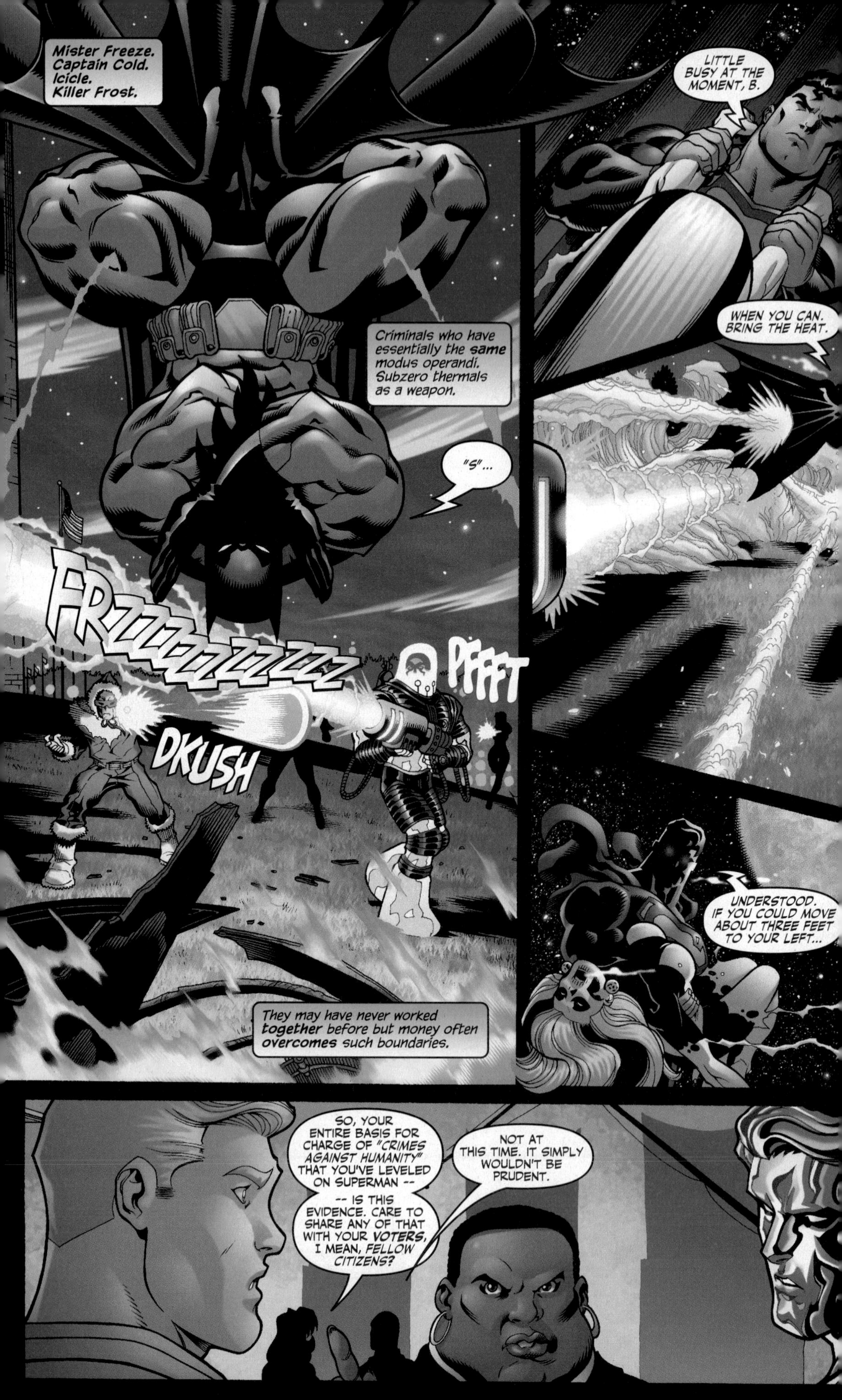

Mister Freeze. Captain Cold. Icicle. Killer Frost.
Criminals who have essentially the **same** modus operandi. Subzero thermals as a weapon.
"S"...
LITTLE BUSY AT THE MOMENT, B.
WHEN YOU CAN. BRING THE HEAT.
FRZZZZZZZZZZZZ
PFFFT
DKUSH
They may have never worked **together** before but money often **overcomes** such boundaries.
UNDERSTOOD. IF YOU COULD MOVE ABOUT THREE FEET TO YOUR LEFT...
SO, YOUR ENTIRE BASIS FOR CHARGE OF *"CRIMES AGAINST HUMANITY"* THAT YOU'VE LEVELED ON SUPERMAN --
-- IS THIS EVIDENCE. CARE TO SHARE ANY OF THAT WITH YOUR *VOTERS*, I MEAN, *FELLOW CITIZENS*?
NOT AT THIS TIME. IT SIMPLY WOULDN'T BE PRUDENT.

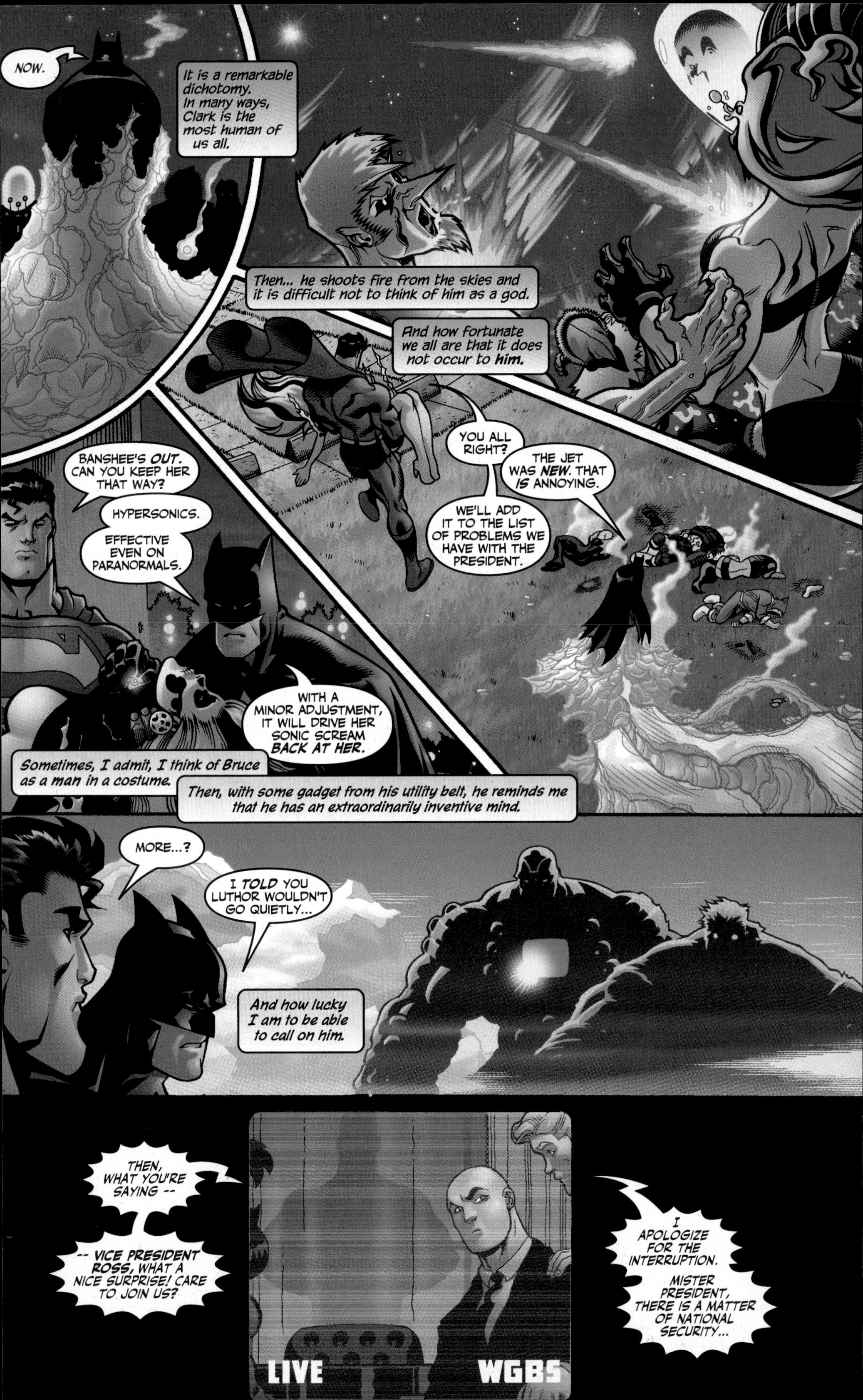

NOW.
It is a remarkable dichotomy. In many ways, Clark is the most human of us all.
Then... he shoots fire from the skies and it is difficult not to think of him as a god.
And how fortunate we all are that it does not occur to him.
YOU ALL RIGHT?
THE JET WAS NEW. THAT IS ANNOYING.
WE'LL ADD IT TO THE LIST OF PROBLEMS WE HAVE WITH THE PRESIDENT.
BANSHEE'S OUT. CAN YOU KEEP HER THAT WAY?
HYPERSONICS.
EFFECTIVE EVEN ON PARANORMALS.
WITH A MINOR ADJUSTMENT, IT WILL DRIVE HER SONIC SCREAM BACK AT HER.
Sometimes, I admit, I think of Bruce as a man in a costume.
Then, with some gadget from his utility belt, he reminds me that he has an extraordinarily inventive mind.
MORE...?
I TOLD YOU LUTHOR WOULDN'T GO QUIETLY...
And how lucky I am to be able to call on him.
THEN, WHAT YOU'RE SAYING --
-- VICE PRESIDENT ROSS, WHAT A NICE SURPRISE! CARE TO JOIN US?
I APOLOGIZE FOR THE INTERRUPTION.
MISTER PRESIDENT, THERE IS A MATTER OF NATIONAL SECURITY...
LIVE
WGBS

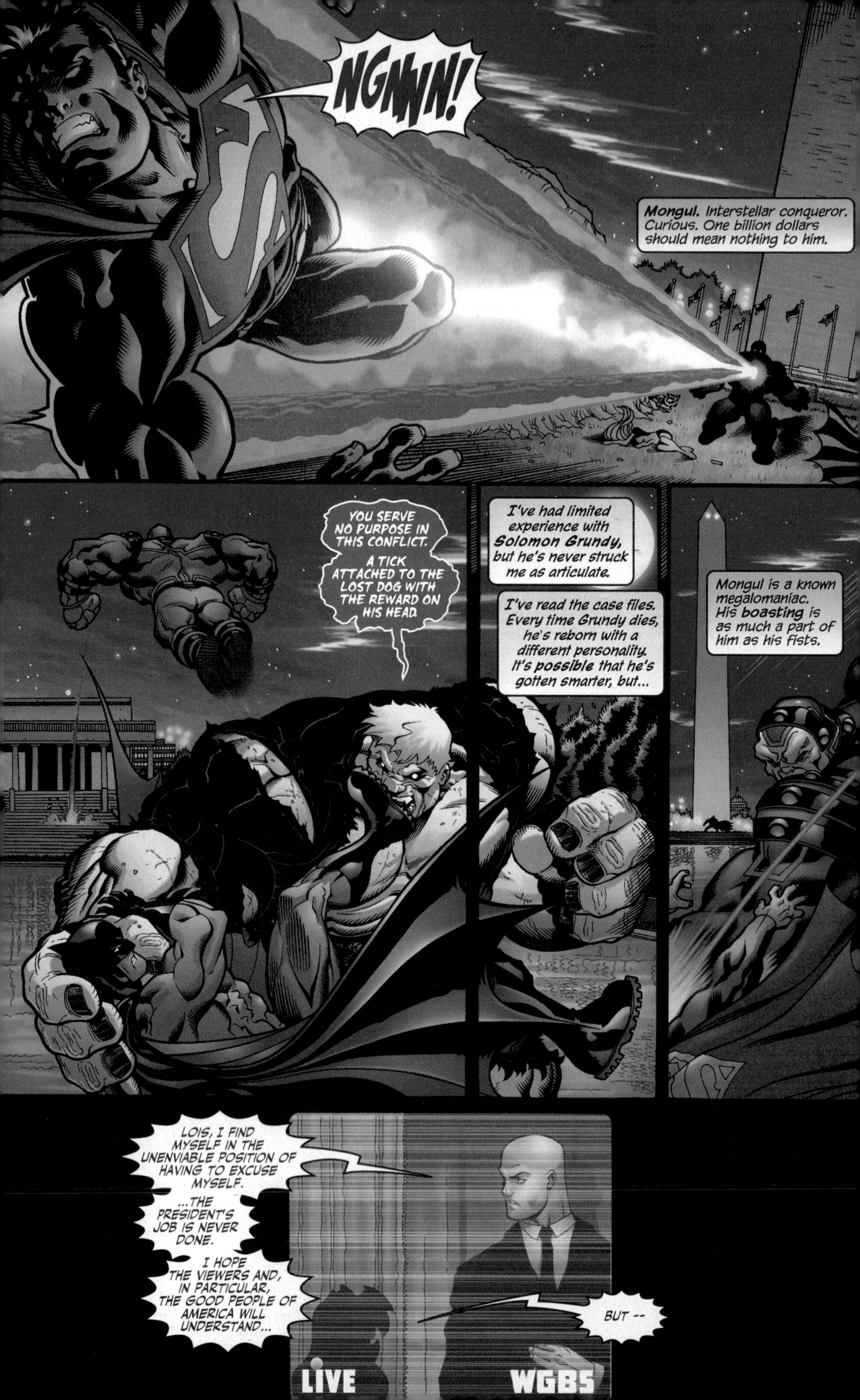
NGNNN!
Mongul. Interstellar conqueror. Curious. One billion dollars should mean nothing to him.
YOU SERVE NO PURPOSE IN THIS CONFLICT.
A TICK ATTACHED TO THE LOST DOG WITH THE REWARD ON HIS HEAD.
I've had limited experience with Solomon Grundy, but he's never struck me as articulate.
I've read the case files. Every time Grundy dies, he's reborn with a different personality. It's possible that he's gotten smarter, but...
Mongul is a known megalomaniac. His boasting is as much a part of him as his fists.
LOIS, I FIND MYSELF IN THE UNENVIABLE POSITION OF HAVING TO EXCUSE MYSELF.
...THE PRESIDENT'S JOB IS NEVER DONE.
I HOPE THE VIEWERS AND, IN PARTICULAR, THE GOOD PEOPLE OF AMERICA WILL UNDERSTAND...
BUT --
LIVE
WGBS

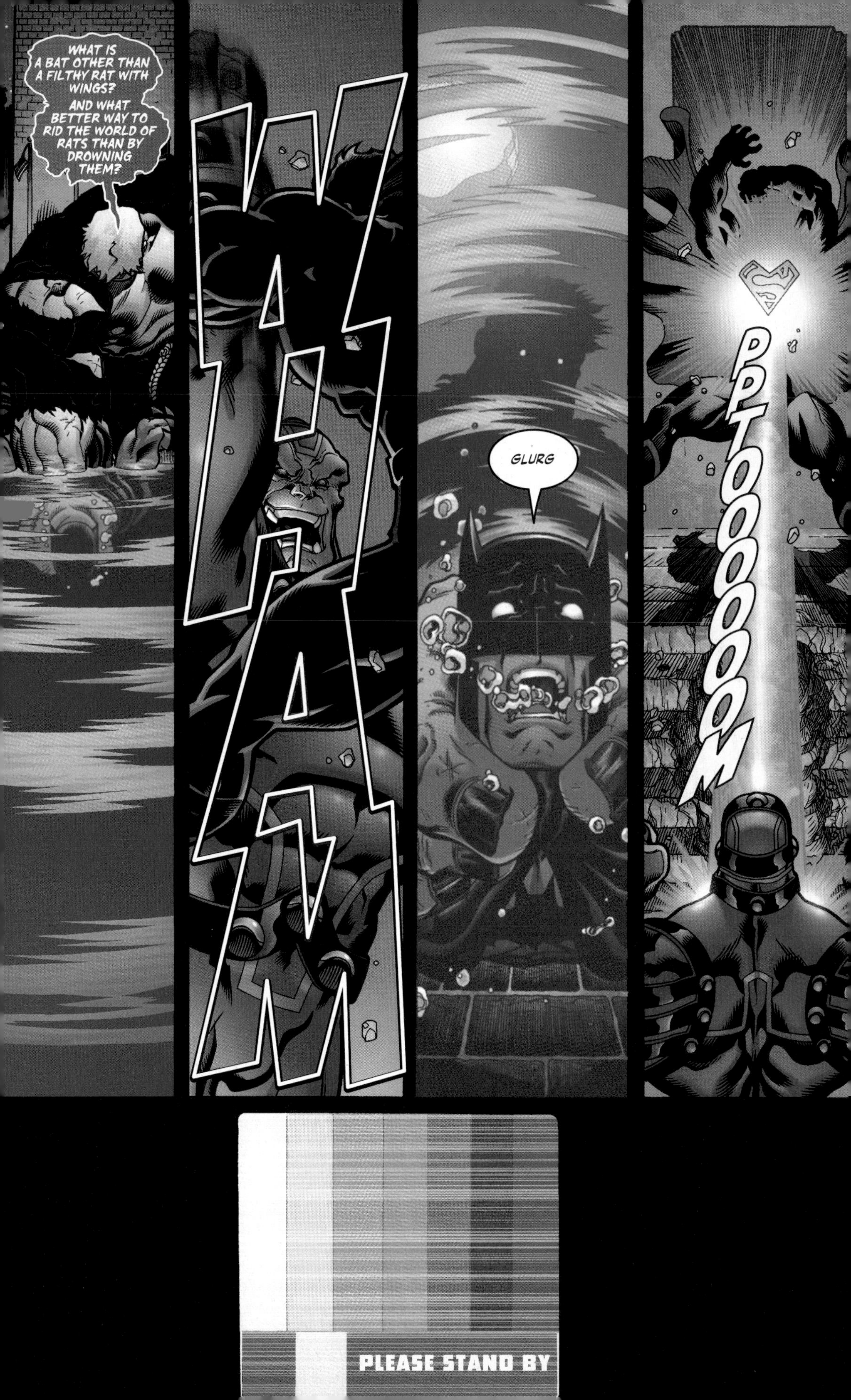
WHAT IS A BAT OTHER THAN A FILTHY RAT WITH WINGS?
AND WHAT BETTER WAY TO RID THE WORLD OF RATS THAN BY DROWNING THEM?
WHAM
GLURG
PPTOOOOOOOM
PLEASE STAND BY

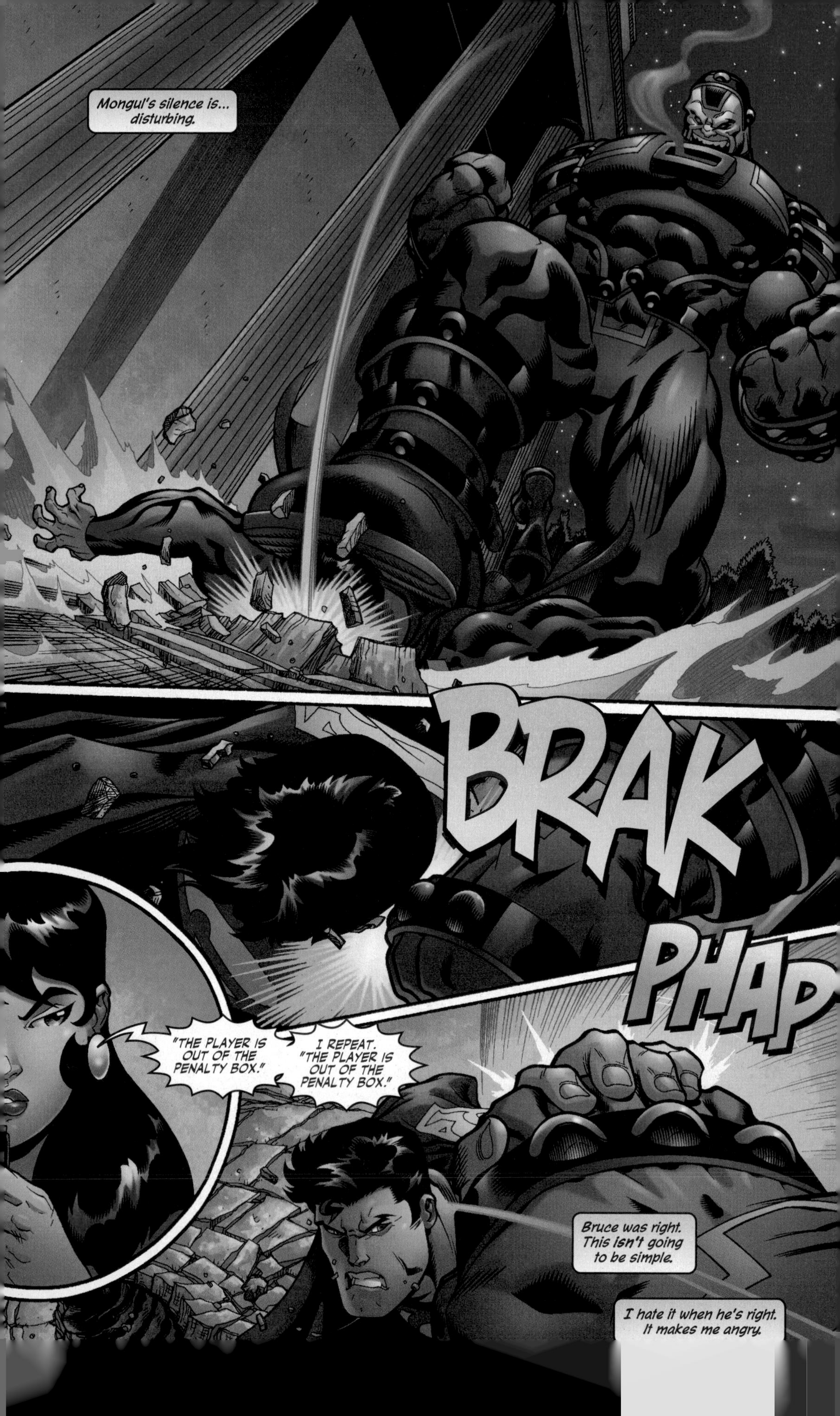

Mongul's silence is... disturbing.
BRAK
PHAP
"THE PLAYER IS OUT OF THE PENALTY BOX."
I REPEAT. "THE PLAYER IS OUT OF THE PENALTY BOX."
Bruce was right. This isn't going to be simple.
I hate it when he's right. It makes me angry.

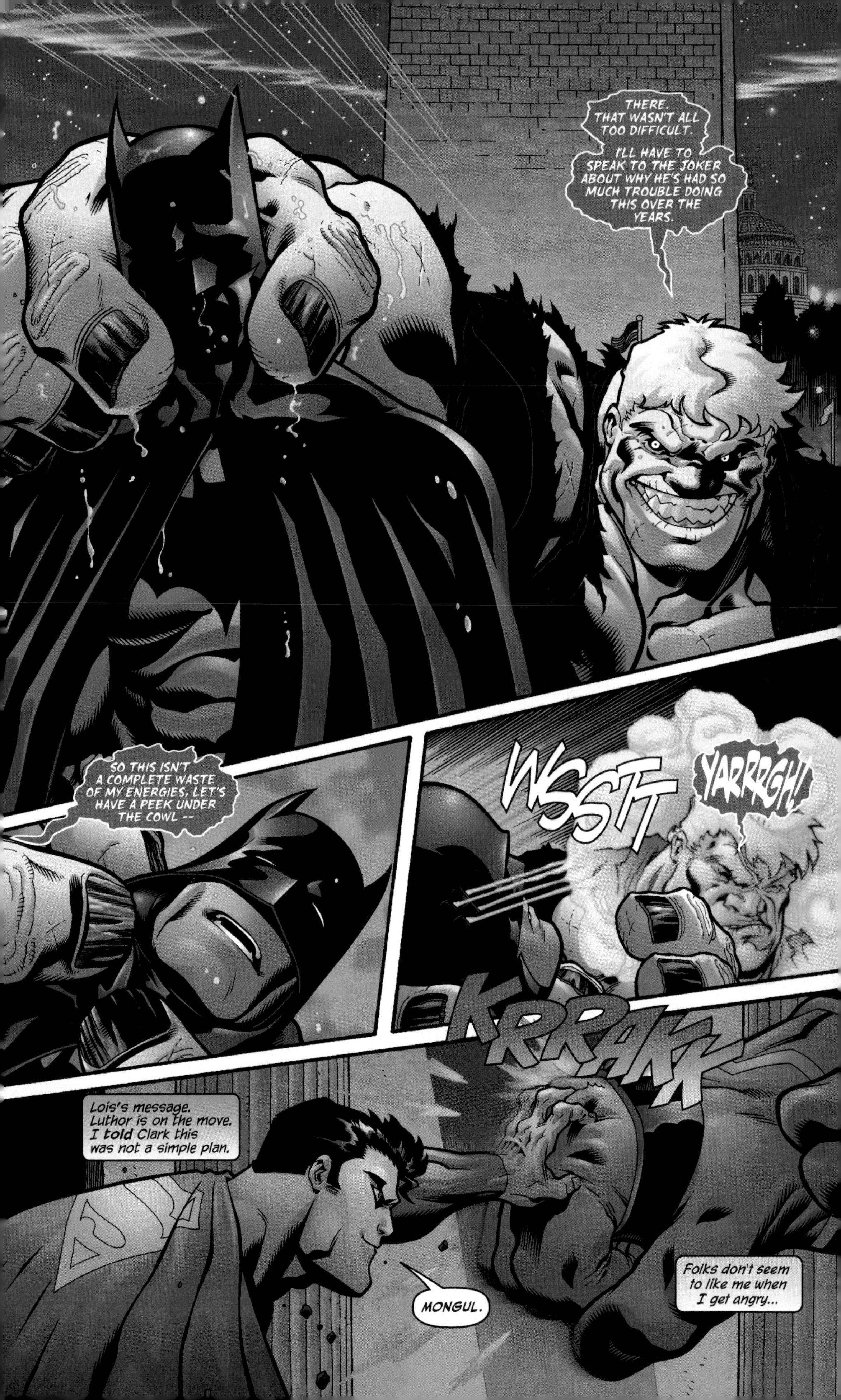
THERE. THAT WASN'T ALL TOO DIFFICULT.
I'LL HAVE TO SPEAK TO THE JOKER ABOUT WHY HE'S HAD SO MUCH TROUBLE DOING THIS OVER THE YEARS.
SO THIS ISN'T A COMPLETE WASTE OF MY ENERGIES, LET'S HAVE A PEEK UNDER THE COWL --
WSSTT
YARRRGH!
KRRAKK
Lois's message. Luthor is on the move. I told Clark this was not a simple plan.
MONGUL.
Folks don't seem to like me when I get angry...

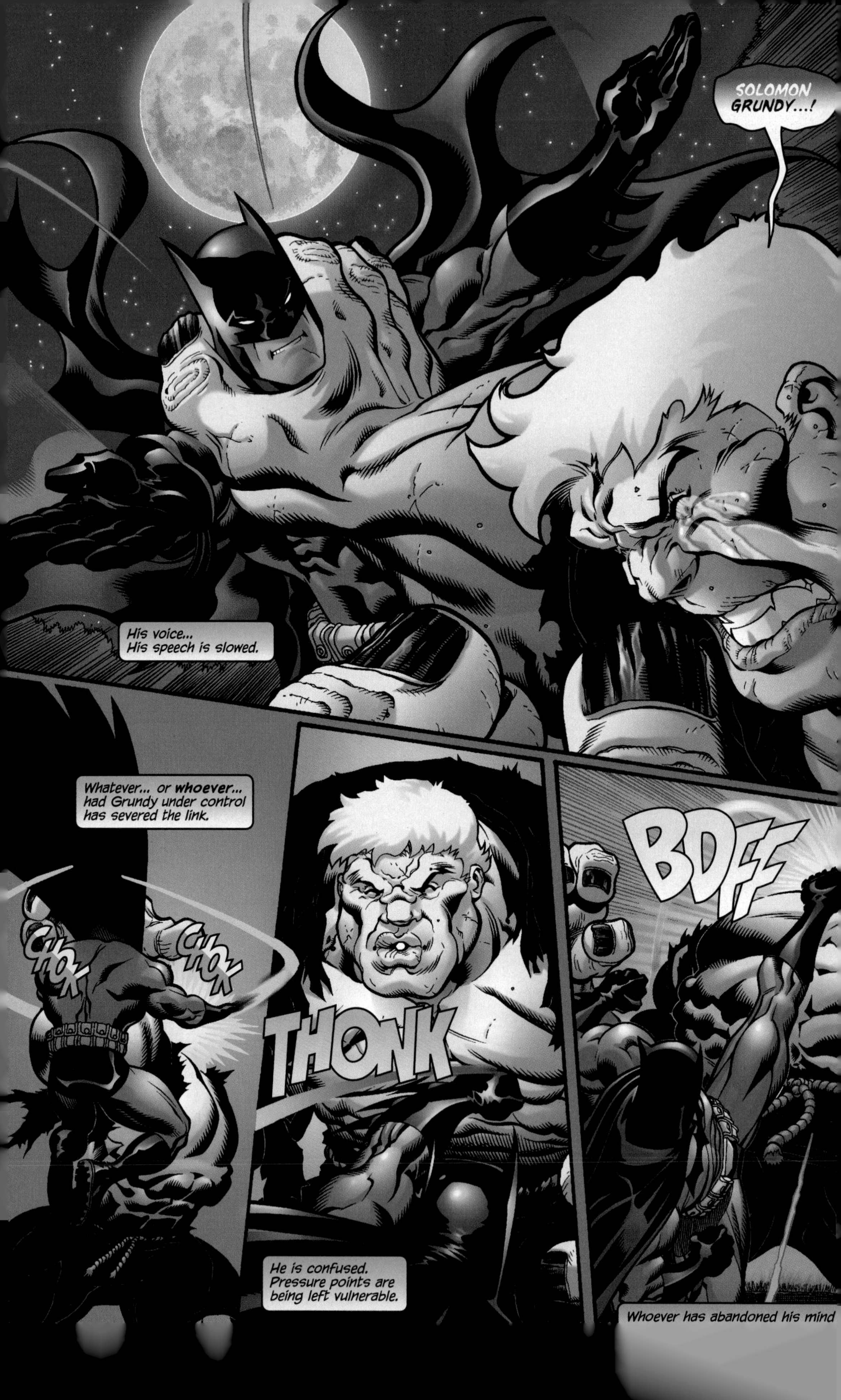
SOLOMON GRUNDY...!
His voice... His speech is slowed.
Whatever... or whoever... had Grundy under control has severed the link.
CHOK
CHOK
THONK
BDFF
He is confused. Pressure points are being left vulnerable.
Whoever has abandoned his mind

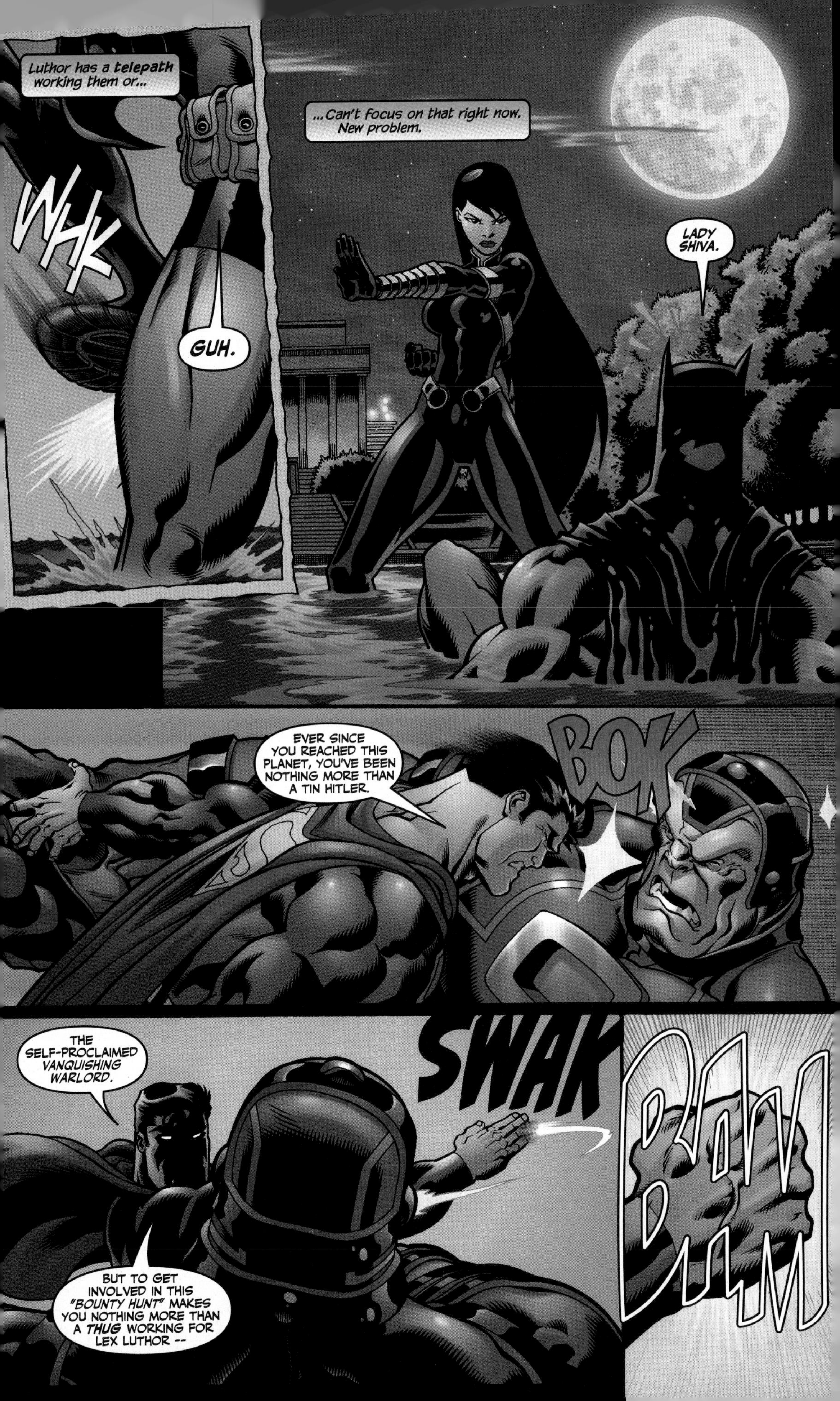

Luthor has a telepath working them or...
WHK
GUH.
...Can't focus on that right now. New problem.
LADY SHIVA.
EVER SINCE YOU REACHED THIS PLANET, YOU'VE BEEN NOTHING MORE THAN A TIN HITLER.
BOK
THE SELF-PROCLAIMED VANQUISHING WARLORD.
SWAK
BUT TO GET INVOLVED IN THIS "BOUNTY HUNT" MAKES YOU NOTHING MORE THAN A THUG WORKING FOR LEX LUTHOR --
BAM

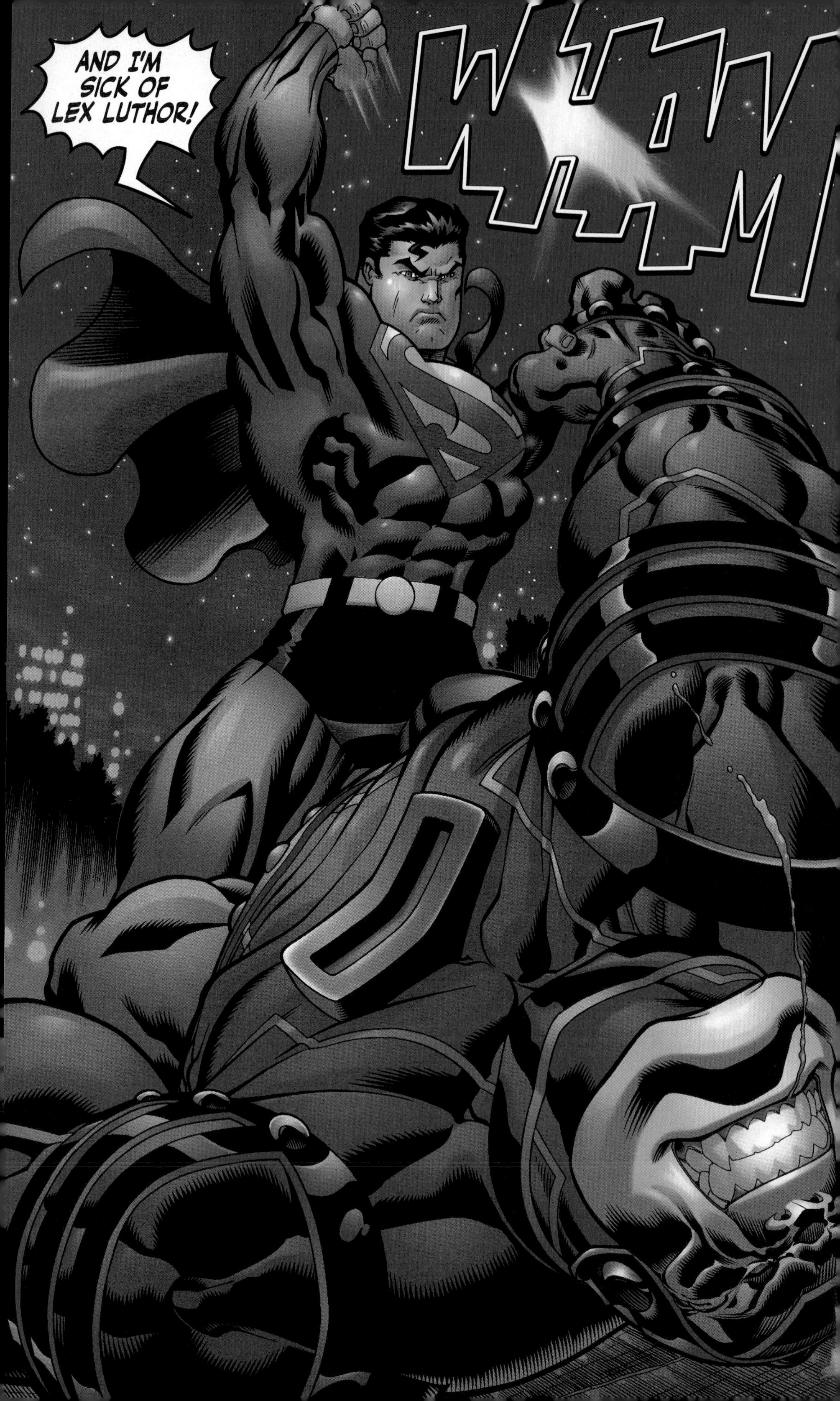
AND I'M SICK OF LEX LUTHOR!
WHAM

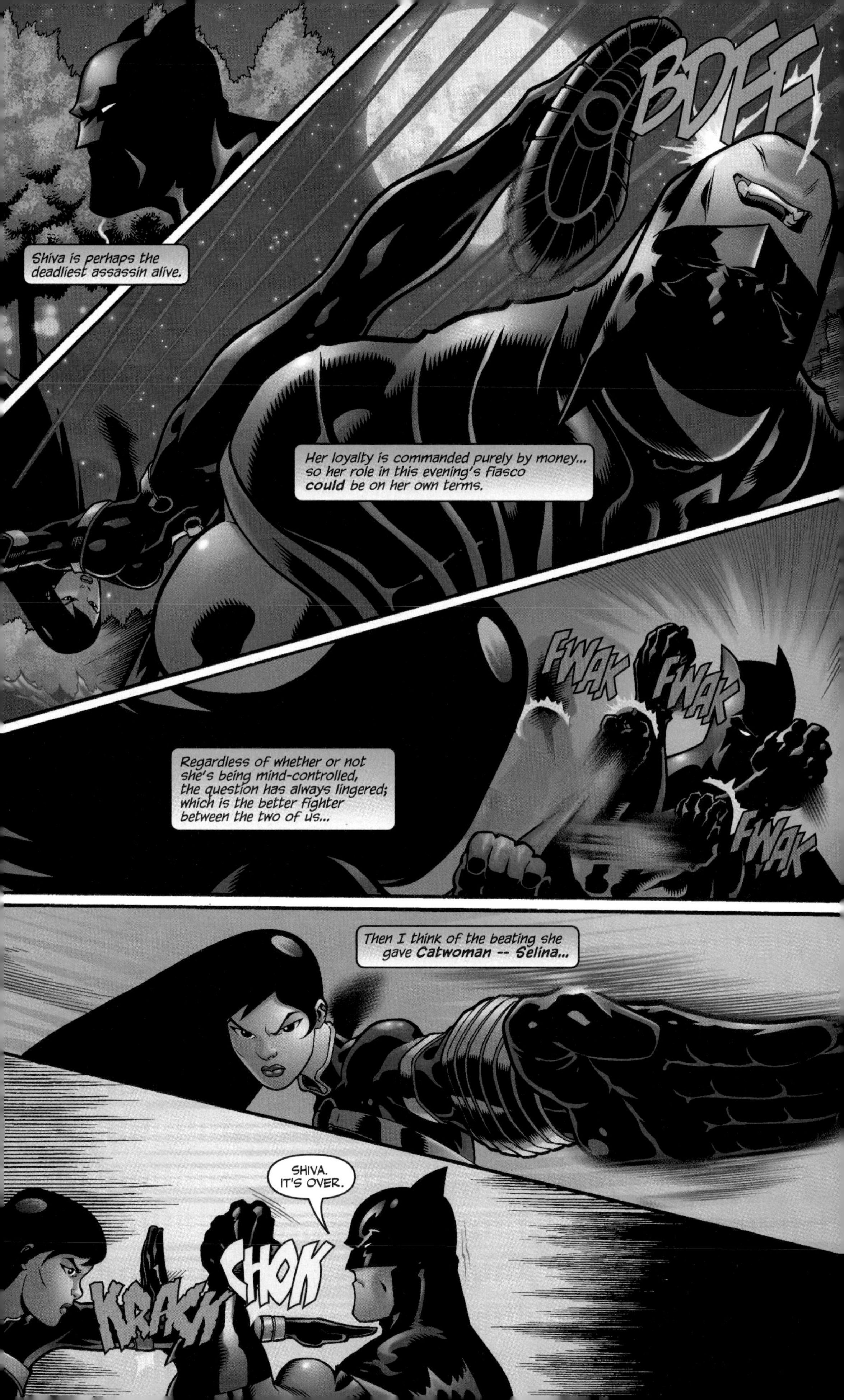
BDFF
Shiva is perhaps the deadliest assassin alive.
Her loyalty is commanded purely by money... so her role in this evening's fiasco **could** be on her own terms.
FWAK
FWAK
Regardless of whether or not she's being mind-controlled, the question has always lingered; which is the better fighter between the two of us...
FWAK
Then I think of the beating she gave **Catwoman -- Selina...**
SHIVA. IT'S OVER.
KRACK
CHOK

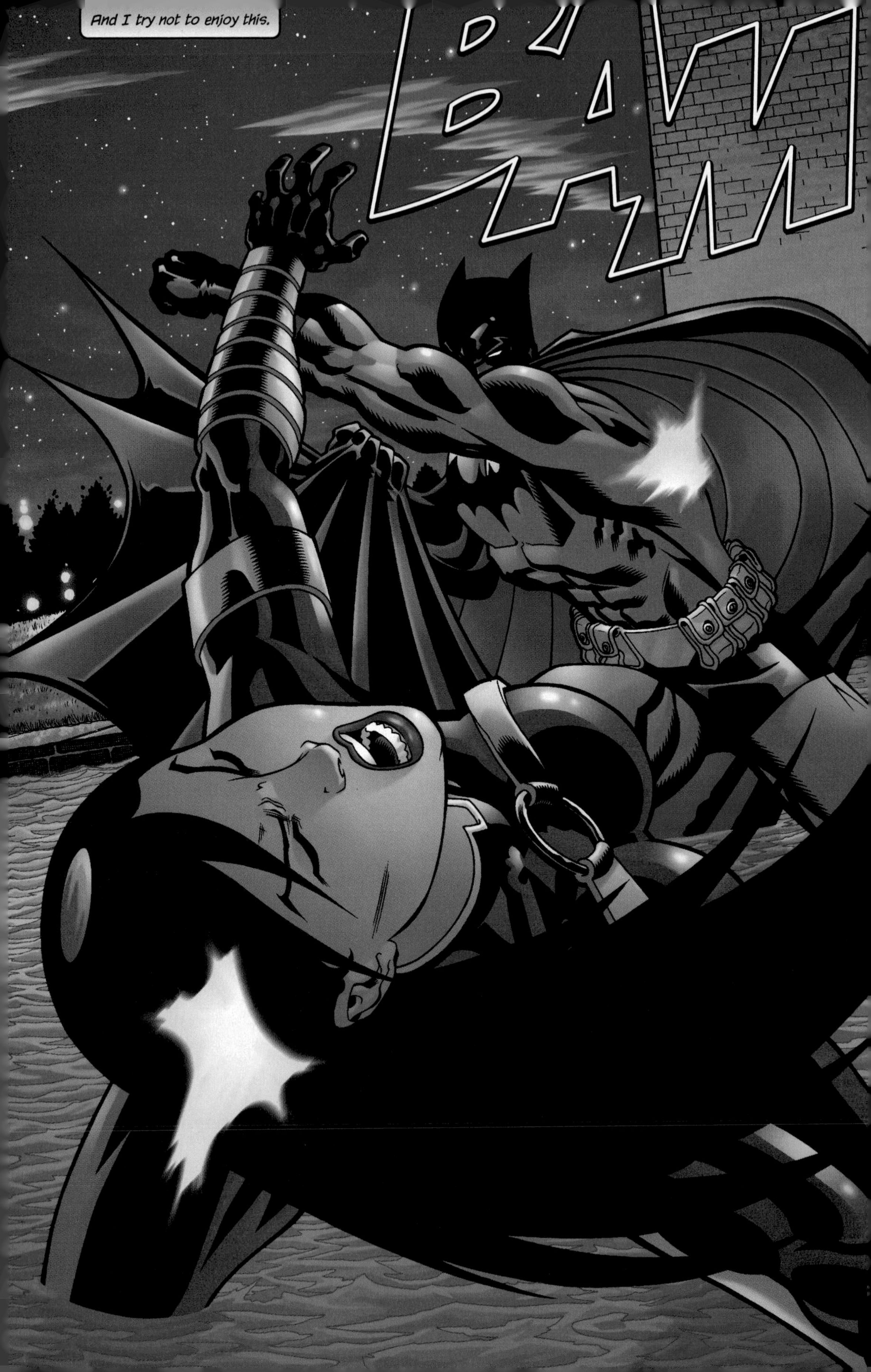
And I try not to enjoy this.
BAM

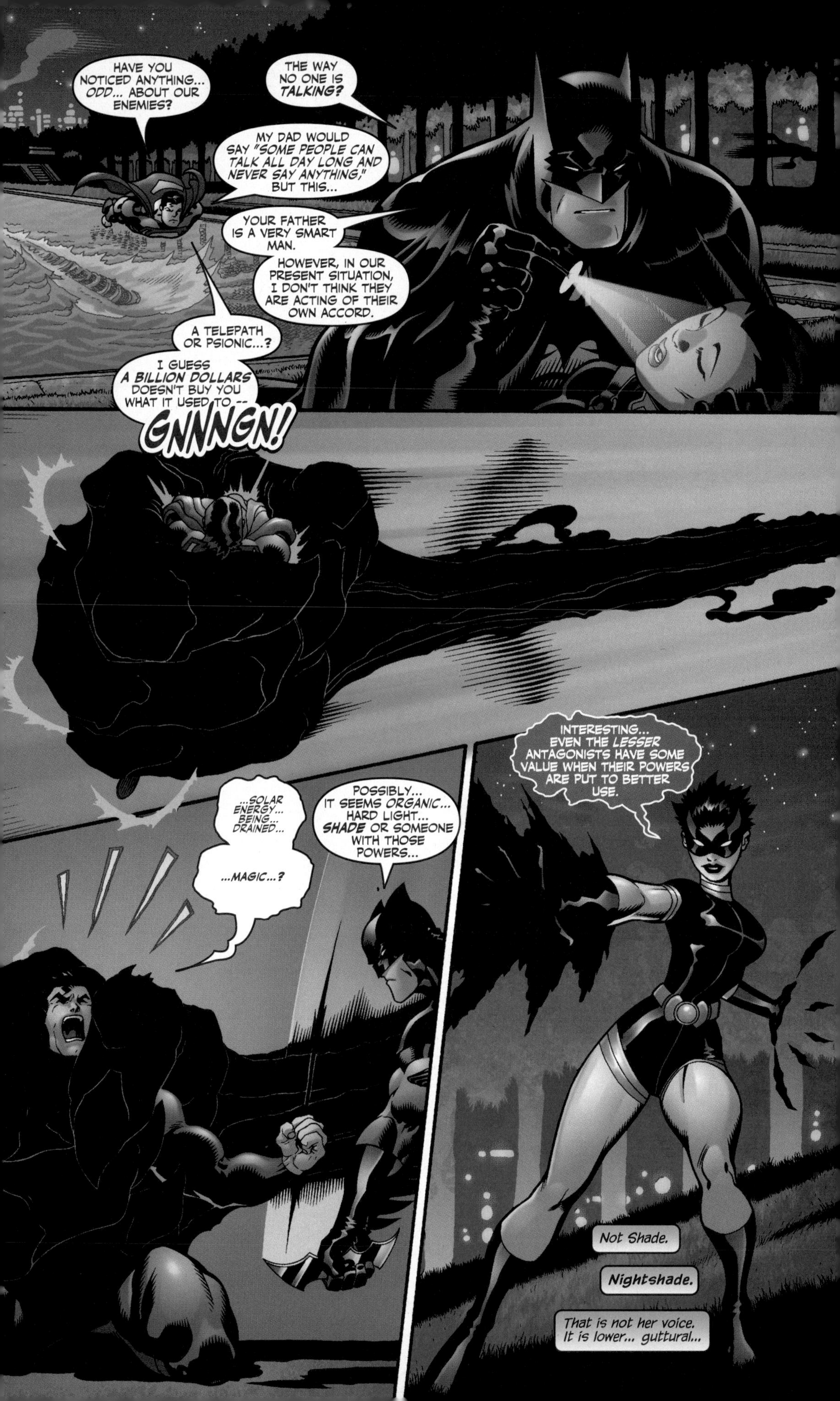

HAVE YOU NOTICED ANYTHING... ODD... ABOUT OUR ENEMIES?
THE WAY NO ONE IS TALKING?
MY DAD WOULD SAY "SOME PEOPLE CAN TALK ALL DAY LONG AND NEVER SAY ANYTHING," BUT THIS...
YOUR FATHER IS A VERY SMART MAN.
HOWEVER, IN OUR PRESENT SITUATION, I DON'T THINK THEY ARE ACTING OF THEIR OWN ACCORD.
A TELEPATH OR PSIONIC...?
I GUESS A BILLION DOLLARS DOESN'T BUY YOU WHAT IT USED TO --
GNNNGN!
...SOLAR ENERGY... BEING... DRAINED...
...MAGIC...?
POSSIBLY... IT SEEMS ORGANIC... HARD LIGHT... SHADE OR SOMEONE WITH THOSE POWERS...
INTERESTING... EVEN THE LESSER ANTAGONISTS HAVE SOME VALUE WHEN THEIR POWERS ARE PUT TO BETTER USE.
Not Shade.
Nightshade.
That is not her voice. It is lower... guttural...

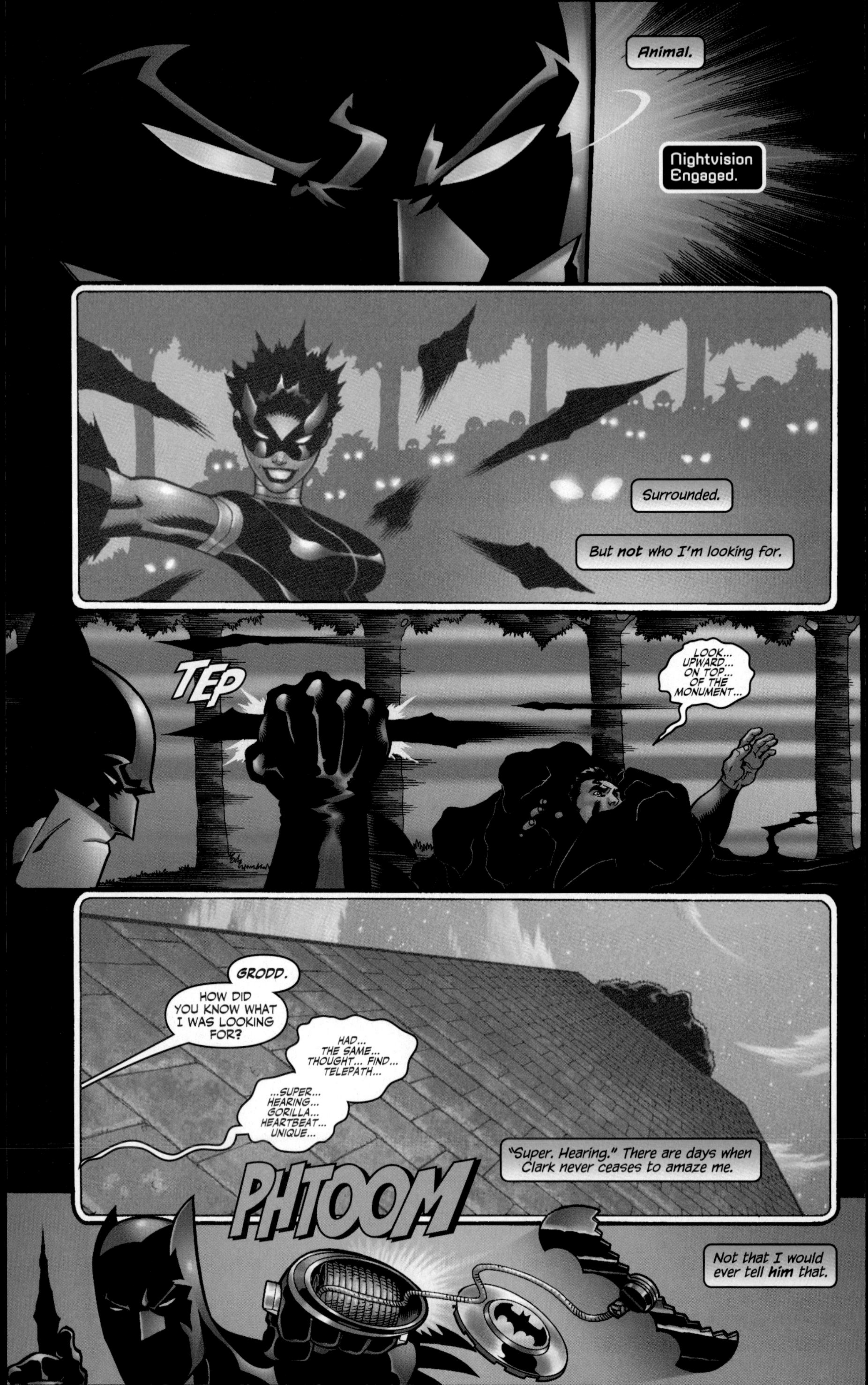
Animal.
Nightvision Engaged.
Surrounded.
But not who I'm looking for.
TEP
LOOK... UPWARD... ON TOP... OF THE MONUMENT...
GRODD.
HOW DID YOU KNOW WHAT I WAS LOOKING FOR?
HAD... THE SAME... THOUGHT... FIND... TELEPATH...
...SUPER... HEARING... GORILLA... HEARTBEAT... UNIQUE...
"Super. Hearing." There are days when Clark never ceases to amaze me.
PHTOOM
Not that I would ever tell him that.

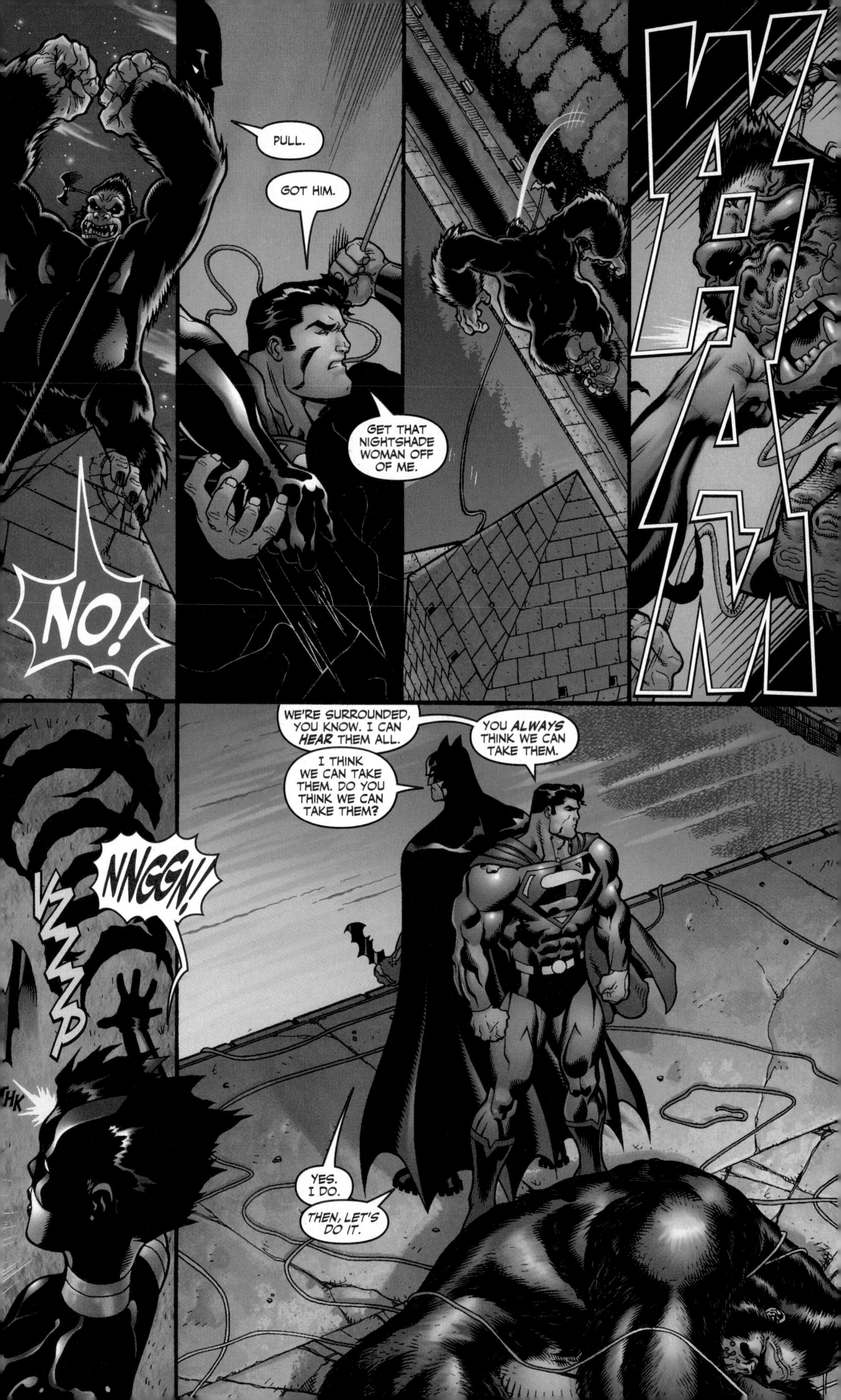
NO!
PULL.
GOT HIM.
GET THAT NIGHTSHADE WOMAN OFF OF ME.
WHAM
NNGGN!
VZZZZP
THK
WE'RE SURROUNDED, YOU KNOW. I CAN HEAR THEM ALL.
YOU ALWAYS THINK WE CAN TAKE THEM.
I THINK WE CAN TAKE THEM. DO YOU THINK WE CAN TAKE THEM?
YES. I DO.
THEN, LET'S DO IT.

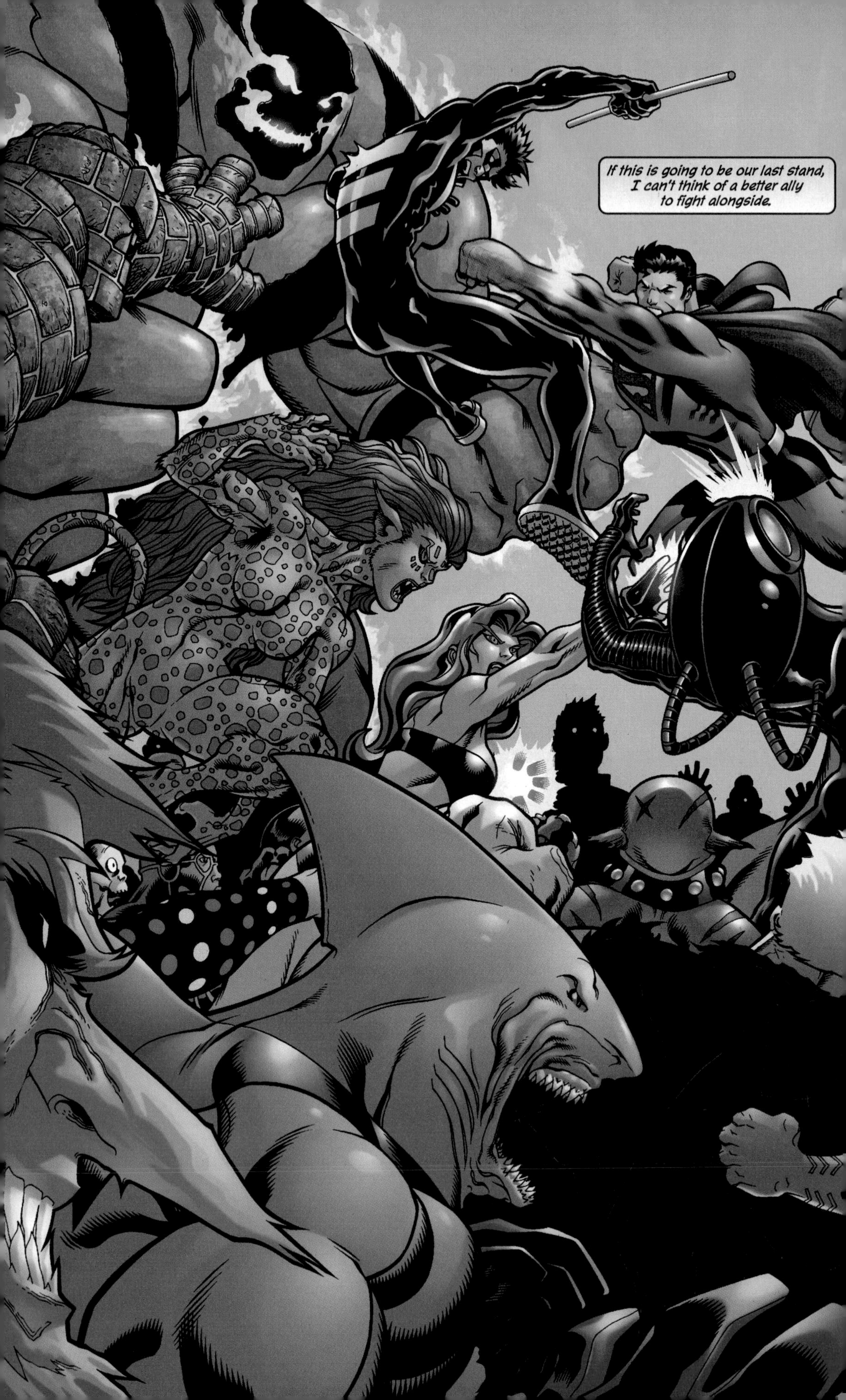
If this is going to be our last stand, I can't think of a better ally to fight alongside.

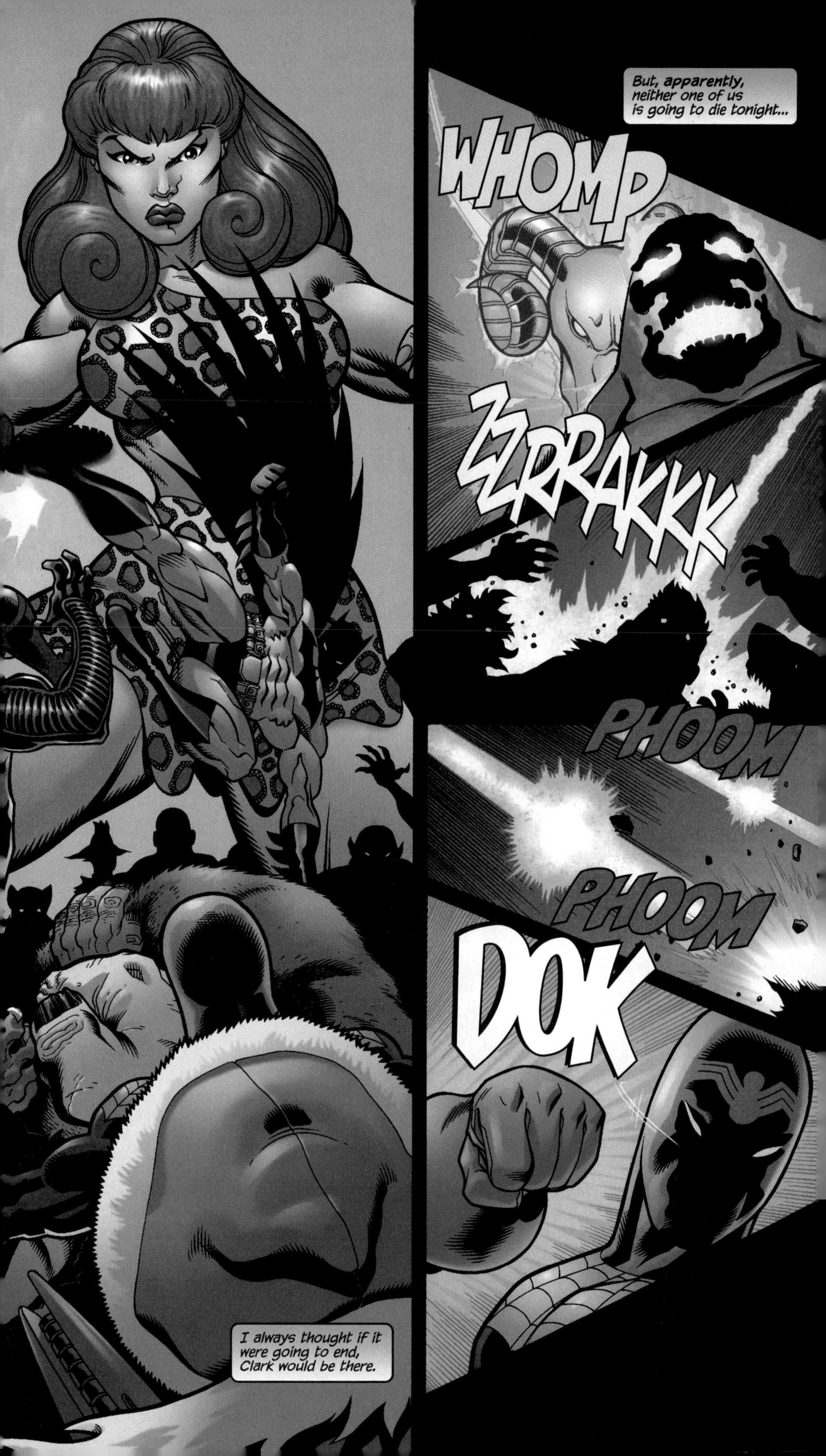
I always thought if it were going to end, Clark would be there.
But, apparently, neither one of us is going to die tonight...
WHOMP
ZZZRRAKKK
PHOOM
PHOOM
DOK

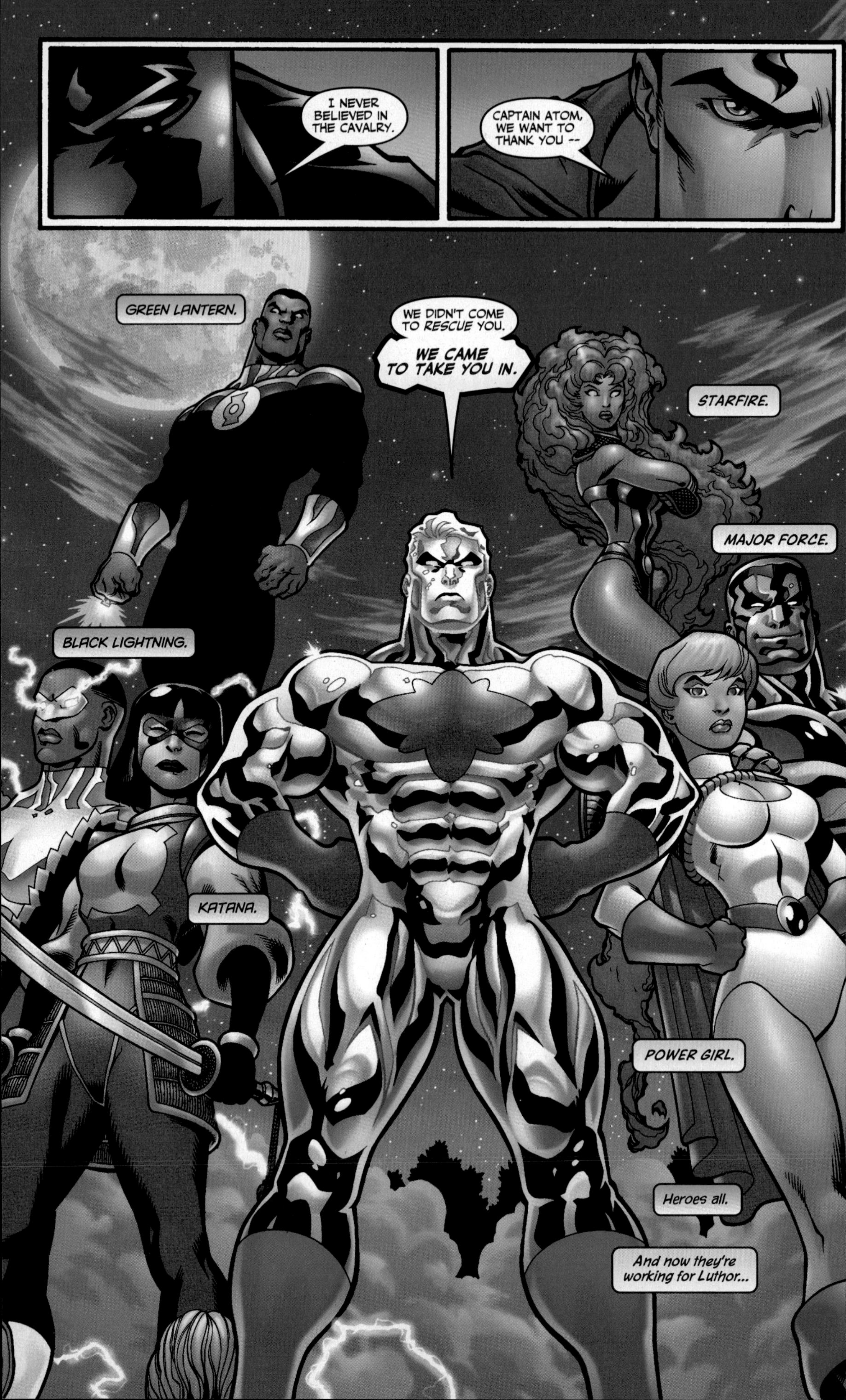
I NEVER BELIEVED IN THE CAVALRY.
CAPTAIN ATOM, WE WANT TO THANK YOU --
GREEN LANTERN.
WE DIDN'T COME TO RESCUE YOU.
WE CAME TO TAKE YOU IN.
STARFIRE.
MAJOR FORCE.
BLACK LIGHTNING.
KATANA.
POWER GIRL.
Heroes all.
And now they're working for Luthor...

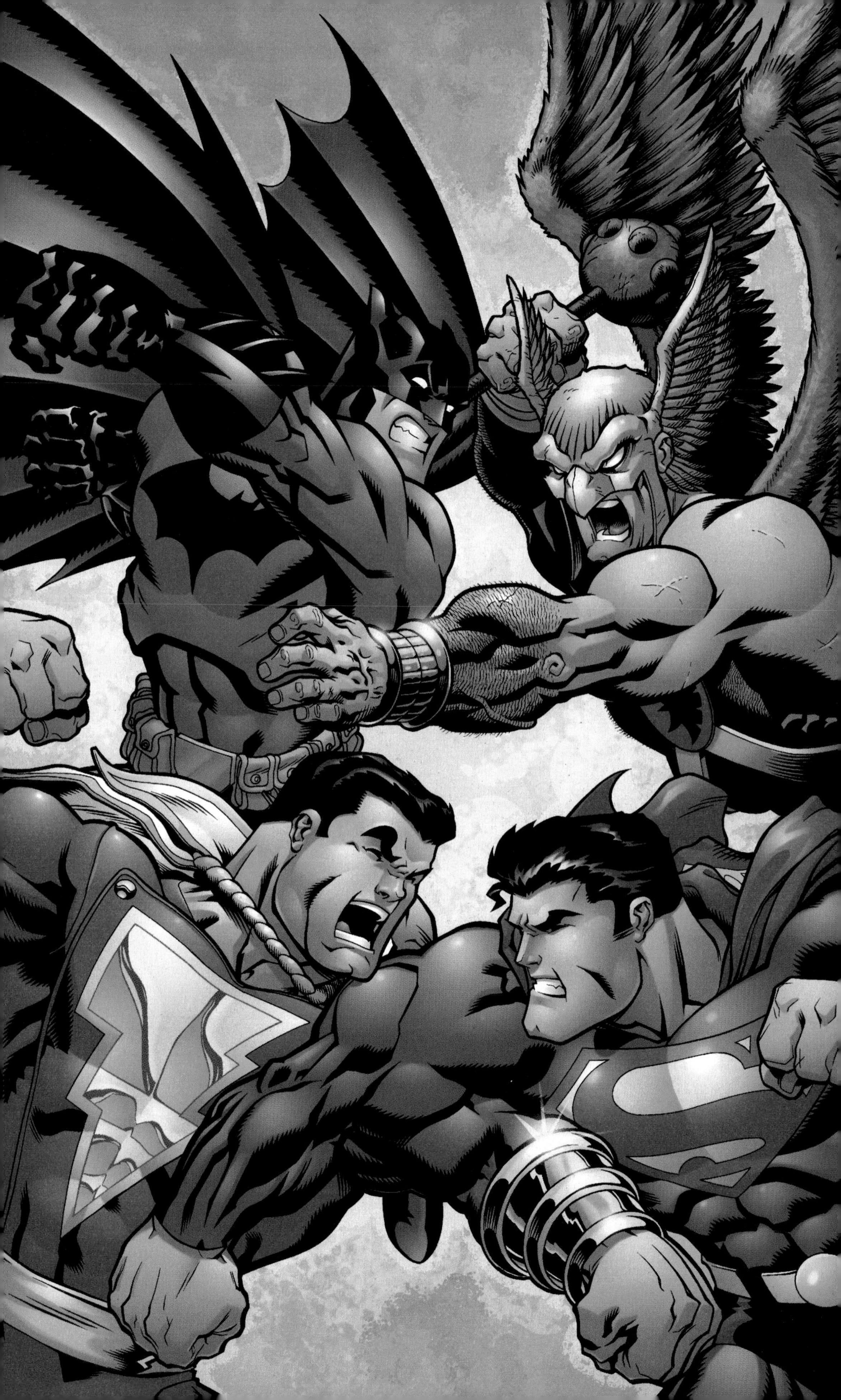

"In times of war, circumstances dictate action."

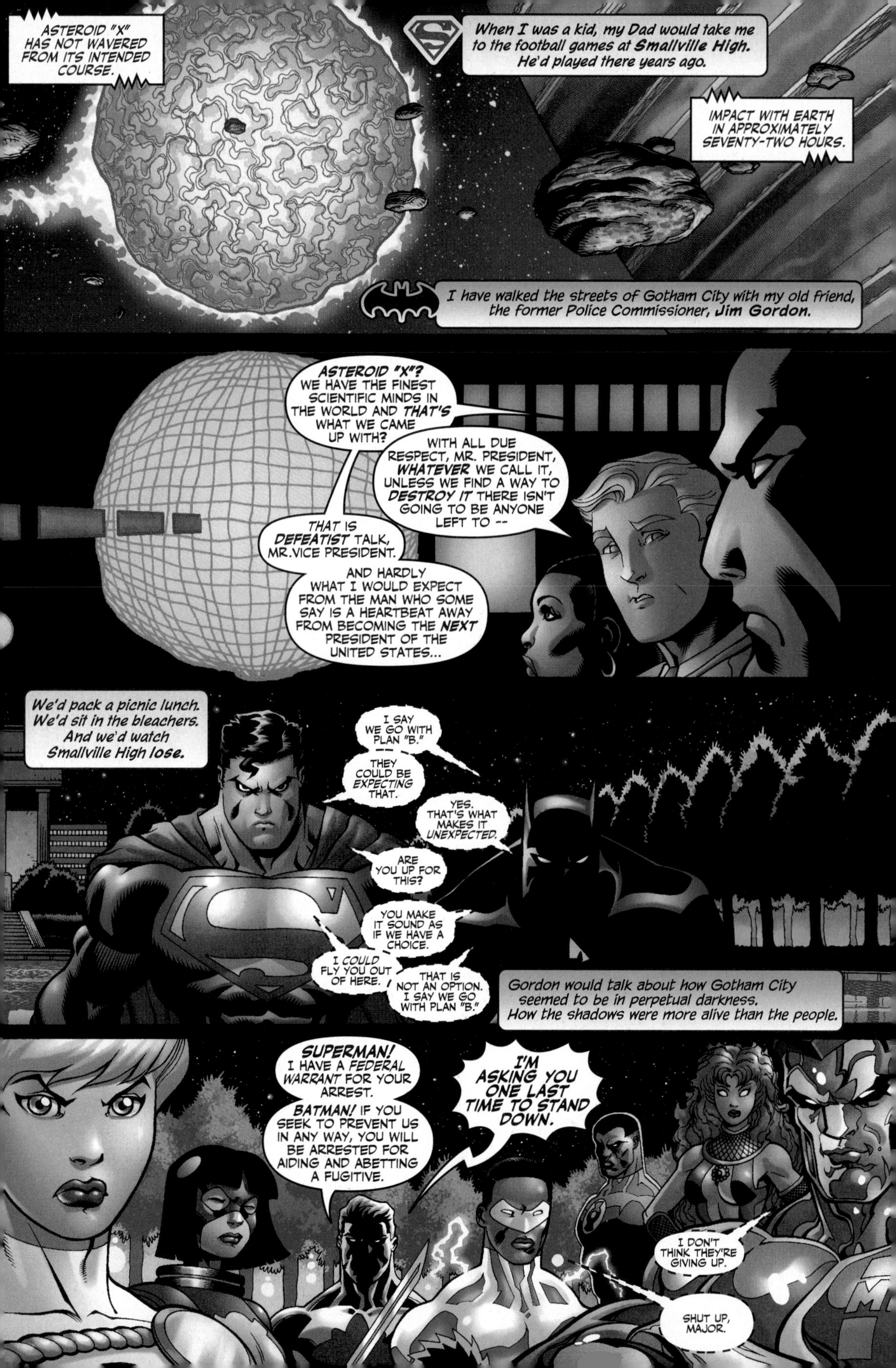
ASTEROID "X" HAS NOT WAVERED FROM ITS INTENDED COURSE.
When I was a kid, my Dad would take me to the football games at Smallville High. He'd played there years ago.
IMPACT WITH EARTH IN APPROXIMATELY SEVENTY-TWO HOURS.
I have walked the streets of Gotham City with my old friend, the former Police Commissioner, Jim Gordon.
ASTEROID "X"? WE HAVE THE FINEST SCIENTIFIC MINDS IN THE WORLD AND THAT'S WHAT WE CAME UP WITH?
WITH ALL DUE RESPECT, MR. PRESIDENT, WHATEVER WE CALL IT, UNLESS WE FIND A WAY TO DESTROY IT THERE ISN'T GOING TO BE ANYONE LEFT TO --
THAT IS DEFEATIST TALK, MR.VICE PRESIDENT.
AND HARDLY WHAT I WOULD EXPECT FROM THE MAN WHO SOME SAY IS A HEARTBEAT AWAY FROM BECOMING THE NEXT PRESIDENT OF THE UNITED STATES...
We'd pack a picnic lunch. We'd sit in the bleachers. And we'd watch Smallville High lose.
I SAY WE GO WITH PLAN "B."
THEY COULD BE EXPECTING THAT.
YES. THAT'S WHAT MAKES IT UNEXPECTED.
ARE YOU UP FOR THIS?
YOU MAKE IT SOUND AS IF WE HAVE A CHOICE.
I COULD FLY YOU OUT OF HERE.
THAT IS NOT AN OPTION. I SAY WE GO WITH PLAN "B."
Gordon would talk about how Gotham City seemed to be in perpetual darkness. How the shadows were more alive than the people.
SUPERMAN! I HAVE A FEDERAL WARRANT FOR YOUR ARREST.
BATMAN! IF YOU SEEK TO PREVENT US IN ANY WAY, YOU WILL BE ARRESTED FOR AIDING AND ABETTING A FUGITIVE.
I'M ASKING YOU ONE LAST TIME TO STAND DOWN.
I DON'T THINK THEY'RE GIVING UP.
SHUT UP, MAJOR.

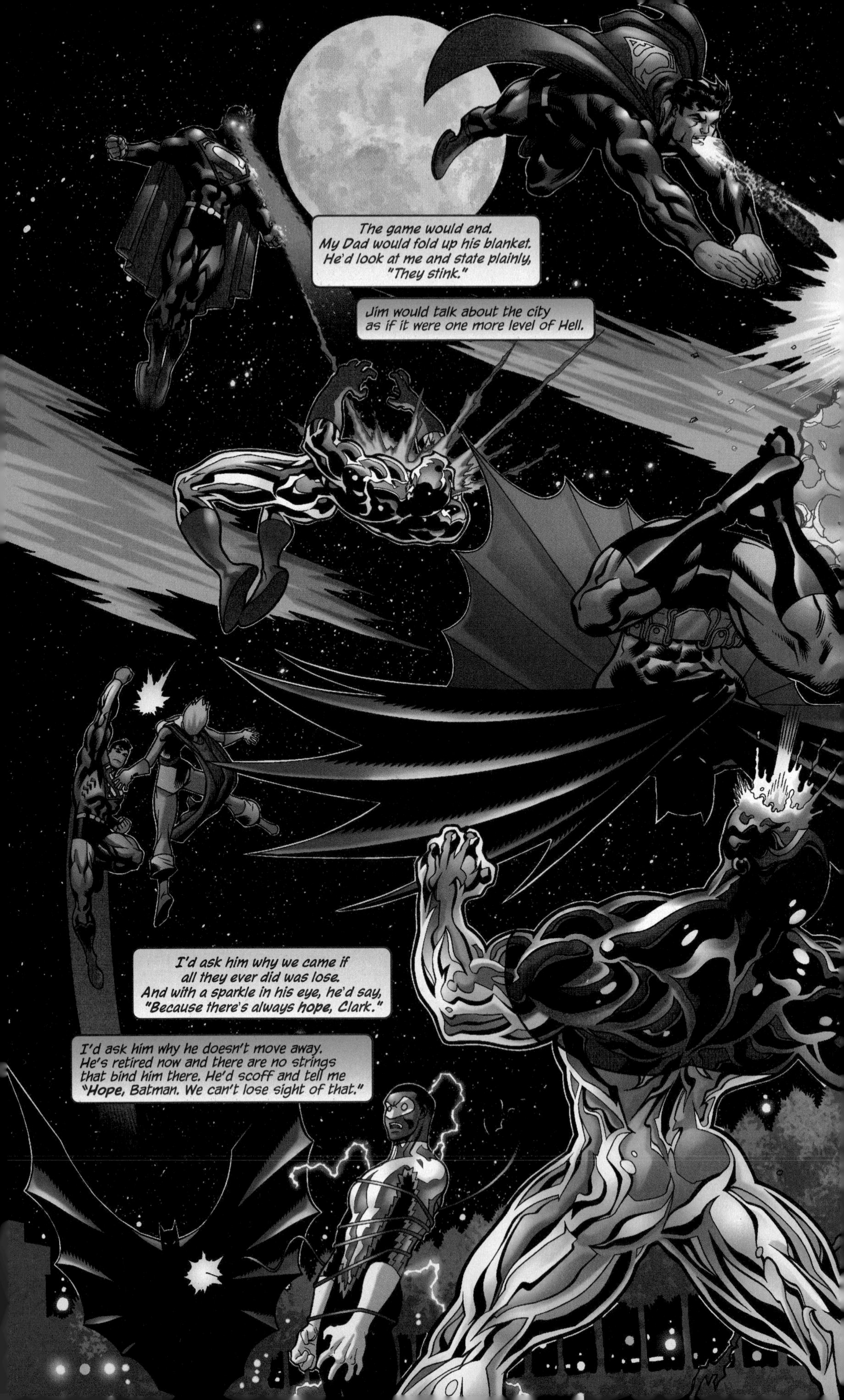
The game would end.
My Dad would fold up his blanket.
He'd look at me and state plainly,
"They stink."
Jim would talk about the city
as if it were one more level of Hell.
I'd ask him why we came if
all they ever did was lose.
And with a sparkle in his eye, he'd say,
"Because there's always hope, Clark."
I'd ask him why he doesn't move away.
He's retired now and there are no strings
that bind him there. He'd scoff and tell me
"Hope, Batman. We can't lose sight of that."

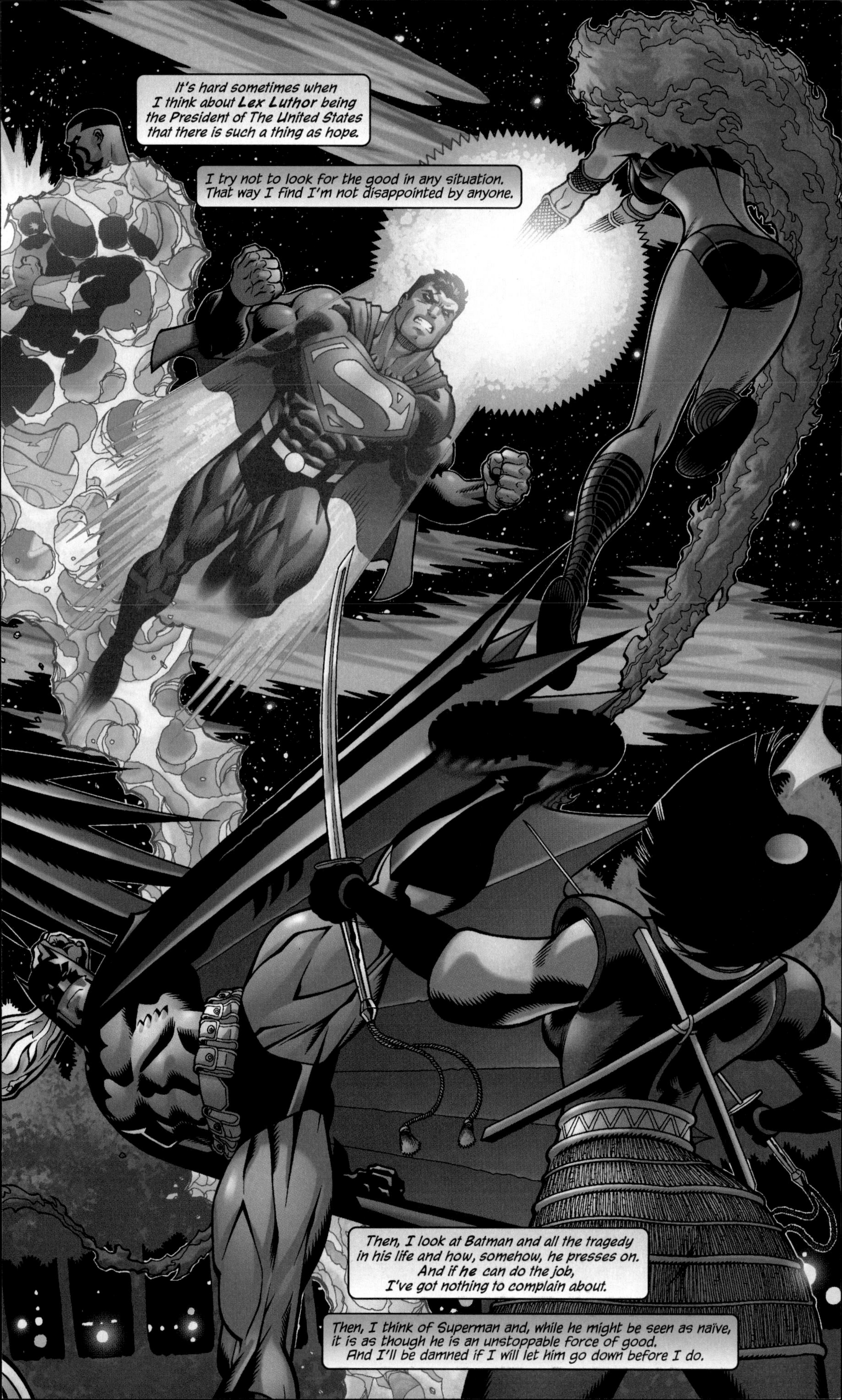
It's hard sometimes when I think about Lex Luthor being the President of The United States that there is such a thing as hope.
I try not to look for the good in any situation. That way I find I'm not disappointed by anyone.
Then, I look at Batman and all the tragedy in his life and how, somehow, he presses on. And if he can do the job, I've got nothing to complain about.
Then, I think of Superman and, while he might be seen as naïve, it is as though he is an unstoppable force of good. And I'll be damned if I will let him go down before I do.

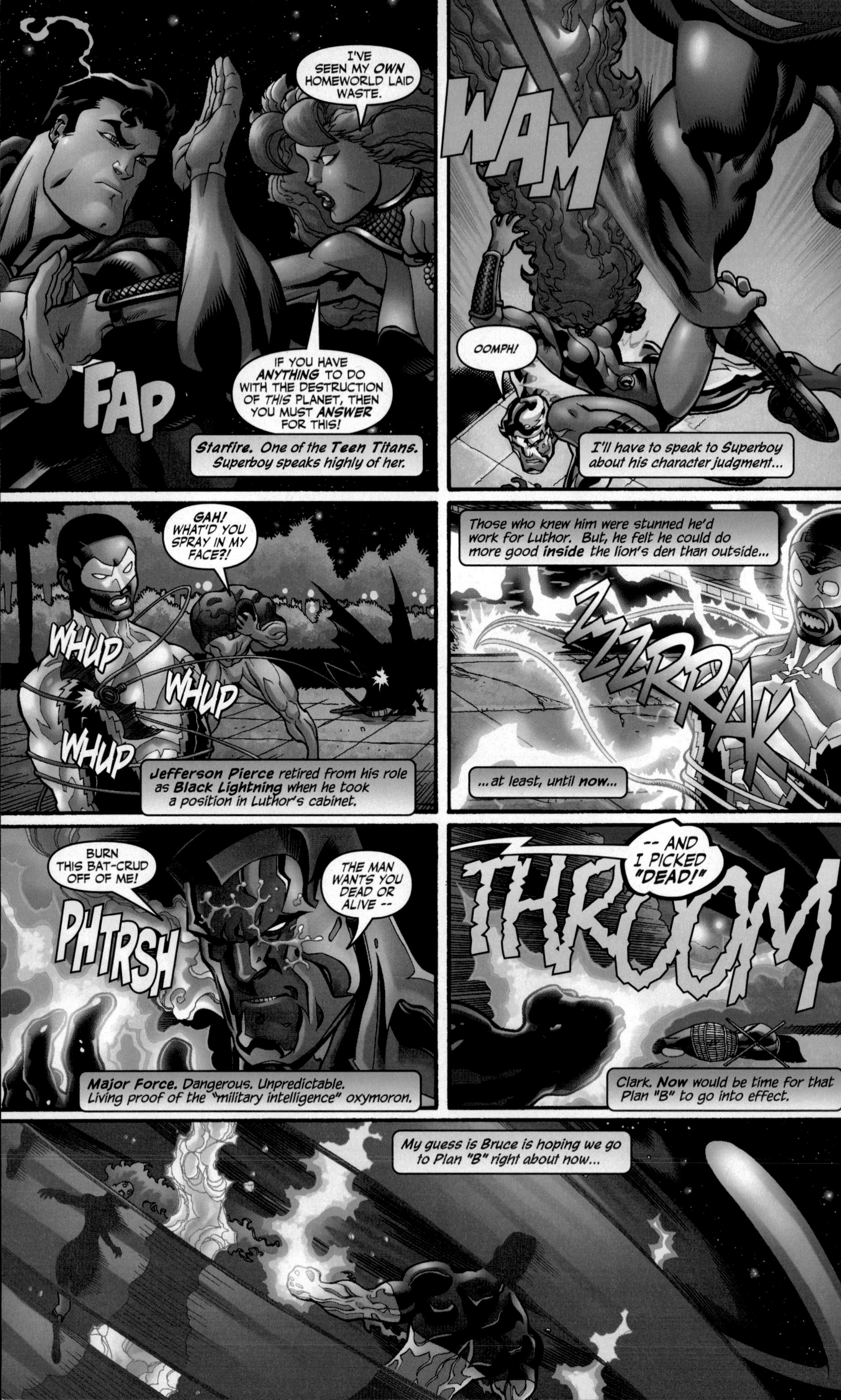
I'VE SEEN MY OWN HOMEWORLD LAID WASTE.
FAP
IF YOU HAVE ANYTHING TO DO WITH THE DESTRUCTION OF THIS PLANET, THEN YOU MUST ANSWER FOR THIS!
Starfire. One of the Teen Titans. Superboy speaks highly of her.
WAM
OOMPH!
I'll have to speak to Superboy about his character judgment...
GAH! WHAT'D YOU SPRAY IN MY FACE?!
WHUP
WHUP
WHUP
Jefferson Pierce retired from his role as Black Lightning when he took a position in Luthor's cabinet.
Those who knew him were stunned he'd work for Luthor. But, he felt he could do more good inside the lion's den than outside...
ZZZRRRAK
...at least, until now...
BURN THIS BAT-CRUD OFF OF ME!
PHTRSH
THE MAN WANTS YOU DEAD OR ALIVE --
Major Force. Dangerous. Unpredictable. Living proof of the "military intelligence" oxymoron.
-- AND I PICKED "DEAD!"
THROOM
Clark. Now would be time for that Plan "B" to go into effect.
My guess is Bruce is hoping we go to Plan "B" right about now...

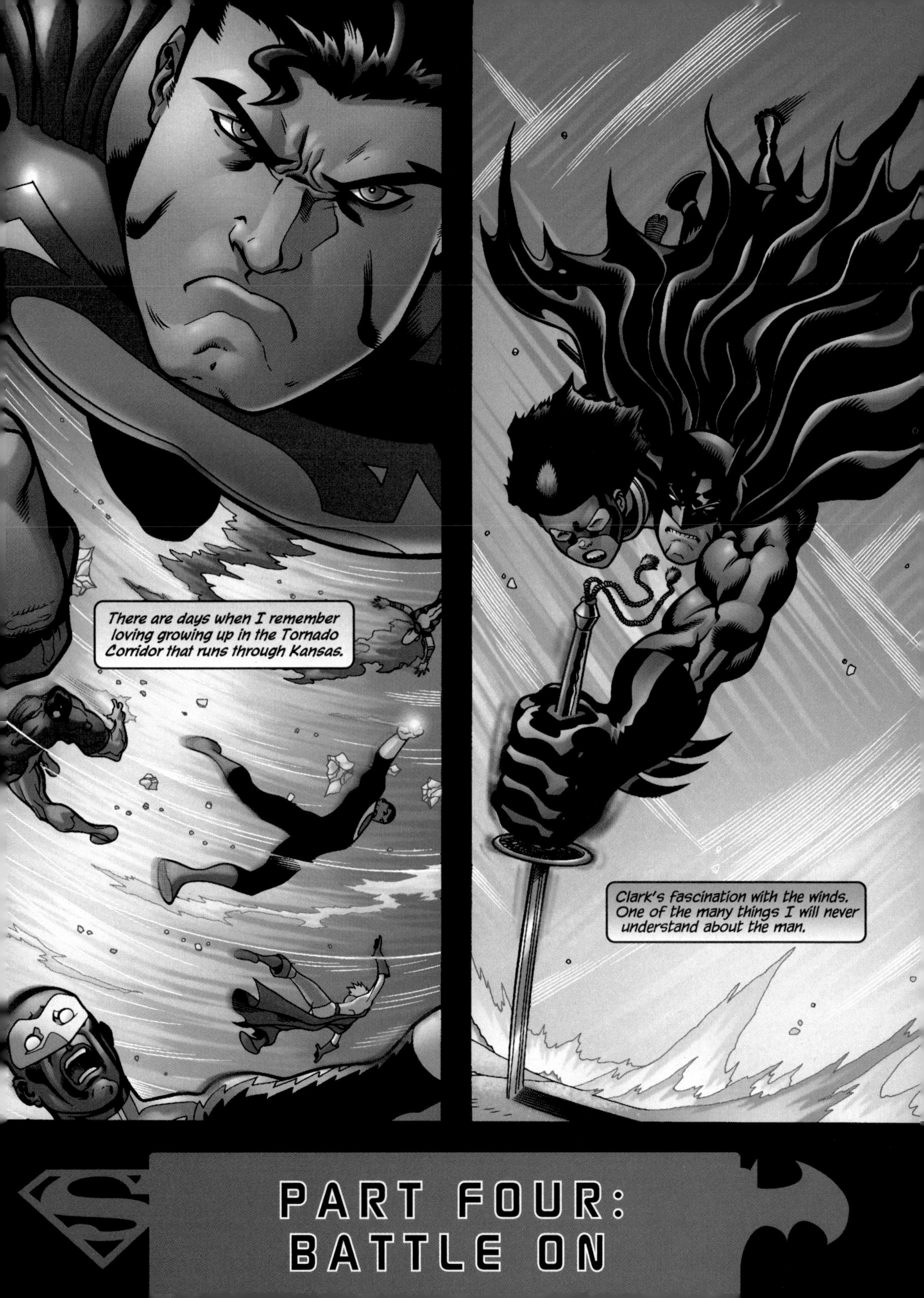
There are days when I remember loving growing up in the Tornado Corridor that runs through Kansas.
Clark's fascination with the winds. One of the many things I will never understand about the man.

PART FOUR: BATTLE ON

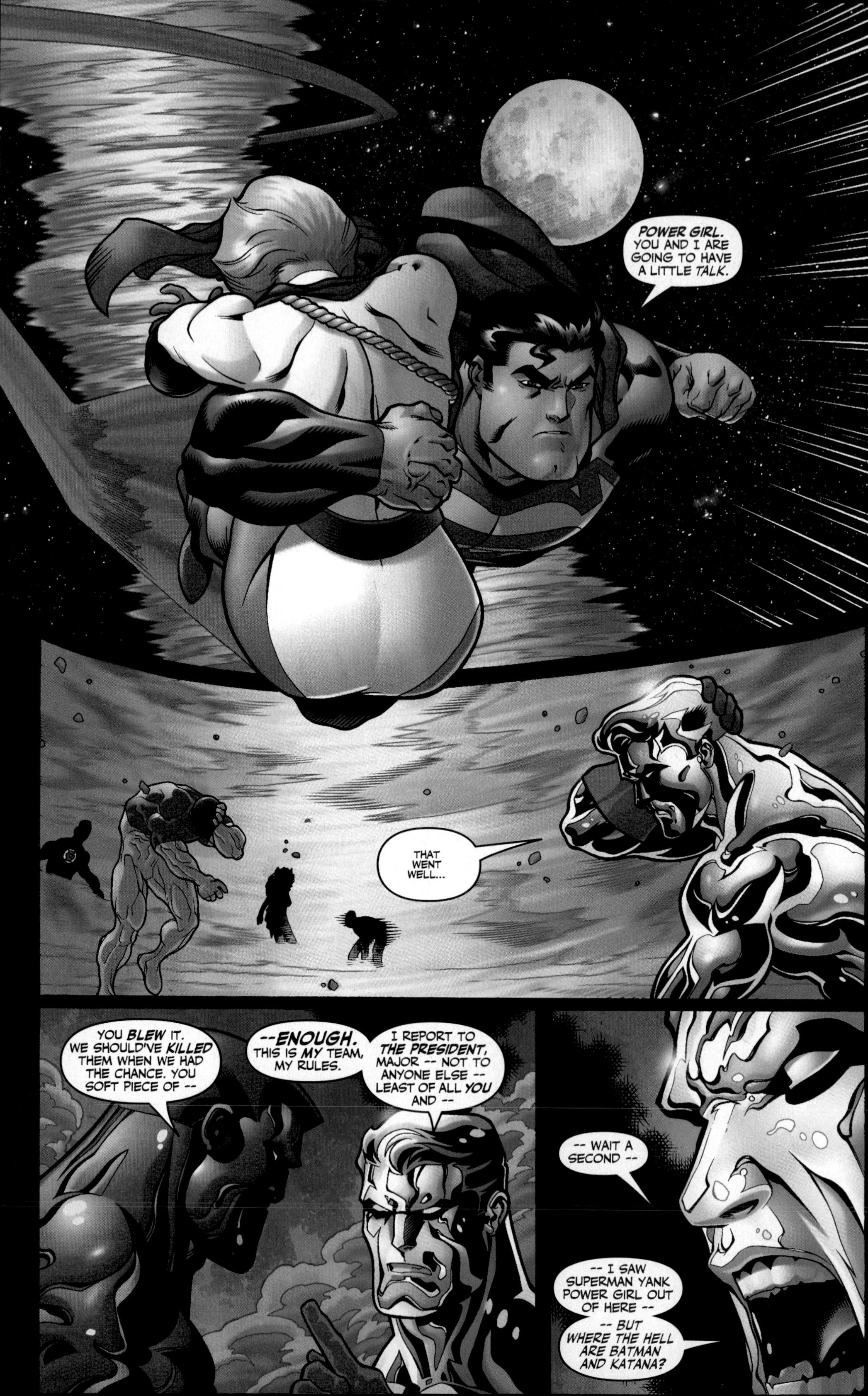
POWER GIRL. YOU AND I ARE GOING TO HAVE A LITTLE TALK.
THAT WENT WELL...
YOU BLEW IT. WE SHOULD'VE KILLED THEM WHEN WE HAD THE CHANCE. YOU SOFT PIECE OF --
--ENOUGH. THIS IS MY TEAM, MY RULES.
I REPORT TO THE PRESIDENT, MAJOR -- NOT TO ANYONE ELSE -- LEAST OF ALL YOU AND --
-- WAIT A SECOND --
-- I SAW SUPERMAN YANK POWER GIRL OUT OF HERE --
-- BUT WHERE THE HELL ARE BATMAN AND KATANA?

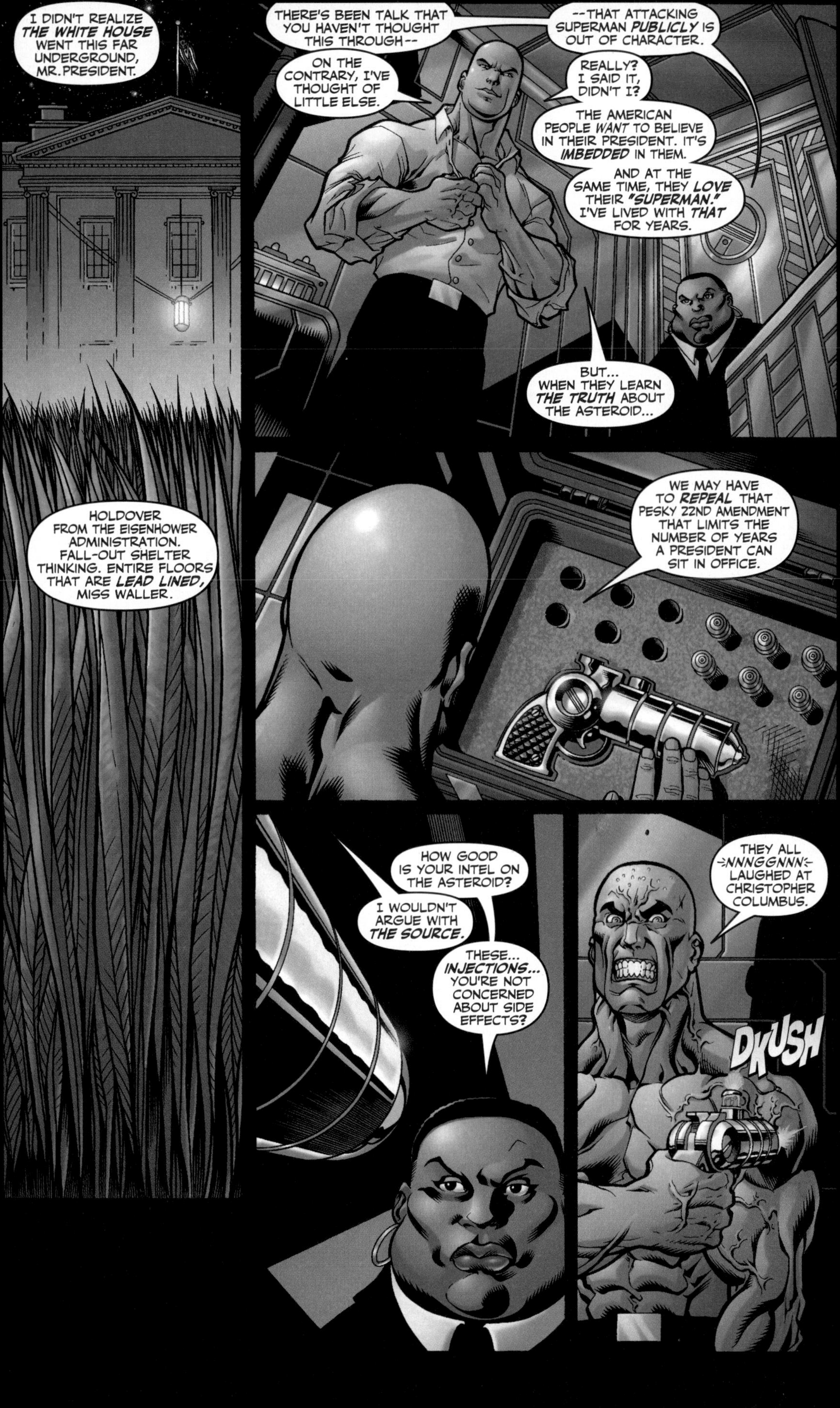
I DIDN'T REALIZE THE WHITE HOUSE WENT THIS FAR UNDERGROUND, MR. PRESIDENT.
HOLDOVER FROM THE EISENHOWER ADMINISTRATION. FALL-OUT SHELTER THINKING. ENTIRE FLOORS THAT ARE LEAD LINED, MISS WALLER.
THERE'S BEEN TALK THAT YOU HAVEN'T THOUGHT THIS THROUGH--
--THAT ATTACKING SUPERMAN PUBLICLY IS OUT OF CHARACTER.
ON THE CONTRARY, I'VE THOUGHT OF LITTLE ELSE.
REALLY? I SAID IT, DIDN'T I?
THE AMERICAN PEOPLE WANT TO BELIEVE IN THEIR PRESIDENT. IT'S IMBEDDED IN THEM.
AND AT THE SAME TIME, THEY LOVE THEIR "SUPERMAN." I'VE LIVED WITH THAT FOR YEARS.
BUT... WHEN THEY LEARN THE TRUTH ABOUT THE ASTEROID...
WE MAY HAVE TO REPEAL THAT PESKY 22ND AMENDMENT THAT LIMITS THE NUMBER OF YEARS A PRESIDENT CAN SIT IN OFFICE.
HOW GOOD IS YOUR INTEL ON THE ASTEROID?
I WOULDN'T ARGUE WITH THE SOURCE.
THESE... INJECTIONS... YOU'RE NOT CONCERNED ABOUT SIDE EFFECTS?
THEY ALL -NNNGGNNN- LAUGHED AT CHRISTOPHER COLUMBUS.
DKUSH

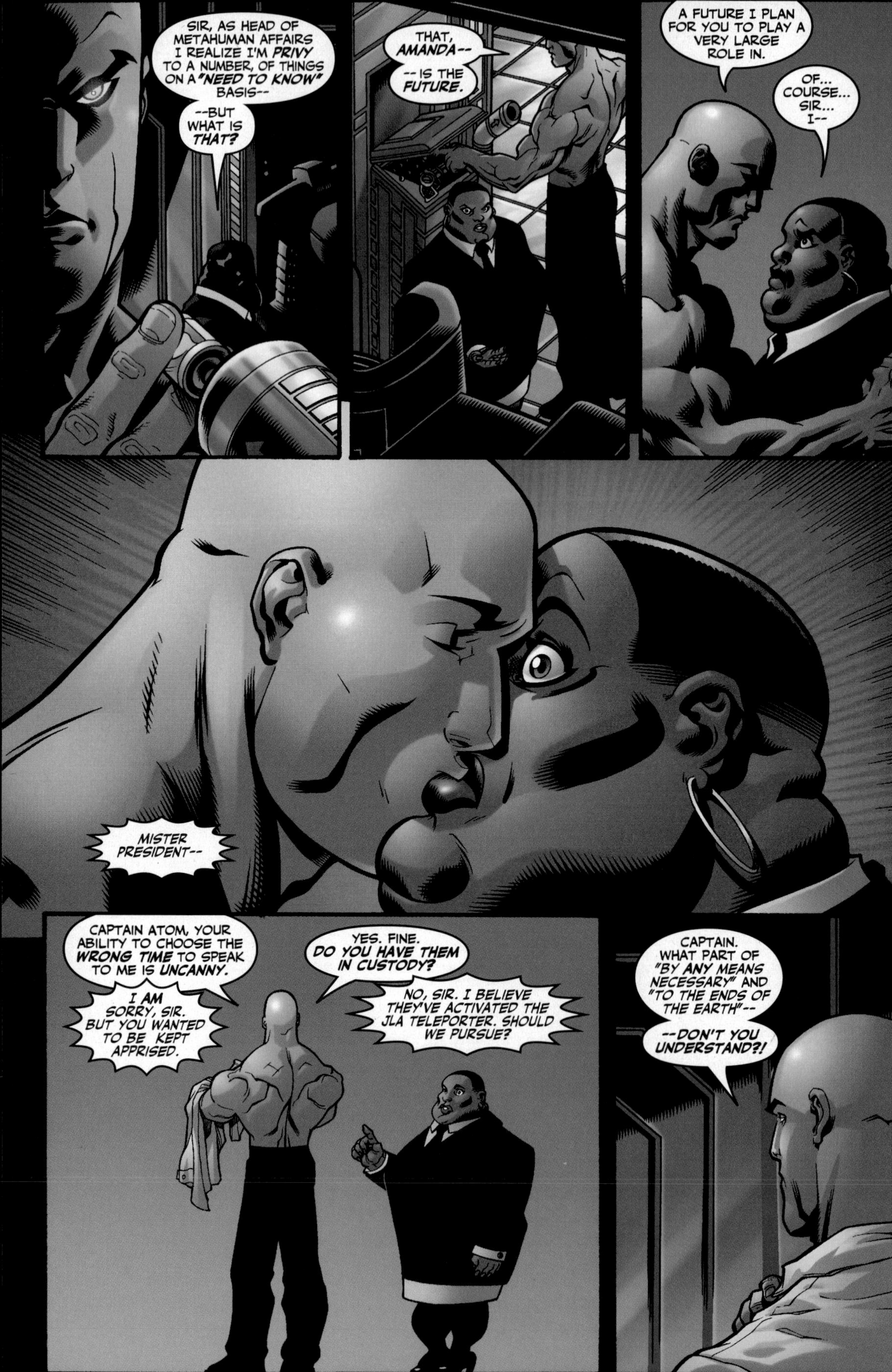
SIR, AS HEAD OF METAHUMAN AFFAIRS I REALIZE I'M PRIVY TO A NUMBER, OF THINGS ON A "NEED TO KNOW" BASIS--
--BUT WHAT IS THAT?
THAT, AMANDA--
--IS THE FUTURE.
A FUTURE I PLAN FOR YOU TO PLAY A VERY LARGE ROLE IN.
OF... COURSE... SIR... I--
MISTER PRESIDENT--
CAPTAIN ATOM, YOUR ABILITY TO CHOOSE THE WRONG TIME TO SPEAK TO ME IS UNCANNY.
I AM SORRY, SIR. BUT YOU WANTED TO BE KEPT APPRISED.
YES. FINE. DO YOU HAVE THEM IN CUSTODY?
NO, SIR. I BELIEVE THEY'VE ACTIVATED THE JLA TELEPORTER. SHOULD WE PURSUE?
CAPTAIN. WHAT PART OF "BY ANY MEANS NECESSARY" AND "TO THE ENDS OF THE EARTH"--
--DON'T YOU UNDERSTAND?!

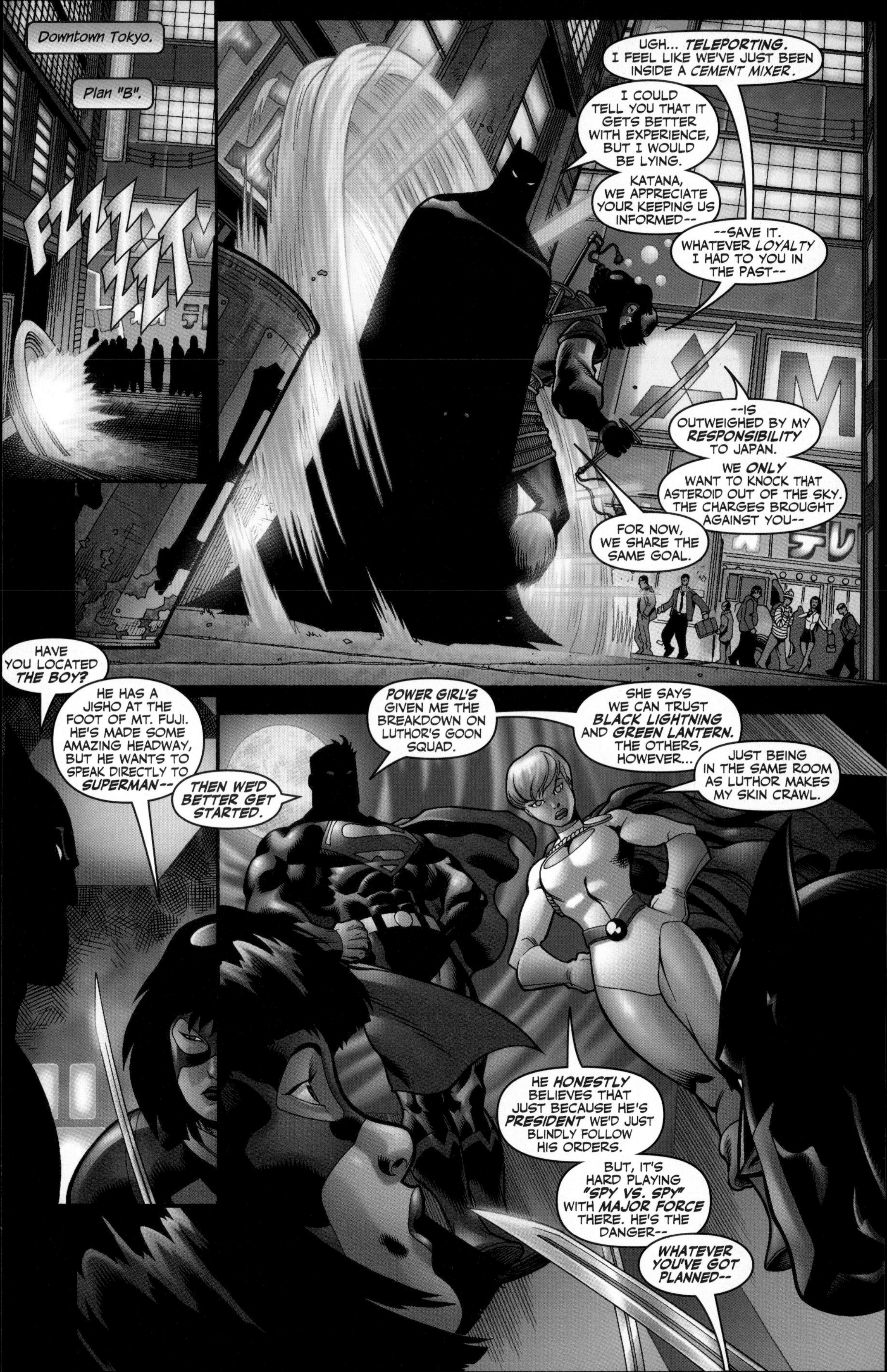
Downtown Tokyo.
Plan "B".
FZZZZZZZTM
UGH... TELEPORTING. I FEEL LIKE WE'VE JUST BEEN INSIDE A CEMENT MIXER.
I COULD TELL YOU THAT IT GETS BETTER WITH EXPERIENCE, BUT I WOULD BE LYING.
KATANA, WE APPRECIATE YOUR KEEPING US INFORMED--
--SAVE IT. WHATEVER LOYALTY I HAD TO YOU IN THE PAST--
--IS OUTWEIGHED BY MY RESPONSIBILITY TO JAPAN.
WE ONLY WANT TO KNOCK THAT ASTEROID OUT OF THE SKY. THE CHARGES BROUGHT AGAINST YOU--
FOR NOW, WE SHARE THE SAME GOAL.
HAVE YOU LOCATED THE BOY?
HE HAS A JISHO AT THE FOOT OF MT. FUJI. HE'S MADE SOME AMAZING HEADWAY, BUT HE WANTS TO SPEAK DIRECTLY TO SUPERMAN--
THEN WE'D BETTER GET STARTED.
POWER GIRL'S GIVEN ME THE BREAKDOWN ON LUTHOR'S GOON SQUAD.
SHE SAYS WE CAN TRUST BLACK LIGHTNING AND GREEN LANTERN. THE OTHERS, HOWEVER...
JUST BEING IN THE SAME ROOM AS LUTHOR MAKES MY SKIN CRAWL.
HE HONESTLY BELIEVES THAT JUST BECAUSE HE'S PRESIDENT WE'D JUST BLINDLY FOLLOW HIS ORDERS.
BUT, IT'S HARD PLAYING "SPY VS. SPY" WITH MAJOR FORCE THERE. HE'S THE DANGER--
WHATEVER YOU'VE GOT PLANNED--

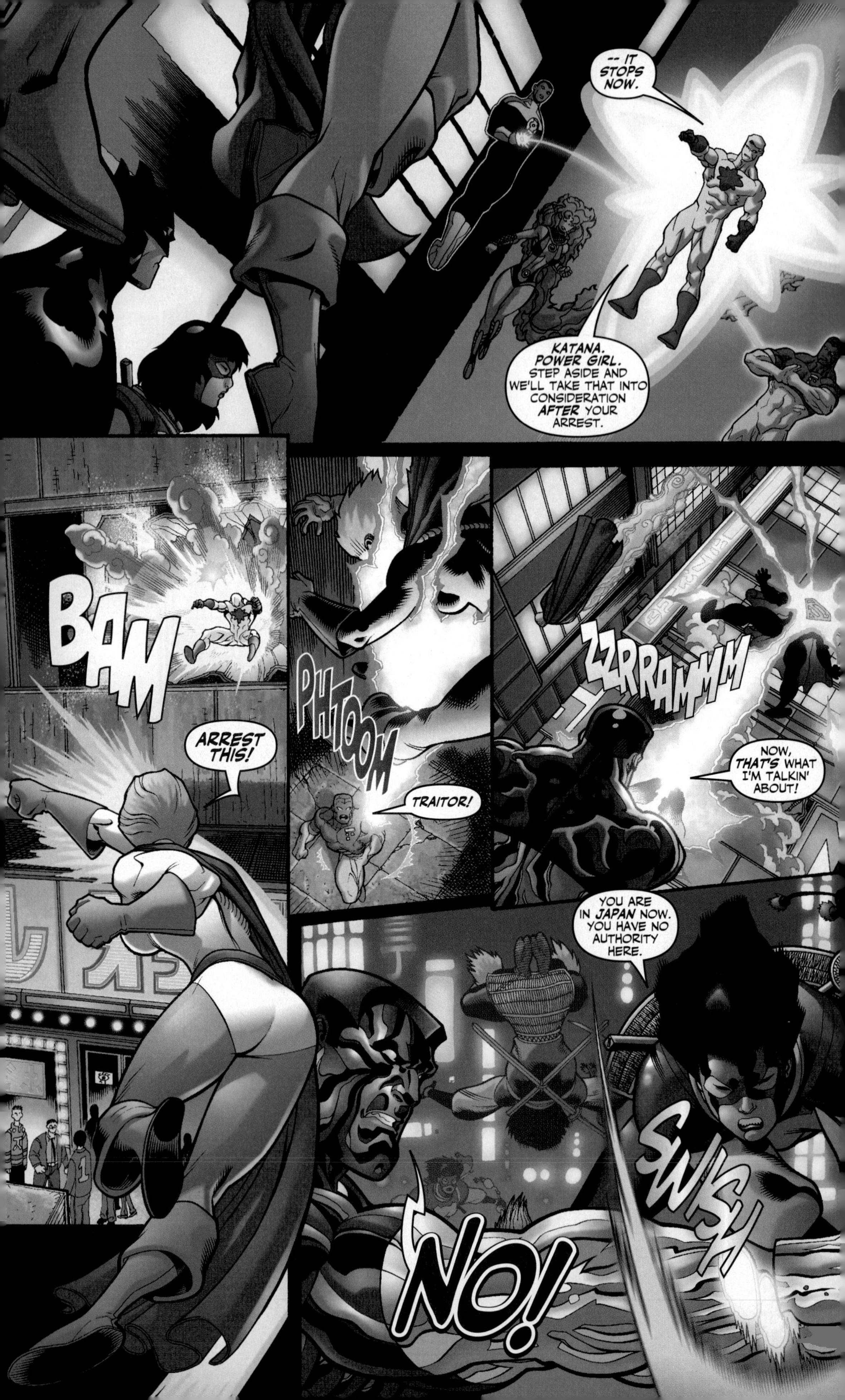
-- IT STOPS NOW.
KATANA. POWER GIRL. STEP ASIDE AND WE'LL TAKE THAT INTO CONSIDERATION AFTER YOUR ARREST.
BAM
ARREST THIS!
PHTOOM
TRAITOR!
ZZRRAMMM
NOW, THAT'S WHAT I'M TALKIN' ABOUT!
YOU ARE IN JAPAN NOW. YOU HAVE NO AUTHORITY HERE.
SWISH
NO!

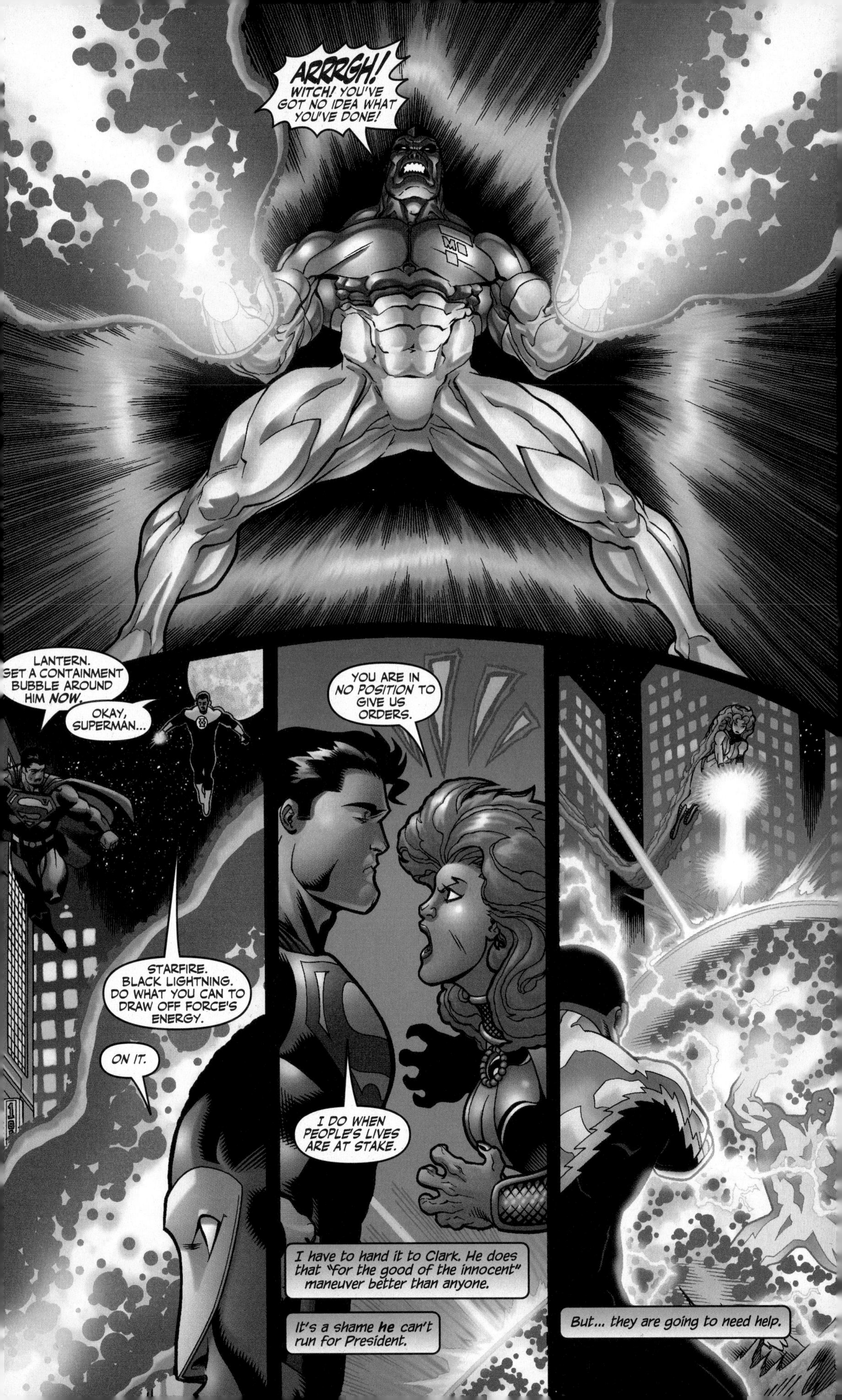
ARRRGH! WITCH! YOU'VE GOT NO IDEA WHAT YOU'VE DONE!
LANTERN. GET A CONTAINMENT BUBBLE AROUND HIM NOW.
OKAY, SUPERMAN...
STARFIRE. BLACK LIGHTNING. DO WHAT YOU CAN TO DRAW OFF FORCE'S ENERGY.
ON IT.
YOU ARE IN NO POSITION TO GIVE US ORDERS.
I DO WHEN PEOPLE'S LIVES ARE AT STAKE.
I have to hand it to Clark. He does that "for the good of the innocent" maneuver better than anyone.
It's a shame he can't run for President.
But... they are going to need help.

CAPTAIN.

YOU HAVE A DILEMMA.

IF WE *SURRENDER* TO YOU, YOU WILL HAVE FULFILLED YOUR MISSION.

AND *TOKYO* WILL BE DECIMATED.

MEN, WOMEN, AND *CHILDREN* WILL HAVE DIED WHILE YOU COMPLETED YOUR *ERRAND*.

I'M UNDER ORDERS TO BRING YOU AND SUPERMAN IN. BY ANY MEANS NECESSARY.

IN TIMES OF WAR, *CIRCUMSTANCES* DICTATE ACTION.

YOU KNOW THAT BETTER THAN ANYONE.

TOKYO HAS *ONE* CHANCE TO SURVIVE. YOU HAVE TO DECIDE.

NOW.

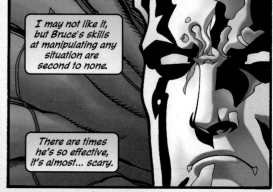

I may not like it, but Bruce's skills at manipulating any situation are second to none.

There are times he's so effective, it's almost... scary.

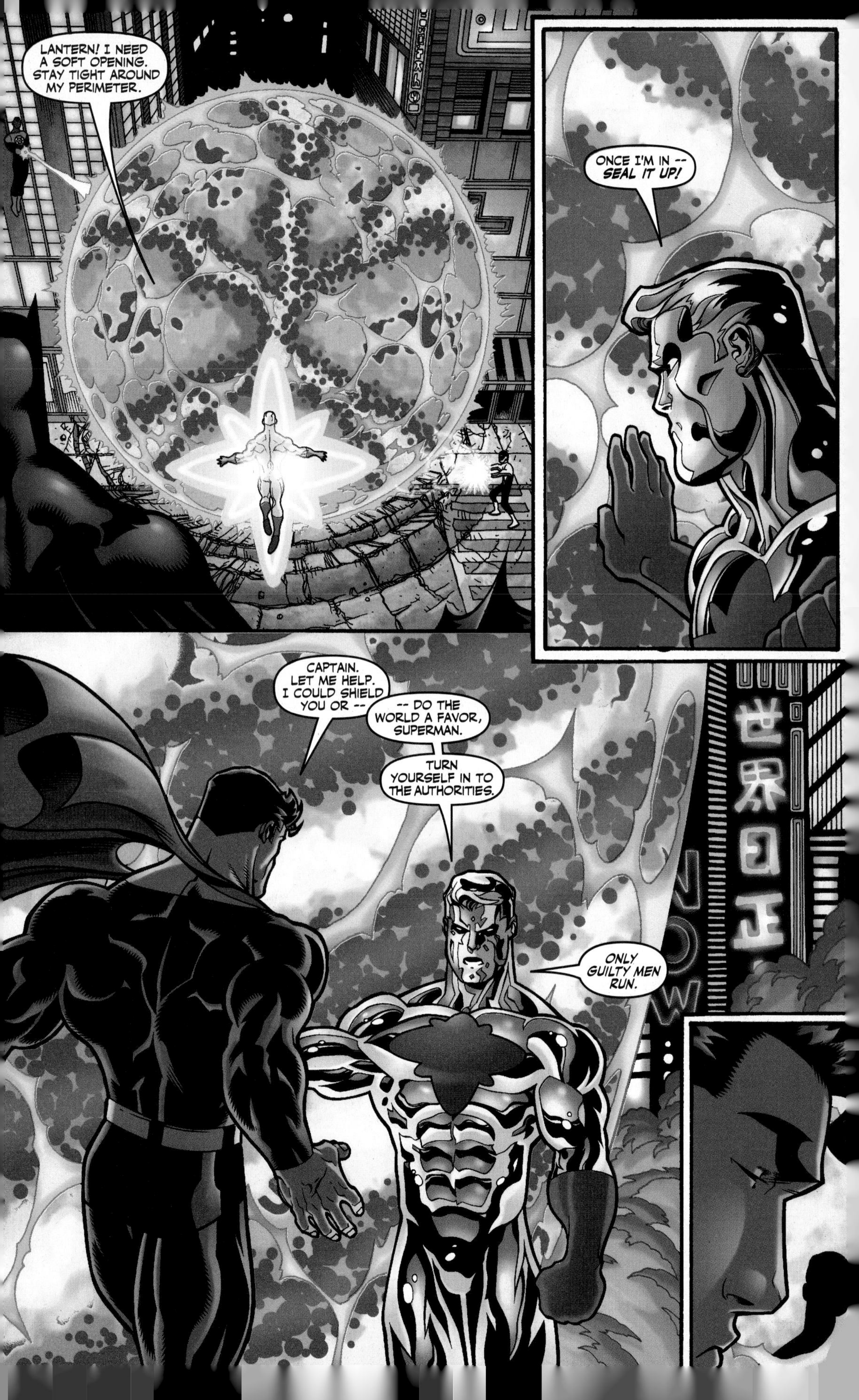
LANTERN! I NEED A SOFT OPENING. STAY TIGHT AROUND MY PERIMETER.
ONCE I'M IN -- SEAL IT UP!
CAPTAIN. LET ME HELP. I COULD SHIELD YOU OR --
-- DO THE WORLD A FAVOR, SUPERMAN.
TURN YOURSELF IN TO THE AUTHORITIES.
ONLY GUILTY MEN RUN.
世界日

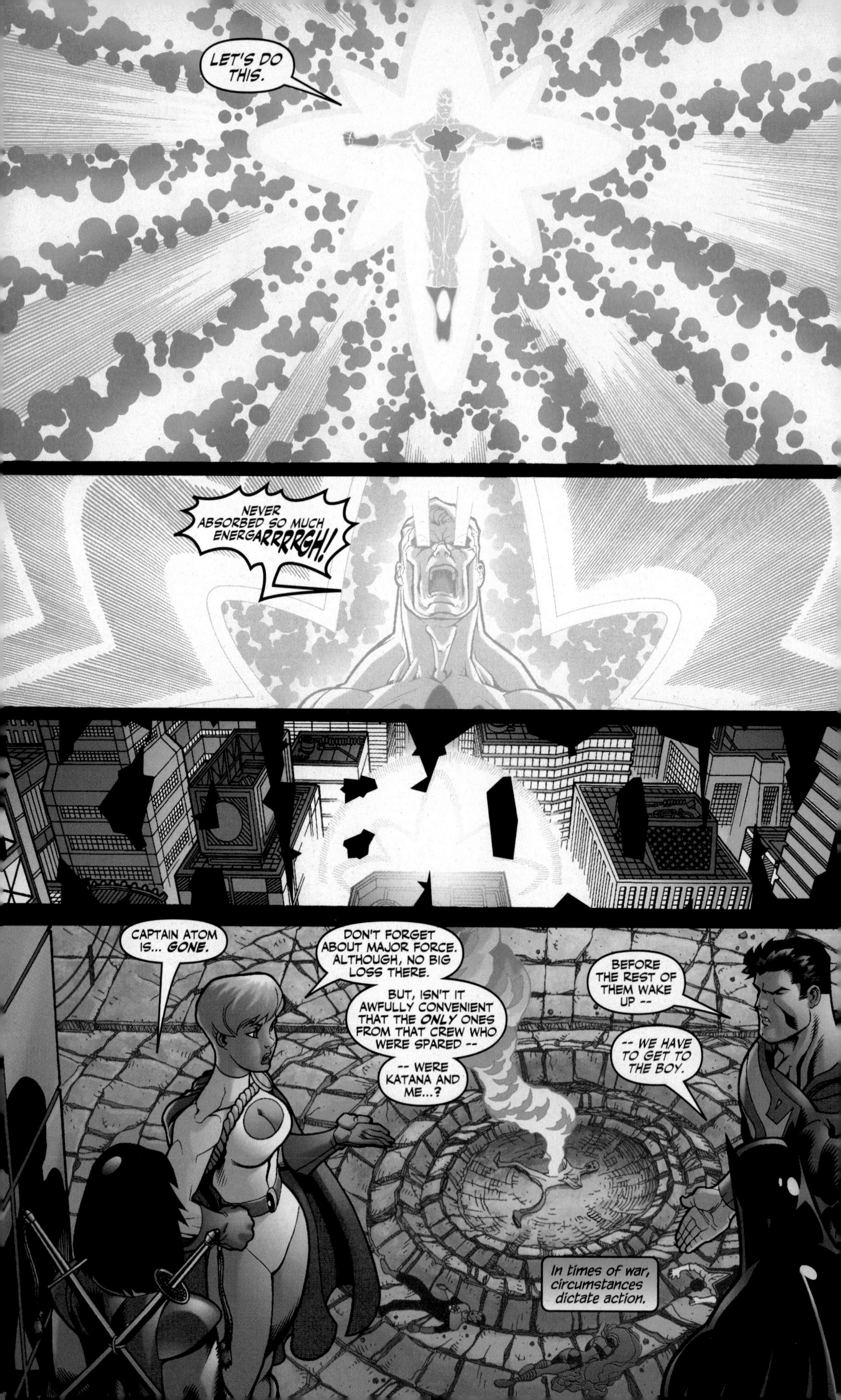

LET'S DO THIS.
NEVER ABSORBED SO MUCH ENERGARRRRGH!
CAPTAIN ATOM IS... GONE.
DON'T FORGET ABOUT MAJOR FORCE. ALTHOUGH, NO BIG LOSS THERE.
BUT, ISN'T IT AWFULLY CONVENIENT THAT THE ONLY ONES FROM THAT CREW WHO WERE SPARED --
-- WERE KATANA AND ME...?
BEFORE THE REST OF THEM WAKE UP --
-- WE HAVE TO GET TO THE BOY.
In times of war, circumstances dictate action.

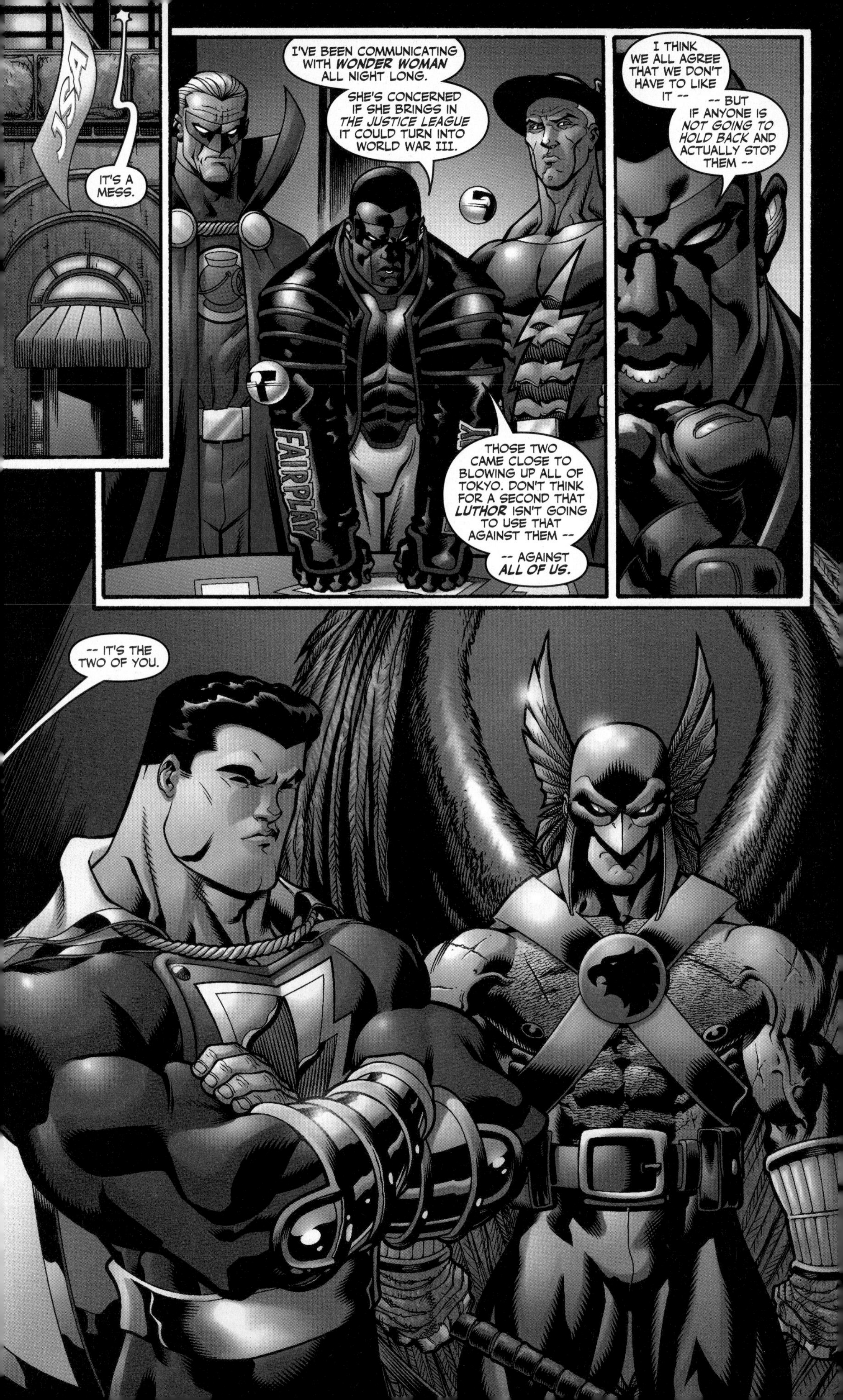
JSA
IT'S A MESS.
I'VE BEEN COMMUNICATING WITH WONDER WOMAN ALL NIGHT LONG.
SHE'S CONCERNED IF SHE BRINGS IN THE JUSTICE LEAGUE IT COULD TURN INTO WORLD WAR III.
FAIRPLAY
THOSE TWO CAME CLOSE TO BLOWING UP ALL OF TOKYO. DON'T THINK FOR A SECOND THAT LUTHOR ISN'T GOING TO USE THAT AGAINST THEM --
-- AGAINST ALL OF US.
I THINK WE ALL AGREE THAT WE DON'T HAVE TO LIKE IT --
-- BUT IF ANYONE IS NOT GOING TO HOLD BACK AND ACTUALLY STOP THEM --
-- IT'S THE TWO OF YOU.

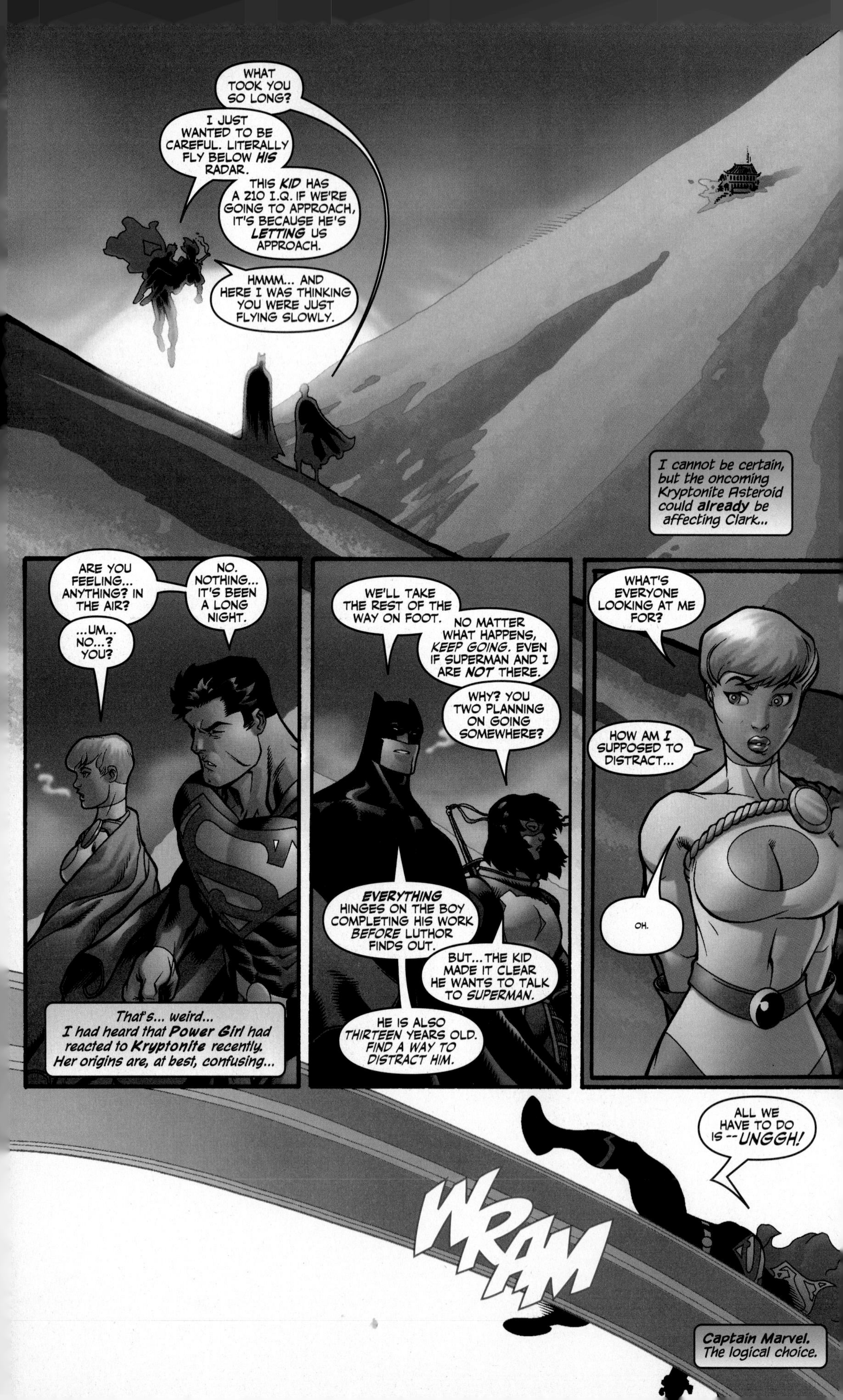

WHAT TOOK YOU SO LONG?
I JUST WANTED TO BE CAREFUL. LITERALLY FLY BELOW HIS RADAR.
THIS KID HAS A 210 I.Q. IF WE'RE GOING TO APPROACH, IT'S BECAUSE HE'S LETTING US APPROACH.
HMMM... AND HERE I WAS THINKING YOU WERE JUST FLYING SLOWLY.
I cannot be certain, but the oncoming Kryptonite Asteroid could already be affecting Clark...
ARE YOU FEELING... ANYTHING? IN THE AIR?
NO. NOTHING... IT'S BEEN A LONG NIGHT.
...UM... NO...? YOU?
That's... weird... I had heard that Power Girl had reacted to Kryptonite recently. Her origins are, at best, confusing...
WE'LL TAKE THE REST OF THE WAY ON FOOT.
NO MATTER WHAT HAPPENS, KEEP GOING. EVEN IF SUPERMAN AND I ARE NOT THERE.
WHY? YOU TWO PLANNING ON GOING SOMEWHERE?
EVERYTHING HINGES ON THE BOY COMPLETING HIS WORK BEFORE LUTHOR FINDS OUT.
BUT... THE KID MADE IT CLEAR HE WANTS TO TALK TO SUPERMAN.
HE IS ALSO THIRTEEN YEARS OLD. FIND A WAY TO DISTRACT HIM.
WHAT'S EVERYONE LOOKING AT ME FOR?
HOW AM I SUPPOSED TO DISTRACT...
OH.
ALL WE HAVE TO DO IS --UNGGH!
WRAM
Captain Marvel. The logical choice.

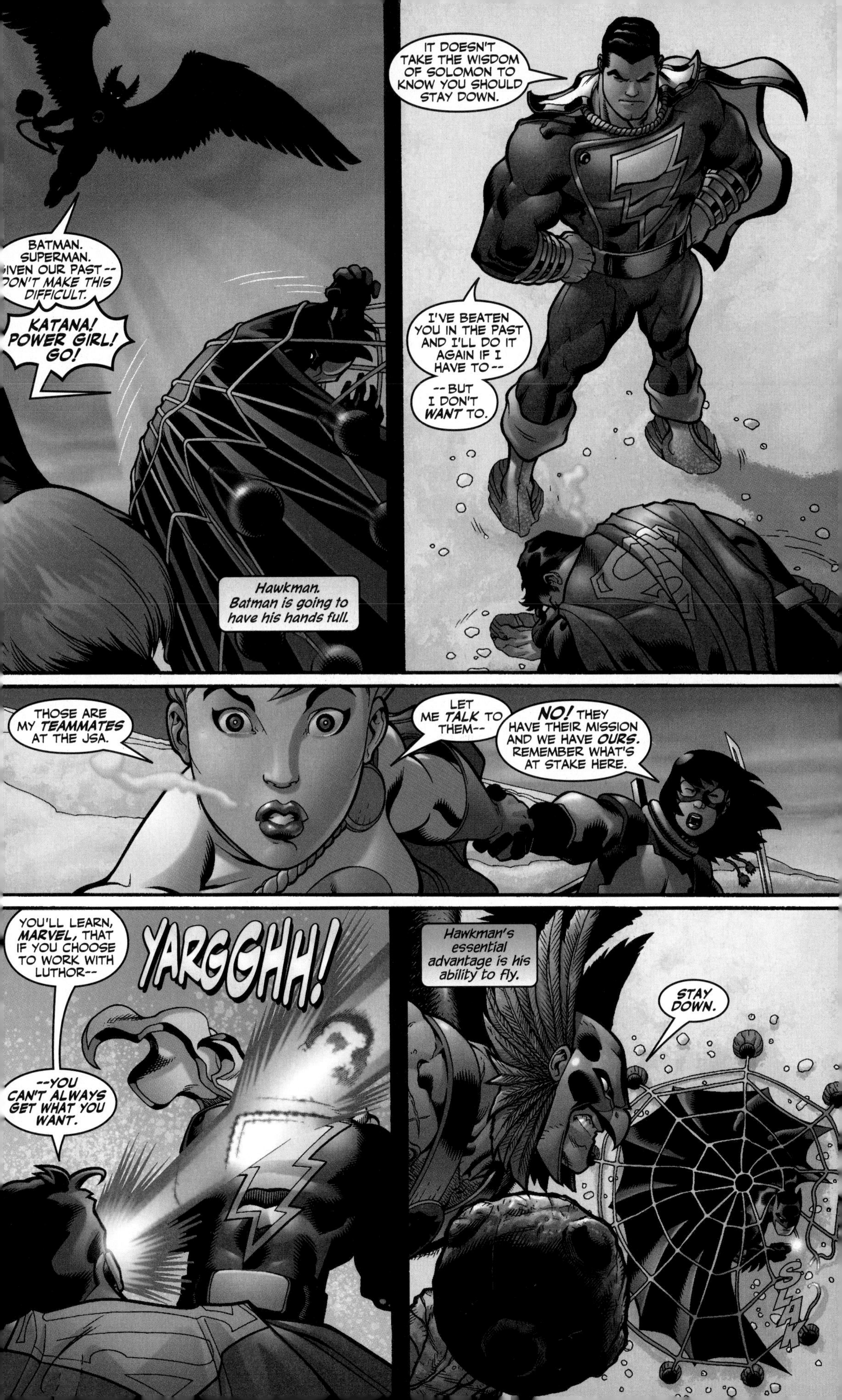
BATMAN. SUPERMAN. GIVEN OUR PAST-- DON'T MAKE THIS DIFFICULT.
KATANA! POWER GIRL! GO!
Hawkman. Batman is going to have his hands full.
IT DOESN'T TAKE THE WISDOM OF SOLOMON TO KNOW YOU SHOULD STAY DOWN.
I'VE BEATEN YOU IN THE PAST AND I'LL DO IT AGAIN IF I HAVE TO--
--BUT I DON'T WANT TO.
THOSE ARE MY TEAMMATES AT THE JSA.
LET ME TALK TO THEM--
NO! THEY HAVE THEIR MISSION AND WE HAVE OURS. REMEMBER WHAT'S AT STAKE HERE.
YOU'LL LEARN, MARVEL, THAT IF YOU CHOOSE TO WORK WITH LUTHOR--
YARGGHH!
--YOU CAN'T ALWAYS GET WHAT YOU WANT.
Hawkman's essential advantage is his ability to fly.
STAY DOWN.

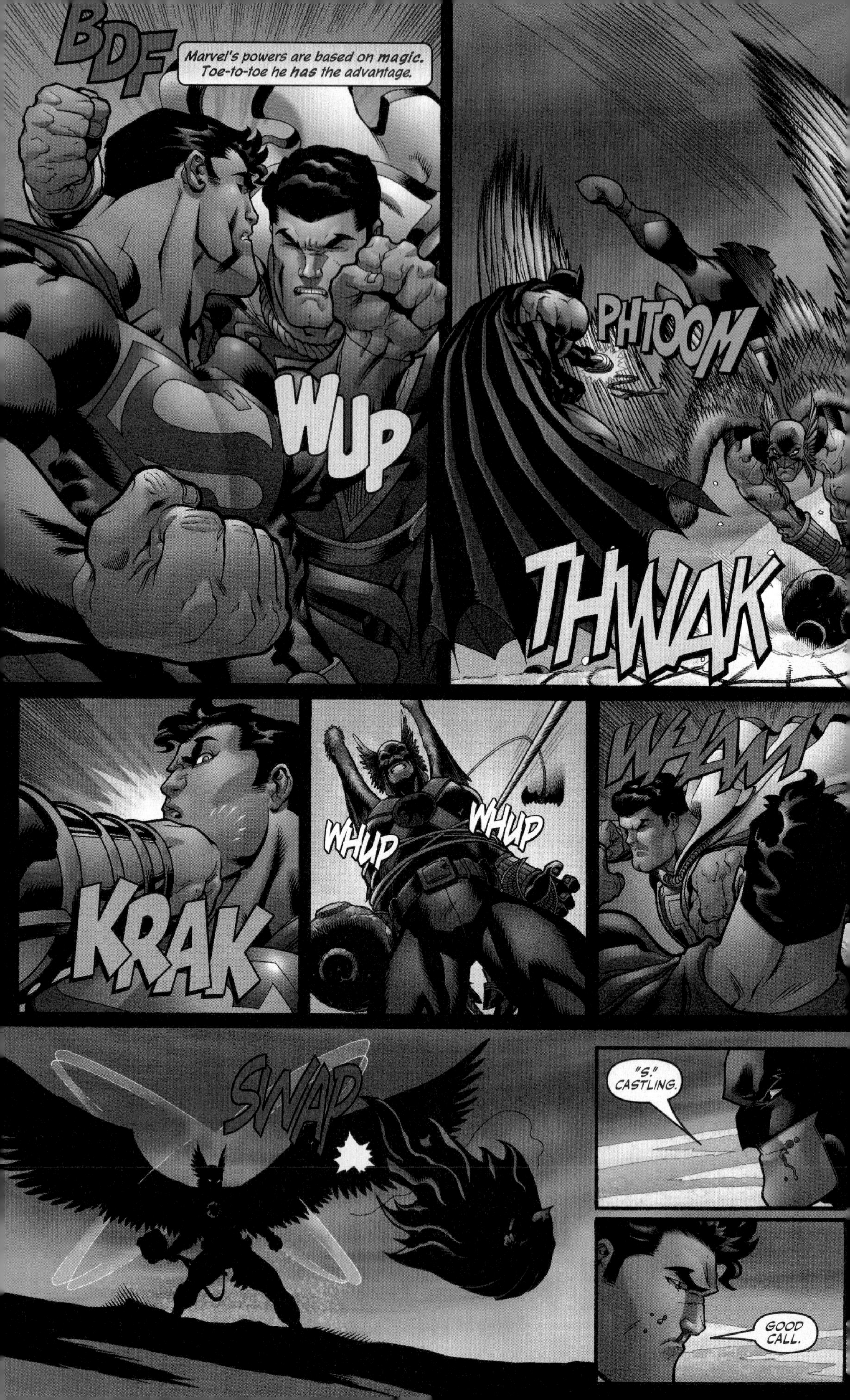
BDF
Marvel's powers are based on magic. Toe-to-toe he has the advantage.
WUP
PHTOOM
THWAK
KRAK
WHUP
WHUP
WHAM
SWAP
"S." CASTLING.
GOOD CALL.

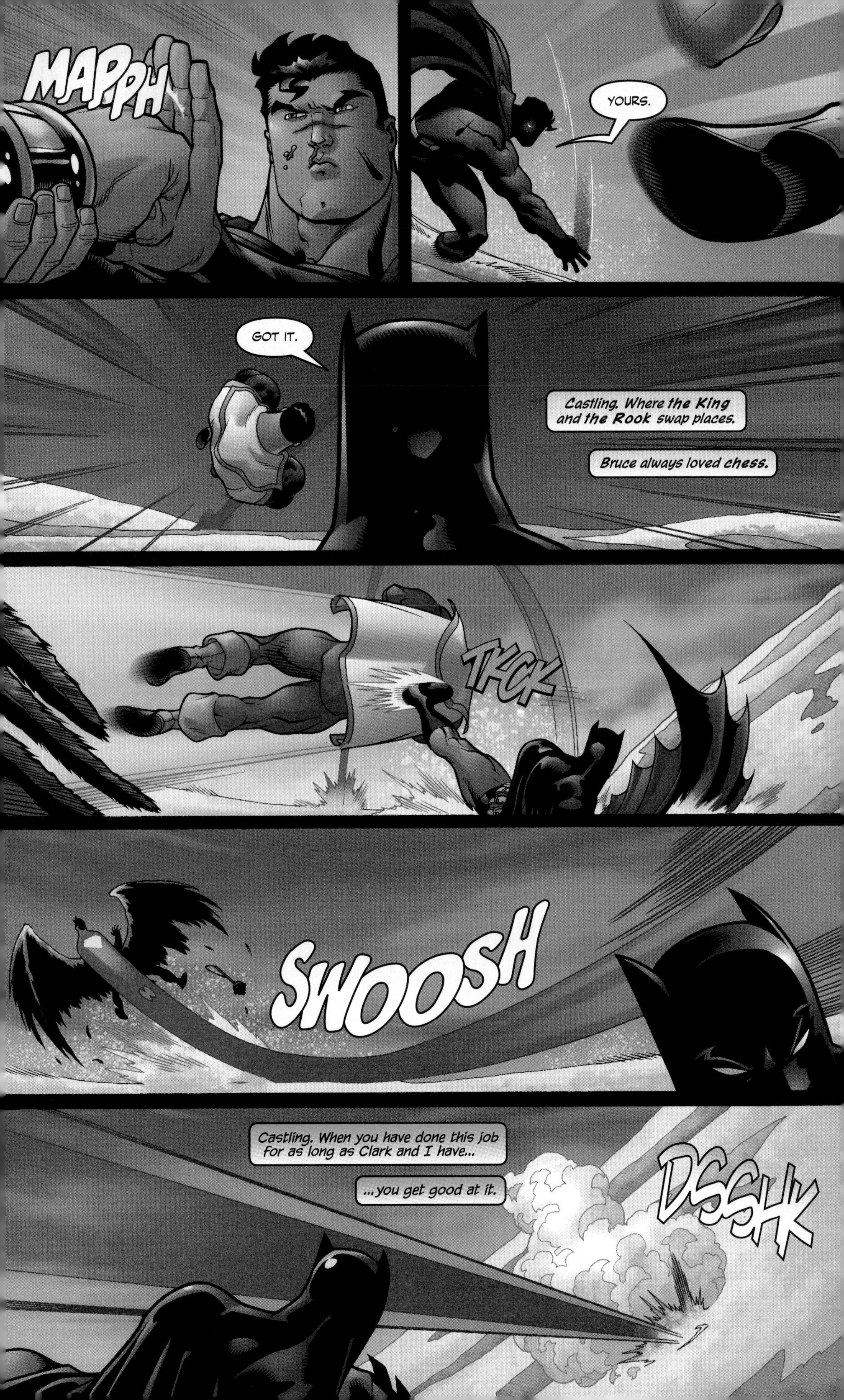
MAPPH
YOURS.
GOT IT.
Castling. Where the King and the Rook swap places.
Bruce always loved chess.
TKCK
SWOOSH
Castling. When you have done this job for as long as Clark and I have...
...you get good at it.
DSSHK

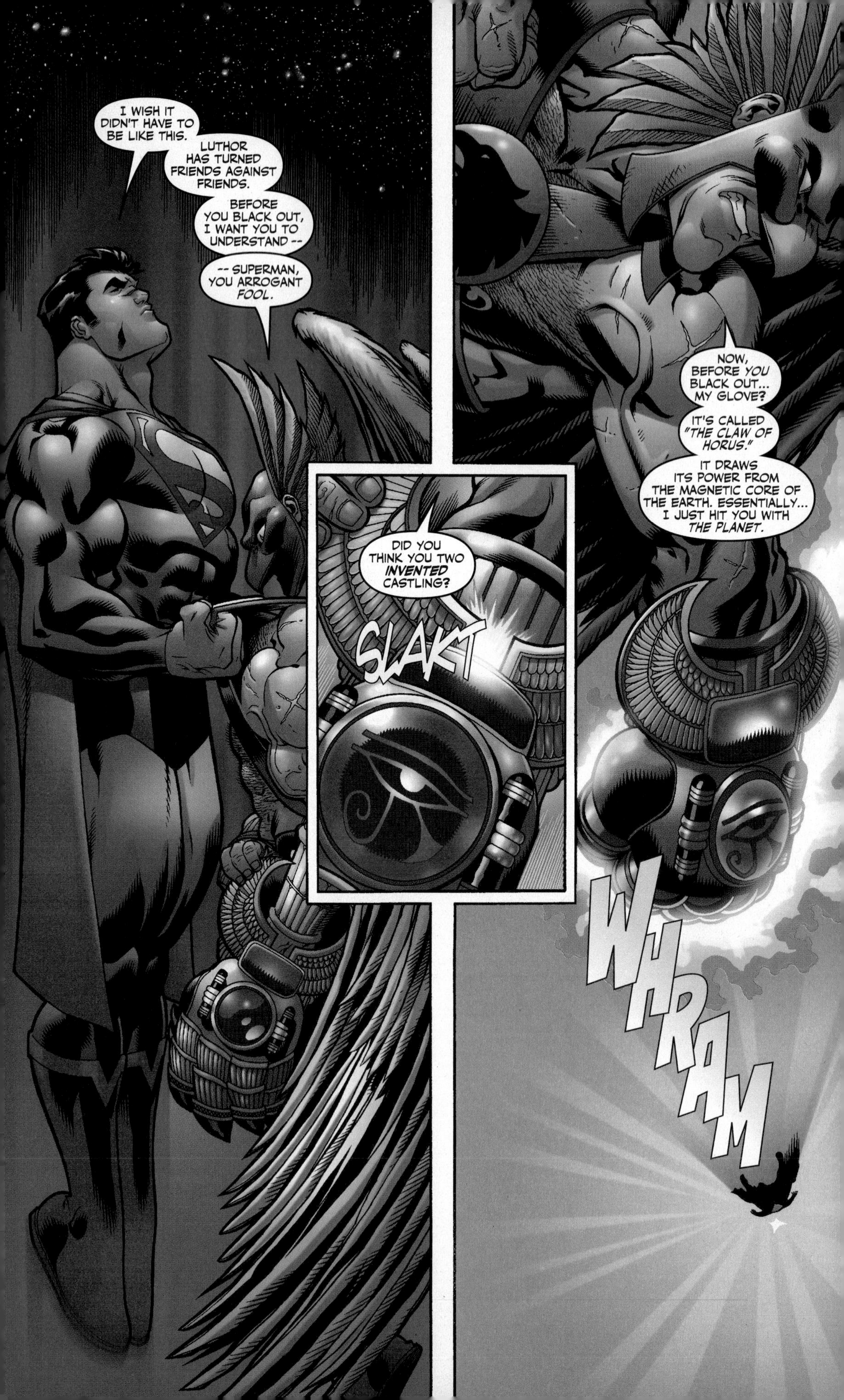
I WISH IT DIDN'T HAVE TO BE LIKE THIS.
LUTHOR HAS TURNED FRIENDS AGAINST FRIENDS.
BEFORE YOU BLACK OUT, I WANT YOU TO UNDERSTAND --
-- SUPERMAN, YOU ARROGANT *FOOL*.
DID YOU THINK YOU TWO ***INVENTED*** CASTLING?
SLAK!
NOW, BEFORE *YOU* BLACK OUT... MY GLOVE?
IT'S CALLED *"THE CLAW OF HORUS."*
IT DRAWS ITS POWER FROM THE MAGNETIC CORE OF THE EARTH. ESSENTIALLY... I JUST HIT YOU WITH *THE PLANET*.
WHRAM

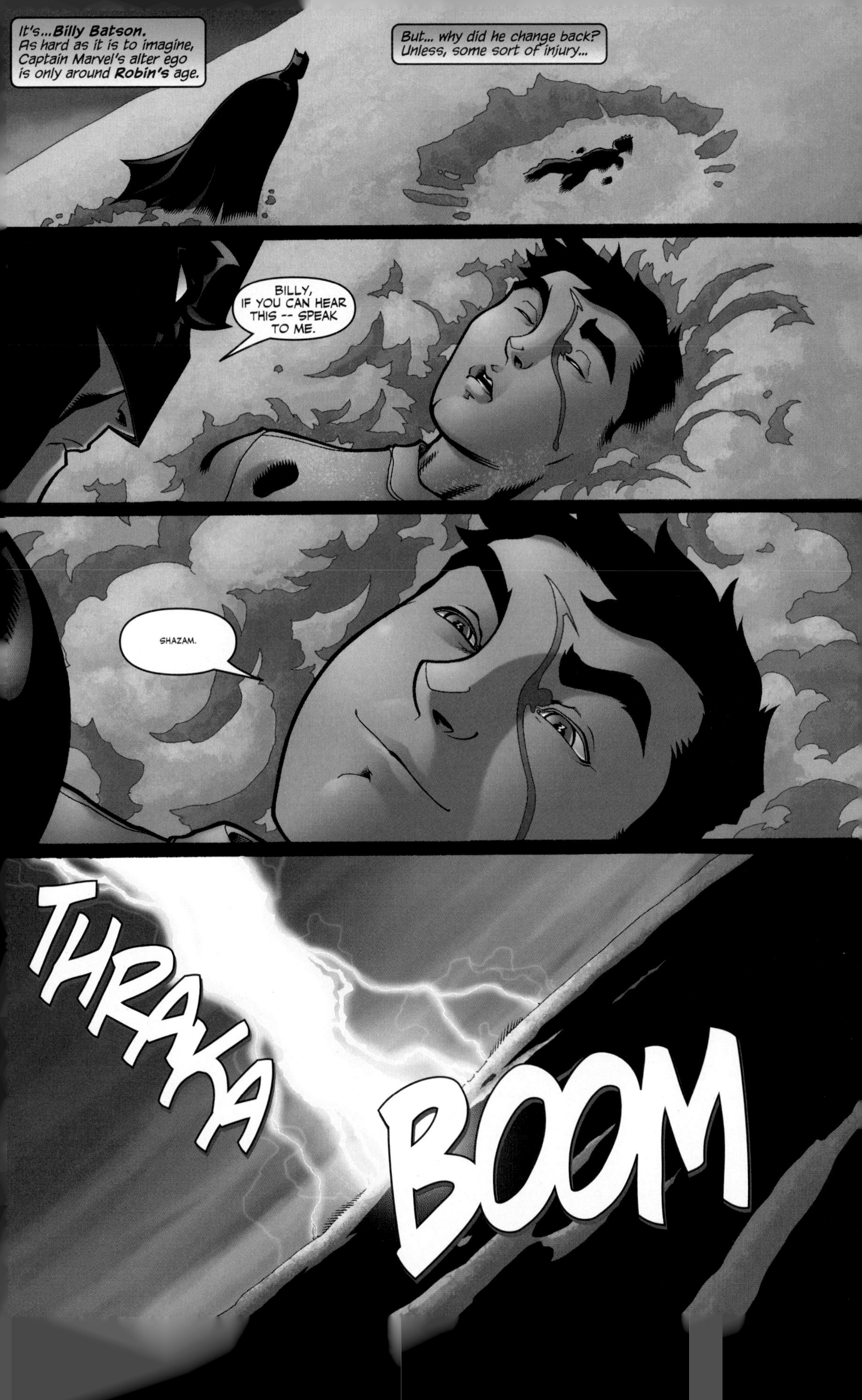
It's...Billy Batson. As hard as it is to imagine, Captain Marvel's alter ego is only around Robin's age.
But... why did he change back? Unless, some sort of injury...
BILLY, IF YOU CAN HEAR THIS -- SPEAK TO ME.
SHAZAM.
THRAKA BOOM

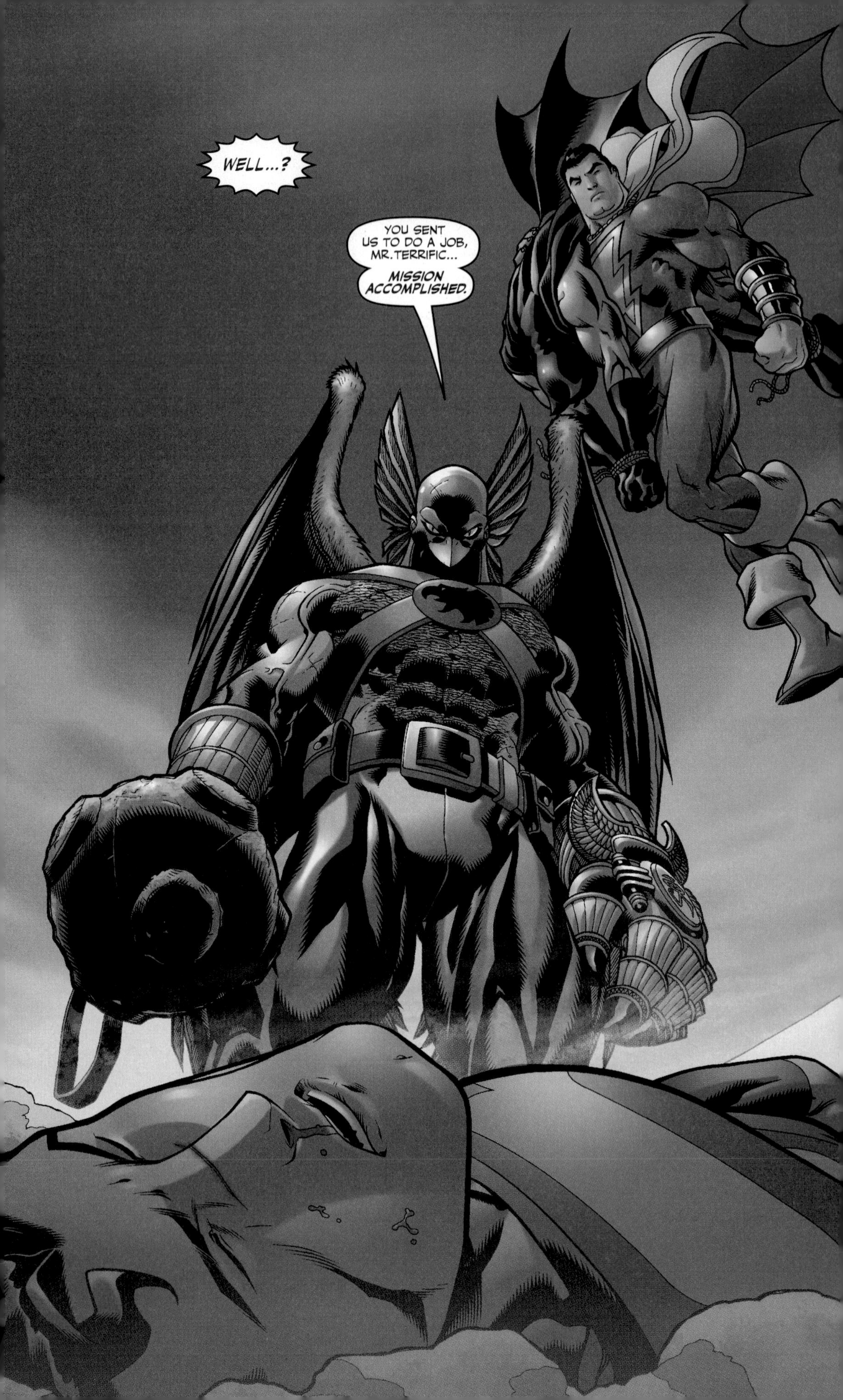
WELL...?
YOU SENT US TO DO A JOB, MR.TERRIFIC... MISSION ACCOMPLISHED.

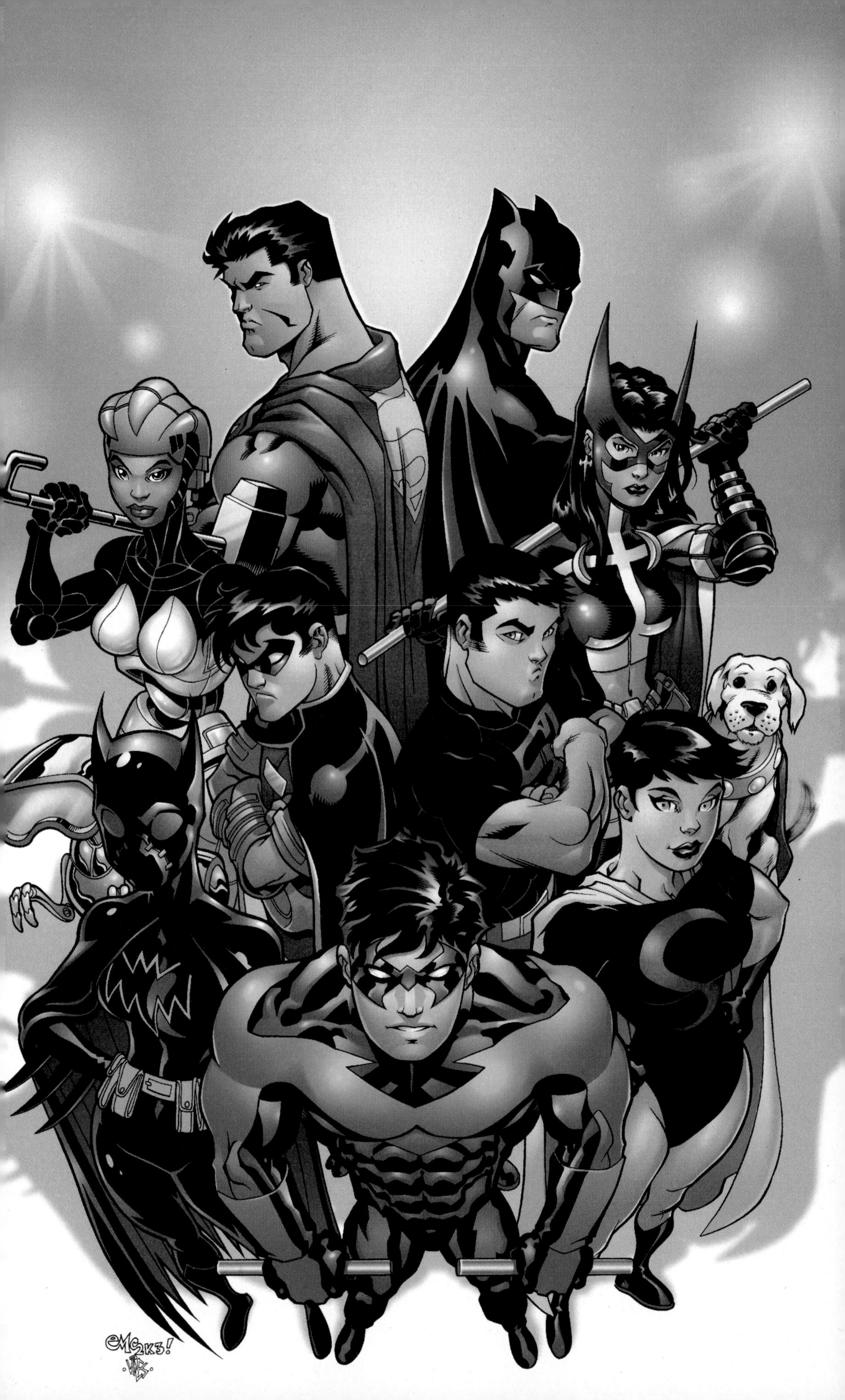

"Give me what I've always wanted — the end of you."

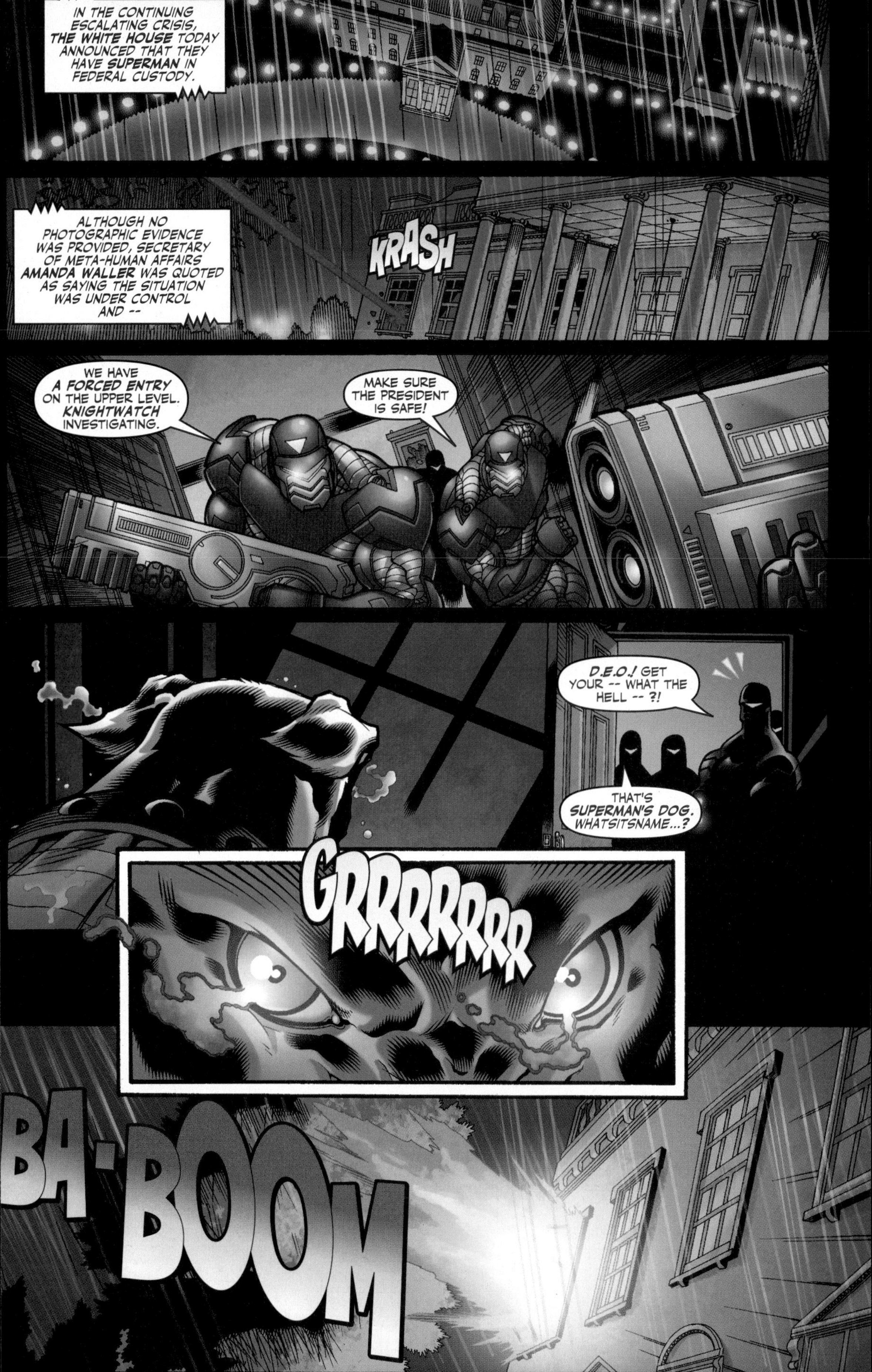
IN THE CONTINUING ESCALATING CRISIS, THE WHITE HOUSE TODAY ANNOUNCED THAT THEY HAVE SUPERMAN IN FEDERAL CUSTODY.
ALTHOUGH NO PHOTOGRAPHIC EVIDENCE WAS PROVIDED, SECRETARY OF META-HUMAN AFFAIRS AMANDA WALLER WAS QUOTED AS SAYING THE SITUATION WAS UNDER CONTROL AND --
KRASH
WE HAVE A FORCED ENTRY ON THE UPPER LEVEL. KNIGHTWATCH INVESTIGATING.
MAKE SURE THE PRESIDENT IS SAFE!
D.E.O.! GET YOUR -- WHAT THE HELL -- ?!
THAT'S SUPERMAN'S DOG. WHATSITSNAME...?
GRRRRRRR
BA-BOOM

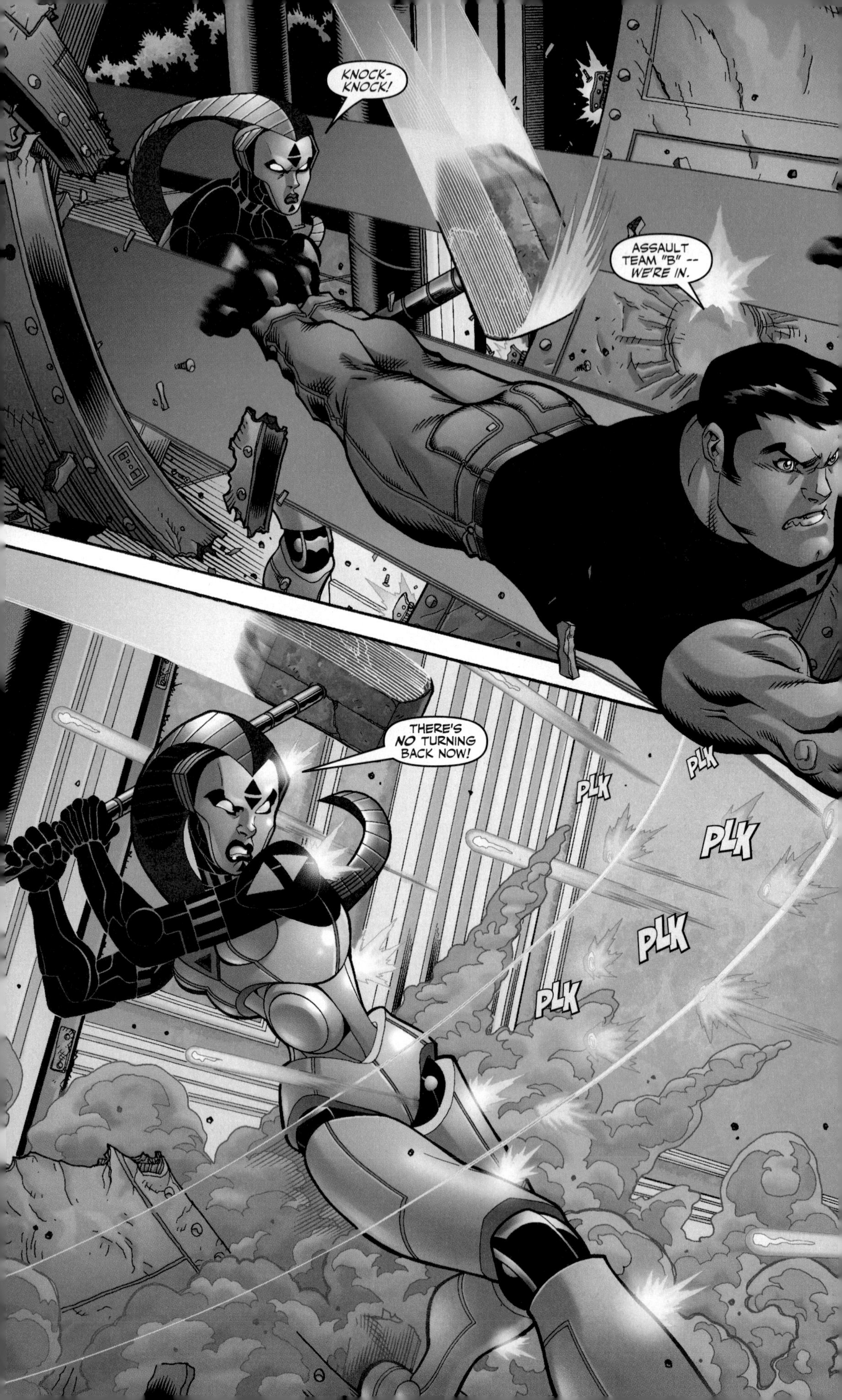
KNOCK-KNOCK!
ASSAULT TEAM "B" -- WE'RE IN.
THERE'S NO TURNING BACK NOW!
PLK
PLK
PLK
PLK
PLK

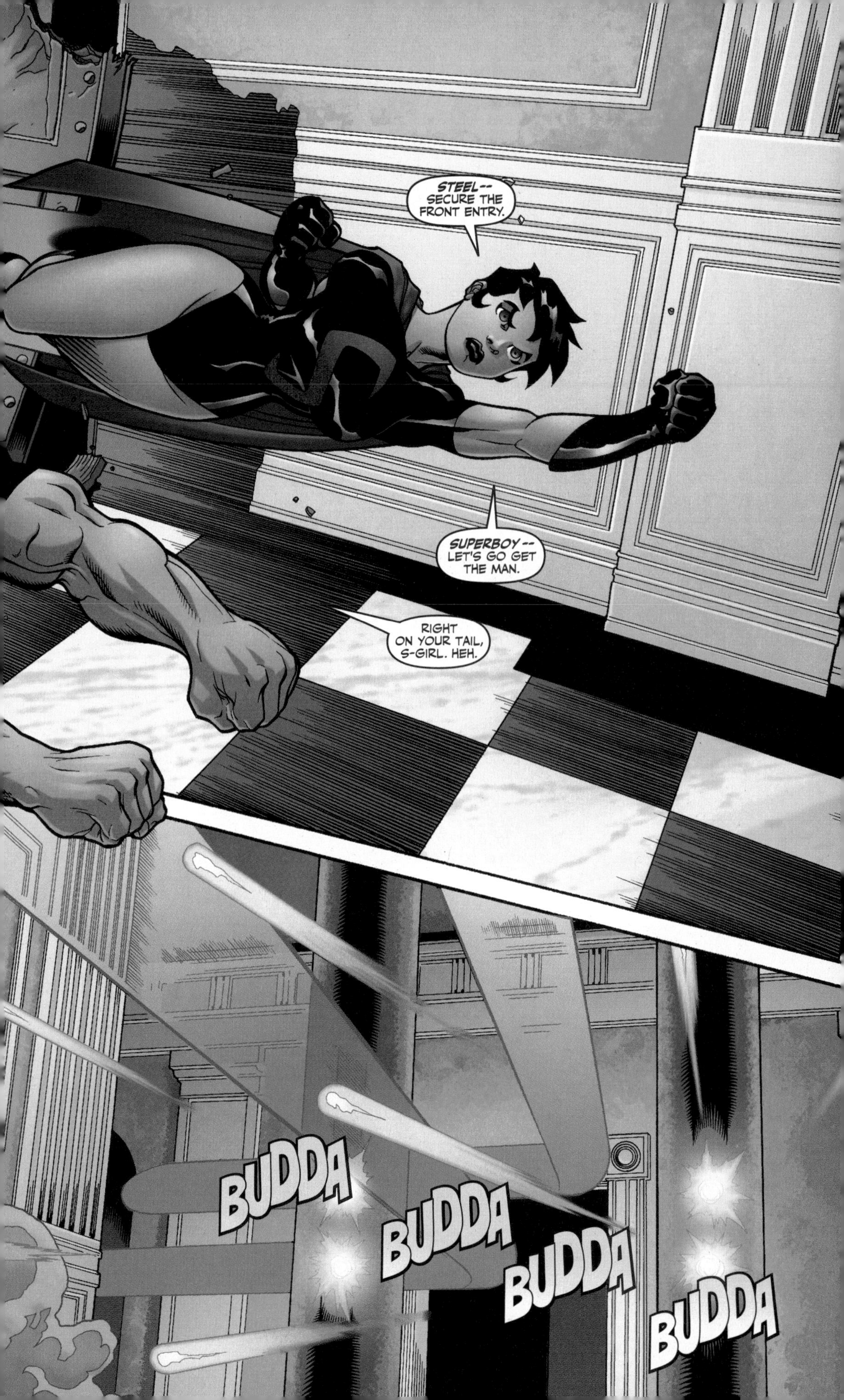
STEEL-- SECURE THE FRONT ENTRY.
SUPERBOY -- LET'S GO GET THE MAN.
RIGHT ON YOUR TAIL, S-GIRL. HEH.
BUDDA
BUDDA
BUDDA
BUDDA

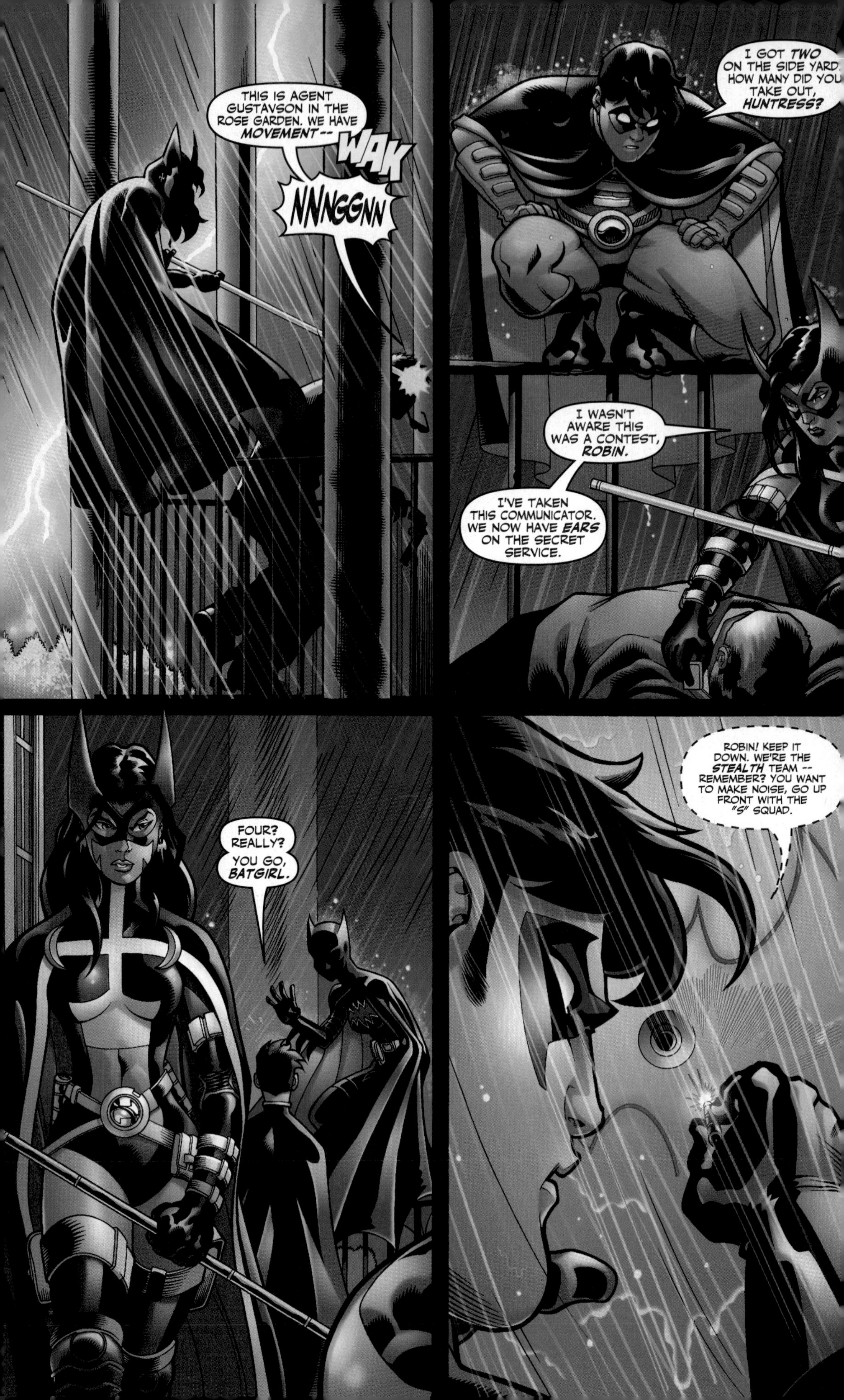
THIS IS AGENT GUSTAVSON IN THE ROSE GARDEN. WE HAVE MOVEMENT--
WAK
NNNGGNN
I GOT TWO ON THE SIDE YARD. HOW MANY DID YOU TAKE OUT, HUNTRESS?
I WASN'T AWARE THIS WAS A CONTEST, ROBIN.
I'VE TAKEN THIS COMMUNICATOR. WE NOW HAVE EARS ON THE SECRET SERVICE.
FOUR? REALLY? YOU GO, BATGIRL.
ROBIN! KEEP IT DOWN. WE'RE THE STEALTH TEAM -- REMEMBER? YOU WANT TO MAKE NOISE, GO UP FRONT WITH THE "S" SQUAD.

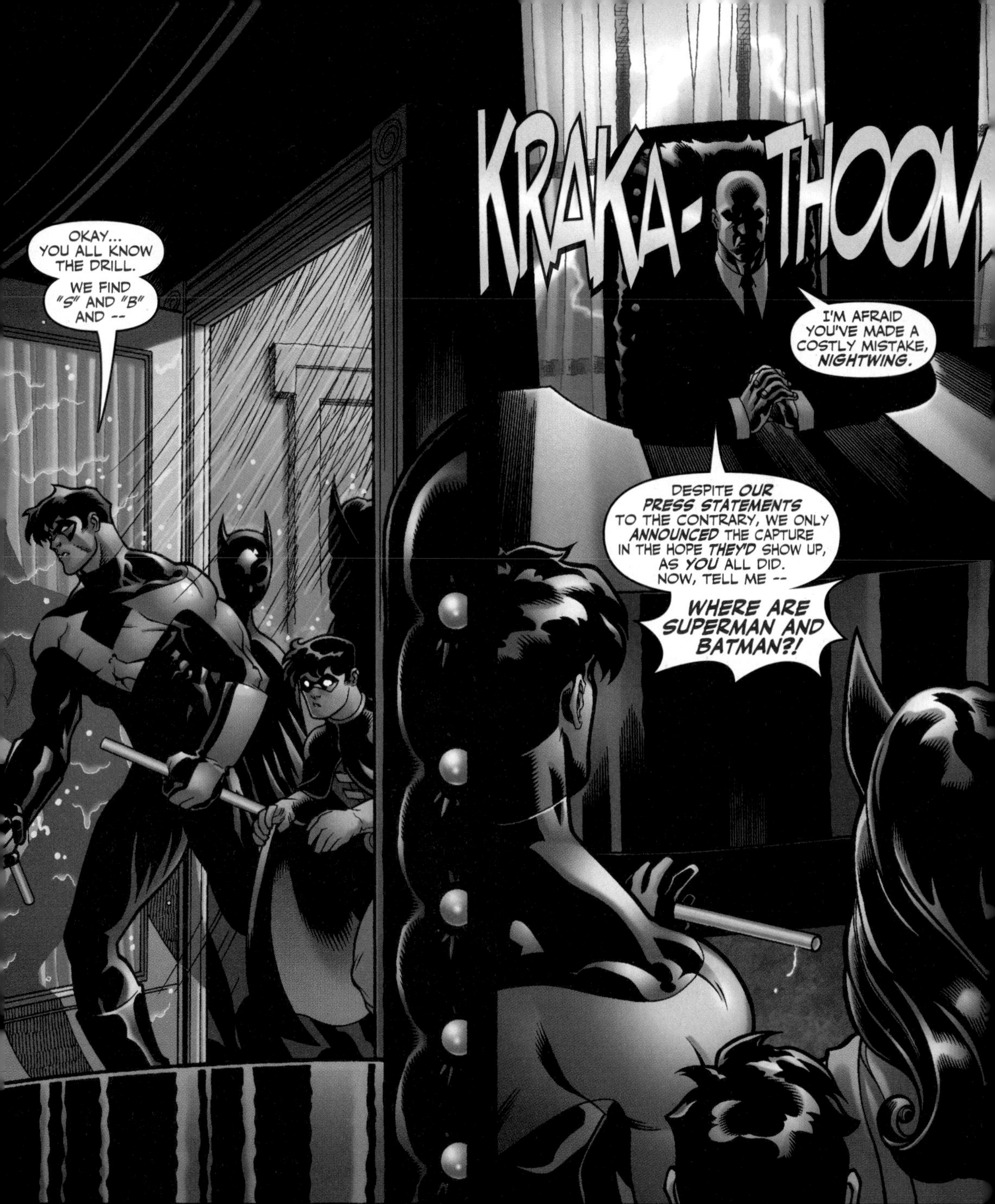
KRAKA-THOOM
OKAY... YOU ALL KNOW THE DRILL.
WE FIND "S" AND "B" AND --
I'M AFRAID YOU'VE MADE A COSTLY MISTAKE, NIGHTWING.
DESPITE OUR PRESS STATEMENTS TO THE CONTRARY, WE ONLY ANNOUNCED THE CAPTURE IN THE HOPE THEY'D SHOW UP, AS YOU ALL DID. NOW, TELL ME --
WHERE ARE SUPERMAN AND BATMAN?!

PART FIVE: STATE OF SIEGE

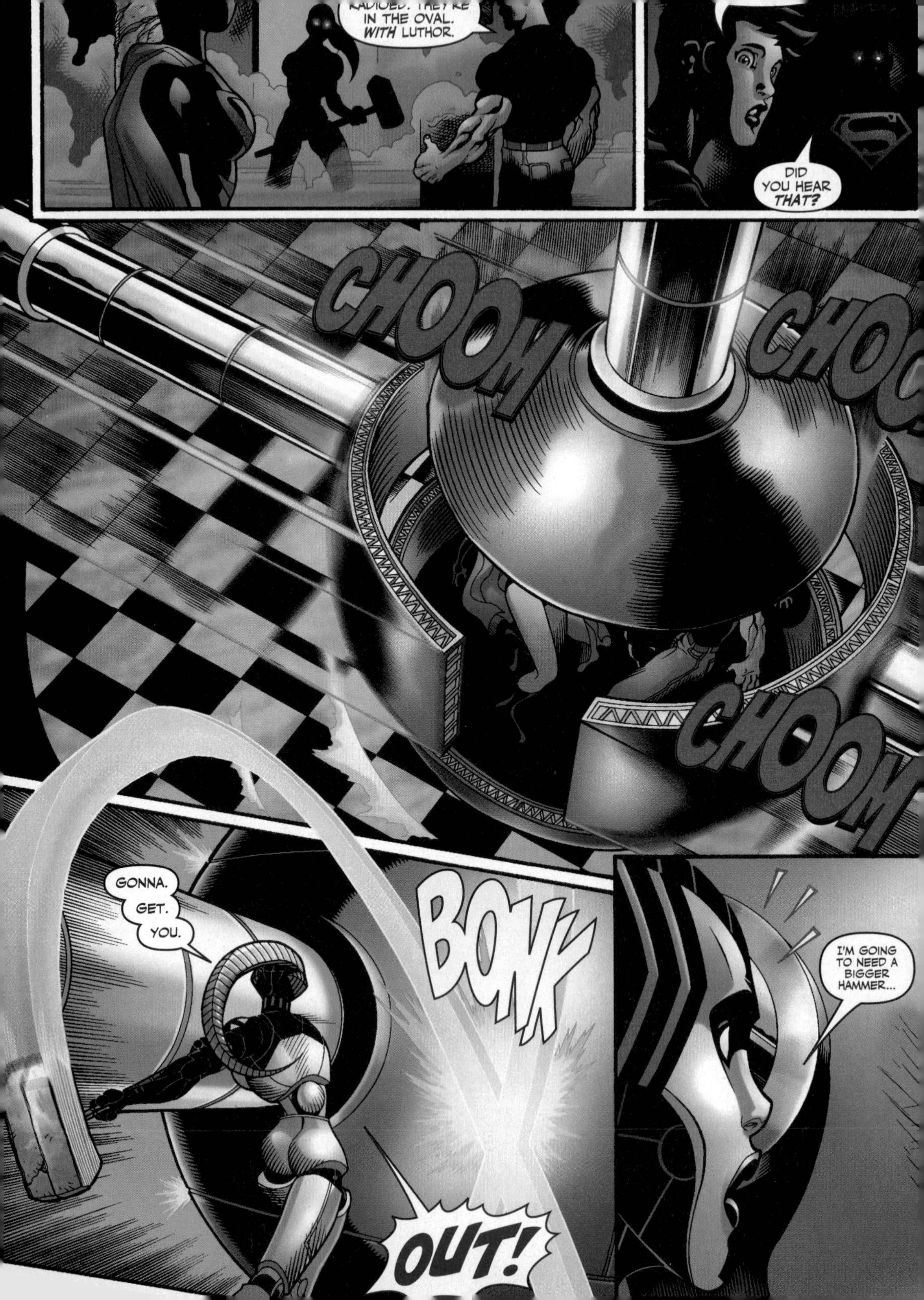
RADIOED. THEY'RE IN THE OVAL. WITH LUTHOR.
DID YOU HEAR THAT?
CHOOM
CHOOM
CHOOM
GONNA.
GET.
YOU.
BONK
OUT!
I'M GOING TO NEED A BIGGER HAMMER...

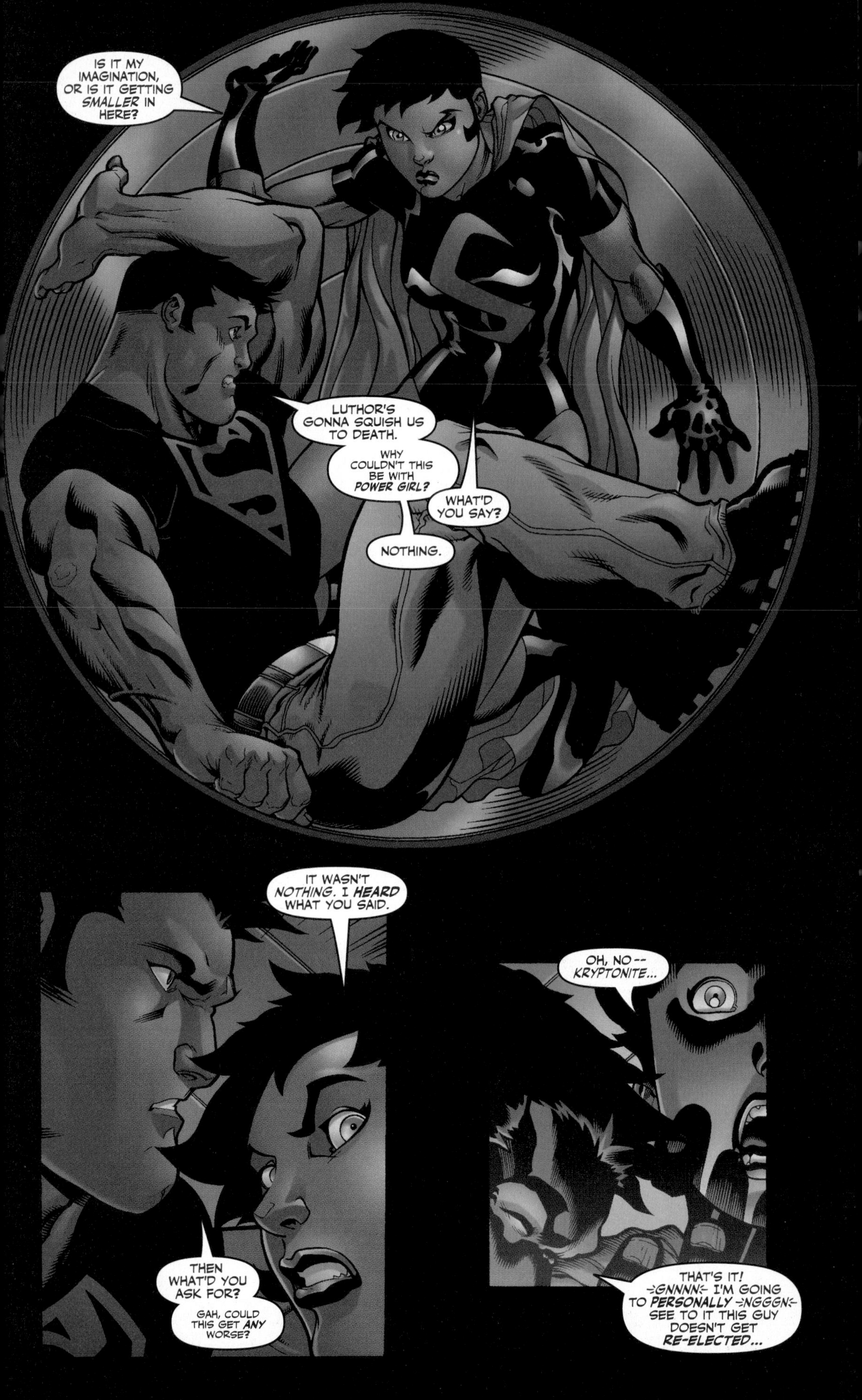
IS IT MY IMAGINATION, OR IS IT GETTING *SMALLER* IN HERE?
LUTHOR'S GONNA SQUISH US TO DEATH.
WHY COULDN'T THIS BE WITH *POWER GIRL?*
WHAT'D YOU SAY?
NOTHING.
IT WASN'T *NOTHING*. I ***HEARD*** WHAT YOU SAID.
THEN WHAT'D YOU ASK FOR?
GAH, COULD THIS GET *ANY* WORSE?
OH, NO-- *KRYPTONITE*...
THAT'S IT! *GNNNN* I'M GOING TO ***PERSONALLY*** *NGGGN* SEE TO IT THIS GUY DOESN'T GET ***RE-ELECTED***...

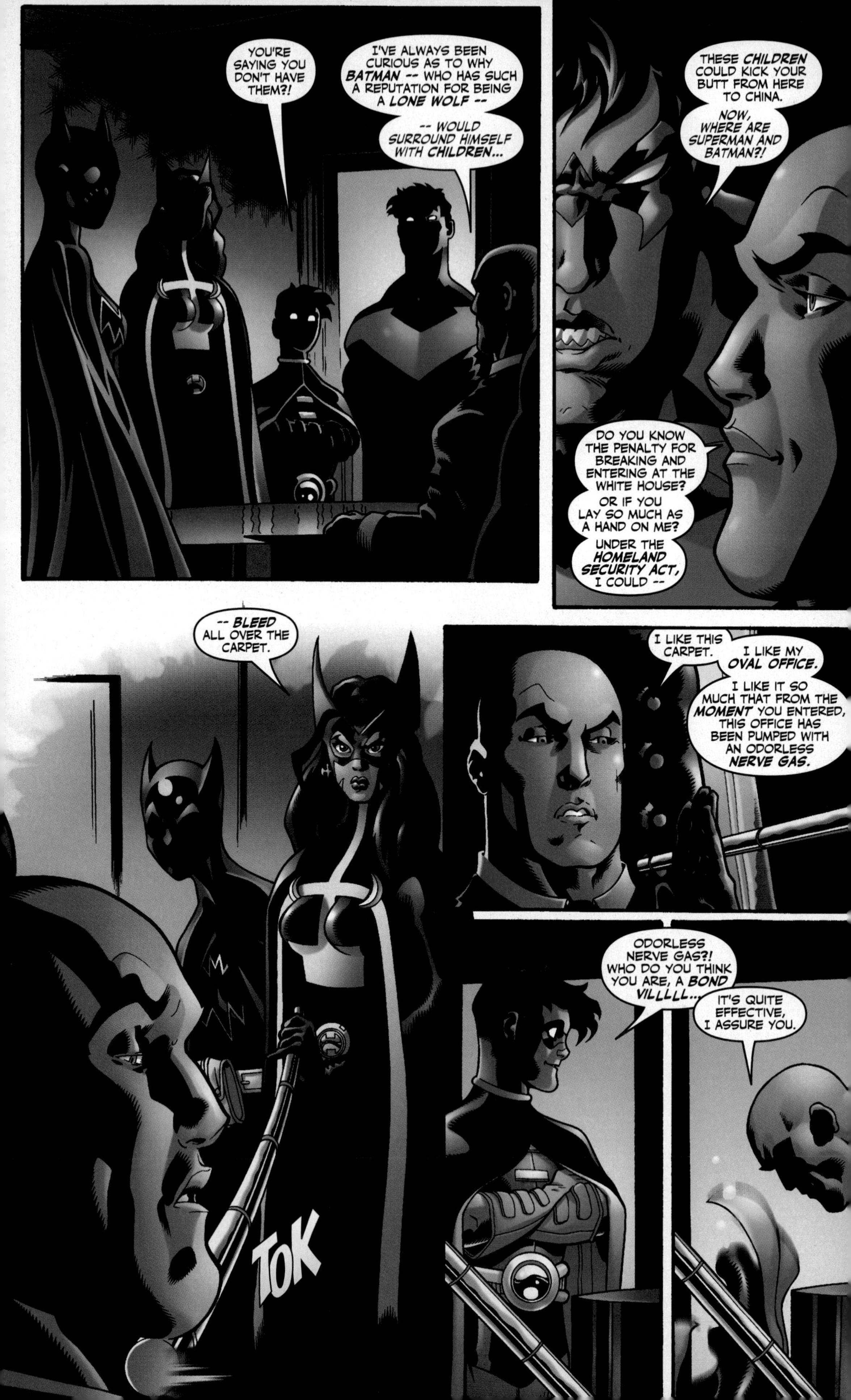
YOU'RE SAYING YOU DON'T HAVE THEM?!
I'VE ALWAYS BEEN CURIOUS AS TO WHY BATMAN -- WHO HAS SUCH A REPUTATION FOR BEING A LONE WOLF --
-- WOULD SURROUND HIMSELF WITH CHILDREN...
THESE CHILDREN COULD KICK YOUR BUTT FROM HERE TO CHINA.
NOW, WHERE ARE SUPERMAN AND BATMAN?!
DO YOU KNOW THE PENALTY FOR BREAKING AND ENTERING AT THE WHITE HOUSE?
OR IF YOU LAY SO MUCH AS A HAND ON ME?
UNDER THE HOMELAND SECURITY ACT, I COULD --
-- BLEED ALL OVER THE CARPET.
TOK
I LIKE THIS CARPET.
I LIKE MY OVAL OFFICE.
I LIKE IT SO MUCH THAT FROM THE MOMENT YOU ENTERED, THIS OFFICE HAS BEEN PUMPED WITH AN ODORLESS NERVE GAS.
ODORLESS NERVE GAS?! WHO DO YOU THINK YOU ARE, A BOND VILLLLL...
IT'S QUITE EFFECTIVE, I ASSURE YOU.

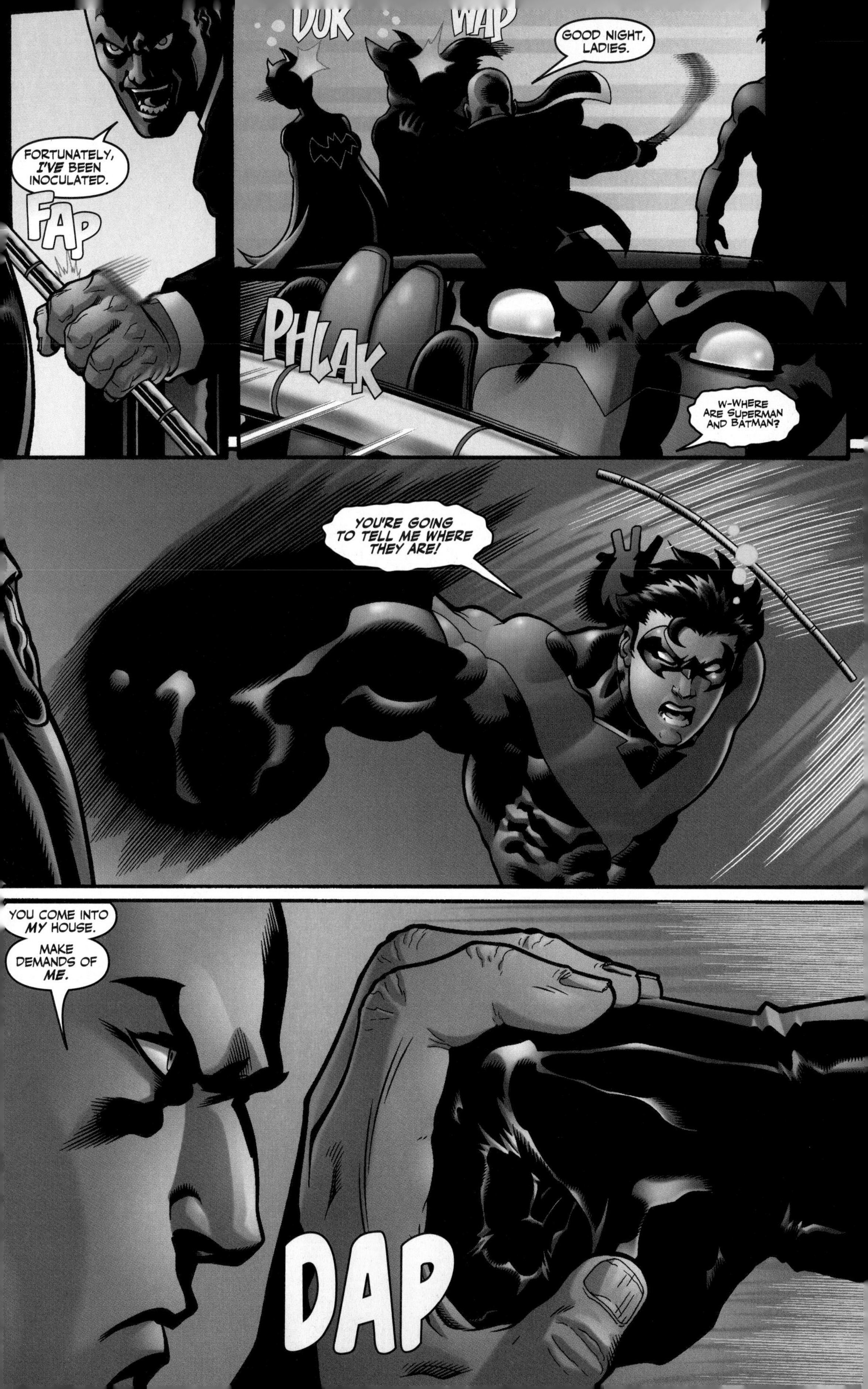
FORTUNATELY, I'VE BEEN INOCULATED.
FAP
DOK
WAP
GOOD NIGHT, LADIES.
PHLAK
W-WHERE ARE SUPERMAN AND BATMAN?
YOU'RE GOING TO TELL ME WHERE THEY ARE!
YOU COME INTO MY HOUSE.
MAKE DEMANDS OF ME.
DAP

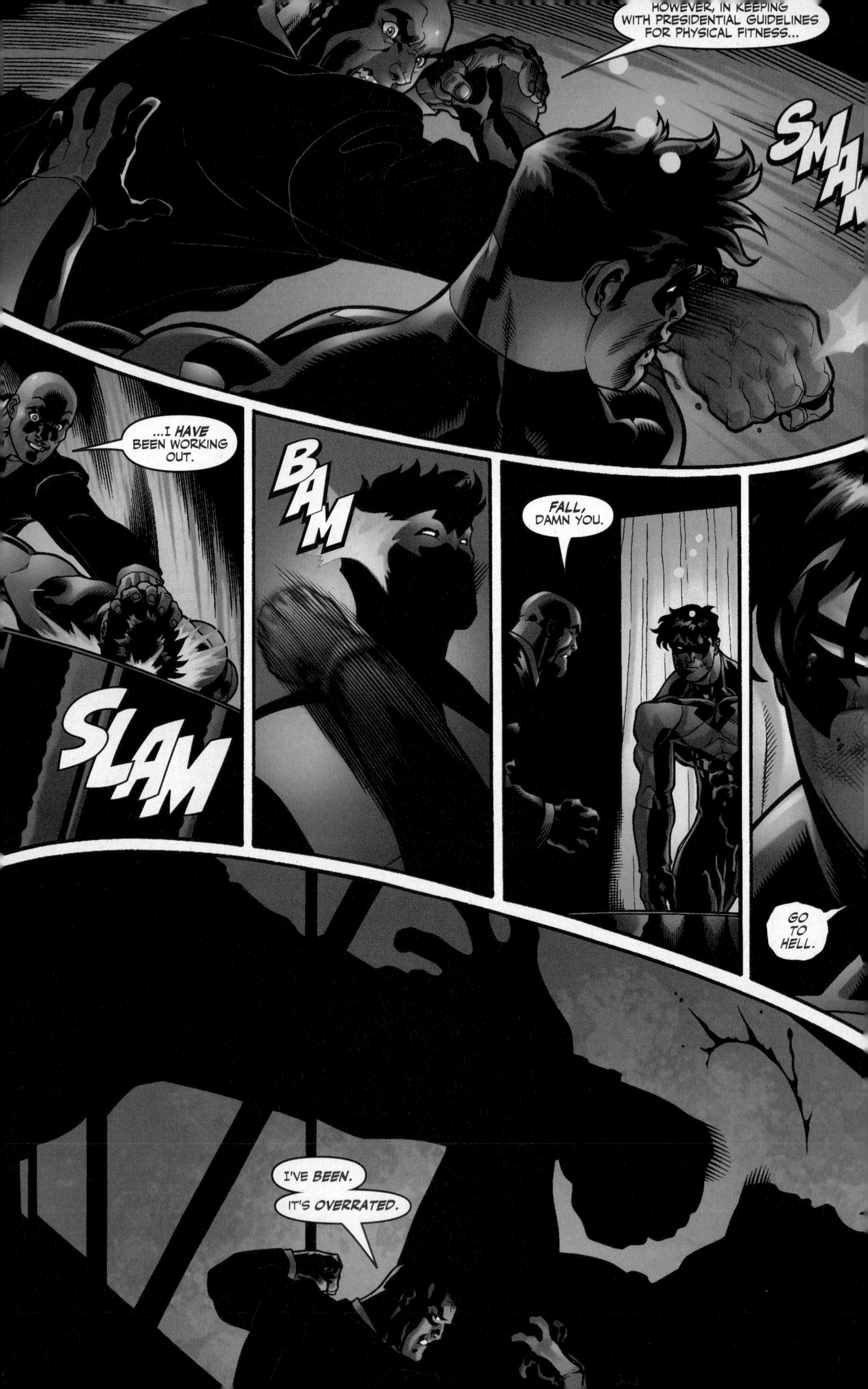
HOWEVER, IN KEEPING WITH PRESIDENTIAL GUIDELINES FOR PHYSICAL FITNESS...
SMAK
...I HAVE BEEN WORKING OUT.
SLAM
BAM
FALL, DAMN YOU.
GO TO HELL.
I'VE BEEN.
IT'S OVERRATED.

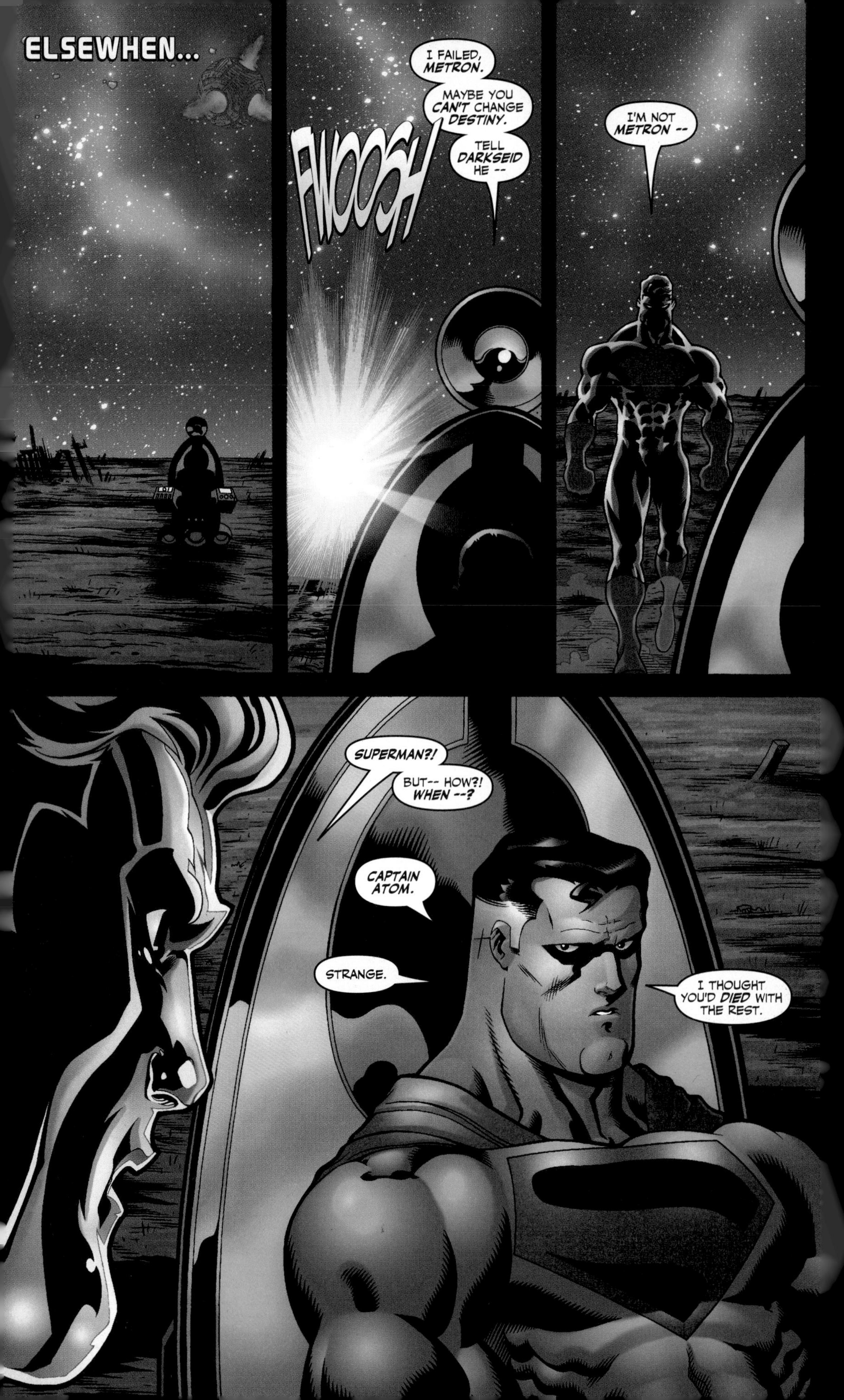
ELSEWHEN...
I FAILED, METRON.
MAYBE YOU CAN'T CHANGE DESTINY.
TELL DARKSEID HE --
FWOOSH
I'M NOT METRON --
SUPERMAN?!
BUT-- HOW?! WHEN --?
CAPTAIN ATOM.
STRANGE.
I THOUGHT YOU'D DIED WITH THE REST.

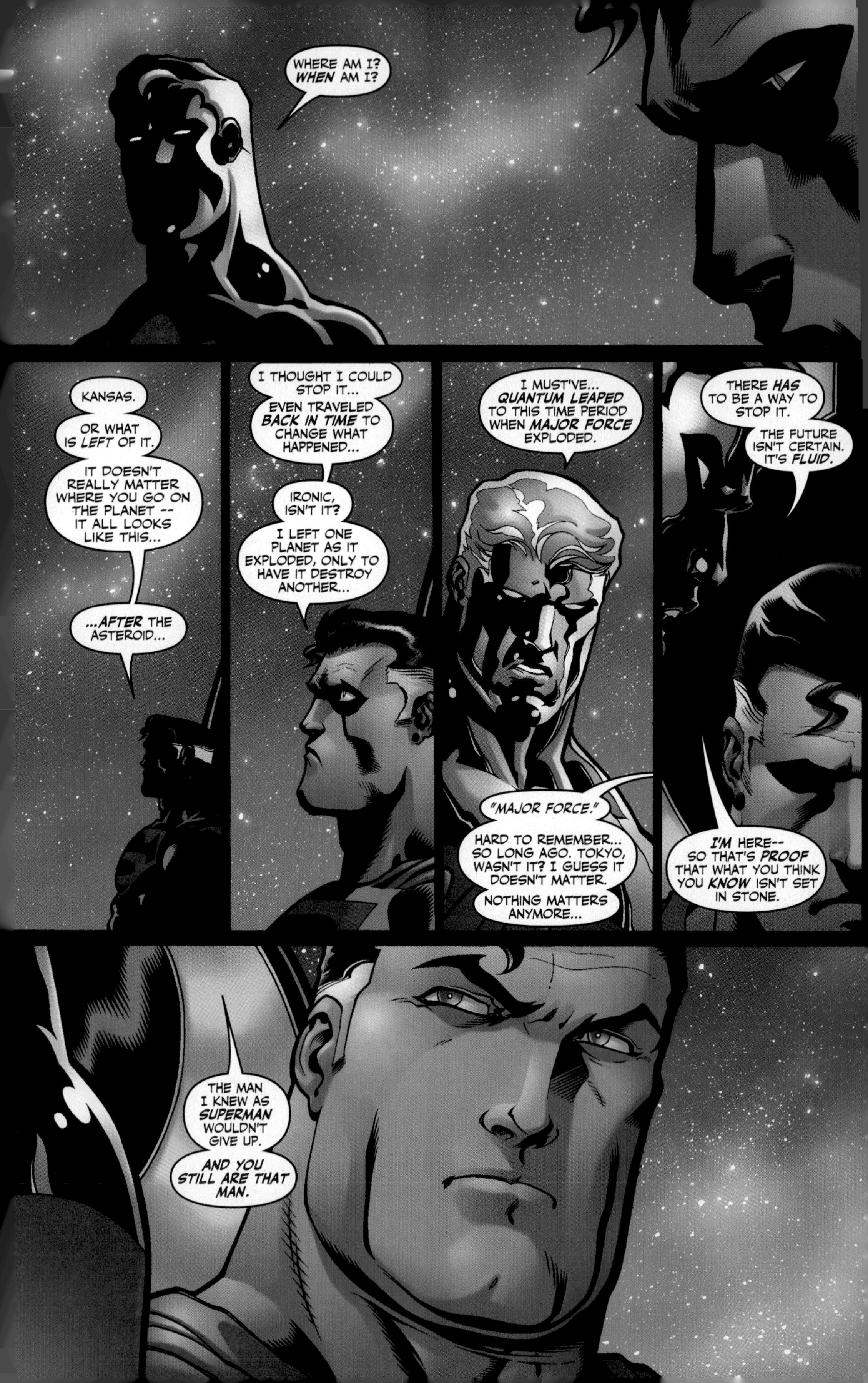
WHERE AM I? WHEN AM I?
KANSAS.
OR WHAT IS LEFT OF IT.
IT DOESN'T REALLY MATTER WHERE YOU GO ON THE PLANET -- IT ALL LOOKS LIKE THIS...
...AFTER THE ASTEROID...
I THOUGHT I COULD STOP IT... EVEN TRAVELED BACK IN TIME TO CHANGE WHAT HAPPENED...
IRONIC, ISN'T IT?
I LEFT ONE PLANET AS IT EXPLODED, ONLY TO HAVE IT DESTROY ANOTHER...
I MUST'VE... QUANTUM LEAPED TO THIS TIME PERIOD WHEN MAJOR FORCE EXPLODED.
"MAJOR FORCE."
HARD TO REMEMBER... SO LONG AGO. TOKYO, WASN'T IT? I GUESS IT DOESN'T MATTER.
NOTHING MATTERS ANYMORE...
THERE HAS TO BE A WAY TO STOP IT.
THE FUTURE ISN'T CERTAIN. IT'S FLUID.
I'M HERE-- SO THAT'S PROOF THAT WHAT YOU THINK YOU KNOW ISN'T SET IN STONE.
THE MAN I KNEW AS SUPERMAN WOULDN'T GIVE UP.
AND YOU STILL ARE THAT MAN.

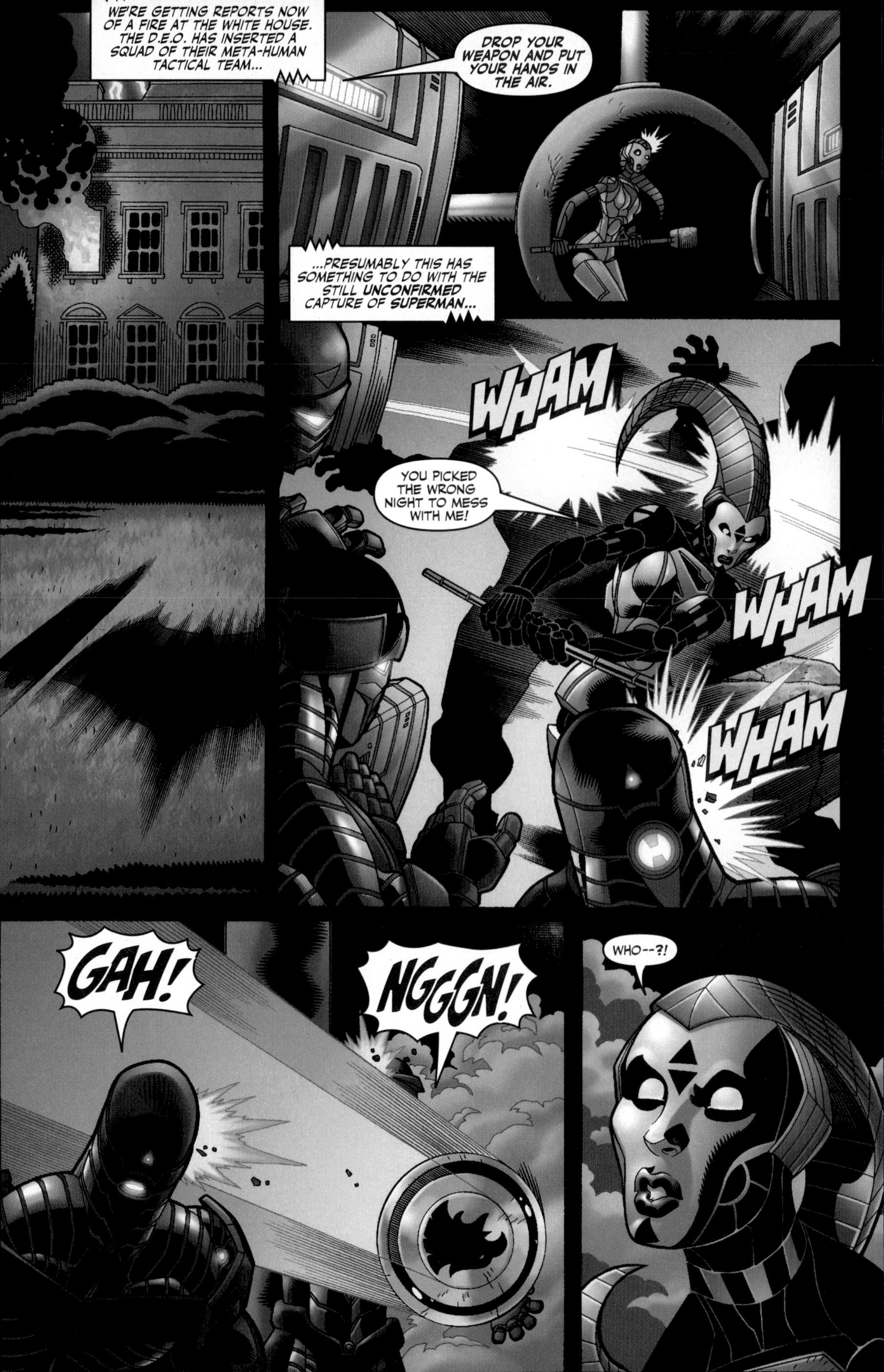
WE'RE GETTING REPORTS NOW OF A FIRE AT THE WHITE HOUSE. THE D.E.O. HAS INSERTED A SQUAD OF THEIR META-HUMAN TACTICAL TEAM...
DROP YOUR WEAPON AND PUT YOUR HANDS IN THE AIR.
...PRESUMABLY THIS HAS SOMETHING TO DO WITH THE STILL UNCONFIRMED CAPTURE OF SUPERMAN...
WHAM
YOU PICKED THE WRONG NIGHT TO MESS WITH ME!
WHAM
WHAM
GAH!
NGGGN!
WHO--?!

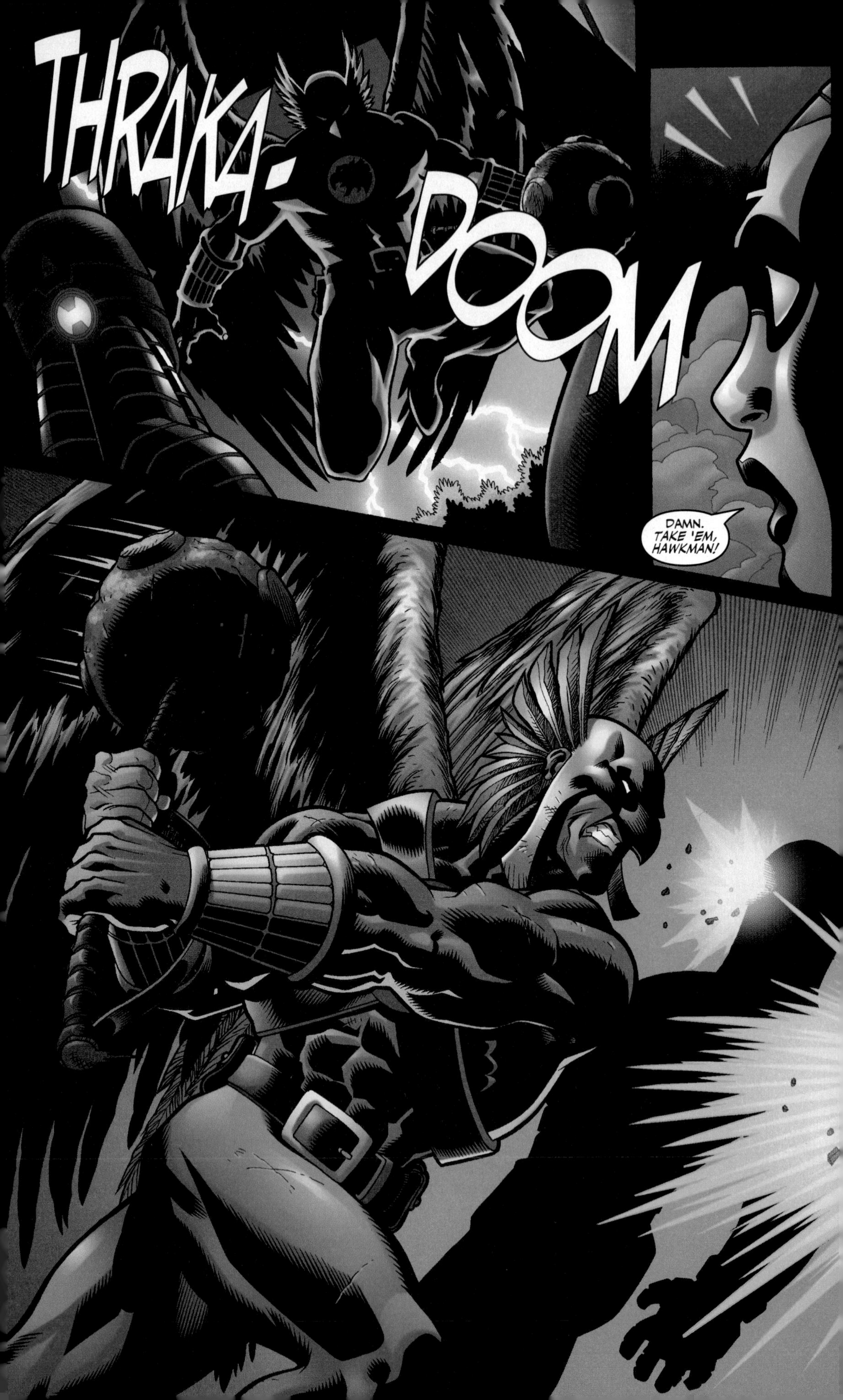
THRAKA-DOOM
DAMN. TAKE 'EM, HAWKMAN!

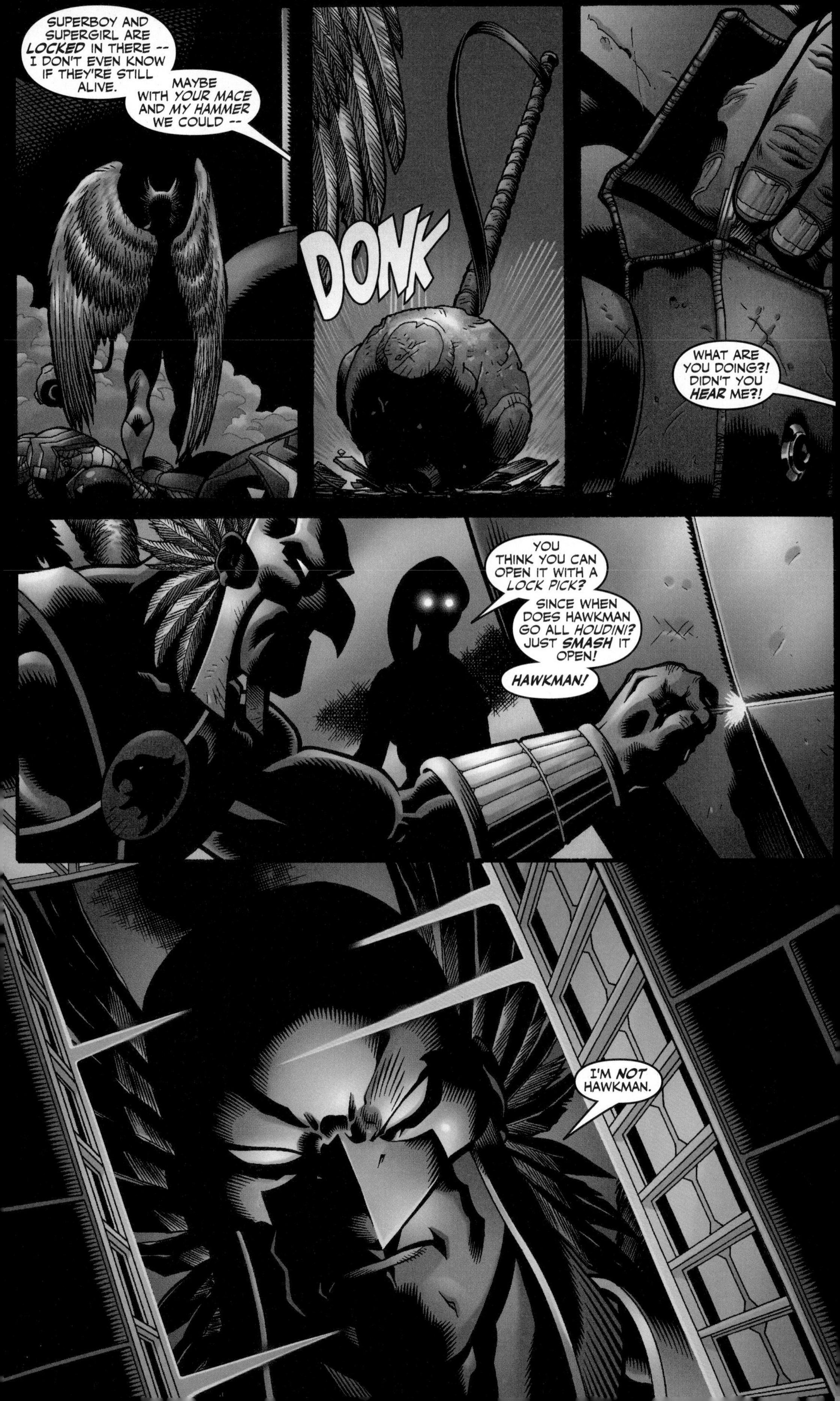
SUPERBOY AND SUPERGIRL ARE LOCKED IN THERE -- I DON'T EVEN KNOW IF THEY'RE STILL ALIVE.
MAYBE WITH YOUR MACE AND MY HAMMER WE COULD --
DONK
WHAT ARE YOU DOING?! DIDN'T YOU HEAR ME?!
YOU THINK YOU CAN OPEN IT WITH A LOCK PICK?
SINCE WHEN DOES HAWKMAN GO ALL HOUDINI? JUST SMASH IT OPEN!
HAWKMAN!
I'M NOT HAWKMAN.

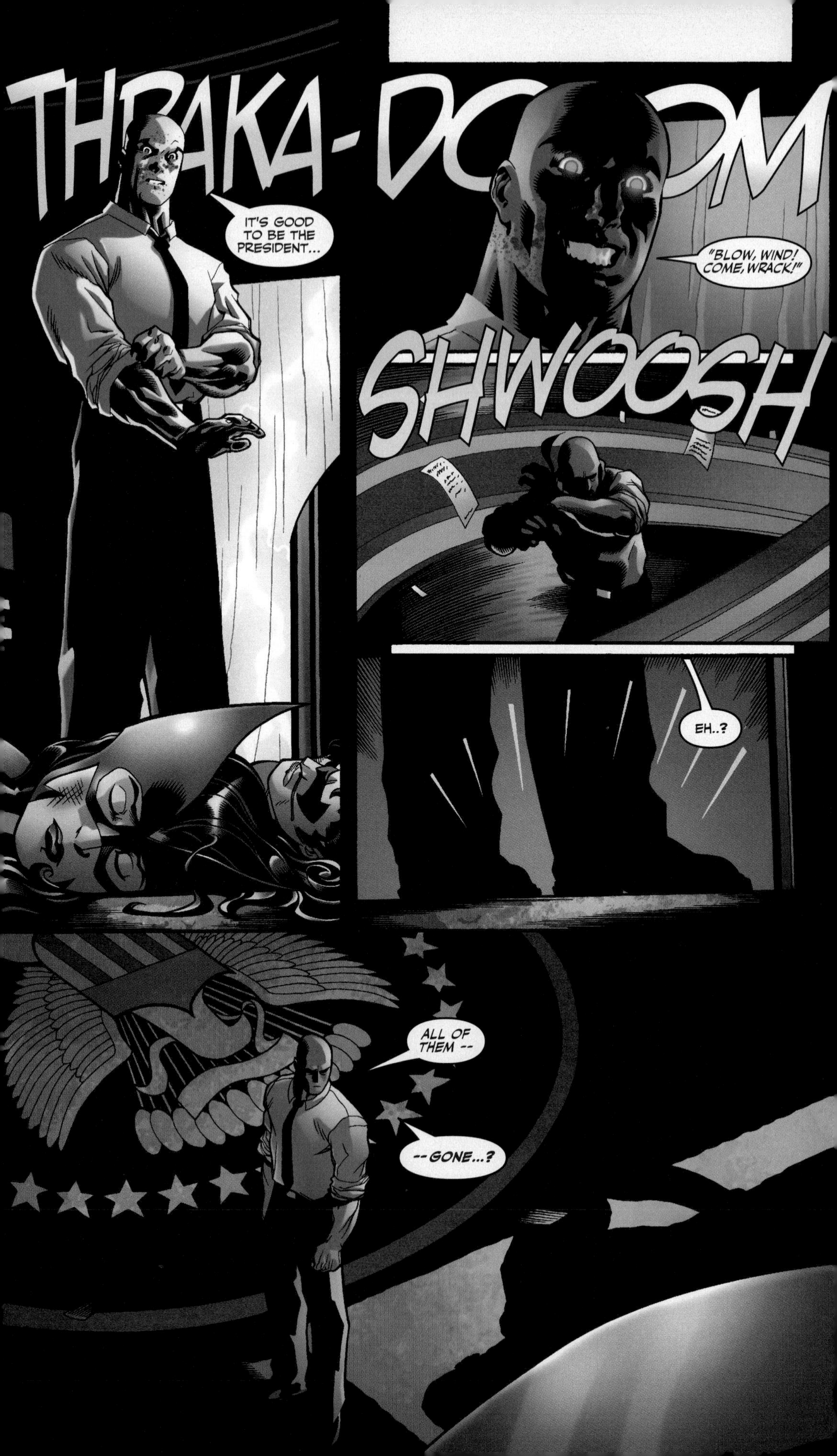
THRAKA-DOOOM
IT'S GOOD TO BE THE PRESIDENT...
"BLOW, WIND! COME, WRACK!"
SHWOOSH
EH..?
ALL OF THEM --
-- GONE...?

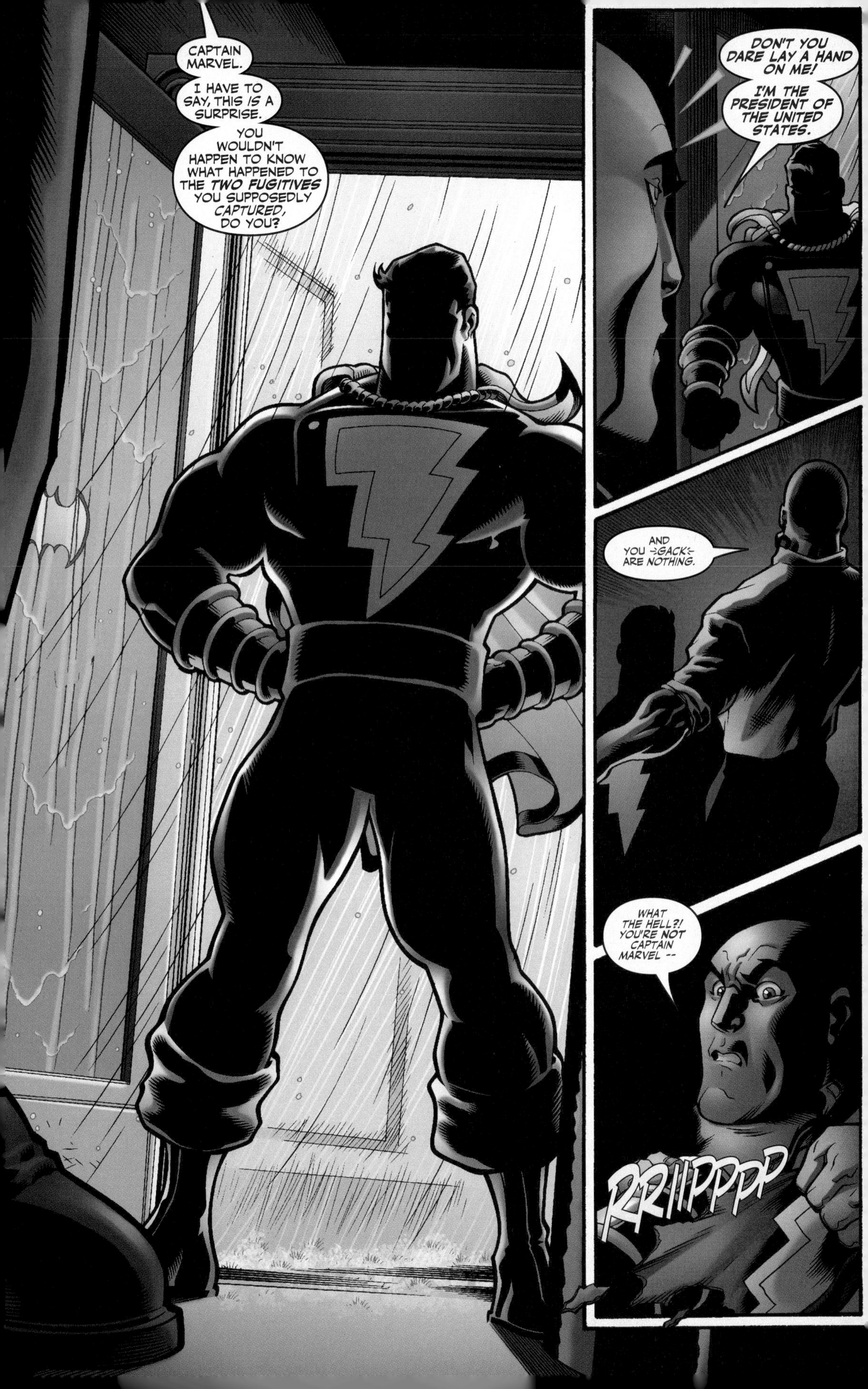
CAPTAIN MARVEL.
I HAVE TO SAY, THIS IS A SURPRISE.
YOU WOULDN'T HAPPEN TO KNOW WHAT HAPPENED TO THE TWO FUGITIVES YOU SUPPOSEDLY CAPTURED, DO YOU?
DON'T YOU DARE LAY A HAND ON ME!
I'M THE PRESIDENT OF THE UNITED STATES.
AND YOU =GACK= ARE NOTHING.
WHAT THE HELL?! YOU'RE NOT CAPTAIN MARVEL --
RRIIPPPP

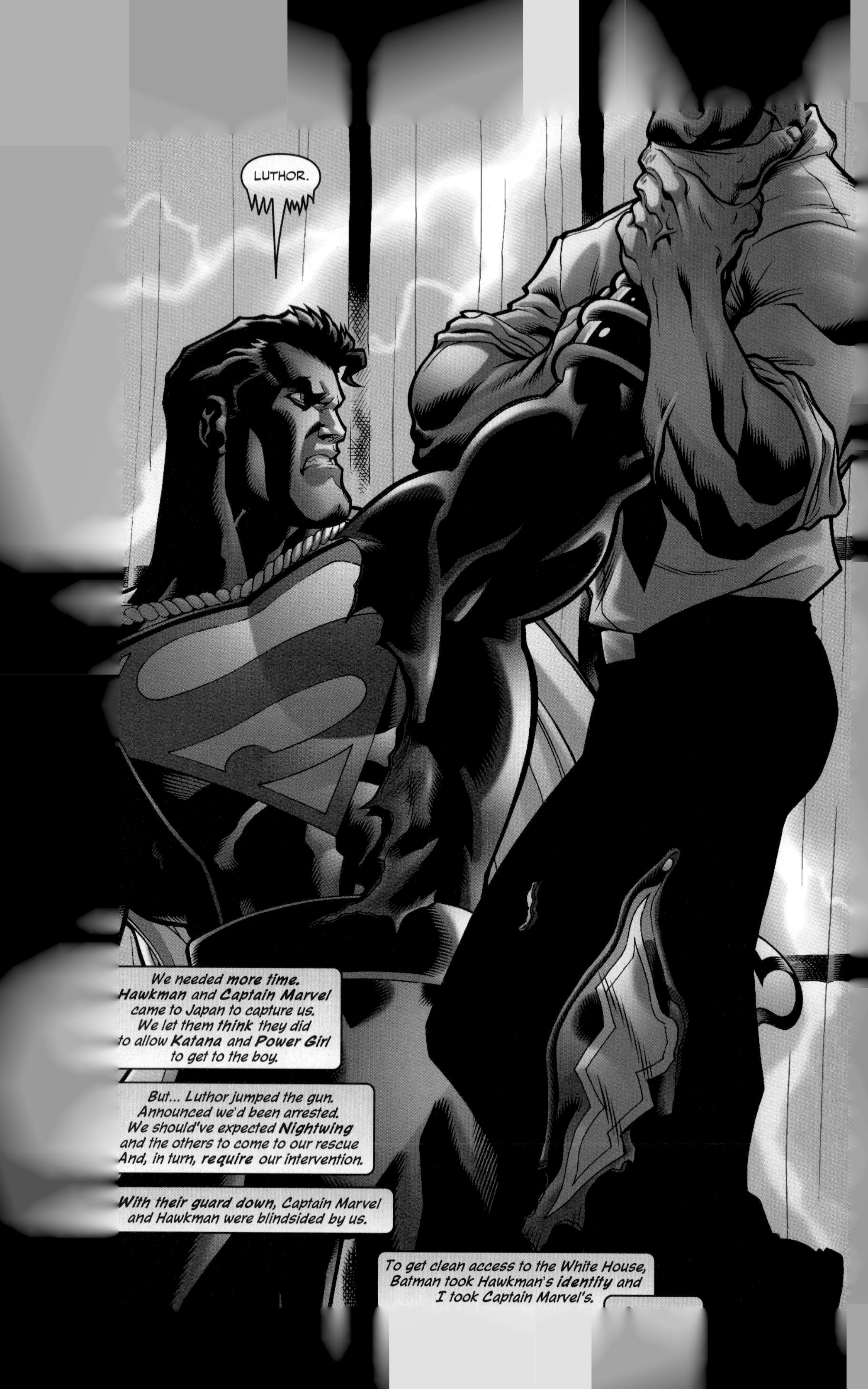
LUTHOR.
We needed more time. Hawkman and Captain Marvel came to Japan to capture us. We let them think they did to allow Katana and Power Girl to get to the boy.
But... Luthor jumped the gun. Announced we'd been arrested. We should've expected Nightwing and the others to come to our rescue And, in turn, require our intervention.
With their guard down, Captain Marvel and Hawkman were blindsided by us.
To get clean access to the White House, Batman took Hawkman's identity and I took Captain Marvel's.

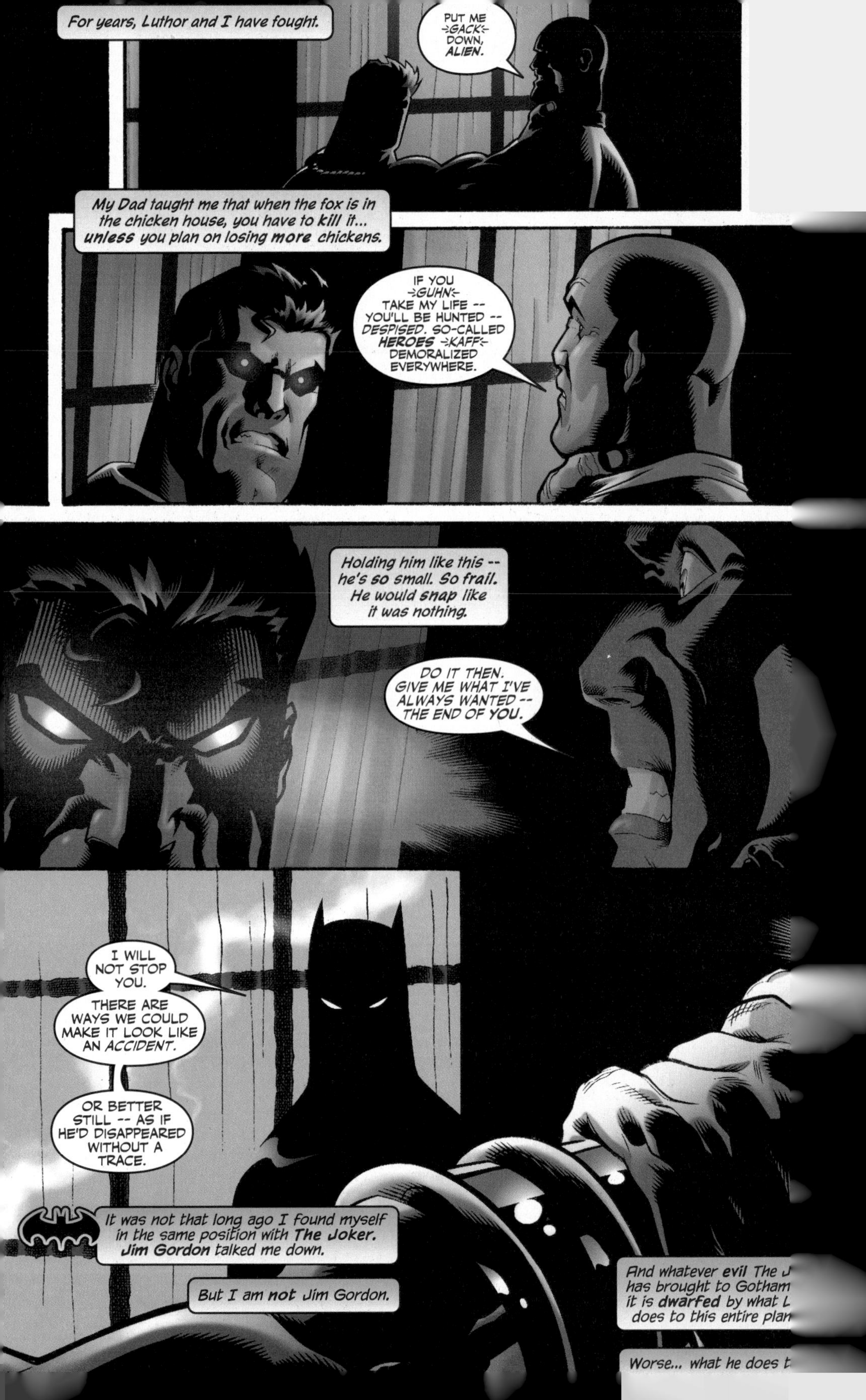
For years, Luthor and I have fought.
PUT ME -GACK- DOWN, ALIEN.
My Dad taught me that when the fox is in the chicken house, you have to kill it... unless you plan on losing more chickens.
IF YOU -GUHN- TAKE MY LIFE -- YOU'LL BE HUNTED -- DESPISED. SO-CALLED HEROES -KAFF- DEMORALIZED EVERYWHERE.
Holding him like this -- he's so small. So frail. He would snap like it was nothing.
DO IT THEN. GIVE ME WHAT I'VE ALWAYS WANTED -- THE END OF YOU.
I WILL NOT STOP YOU.
THERE ARE WAYS WE COULD MAKE IT LOOK LIKE AN ACCIDENT.
OR BETTER STILL -- AS IF HE'D DISAPPEARED WITHOUT A TRACE.
It was not that long ago I found myself in the same position with The Joker. Jim Gordon talked me down.
But I am not Jim Gordon.

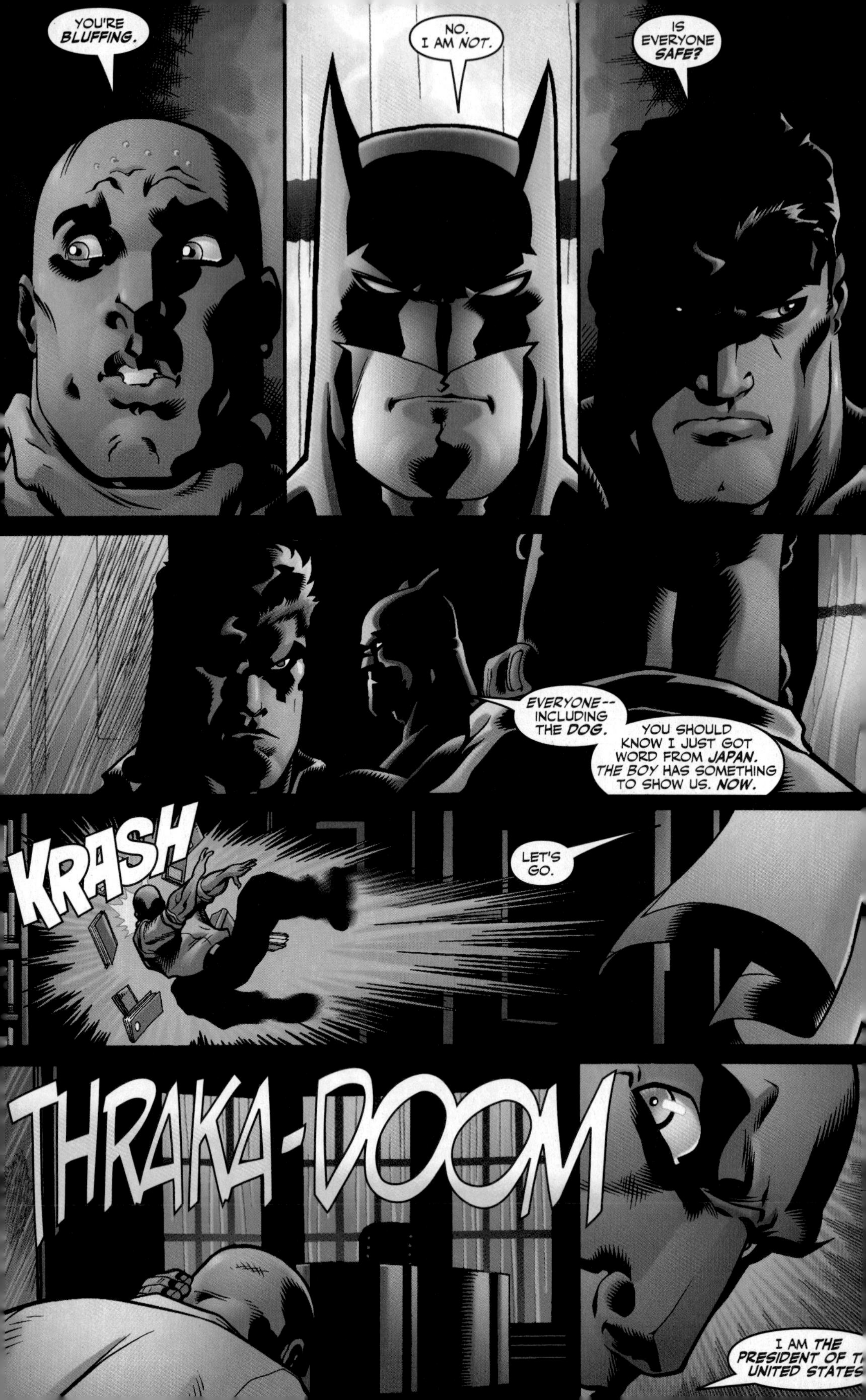
YOU'RE BLUFFING.
NO. I AM NOT.
IS EVERYONE SAFE?
EVERYONE-- INCLUDING THE DOG.
YOU SHOULD KNOW I JUST GOT WORD FROM JAPAN. THE BOY HAS SOMETHING TO SHOW US. NOW.
KRASH
LET'S GO.
THRAKA-DOOM
I AM THE PRESIDENT OF T UNITED STATES

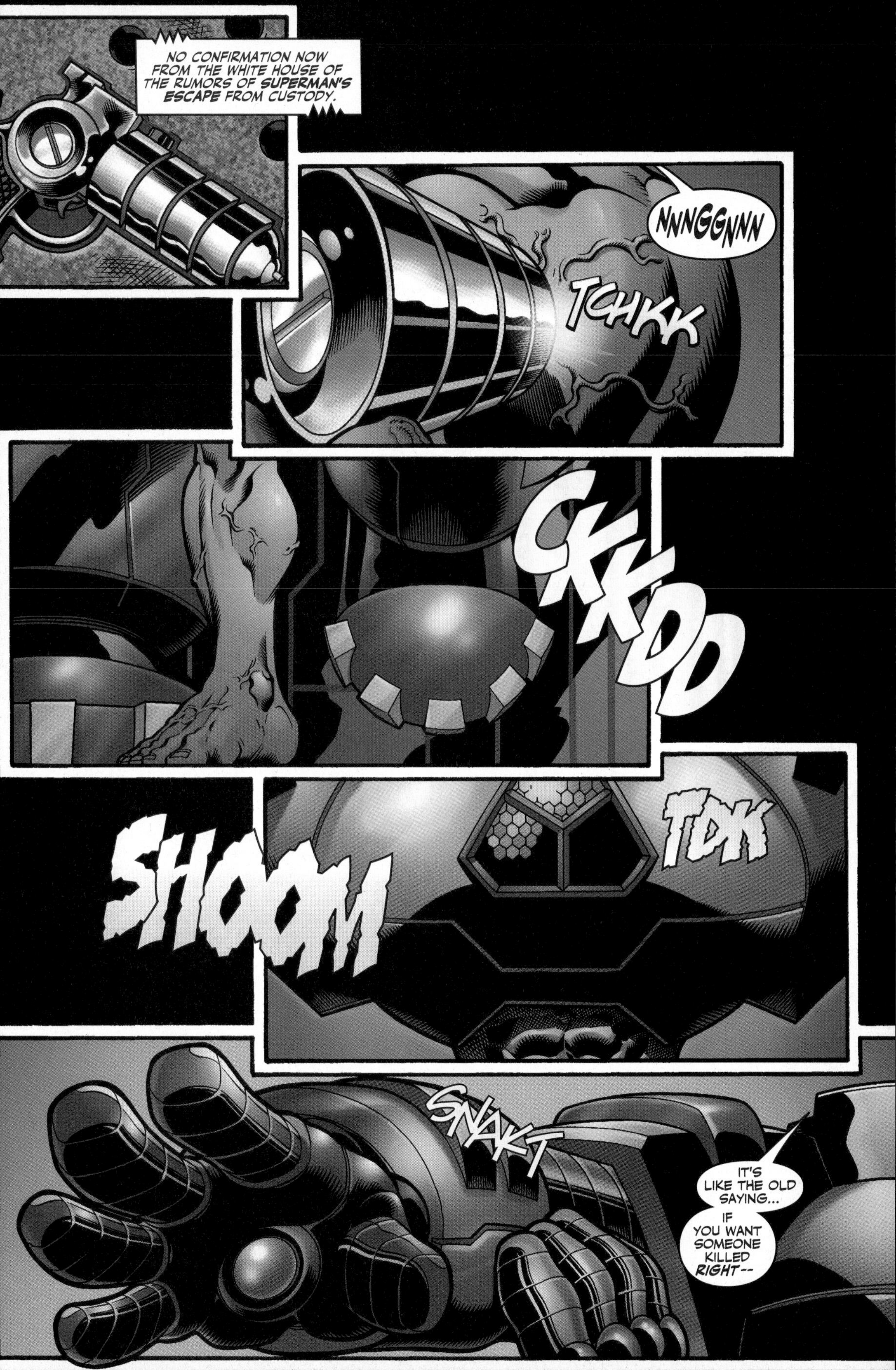
NO CONFIRMATION NOW FROM THE WHITE HOUSE OF THE RUMORS OF SUPERMAN'S ESCAPE FROM CUSTODY.
NNNGGNNN
TCHKK
CKKDD
SHOOM
TDK
SNAKT
IT'S LIKE THE OLD SAYING...
IF YOU WANT SOMEONE KILLED RIGHT--

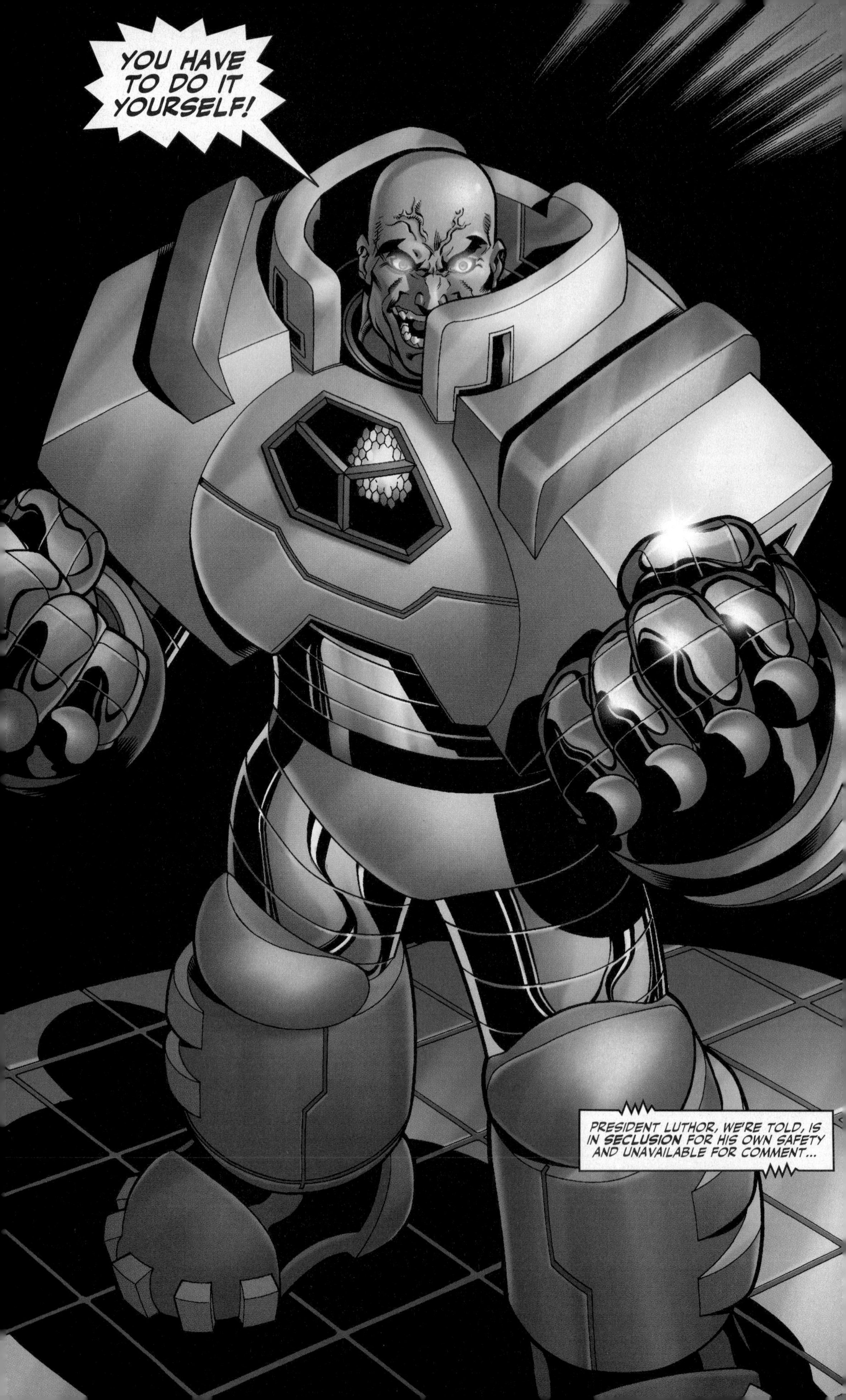
YOU HAVE TO DO IT YOURSELF!
PRESIDENT LUTHOR, WE'RE TOLD, IS IN SECLUSION FOR HIS OWN SAFETY AND UNAVAILABLE FOR COMMENT...

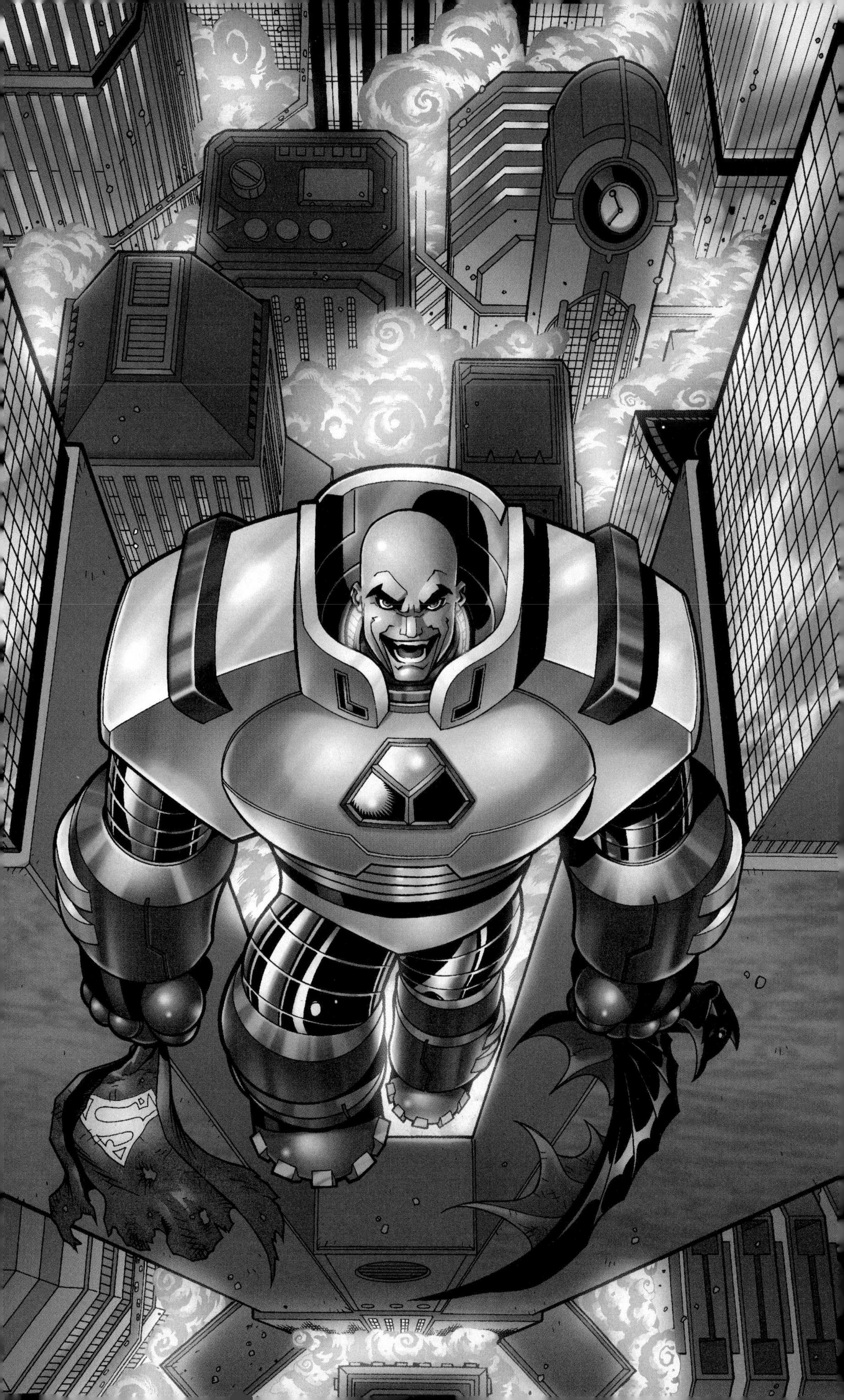

"When does it end, Luthor?"

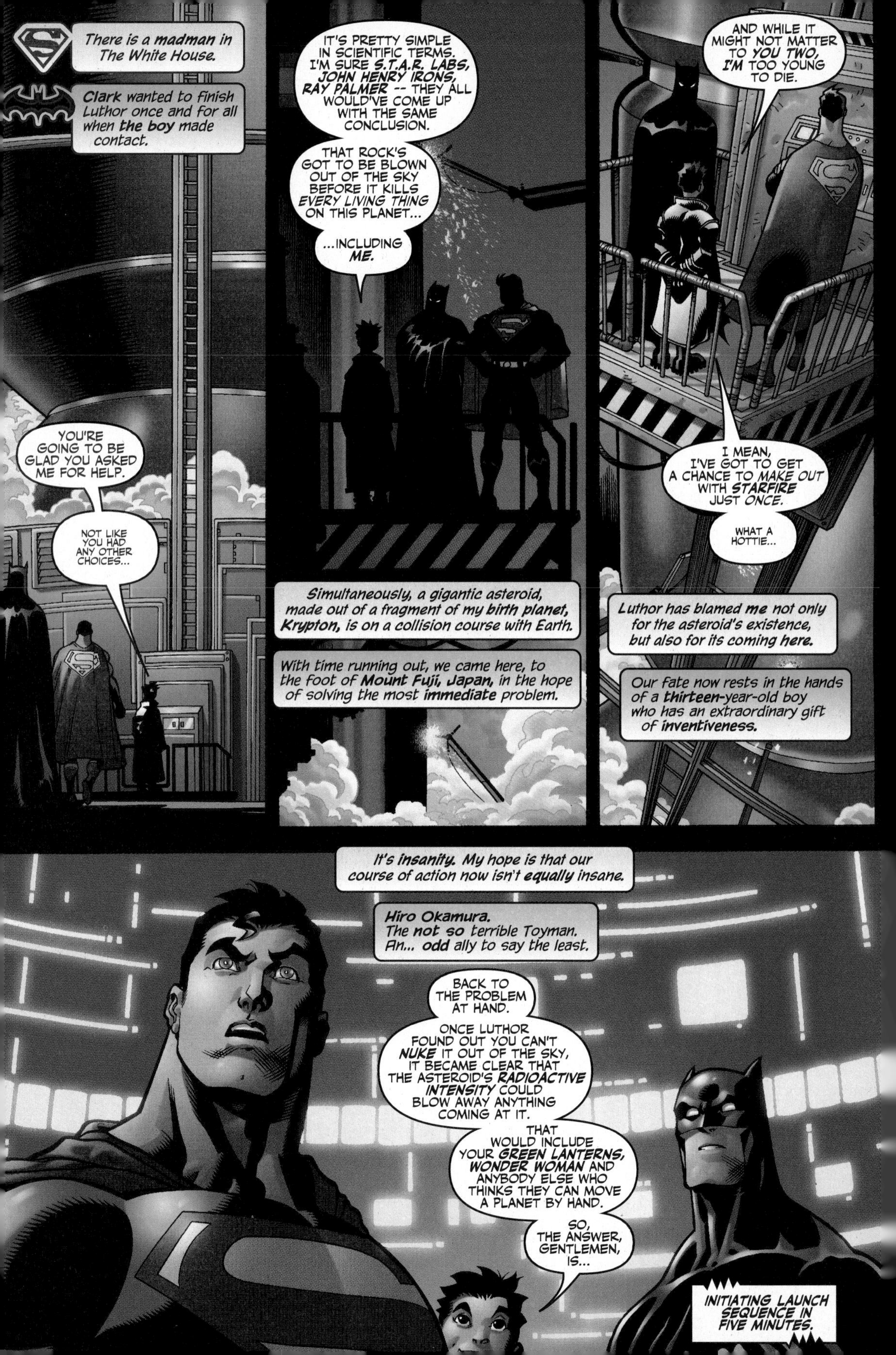
There is a madman in The White House.
Clark wanted to finish Luthor once and for all when the boy made contact.
YOU'RE GOING TO BE GLAD YOU ASKED ME FOR HELP.
NOT LIKE YOU HAD ANY OTHER CHOICES...
IT'S PRETTY SIMPLE IN SCIENTIFIC TERMS. I'M SURE S.T.A.R. LABS, JOHN HENRY IRONS, RAY PALMER -- THEY ALL WOULD'VE COME UP WITH THE SAME CONCLUSION.
THAT ROCK'S GOT TO BE BLOWN OUT OF THE SKY BEFORE IT KILLS EVERY LIVING THING ON THIS PLANET...
...INCLUDING ME.
Simultaneously, a gigantic asteroid, made out of a fragment of my birth planet, Krypton, is on a collision course with Earth.
With time running out, we came here, to the foot of Mount Fuji, Japan, in the hope of solving the most immediate problem.
AND WHILE IT MIGHT NOT MATTER TO YOU TWO, I'M TOO YOUNG TO DIE.
I MEAN, I'VE GOT TO GET A CHANCE TO MAKE OUT WITH STARFIRE JUST ONCE.
WHAT A HOTTIE...
Luthor has blamed me not only for the asteroid's existence, but also for its coming here.
Our fate now rests in the hands of a thirteen-year-old boy who has an extraordinary gift of inventiveness.
It's insanity. My hope is that our course of action now isn't equally insane.
Hiro Okamura. The not so terrible Toyman. An... odd ally to say the least.
BACK TO THE PROBLEM AT HAND.
ONCE LUTHOR FOUND OUT YOU CAN'T NUKE IT OUT OF THE SKY, IT BECAME CLEAR THAT THE ASTEROID'S RADIOACTIVE INTENSITY COULD BLOW AWAY ANYTHING COMING AT IT.
THAT WOULD INCLUDE YOUR GREEN LANTERNS, WONDER WOMAN AND ANYBODY ELSE WHO THINKS THEY CAN MOVE A PLANET BY HAND.
SO, THE ANSWER, GENTLEMEN, IS...
INITIATING LAUNCH SEQUENCE IN FIVE MINUTES.

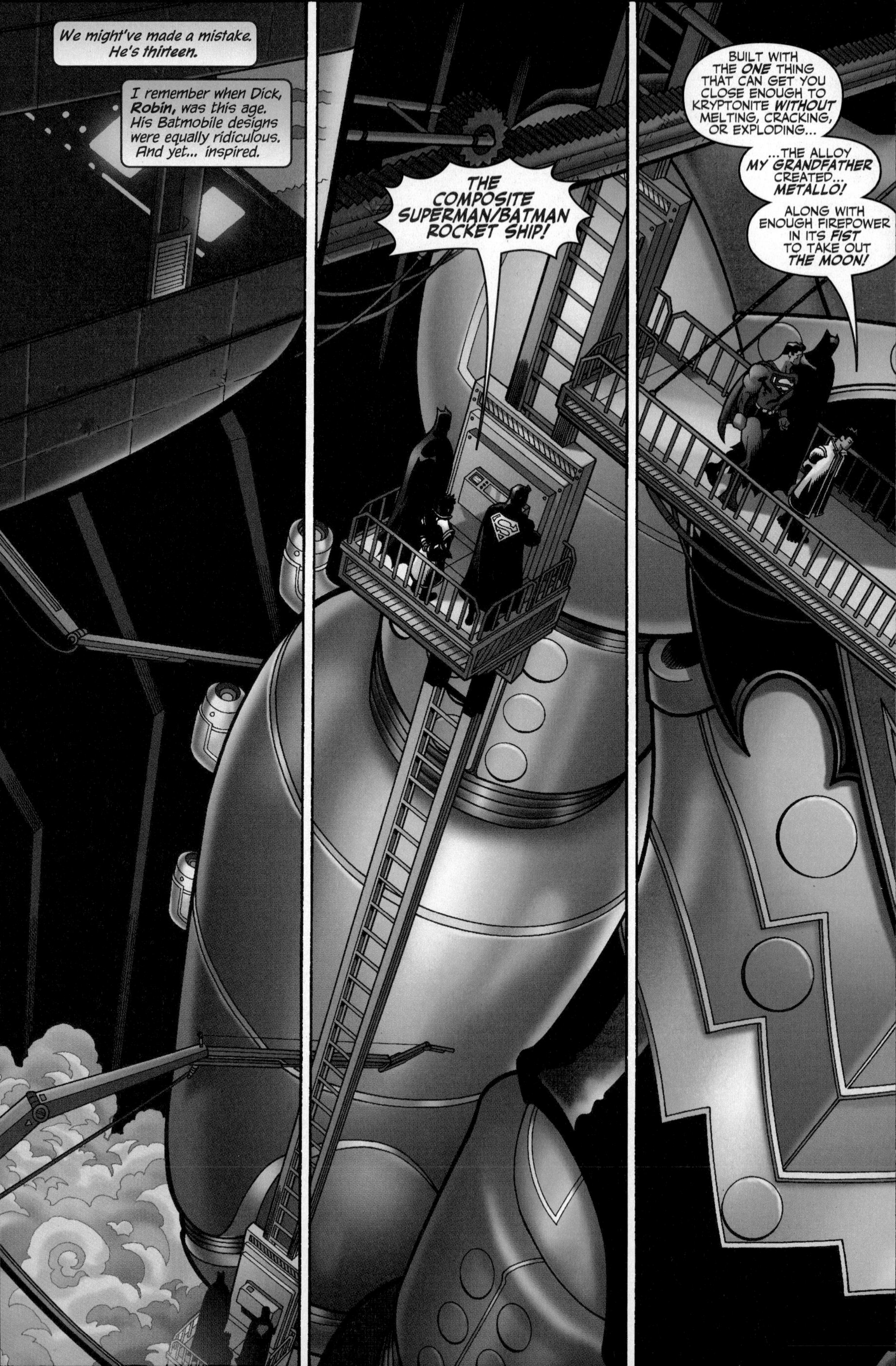
We might've made a mistake. He's thirteen.
I remember when Dick, Robin, was this age. His Batmobile designs were equally ridiculous. And yet... inspired.
THE COMPOSITE SUPERMAN/BATMAN ROCKET SHIP!
BUILT WITH THE ONE THING THAT CAN GET YOU CLOSE ENOUGH TO KRYPTONITE WITHOUT MELTING, CRACKING, OR EXPLODING...
...THE ALLOY MY GRANDFATHER CREATED... METALLO!
ALONG WITH ENOUGH FIREPOWER IN ITS FIST TO TAKE OUT THE MOON!

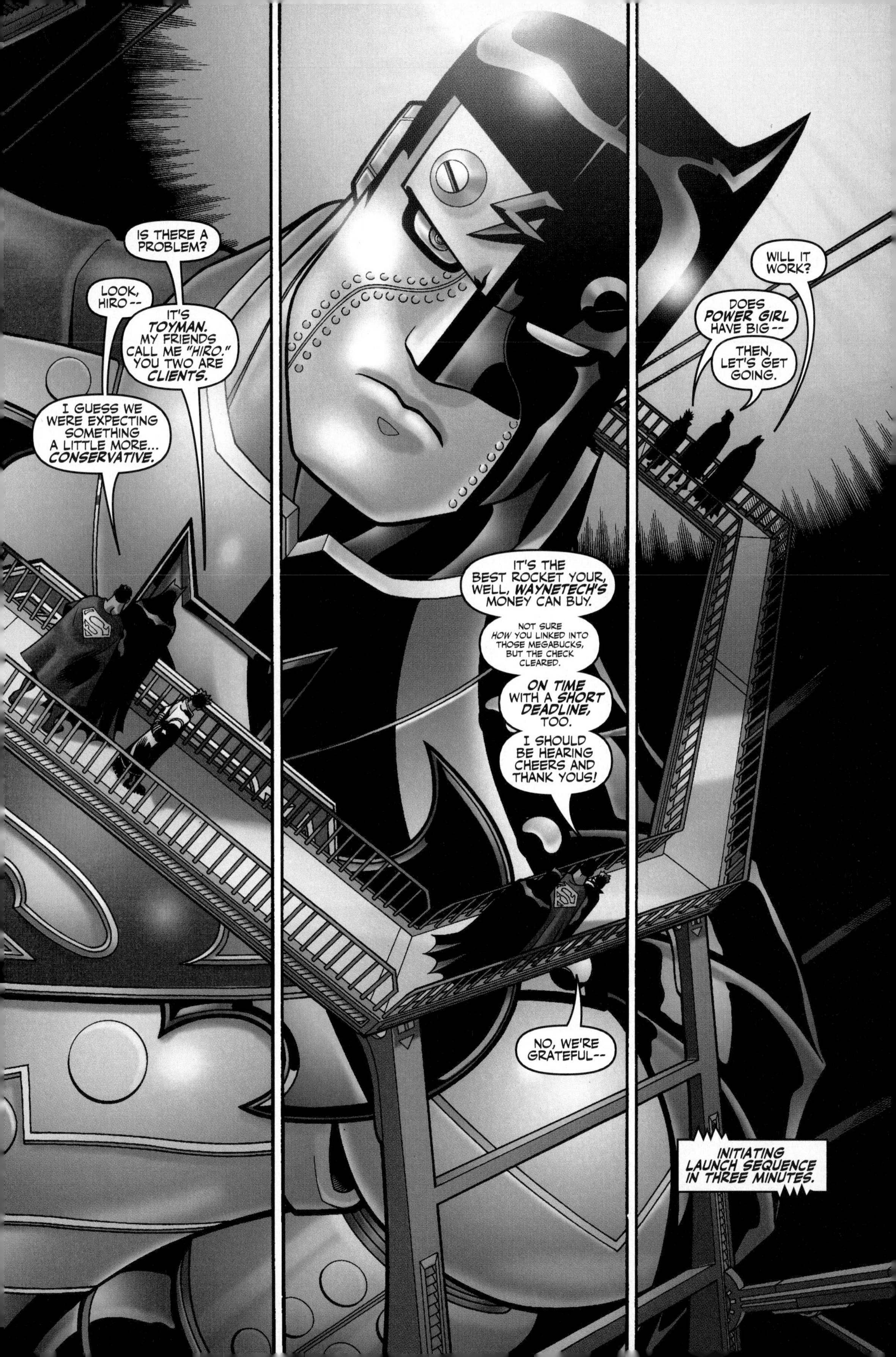
IS THERE A PROBLEM?
LOOK, HIRO--
IT'S TOYMAN. MY FRIENDS CALL ME "HIRO." YOU TWO ARE CLIENTS.
I GUESS WE WERE EXPECTING SOMETHING A LITTLE MORE... CONSERVATIVE.
IT'S THE BEST ROCKET YOUR, WELL, WAYNETECH'S MONEY CAN BUY.
NOT SURE HOW YOU LINKED INTO THOSE MEGABUCKS, BUT THE CHECK CLEARED.
ON TIME WITH A SHORT DEADLINE, TOO.
I SHOULD BE HEARING CHEERS AND THANK YOUS!
NO, WE'RE GRATEFUL--
WILL IT WORK?
DOES POWER GIRL HAVE BIG--
THEN, LET'S GET GOING.
INITIATING LAUNCH SEQUENCE IN THREE MINUTES.

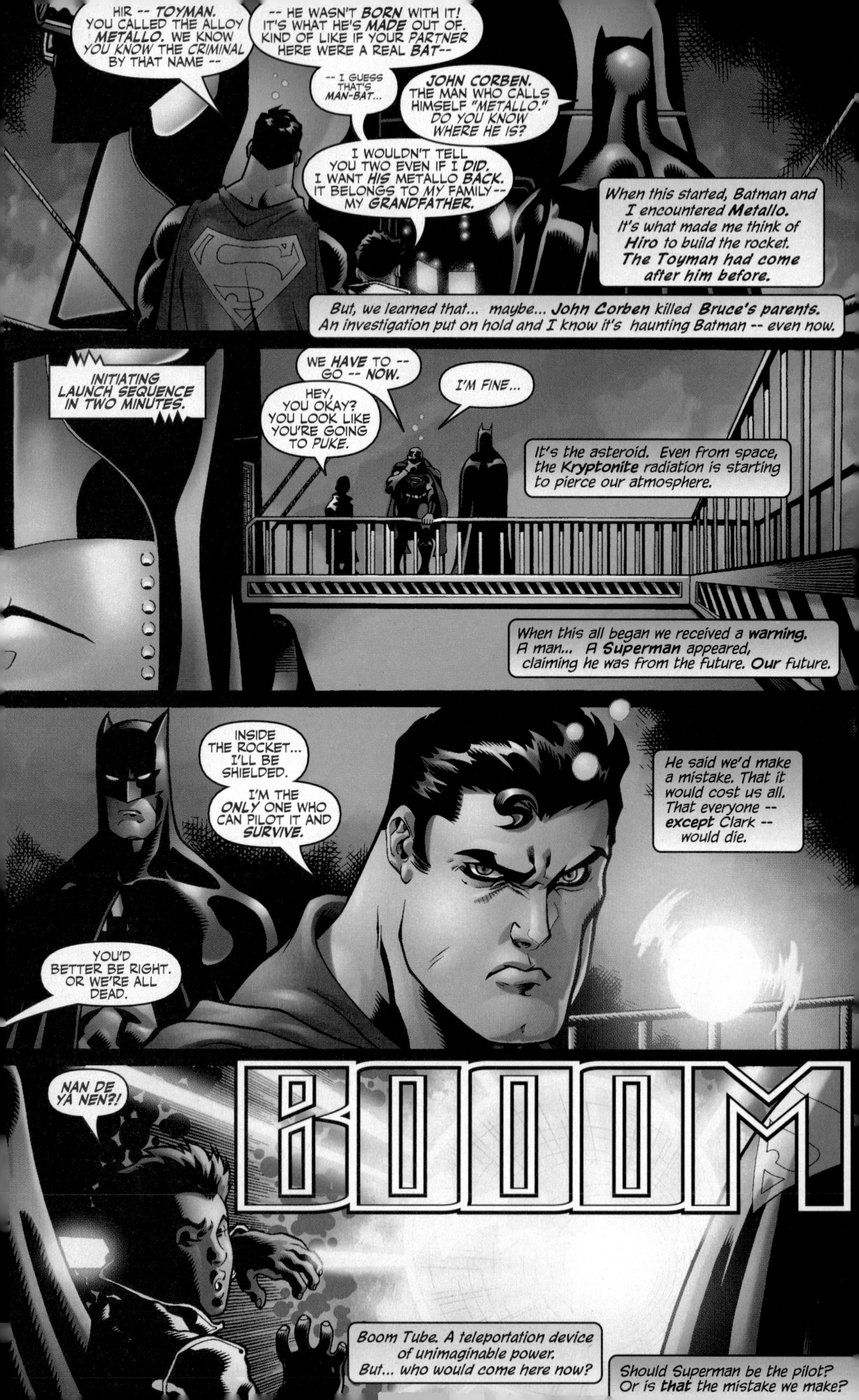
HIR -- TOYMAN. YOU CALLED THE ALLOY METALLO. WE KNOW YOU KNOW THE CRIMINAL BY THAT NAME --
-- HE WASN'T BORN WITH IT! IT'S WHAT HE'S MADE OUT OF. KIND OF LIKE IF YOUR PARTNER HERE WERE A REAL BAT--
-- I GUESS THAT'S MAN-BAT...
JOHN CORBEN. THE MAN WHO CALLS HIMSELF "METALLO." DO YOU KNOW WHERE HE IS?
I WOULDN'T TELL YOU TWO EVEN IF I DID. I WANT HIS METALLO BACK. IT BELONGS TO MY FAMILY-- MY GRANDFATHER.
When this started, Batman and I encountered Metallo. It's what made me think of Hiro to build the rocket. The Toyman had come after him before.
But, we learned that... maybe... John Corben killed Bruce's parents. An investigation put on hold and I know it's haunting Batman -- even now.
INITIATING LAUNCH SEQUENCE IN TWO MINUTES.
WE HAVE TO -- GO -- NOW.
HEY, YOU OKAY? YOU LOOK LIKE YOU'RE GOING TO PUKE.
I'M FINE...
It's the asteroid. Even from space, the Kryptonite radiation is starting to pierce our atmosphere.
When this all began we received a warning. A man... A Superman appeared, claiming he was from the future. Our future.
INSIDE THE ROCKET... I'LL BE SHIELDED.
I'M THE ONLY ONE WHO CAN PILOT IT AND SURVIVE.
He said we'd make a mistake. That it would cost us all. That everyone -- except Clark -- would die.
YOU'D BETTER BE RIGHT. OR WE'RE ALL DEAD.
NAN DE YA NEN?!
BOOOM
Boom Tube. A teleportation device of unimaginable power. But... who would come here now?
Should Superman be the pilot? Or is that the mistake we make?

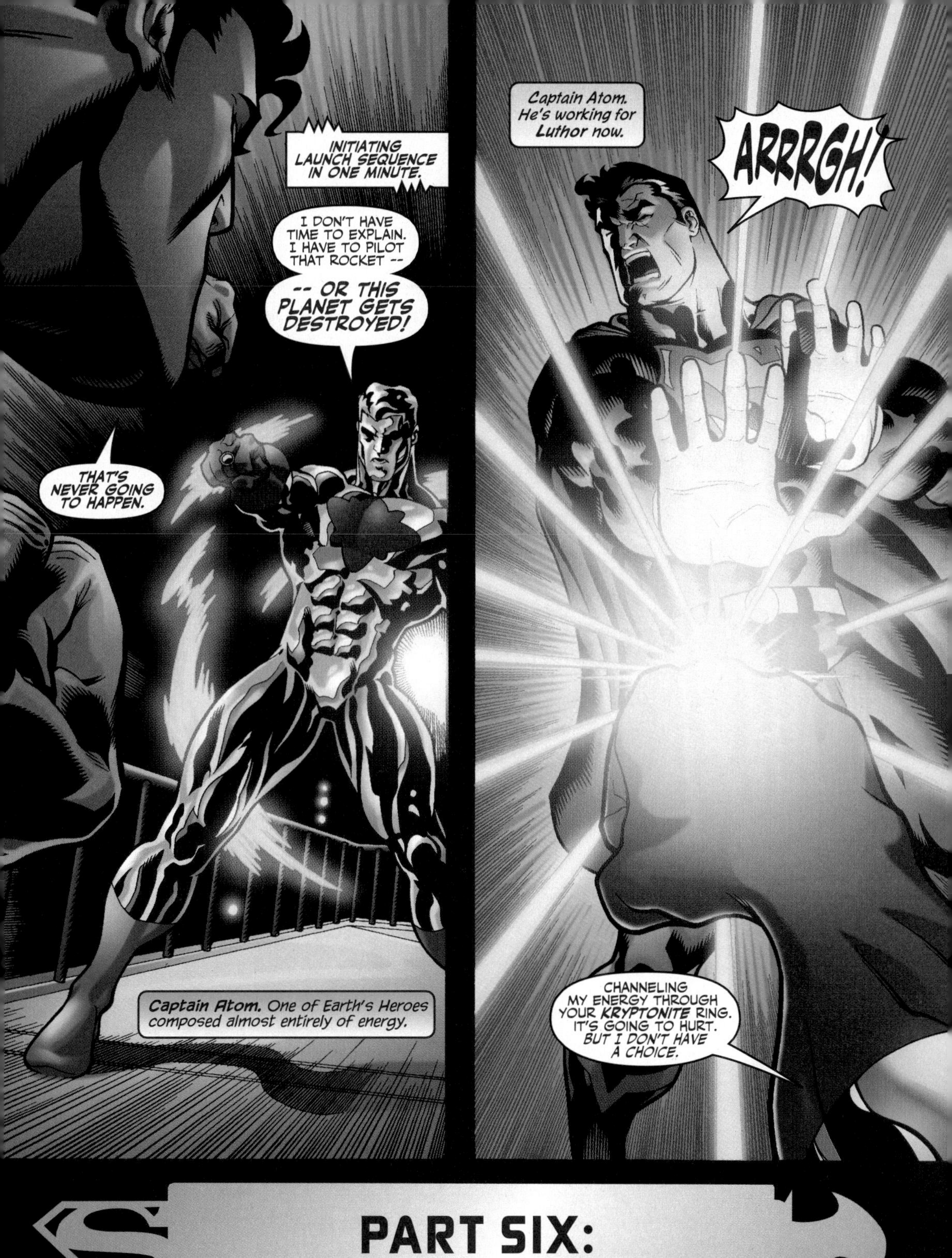

INITIATING LAUNCH SEQUENCE IN ONE MINUTE.
I DON'T HAVE TIME TO EXPLAIN. I HAVE TO PILOT THAT ROCKET --
-- OR THIS PLANET GETS DESTROYED!
THAT'S NEVER GOING TO HAPPEN.
Captain Atom. One of Earth's Heroes composed almost entirely of energy.
Captain Atom. He's working for Luthor now.
ARRRGH!
CHANNELING MY ENERGY THROUGH YOUR KRYPTONITE RING. IT'S GOING TO HURT. BUT I DON'T HAVE A CHOICE.

PART SIX: FINAL COUNTDOWN

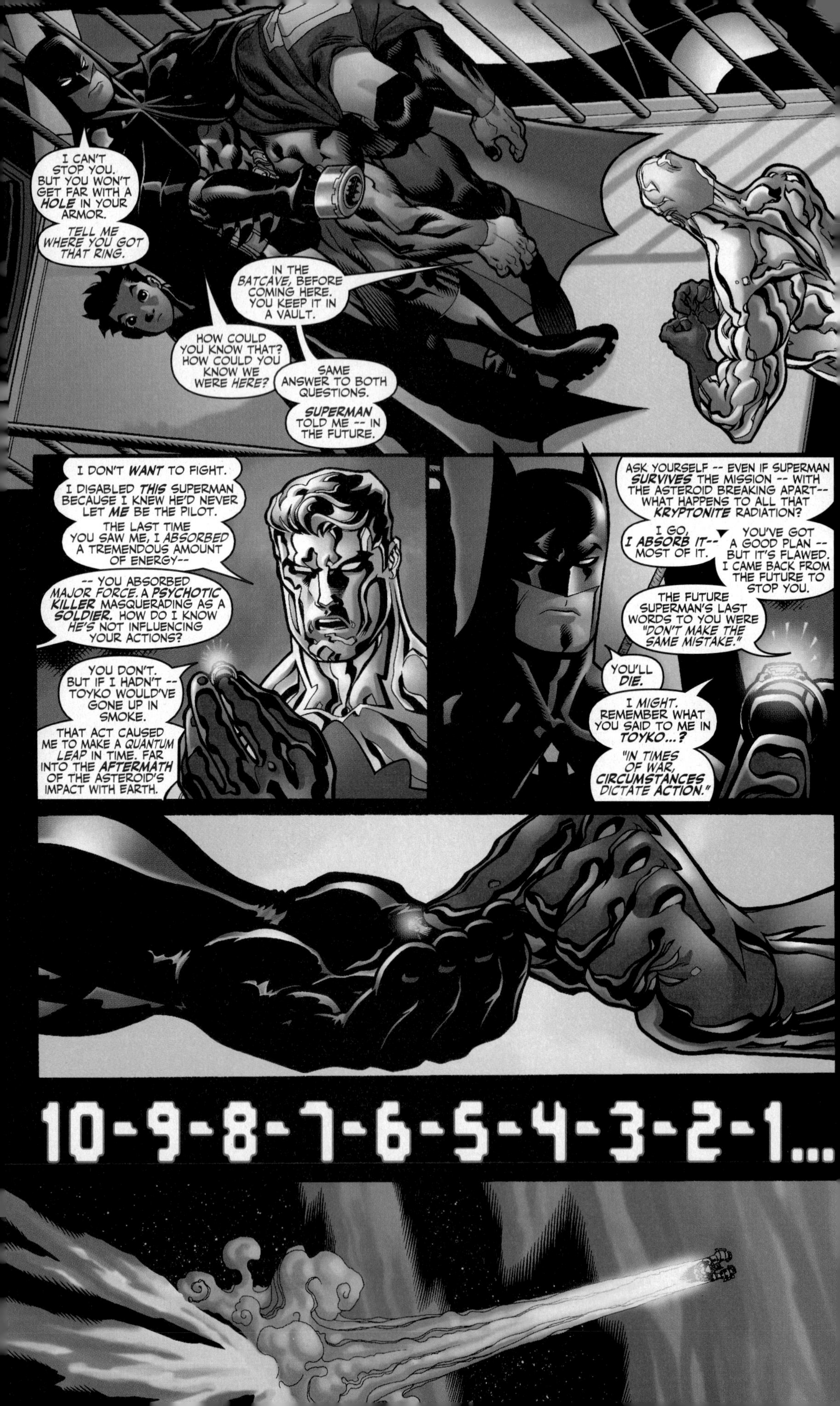
I CAN'T STOP YOU. BUT YOU WON'T GET FAR WITH A HOLE IN YOUR ARMOR.
TELL ME WHERE YOU GOT THAT RING.
IN THE BATCAVE, BEFORE COMING HERE. YOU KEEP IT IN A VAULT.
HOW COULD YOU KNOW THAT? HOW COULD YOU KNOW WE WERE HERE?
SAME ANSWER TO BOTH QUESTIONS.
SUPERMAN TOLD ME -- IN THE FUTURE.
I DON'T WANT TO FIGHT.
I DISABLED THIS SUPERMAN BECAUSE I KNEW HE'D NEVER LET ME BE THE PILOT.
THE LAST TIME YOU SAW ME, I ABSORBED A TREMENDOUS AMOUNT OF ENERGY--
-- YOU ABSORBED MAJOR FORCE. A PSYCHOTIC KILLER MASQUERADING AS A SOLDIER. HOW DO I KNOW HE'S NOT INFLUENCING YOUR ACTIONS?
YOU DON'T. BUT IF I HADN'T -- TOYKO WOULD'VE GONE UP IN SMOKE.
THAT ACT CAUSED ME TO MAKE A QUANTUM LEAP IN TIME. FAR INTO THE AFTERMATH OF THE ASTEROID'S IMPACT WITH EARTH.
ASK YOURSELF -- EVEN IF SUPERMAN SURVIVES THE MISSION -- WITH THE ASTEROID BREAKING APART-- WHAT HAPPENS TO ALL THAT KRYPTONITE RADIATION?
I GO, I ABSORB IT-- MOST OF IT.
YOU'VE GOT A GOOD PLAN -- BUT IT'S FLAWED. I CAME BACK FROM THE FUTURE TO STOP YOU.
THE FUTURE SUPERMAN'S LAST WORDS TO YOU WERE "DON'T MAKE THE SAME MISTAKE."
YOU'LL DIE.
I MIGHT. REMEMBER WHAT YOU SAID TO ME IN TOYKO...?
"IN TIMES OF WAR, CIRCUMSTANCES DICTATE ACTION."
10-9-8-7-6-5-4-3-2-1...

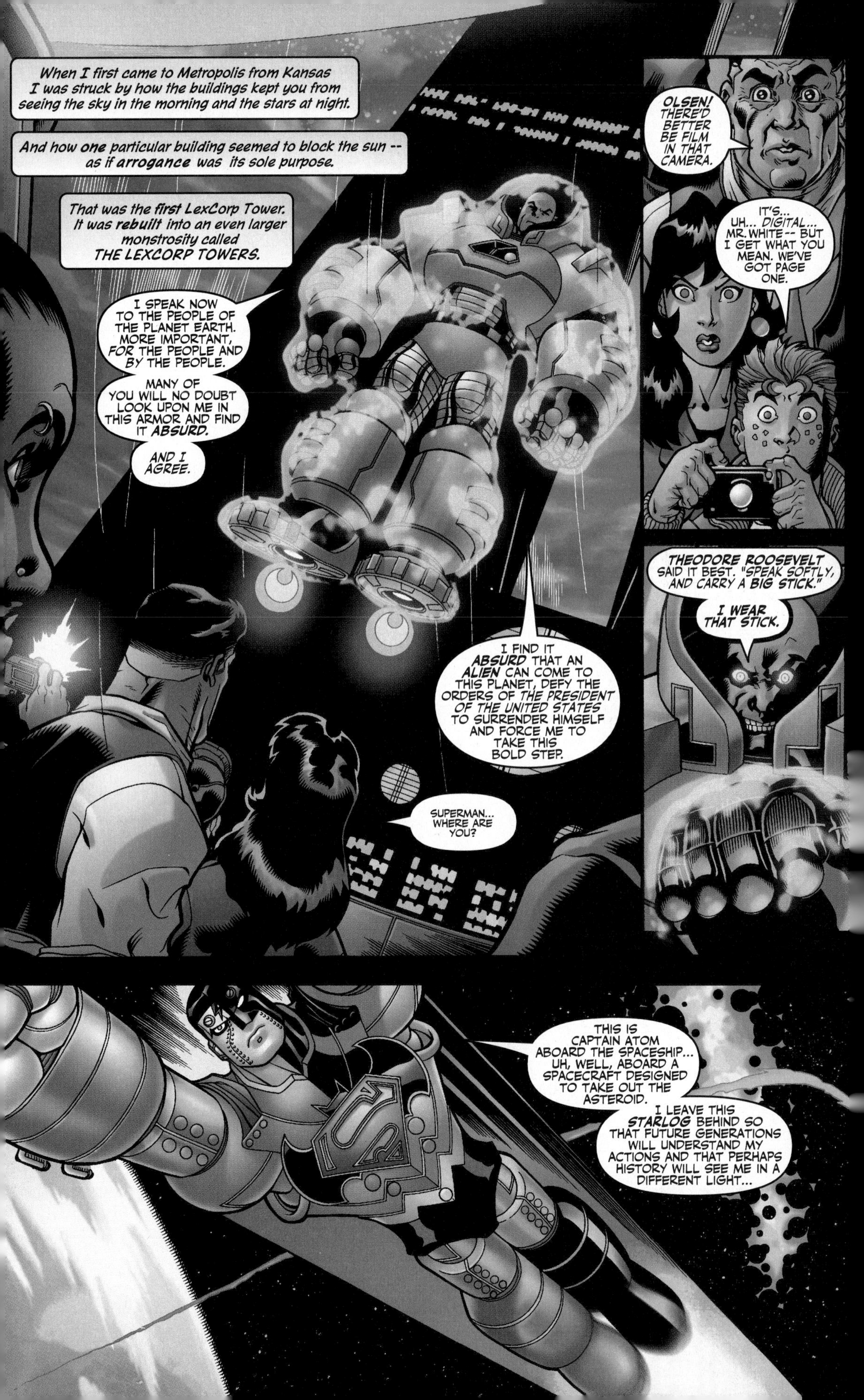
When I first came to Metropolis from Kansas I was struck by how the buildings kept you from seeing the sky in the morning and the stars at night.
And how one particular building seemed to block the sun -- as if arrogance was its sole purpose.
That was the first LexCorp Tower. It was rebuilt into an even larger monstrosity called THE LEXCORP TOWERS.
I SPEAK NOW TO THE PEOPLE OF THE PLANET EARTH. MORE IMPORTANT, FOR THE PEOPLE AND BY THE PEOPLE.
MANY OF YOU WILL NO DOUBT LOOK UPON ME IN THIS ARMOR AND FIND IT ABSURD.
AND I AGREE.
OLSEN! THERE'D BETTER BE FILM IN THAT CAMERA.
IT'S... UH... DIGITAL... MR. WHITE -- BUT I GET WHAT YOU MEAN. WE'VE GOT PAGE ONE.
I FIND IT ABSURD THAT AN ALIEN CAN COME TO THIS PLANET, DEFY THE ORDERS OF THE PRESIDENT OF THE UNITED STATES TO SURRENDER HIMSELF AND FORCE ME TO TAKE THIS BOLD STEP.
THEODORE ROOSEVELT SAID IT BEST. "SPEAK SOFTLY, AND CARRY A BIG STICK."
I WEAR THAT STICK.
SUPERMAN... WHERE ARE YOU?
THIS IS CAPTAIN ATOM ABOARD THE SPACESHIP... UH, WELL, ABOARD A SPACECRAFT DESIGNED TO TAKE OUT THE ASTEROID.
I LEAVE THIS STARLOG BEHIND SO THAT FUTURE GENERATIONS WILL UNDERSTAND MY ACTIONS AND THAT PERHAPS HISTORY WILL SEE ME IN A DIFFERENT LIGHT...

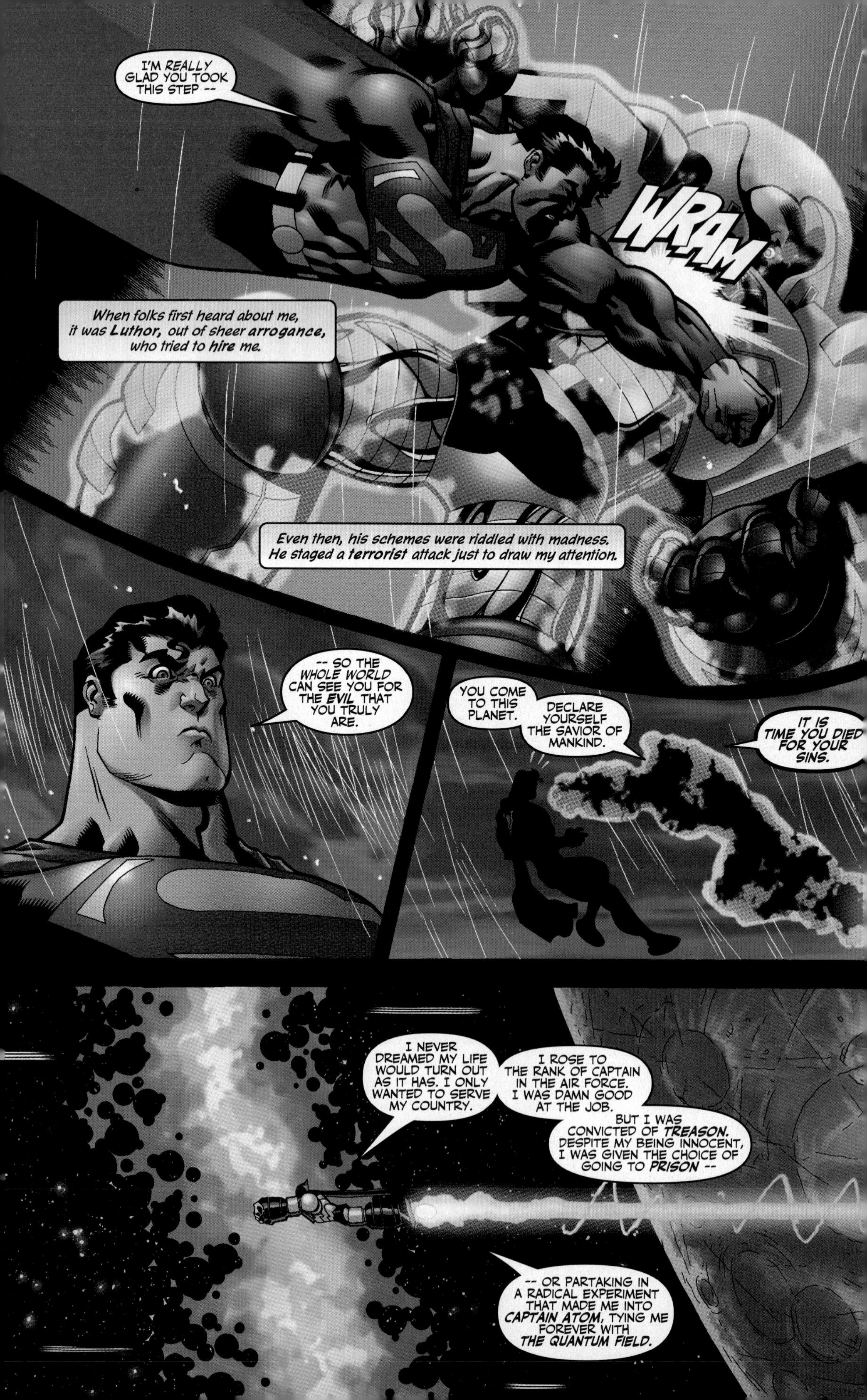
I'M REALLY GLAD YOU TOOK THIS STEP --
WRAM
When folks first heard about me, it was Luthor, out of sheer arrogance, who tried to hire me.
Even then, his schemes were riddled with madness. He staged a terrorist attack just to draw my attention.
-- SO THE WHOLE WORLD CAN SEE YOU FOR THE EVIL THAT YOU TRULY ARE.
YOU COME TO THIS PLANET.
DECLARE YOURSELF THE SAVIOR OF MANKIND.
IT IS TIME YOU DIED FOR YOUR SINS.
I NEVER DREAMED MY LIFE WOULD TURN OUT AS IT HAS. I ONLY WANTED TO SERVE MY COUNTRY.
I ROSE TO THE RANK OF CAPTAIN IN THE AIR FORCE. I WAS DAMN GOOD AT THE JOB.
BUT I WAS CONVICTED OF TREASON. DESPITE MY BEING INNOCENT, I WAS GIVEN THE CHOICE OF GOING TO PRISON --
-- OR PARTAKING IN A RADICAL EXPERIMENT THAT MADE ME INTO CAPTAIN ATOM, TYING ME FOREVER WITH THE QUANTUM FIELD.

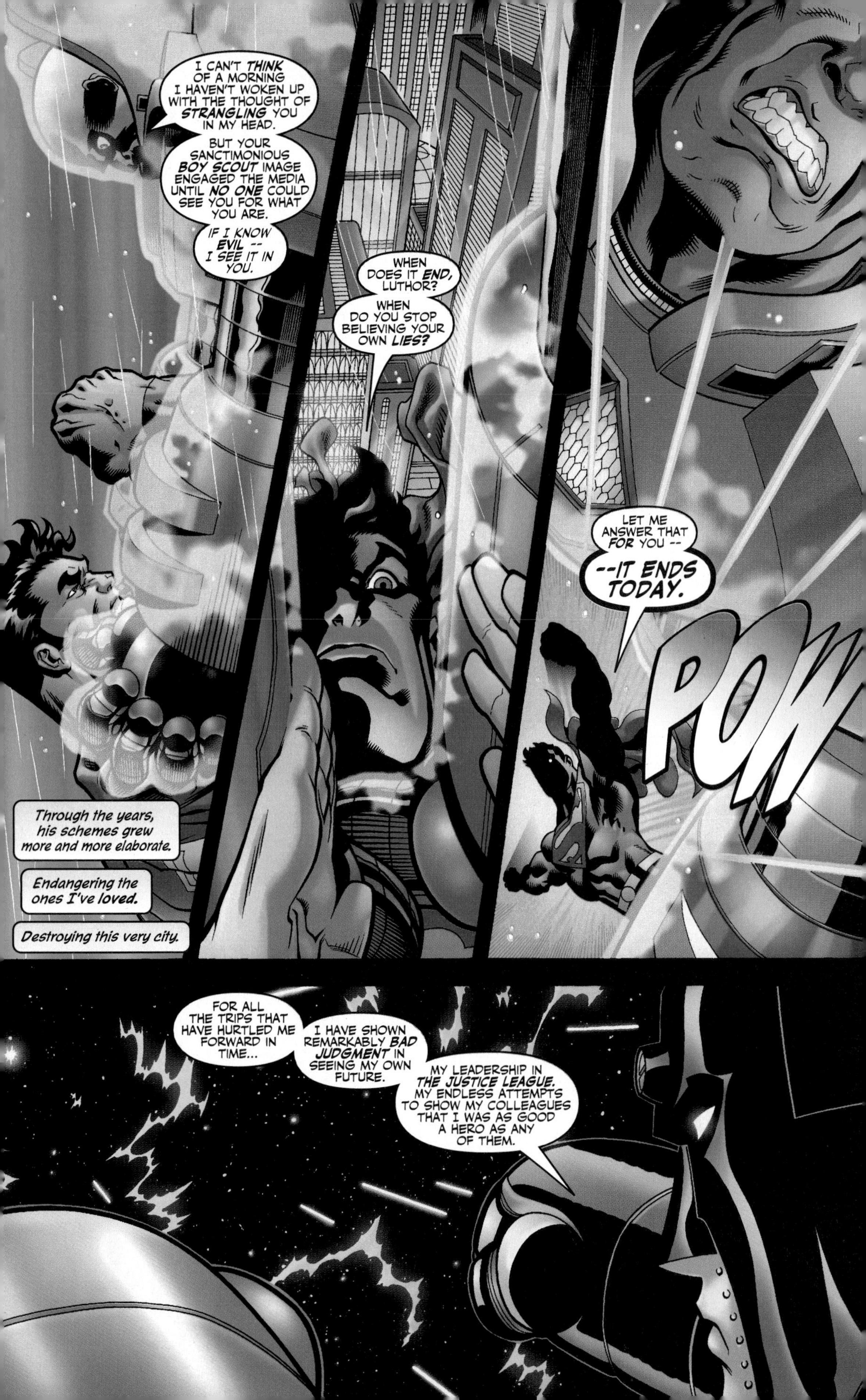
I CAN'T THINK OF A MORNING I HAVEN'T WOKEN UP WITH THE THOUGHT OF STRANGLING YOU IN MY HEAD.
BUT YOUR SANCTIMONIOUS BOY SCOUT IMAGE ENGAGED THE MEDIA UNTIL NO ONE COULD SEE YOU FOR WHAT YOU ARE.
IF I KNOW EVIL -- I SEE IT IN YOU.
Through the years, his schemes grew more and more elaborate.
Endangering the ones I've loved.
Destroying this very city.
WHEN DOES IT END, LUTHOR?
WHEN DO YOU STOP BELIEVING YOUR OWN LIES?
LET ME ANSWER THAT FOR YOU --
--IT ENDS TODAY.
POW
FOR ALL THE TRIPS THAT HAVE HURTLED ME FORWARD IN TIME...
I HAVE SHOWN REMARKABLY BAD JUDGMENT IN SEEING MY OWN FUTURE.
MY LEADERSHIP IN THE JUSTICE LEAGUE. MY ENDLESS ATTEMPTS TO SHOW MY COLLEAGUES THAT I WAS AS GOOD A HERO AS ANY OF THEM.

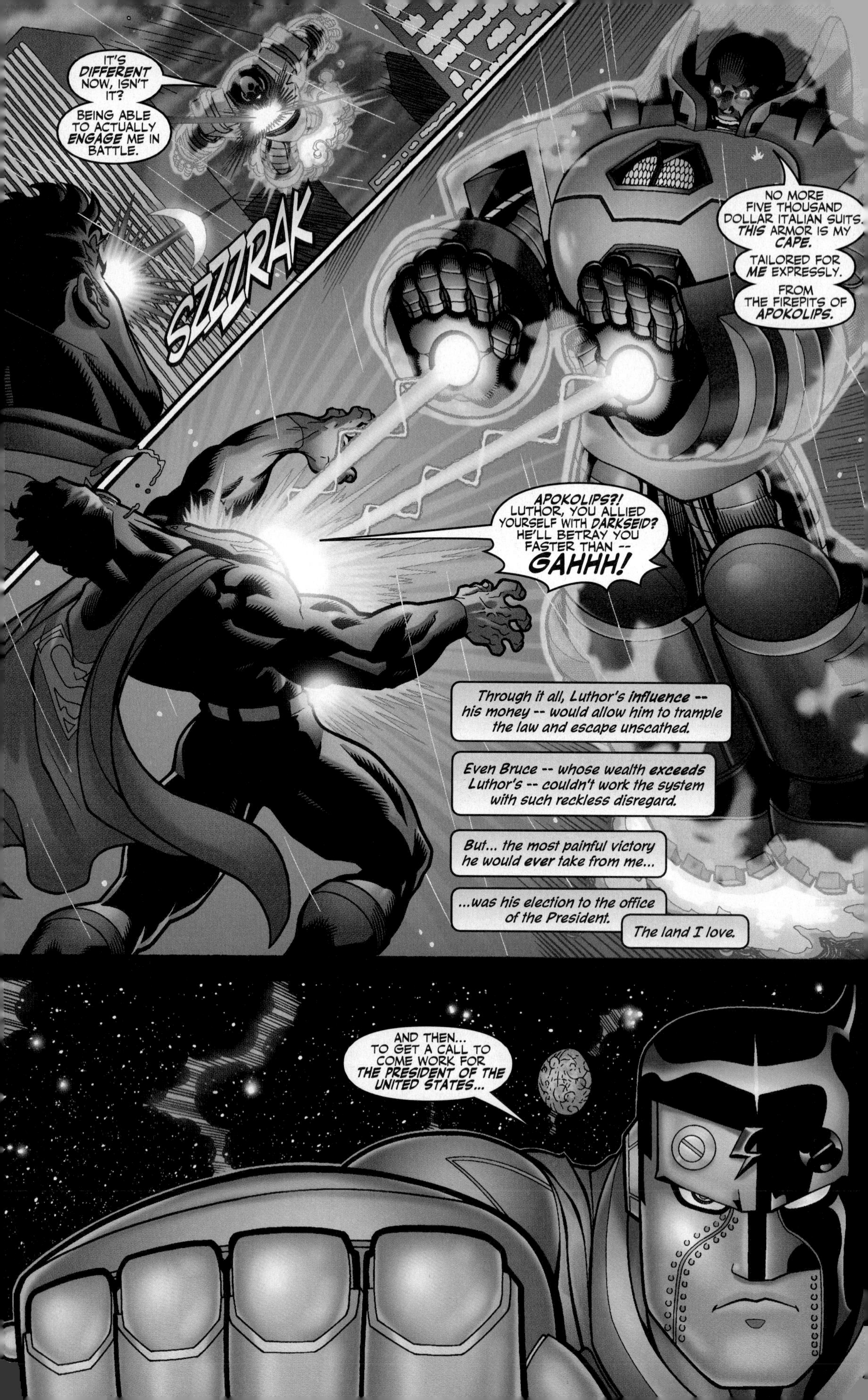
IT'S DIFFERENT NOW, ISN'T IT?
BEING ABLE TO ACTUALLY ENGAGE ME IN BATTLE.
SZZZRAK
NO MORE FIVE THOUSAND DOLLAR ITALIAN SUITS. THIS ARMOR IS MY CAPE.
TAILORED FOR ME EXPRESSLY.
FROM THE FIREPITS OF APOKOLIPS.
APOKOLIPS?! LUTHOR, YOU ALLIED YOURSELF WITH DARKSEID? HE'LL BETRAY YOU FASTER THAN -- GAHHH!
Through it all, Luthor's influence -- his money -- would allow him to trample the law and escape unscathed.
Even Bruce -- whose wealth exceeds Luthor's -- couldn't work the system with such reckless disregard.
But... the most painful victory he would ever take from me...
...was his election to the office of the President.
The land I love.
AND THEN... TO GET A CALL TO COME WORK FOR THE PRESIDENT OF THE UNITED STATES...

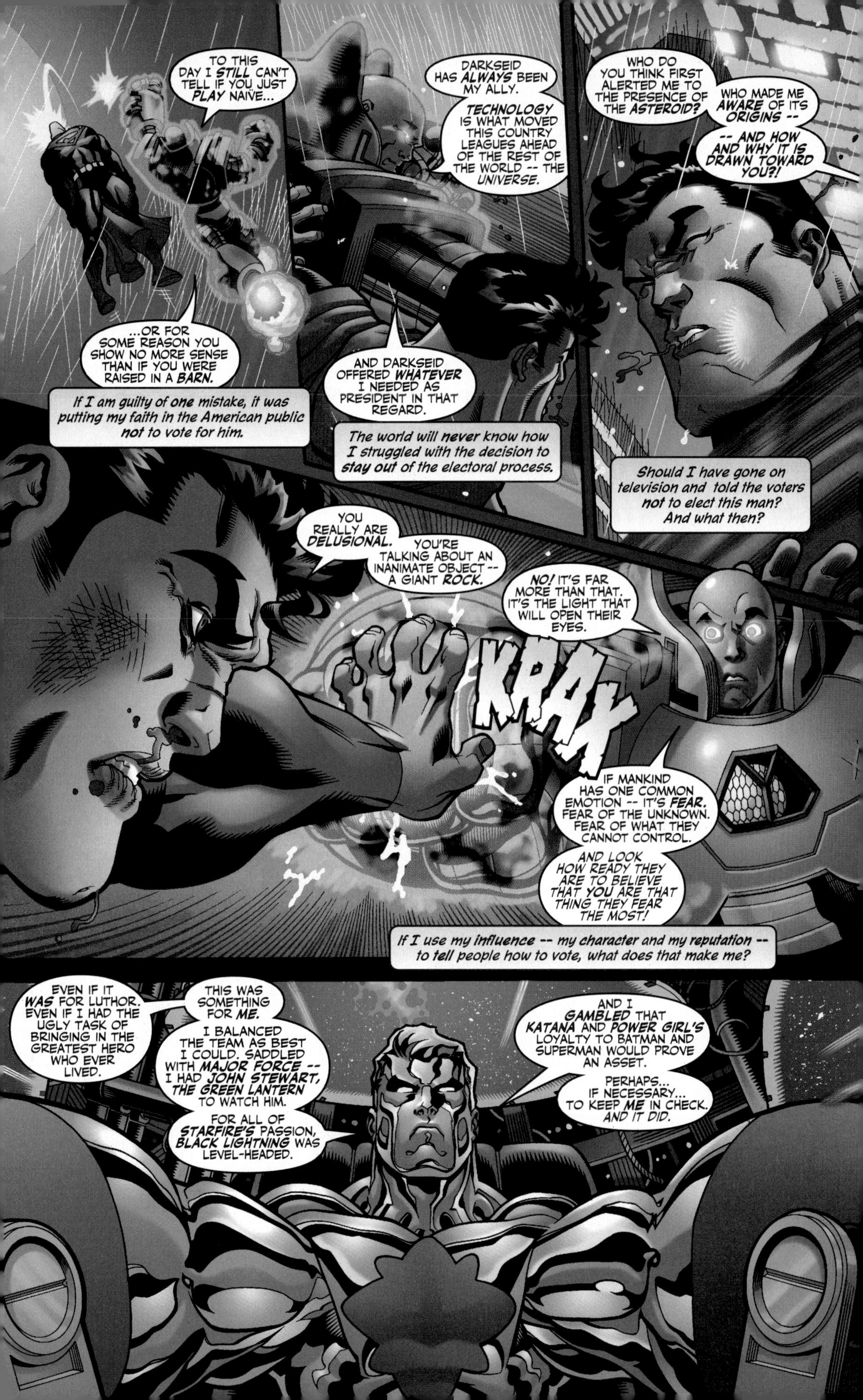

TO THIS DAY I STILL CAN'T TELL IF YOU JUST PLAY NAÏVE...
...OR FOR SOME REASON YOU SHOW NO MORE SENSE THAN IF YOU WERE RAISED IN A BARN.
If I am guilty of one mistake, it was putting my faith in the American public not to vote for him.
DARKSEID HAS ALWAYS BEEN MY ALLY.
TECHNOLOGY IS WHAT MOVED THIS COUNTRY LEAGUES AHEAD OF THE REST OF THE WORLD -- THE UNIVERSE.
AND DARKSEID OFFERED WHATEVER I NEEDED AS PRESIDENT IN THAT REGARD.
The world will never know how I struggled with the decision to stay out of the electoral process.
WHO DO YOU THINK FIRST ALERTED ME TO THE PRESENCE OF THE ASTEROID?
WHO MADE ME AWARE OF ITS ORIGINS --
-- AND HOW AND WHY IT IS DRAWN TOWARD YOU?!
Should I have gone on television and told the voters not to elect this man? And what then?
YOU REALLY ARE DELUSIONAL.
YOU'RE TALKING ABOUT AN INANIMATE OBJECT -- A GIANT ROCK.
NO! IT'S FAR MORE THAN THAT. IT'S THE LIGHT THAT WILL OPEN THEIR EYES.
KRAK
IF MANKIND HAS ONE COMMON EMOTION -- IT'S FEAR. FEAR OF THE UNKNOWN. FEAR OF WHAT THEY CANNOT CONTROL.
AND LOOK HOW READY THEY ARE TO BELIEVE THAT YOU ARE THAT THING THEY FEAR THE MOST!
If I use my influence -- my character and my reputation -- to tell people how to vote, what does that make me?
EVEN IF IT WAS FOR LUTHOR. EVEN IF I HAD THE UGLY TASK OF BRINGING IN THE GREATEST HERO WHO EVER LIVED.
THIS WAS SOMETHING FOR ME.
I BALANCED THE TEAM AS BEST I COULD. SADDLED WITH MAJOR FORCE -- I HAD JOHN STEWART, THE GREEN LANTERN TO WATCH HIM.
FOR ALL OF STARFIRE'S PASSION, BLACK LIGHTNING WAS LEVEL-HEADED.
AND I GAMBLED THAT KATANA AND POWER GIRL'S LOYALTY TO BATMAN AND SUPERMAN WOULD PROVE AN ASSET.
PERHAPS... IF NECESSARY... TO KEEP ME IN CHECK. AND IT DID.

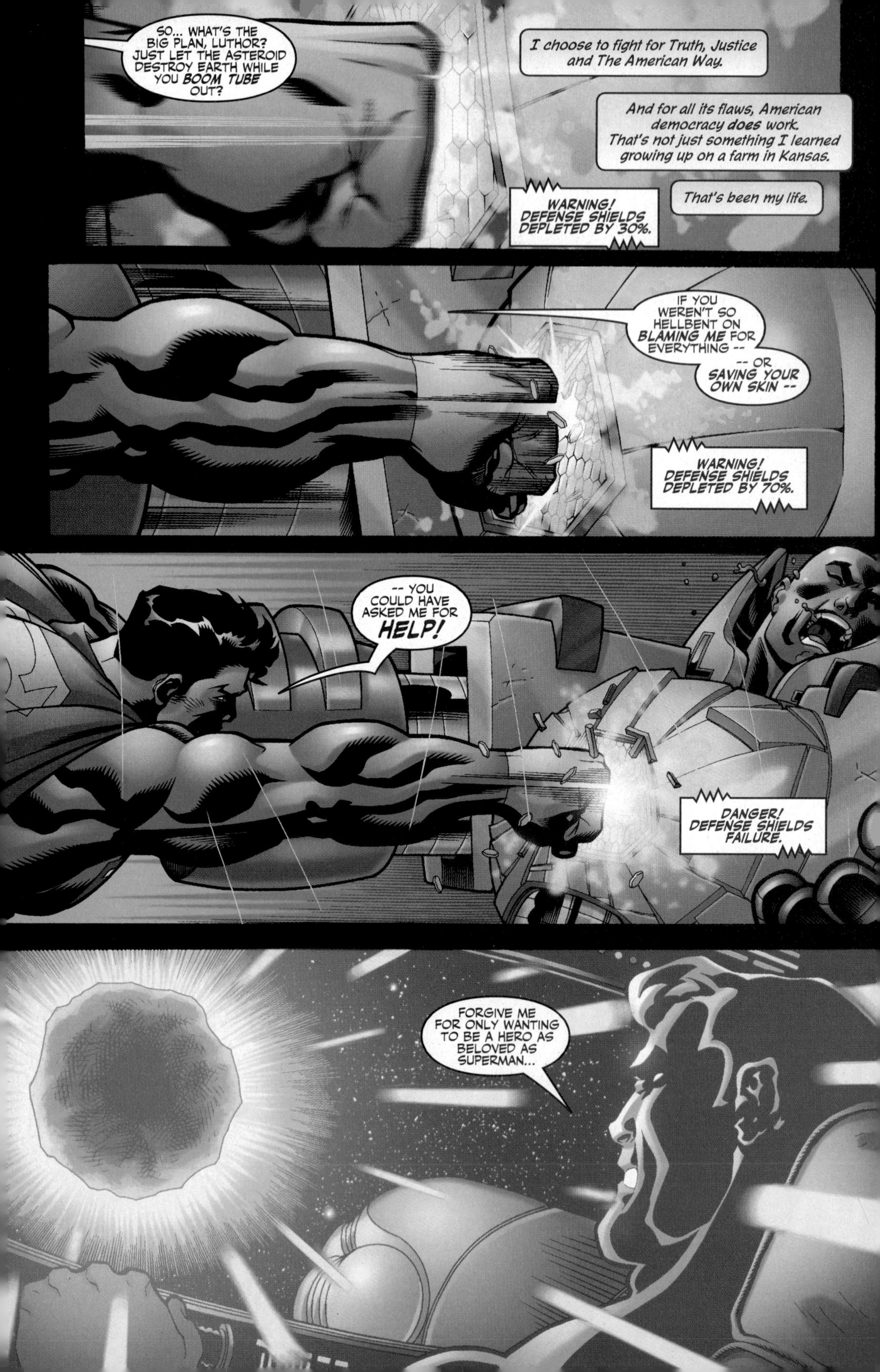
SO... WHAT'S THE BIG PLAN, LUTHOR? JUST LET THE ASTEROID DESTROY EARTH WHILE YOU BOOM TUBE OUT?
I choose to fight for Truth, Justice and The American Way.
And for all its flaws, American democracy does work. That's not just something I learned growing up on a farm in Kansas.
That's been my life.
WARNING! DEFENSE SHIELDS DEPLETED BY 30%.
IF YOU WEREN'T SO HELLBENT ON BLAMING ME FOR EVERYTHING --
-- OR SAVING YOUR OWN SKIN --
WARNING! DEFENSE SHIELDS DEPLETED BY 70%.
-- YOU COULD HAVE ASKED ME FOR HELP!
DANGER! DEFENSE SHIELDS FAILURE.
FORGIVE ME FOR ONLY WANTING TO BE A HERO AS BELOVED AS SUPERMAN...

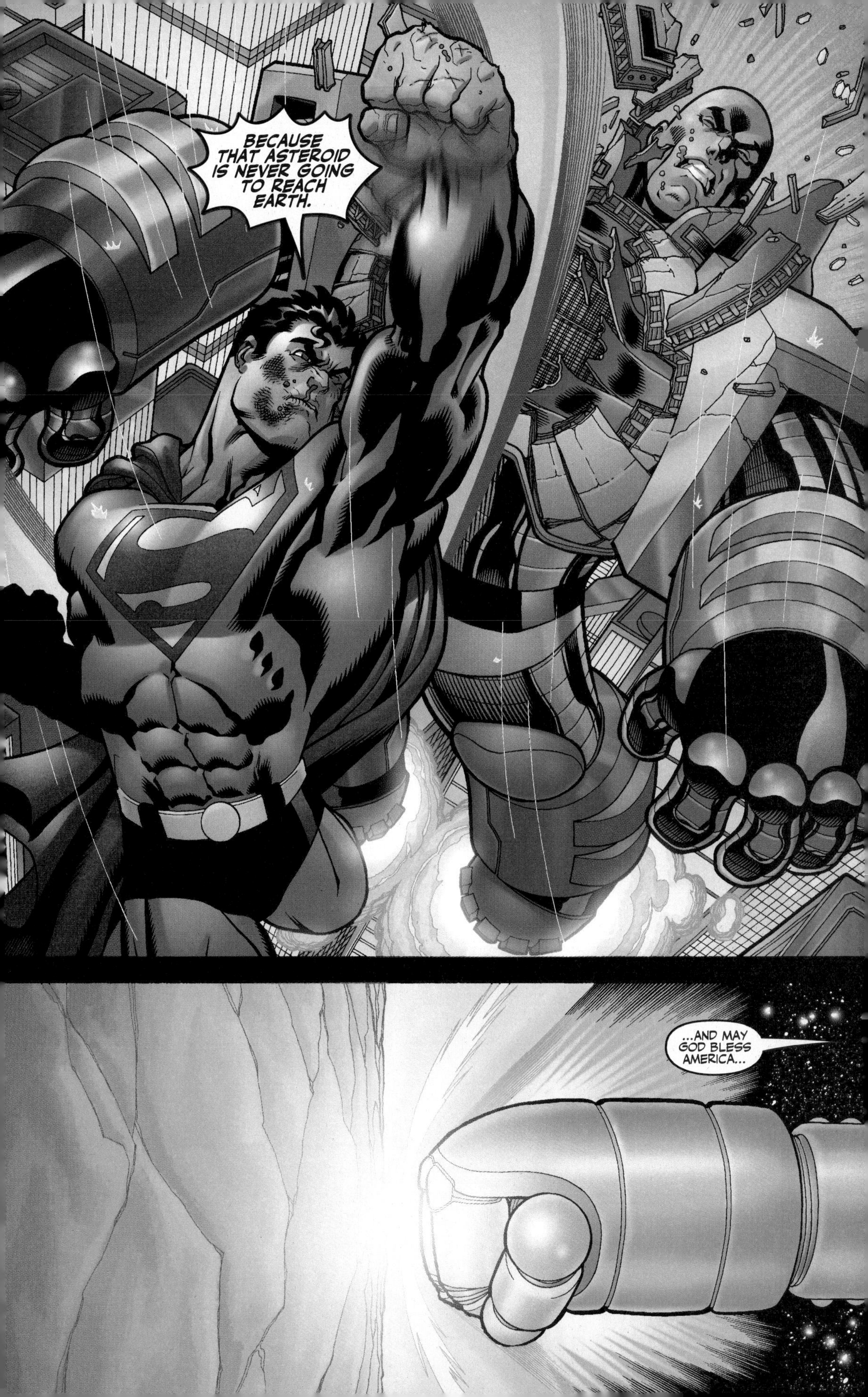
BECAUSE THAT ASTEROID IS NEVER GOING TO REACH EARTH.
...AND MAY GOD BLESS AMERICA...

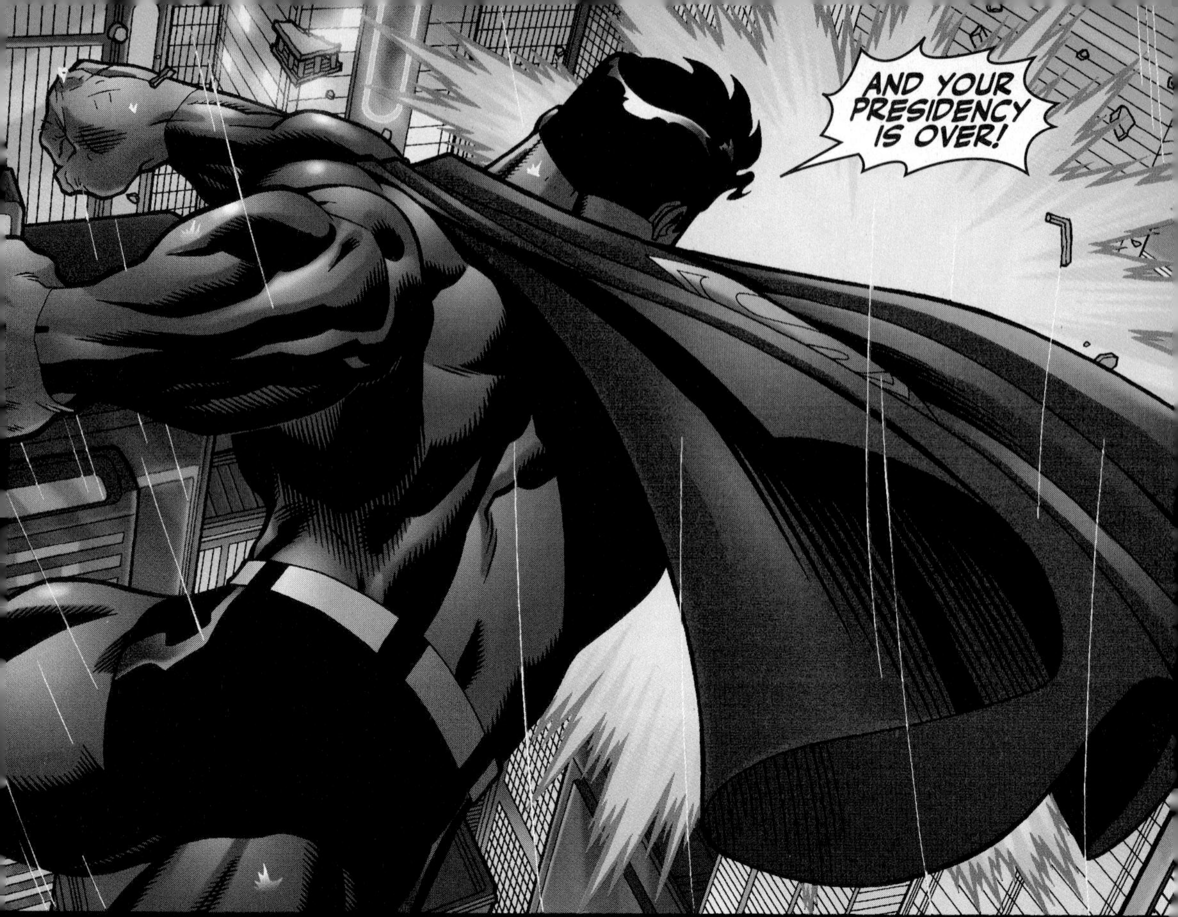
AND YOUR PRESIDENCY IS OVER!

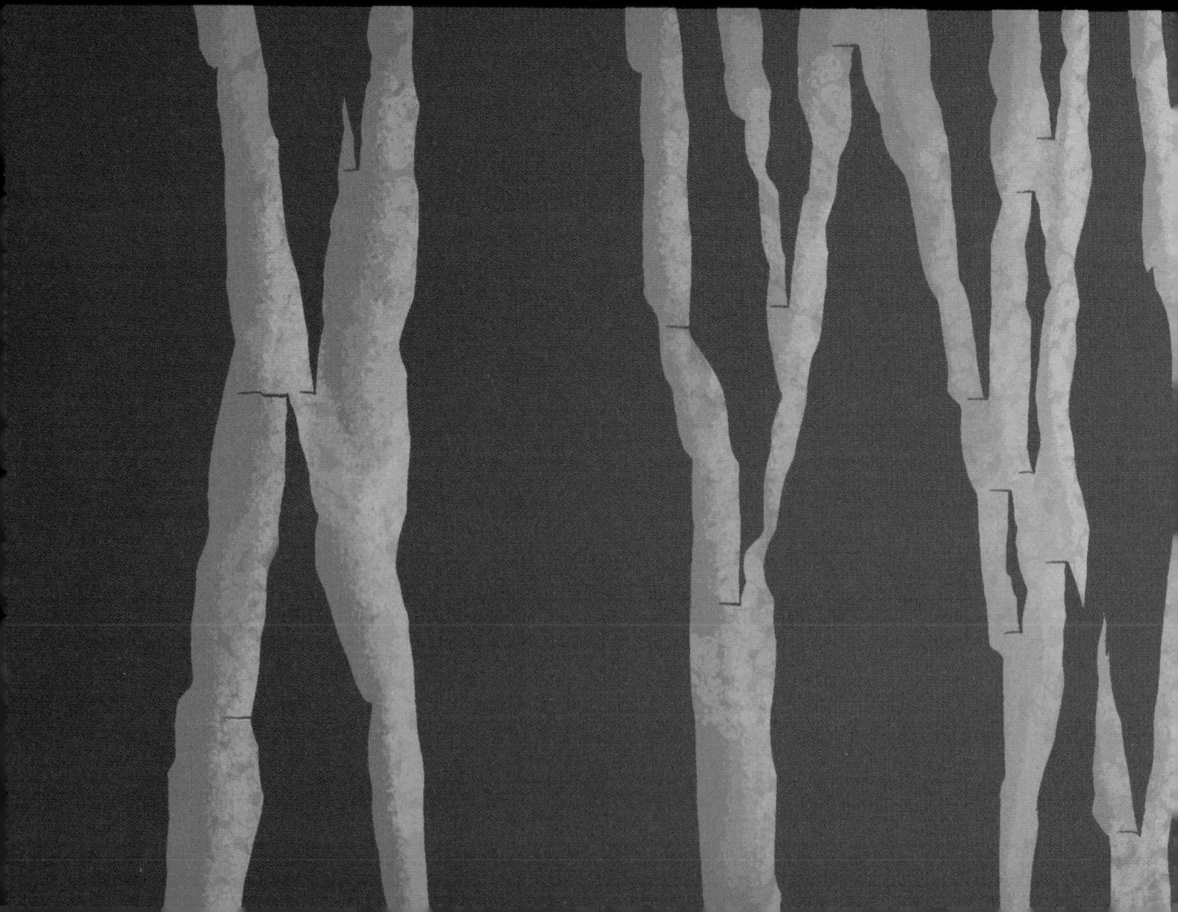

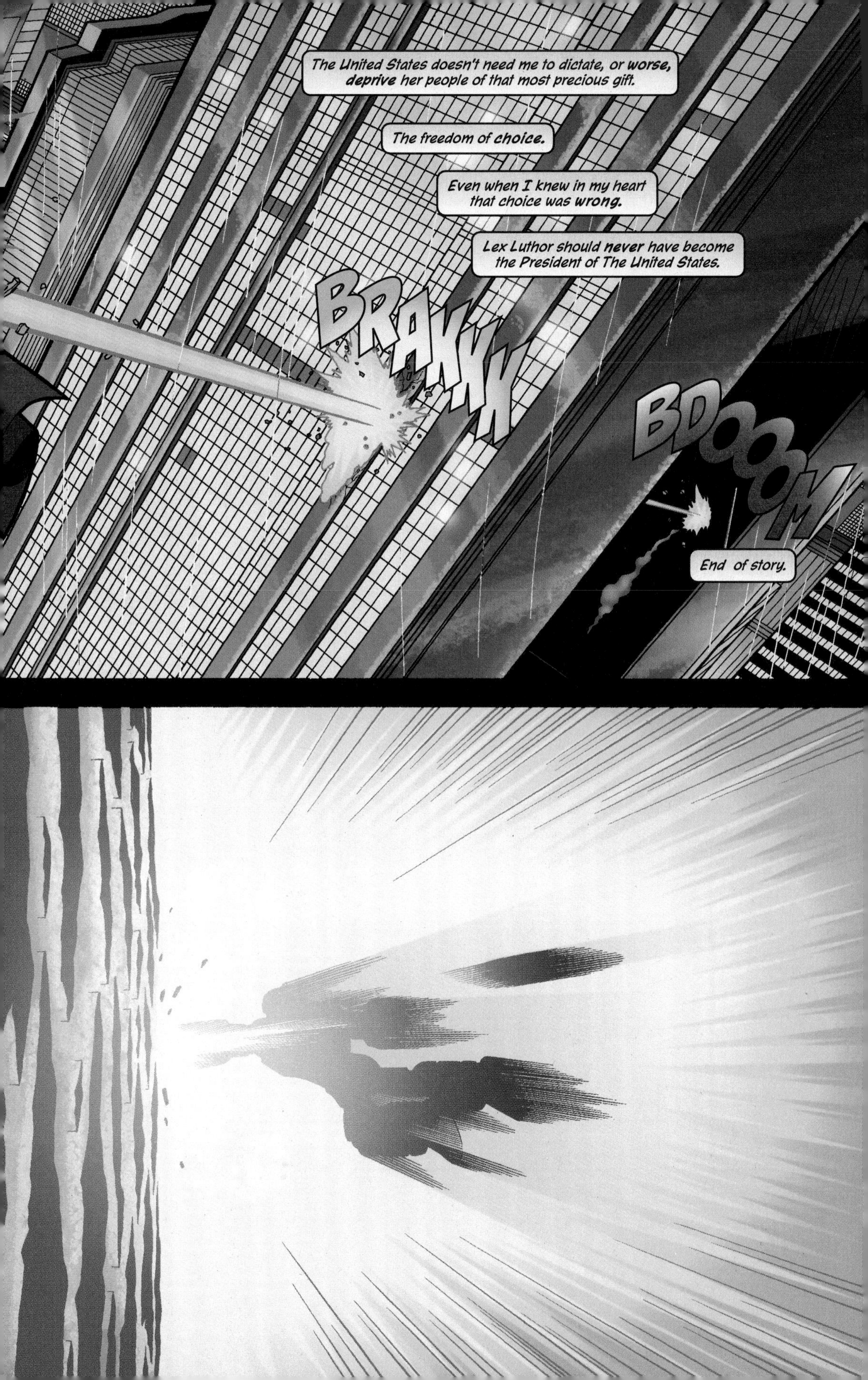
The United States doesn't need me to dictate, or worse, deprive her people of that most precious gift.
The freedom of choice.
Even when I knew in my heart that choice was wrong.
Lex Luthor should never have become the President of The United States.
BRAKKKK
BDOOOOM
End of story.

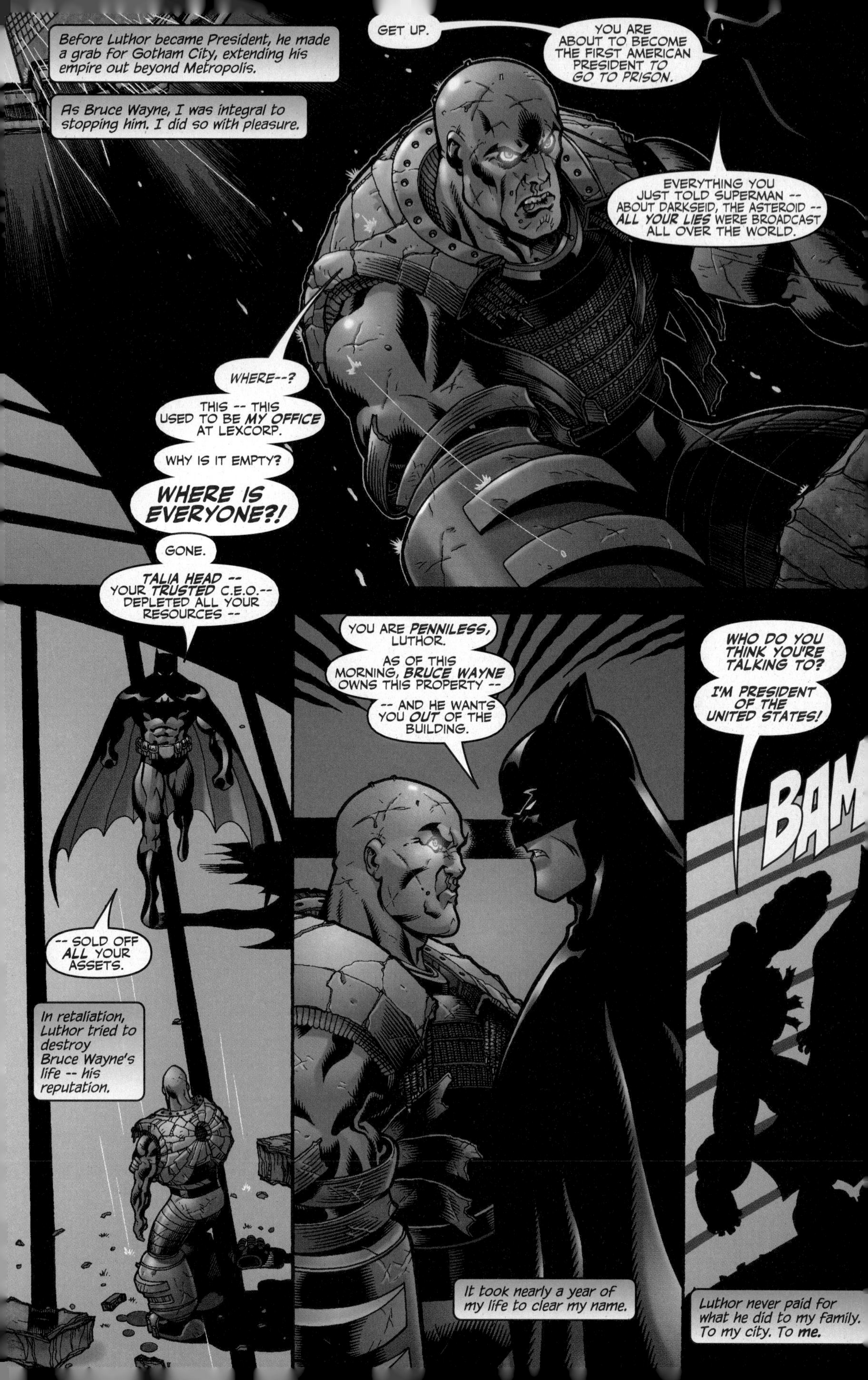
Before Luthor became President, he made a grab for Gotham City, extending his empire out beyond Metropolis.
As Bruce Wayne, I was integral to stopping him. I did so with pleasure.
GET UP.
YOU ARE ABOUT TO BECOME THE FIRST AMERICAN PRESIDENT TO GO TO PRISON.
EVERYTHING YOU JUST TOLD SUPERMAN -- ABOUT DARKSEID, THE ASTEROID -- ALL YOUR LIES WERE BROADCAST ALL OVER THE WORLD.
WHERE--?
THIS -- THIS USED TO BE MY OFFICE AT LEXCORP.
WHY IS IT EMPTY?
WHERE IS EVERYONE?!
GONE.
TALIA HEAD -- YOUR TRUSTED C.E.O.-- DEPLETED ALL YOUR RESOURCES --
-- SOLD OFF ALL YOUR ASSETS.
In retaliation, Luthor tried to destroy Bruce Wayne's life -- his reputation.
YOU ARE PENNILESS, LUTHOR.
AS OF THIS MORNING, BRUCE WAYNE OWNS THIS PROPERTY --
-- AND HE WANTS YOU OUT OF THE BUILDING.
It took nearly a year of my life to clear my name.
WHO DO YOU THINK YOU'RE TALKING TO?
I'M PRESIDENT OF THE UNITED STATES!
BAM
Luthor never paid for what he did to my family. To my city. To me.

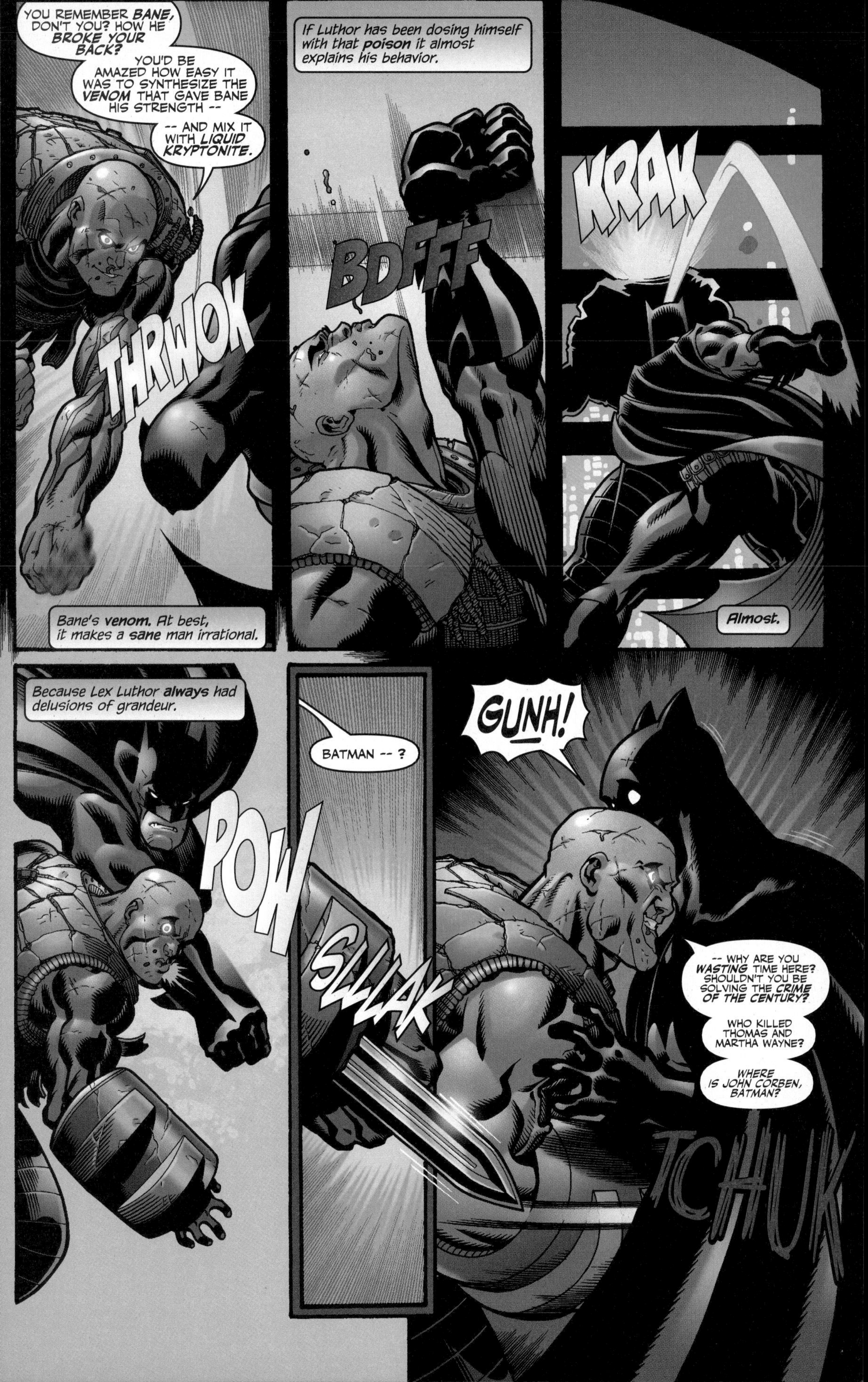

YOU REMEMBER BANE, DON'T YOU? HOW HE BROKE YOUR BACK?
YOU'D BE AMAZED HOW EASY IT WAS TO SYNTHESIZE THE VENOM THAT GAVE BANE HIS STRENGTH --
-- AND MIX IT WITH LIQUID KRYPTONITE.
THRWOK
Bane's venom. At best, it makes a sane man irrational.
If Luthor has been dosing himself with that poison it almost explains his behavior.
BDFFF
KRAK
Almost.
Because Lex Luthor always had delusions of grandeur.
POW
BATMAN -- ?
SLLLAK
GUNH!
-- WHY ARE YOU WASTING TIME HERE? SHOULDN'T YOU BE SOLVING THE CRIME OF THE CENTURY?
WHO KILLED THOMAS AND MARTHA WAYNE?
WHERE IS JOHN CORBEN, BATMAN?
TCHUK

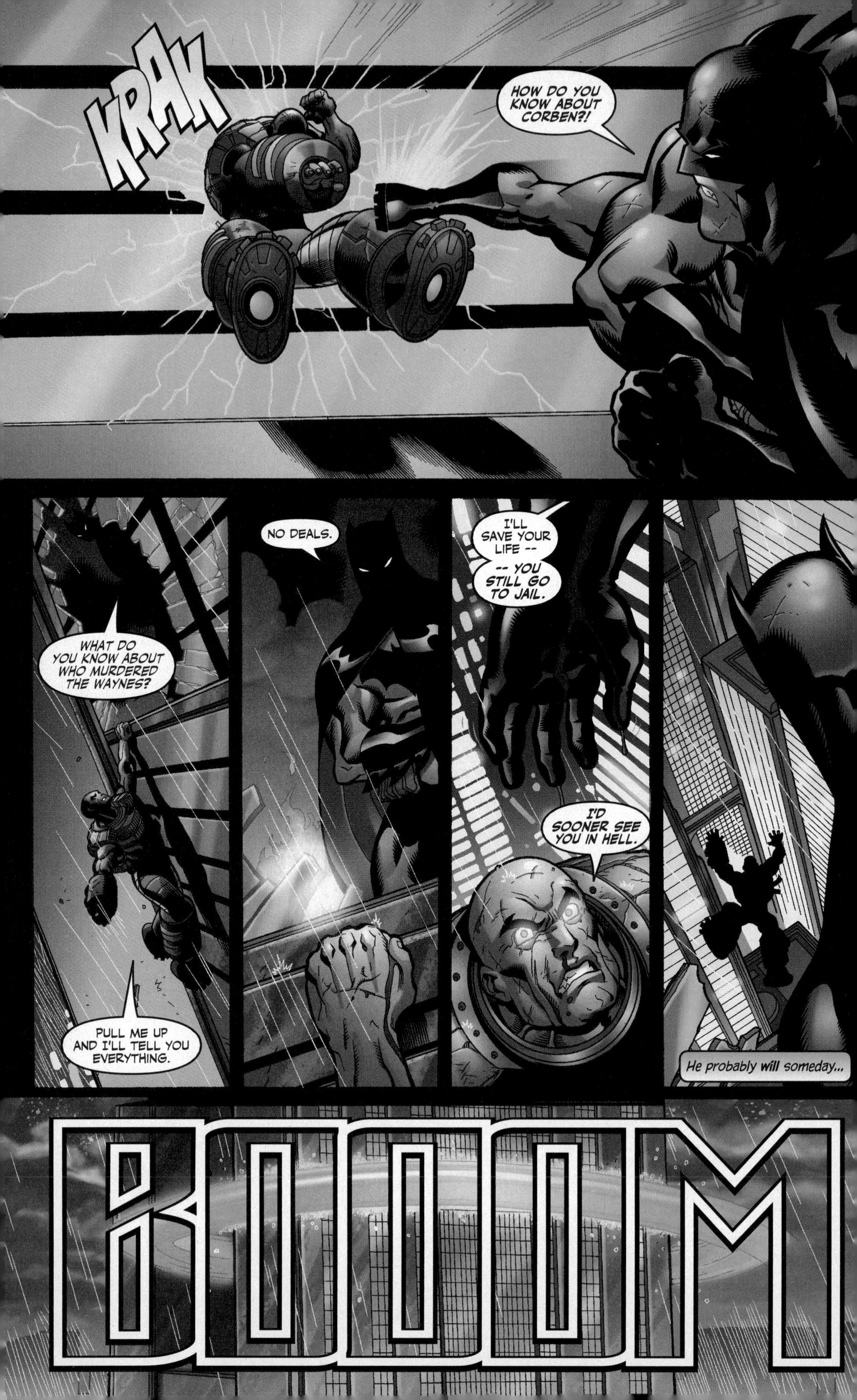
KRAK
HOW DO YOU KNOW ABOUT CORBEN?!
WHAT DO YOU KNOW ABOUT WHO MURDERED THE WAYNES?
PULL ME UP AND I'LL TELL YOU EVERYTHING.
NO DEALS.
I'LL SAVE YOUR LIFE --
-- YOU STILL GO TO JAIL.
I'D SOONER SEE YOU IN HELL.
He probably will someday...
BOOOM

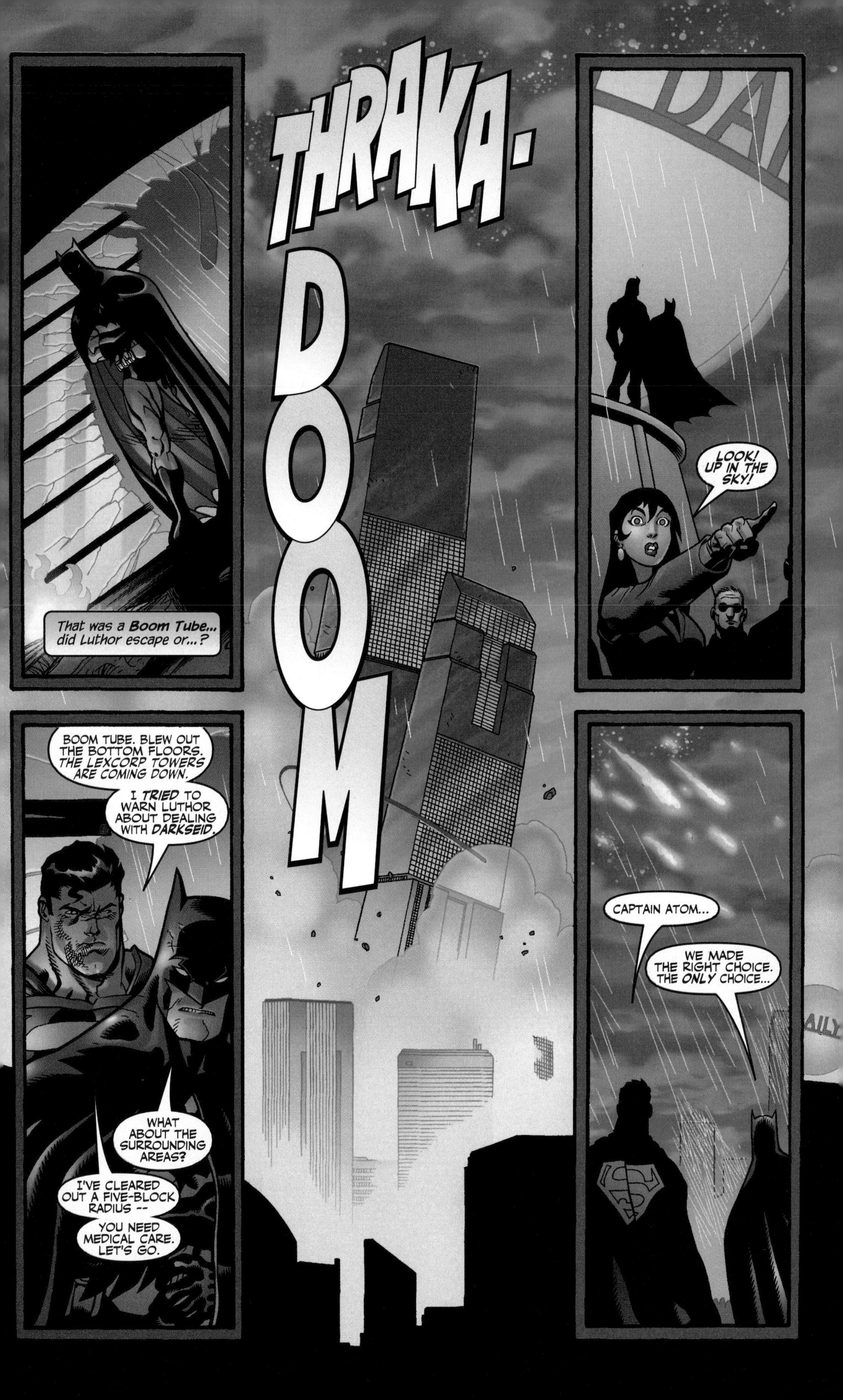
THRAKA-DOOM
That was a Boom Tube... did Luthor escape or...?
LOOK! UP IN THE SKY!
BOOM TUBE. BLEW OUT THE BOTTOM FLOORS. THE LEXCORP TOWERS ARE COMING DOWN.
I TRIED TO WARN LUTHOR ABOUT DEALING WITH DARKSEID.
WHAT ABOUT THE SURROUNDING AREAS?
I'VE CLEARED OUT A FIVE-BLOCK RADIUS --
YOU NEED MEDICAL CARE. LET'S GO.
CAPTAIN ATOM...
WE MADE THE RIGHT CHOICE. THE ONLY CHOICE...

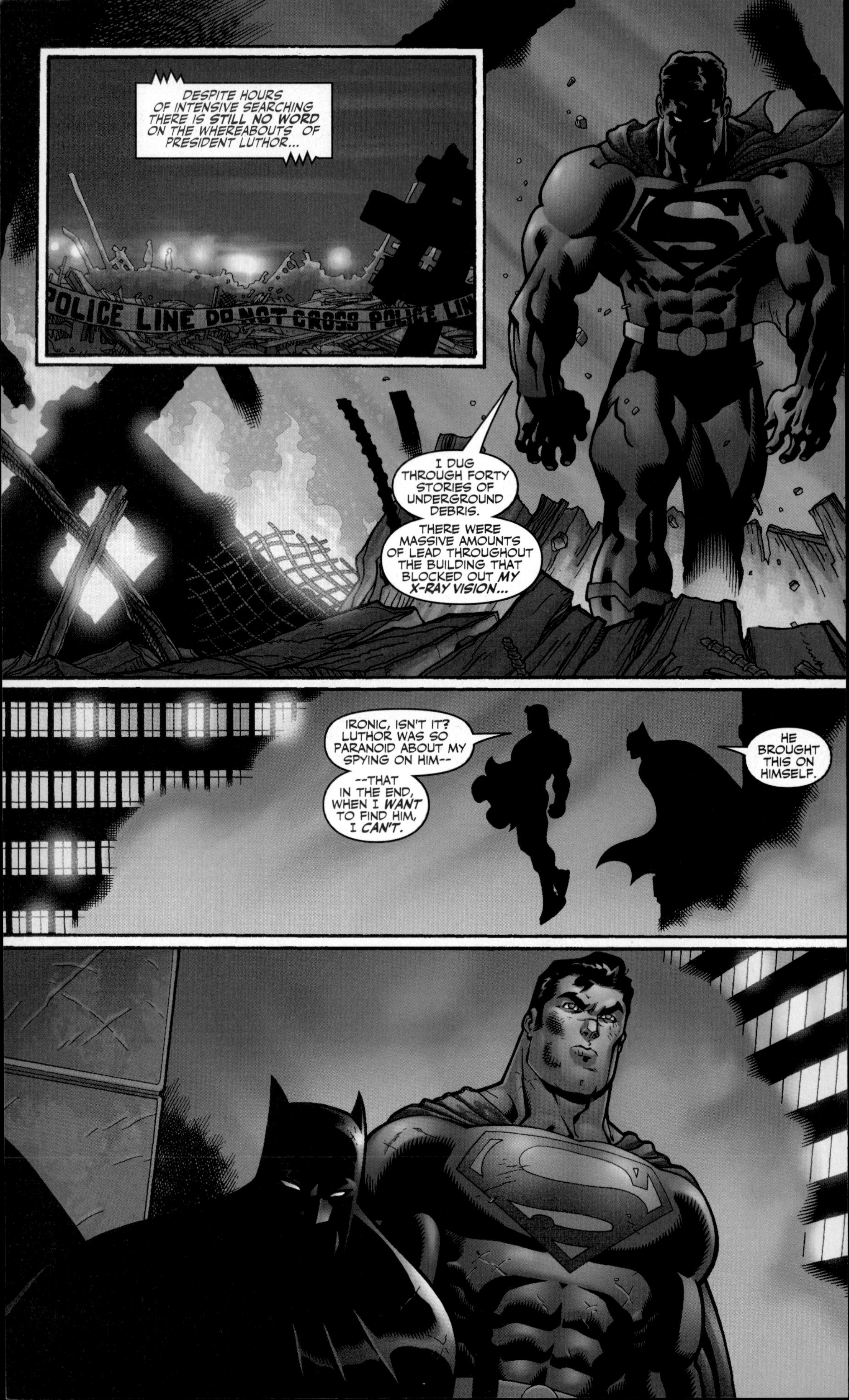
DESPITE HOURS OF INTENSIVE SEARCHING THERE IS STILL NO WORD ON THE WHEREABOUTS OF PRESIDENT LUTHOR...
POLICE LINE DO NOT CROSS POLICE LIN
I DUG THROUGH FORTY STORIES OF UNDERGROUND DEBRIS.
THERE WERE MASSIVE AMOUNTS OF LEAD THROUGHOUT THE BUILDING THAT BLOCKED OUT MY X-RAY VISION...
IRONIC, ISN'T IT? LUTHOR WAS SO PARANOID ABOUT MY SPYING ON HIM--
--THAT IN THE END, WHEN I WANT TO FIND HIM, I CAN'T.
HE BROUGHT THIS ON HIMSELF.

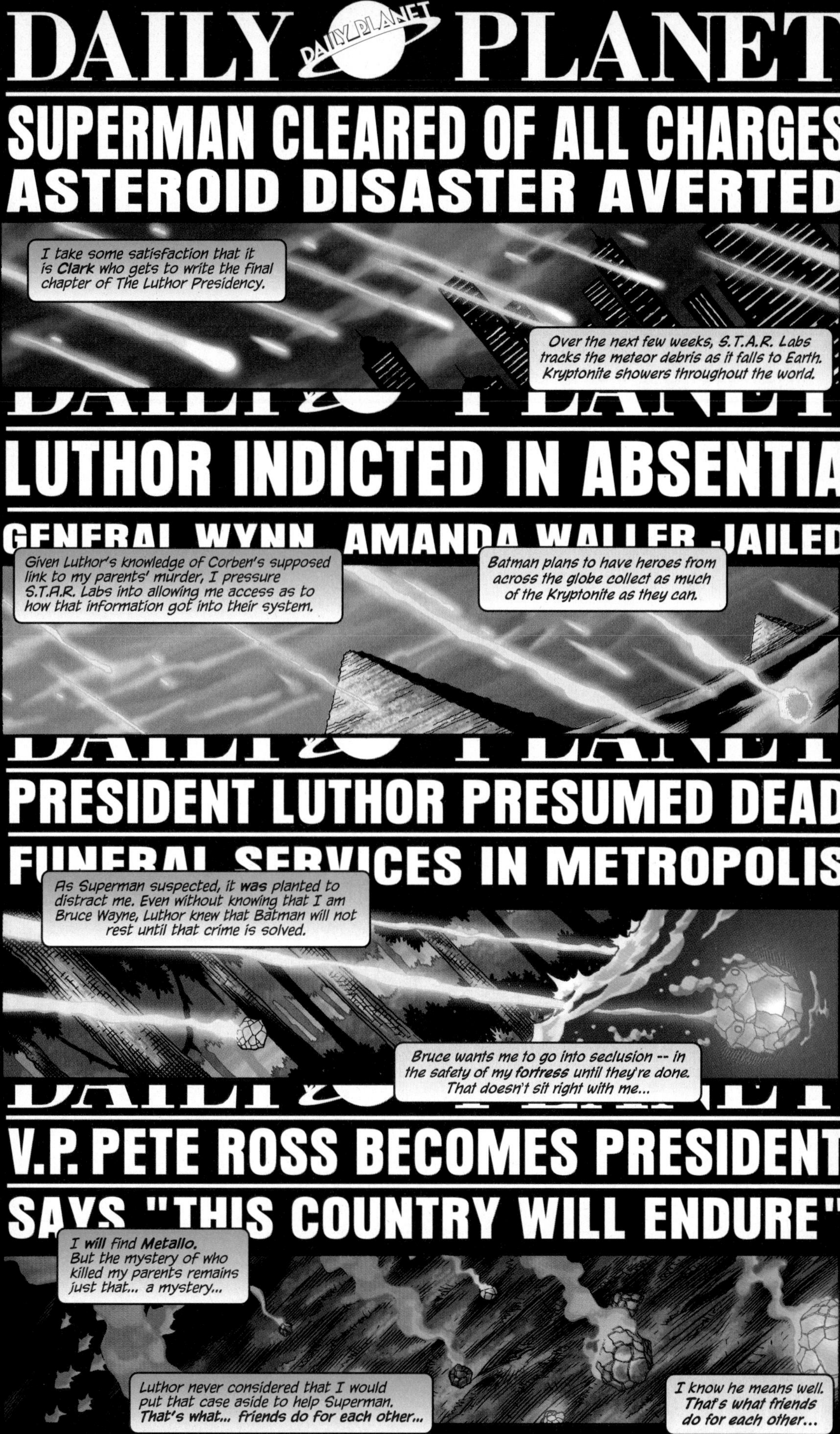
DAILY PLANET
DAILY PLANET
SUPERMAN CLEARED OF ALL CHARGES
ASTEROID DISASTER AVERTED
I take some satisfaction that it is Clark who gets to write the final chapter of The Luthor Presidency.
Over the next few weeks, S.T.A.R. Labs tracks the meteor debris as it falls to Earth. Kryptonite showers throughout the world.
LUTHOR INDICTED IN ABSENTIA
GENERAL WYNN, AMANDA WALLER JAILED
Given Luthor's knowledge of Corben's supposed link to my parents' murder, I pressure S.T.A.R. Labs into allowing me access as to how that information got into their system.
Batman plans to have heroes from across the globe collect as much of the Kryptonite as they can.
PRESIDENT LUTHOR PRESUMED DEAD
FUNERAL SERVICES IN METROPOLIS
As Superman suspected, it was planted to distract me. Even without knowing that I am Bruce Wayne, Luthor knew that Batman will not rest until that crime is solved.
Bruce wants me to go into seclusion -- in the safety of my fortress until they're done. That doesn't sit right with me...
V.P. PETE ROSS BECOMES PRESIDENT
SAYS "THIS COUNTRY WILL ENDURE"
I will find Metallo. But the mystery of who killed my parents remains just that... a mystery...
Luthor never considered that I would put that case aside to help Superman. That's what... friends do for each other...
I know he means well. That's what friends do for each other...

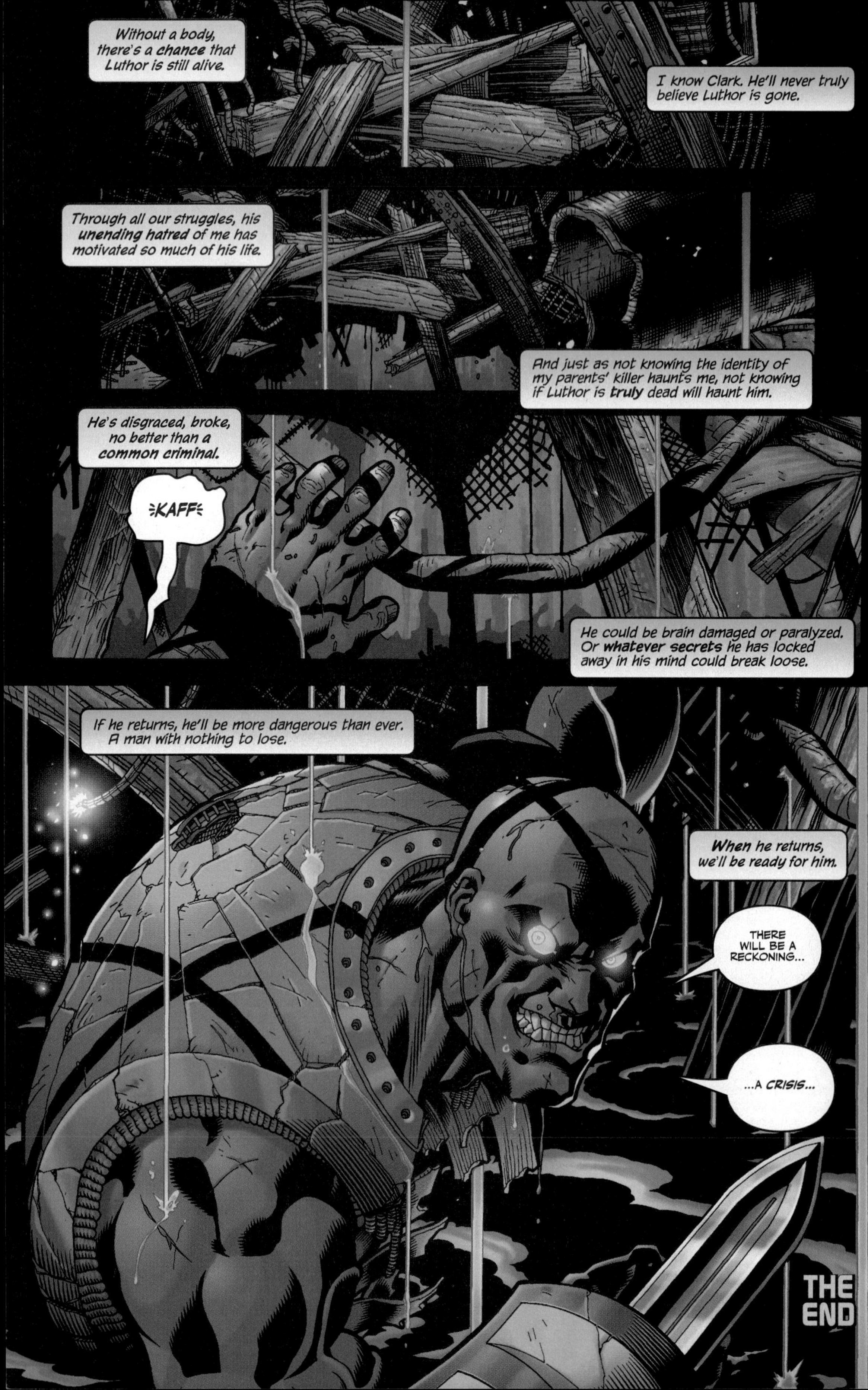
Without a body, there's a chance that Luthor is still alive.
I know Clark. He'll never truly believe Luthor is gone.
Through all our struggles, his unending hatred of me has motivated so much of his life.
And just as not knowing the identity of my parents' killer haunts me, not knowing if Luthor is truly dead will haunt him.
He's disgraced, broke, no better than a common criminal.
KAFF
He could be brain damaged or paralyzed. Or whatever secrets he has locked away in his mind could break loose.
If he returns, he'll be more dangerous than ever. A man with nothing to lose.
When he returns, we'll be ready for him.
THERE WILL BE A RECKONING...
...A CRISIS...
THE END

SKETCHES ED McGUINNESS

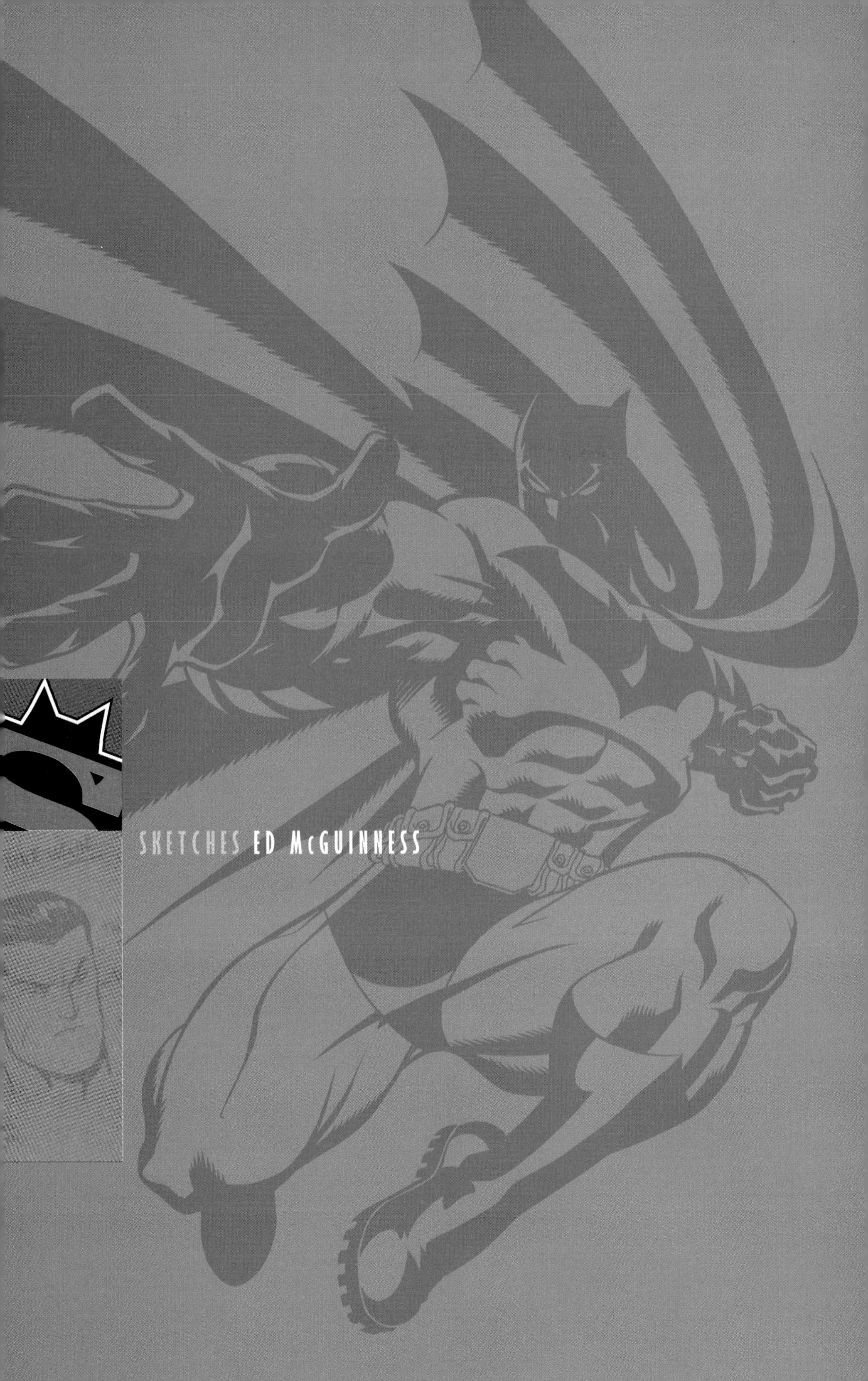

Early variant pose of Batman for front cover.

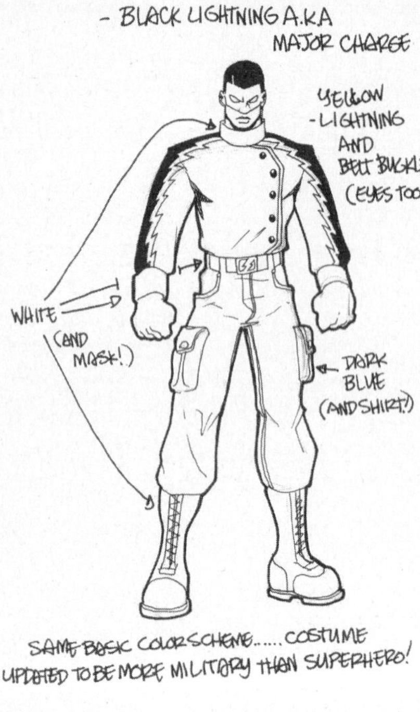

- BLACK LIGHTNING A.K.A
MAJOR CHARGE
YELLOW
- LIGHTNING
AND
BELT BUCKLE
(EYES TOO!)
WHITE
(AND
MASK!)
DARK
BLUE
(AND SHIRT!)
SAME BASIC COLOR SCHEME...... COSTUME
UPDATED TO BE MORE MILITARY THAN SUPERHERO!

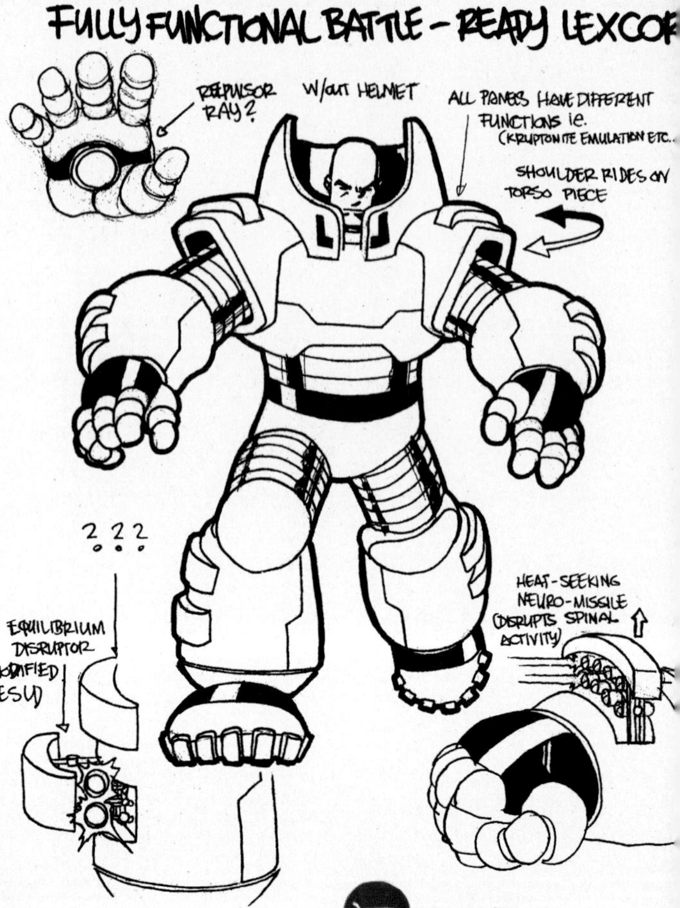

FULLY FUNCTIONAL BATTLE - READY LEXCOR
REPULSOR
RAY?
W/OUT HELMET
ALL PANELS HAVE DIFFERENT
FUNCTIONS i.e.
(KRYPTONITE EMULATION ETC..
SHOULDER RIDES ON
TORSO PIECE
? ? ?
EQUILIBRIUM
DISRUPTOR
MODIFIED
ESU
HEAT-SEEKING
NEURO-MISSILE
(DISRUPTS SPINAL
ACTIVITY)

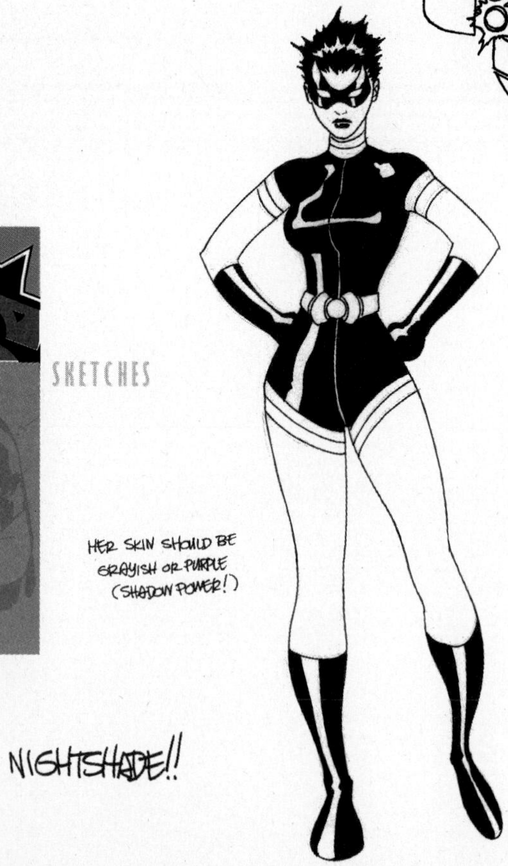

HER SKIN SHOULD BE
GRAYISH OR PURPLE
(SHADOW POWER!)
NIGHTSHADE!!

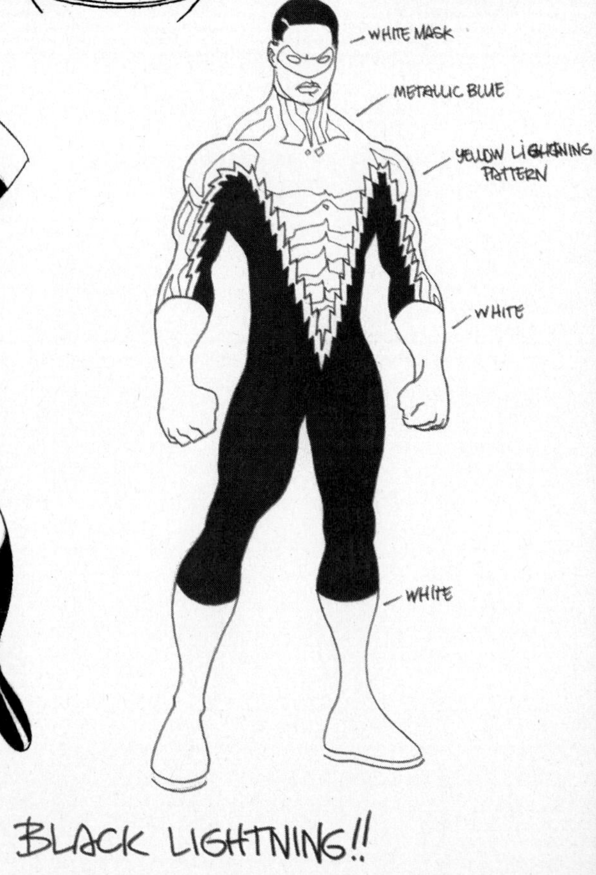

WHITE MASK
METALLIC BLUE
YELLOW LIGHTNING
PATTERN
WHITE
WHITE
BLACK LIGHTNING!!

Early drawing of older Superman (modeled after the version seen in KINGDOM COME).

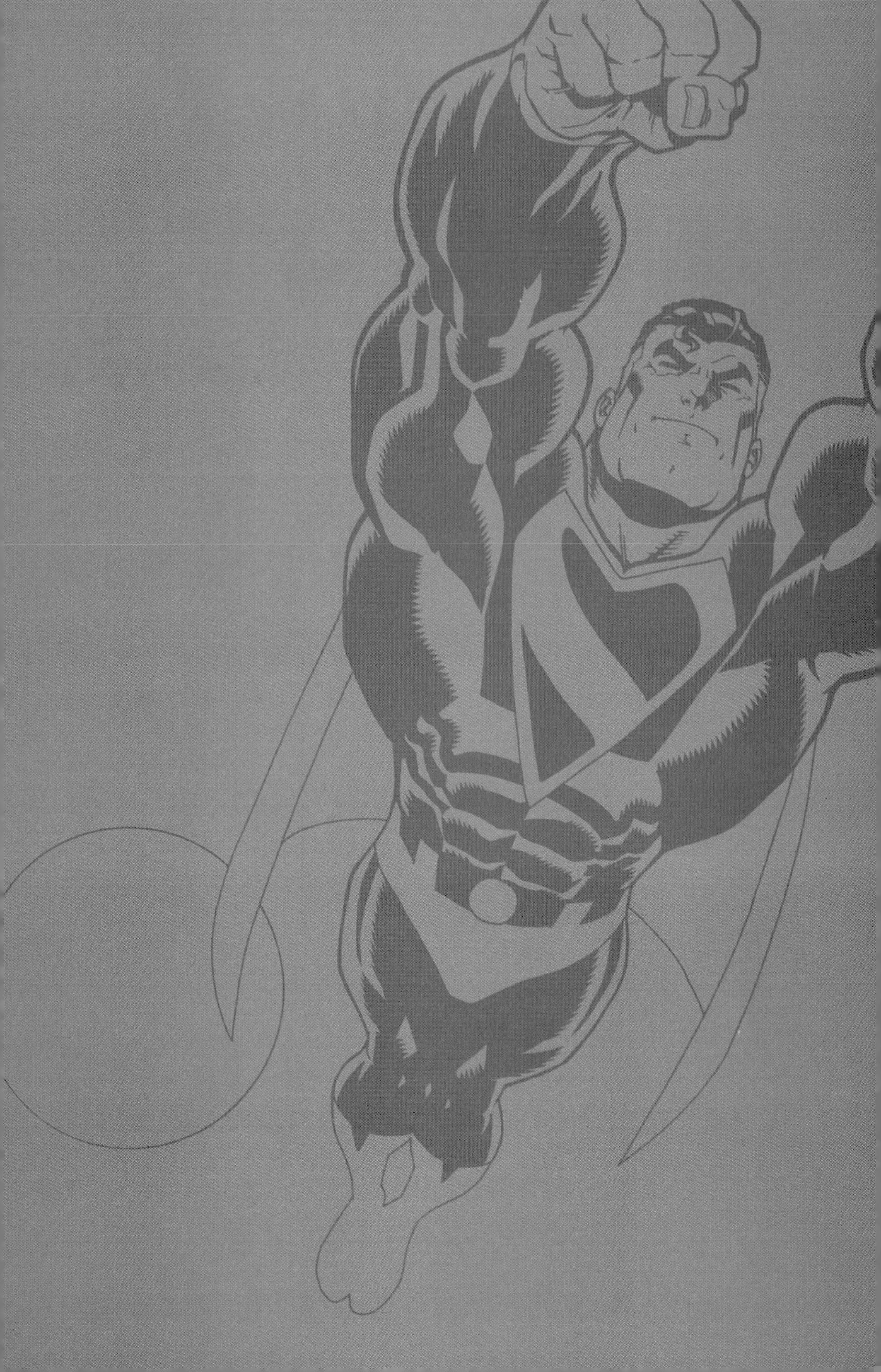

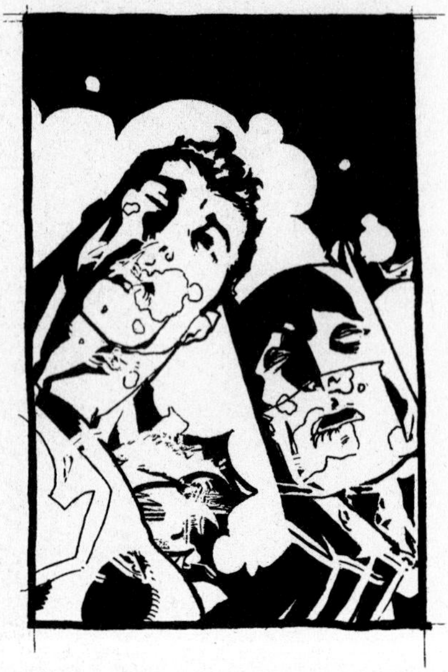

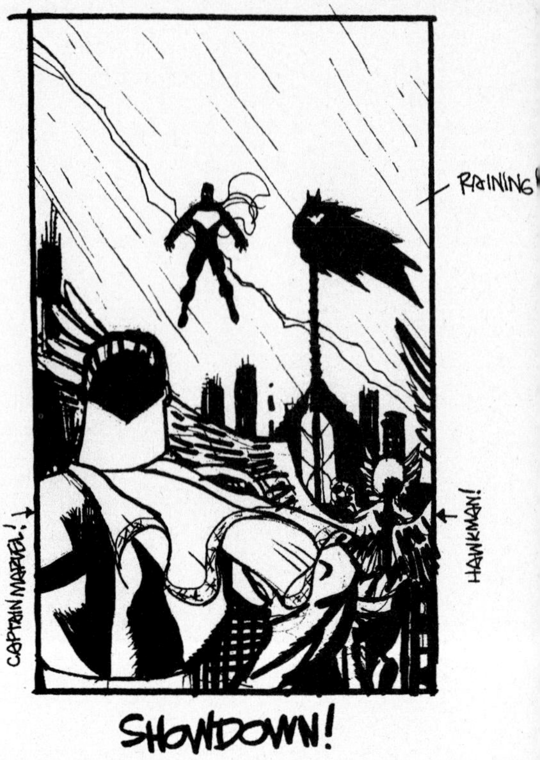
RAINING!
CAPTAIN MARVEL!
HAWKMAN!
SHOWDOWN!

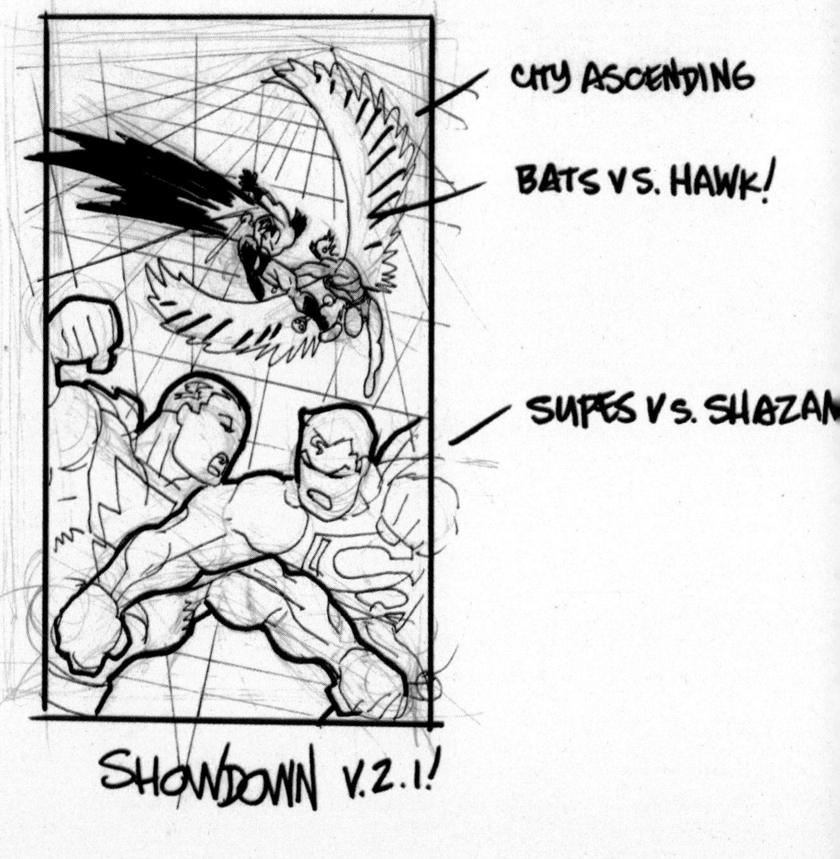
CITY ASCENDING
BATS VS. HAWK!
SUPES VS. SHAZAM
SHOWDOWN V.2.1!

Alternative cover sketches for issues #2 and #4.

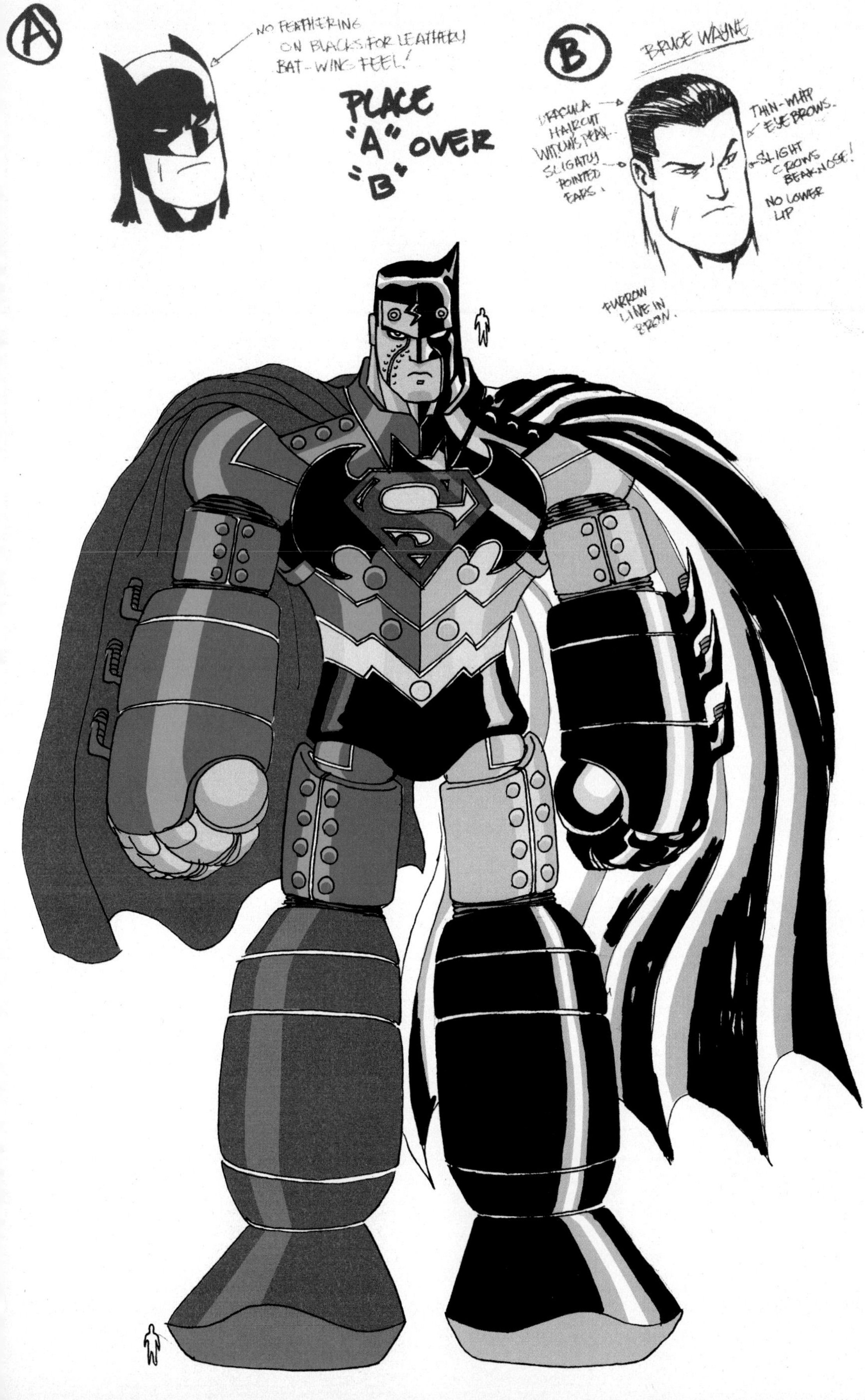
A
NO FEATHERING ON BLACKS FOR LEATHERY BAT-WING FEEL!
PLACE "A" OVER "B"
B
BRUCE WAYNE
DRACULA HAIRCUT WIDOW'S PEAK.
SLIGHTLY POINTED EARS.
THIN-WHIP EYEBROWS.
SLIGHT CROWS BEAK NOSE!
NO LOWER LIP
FURROW LINE IN BROW.

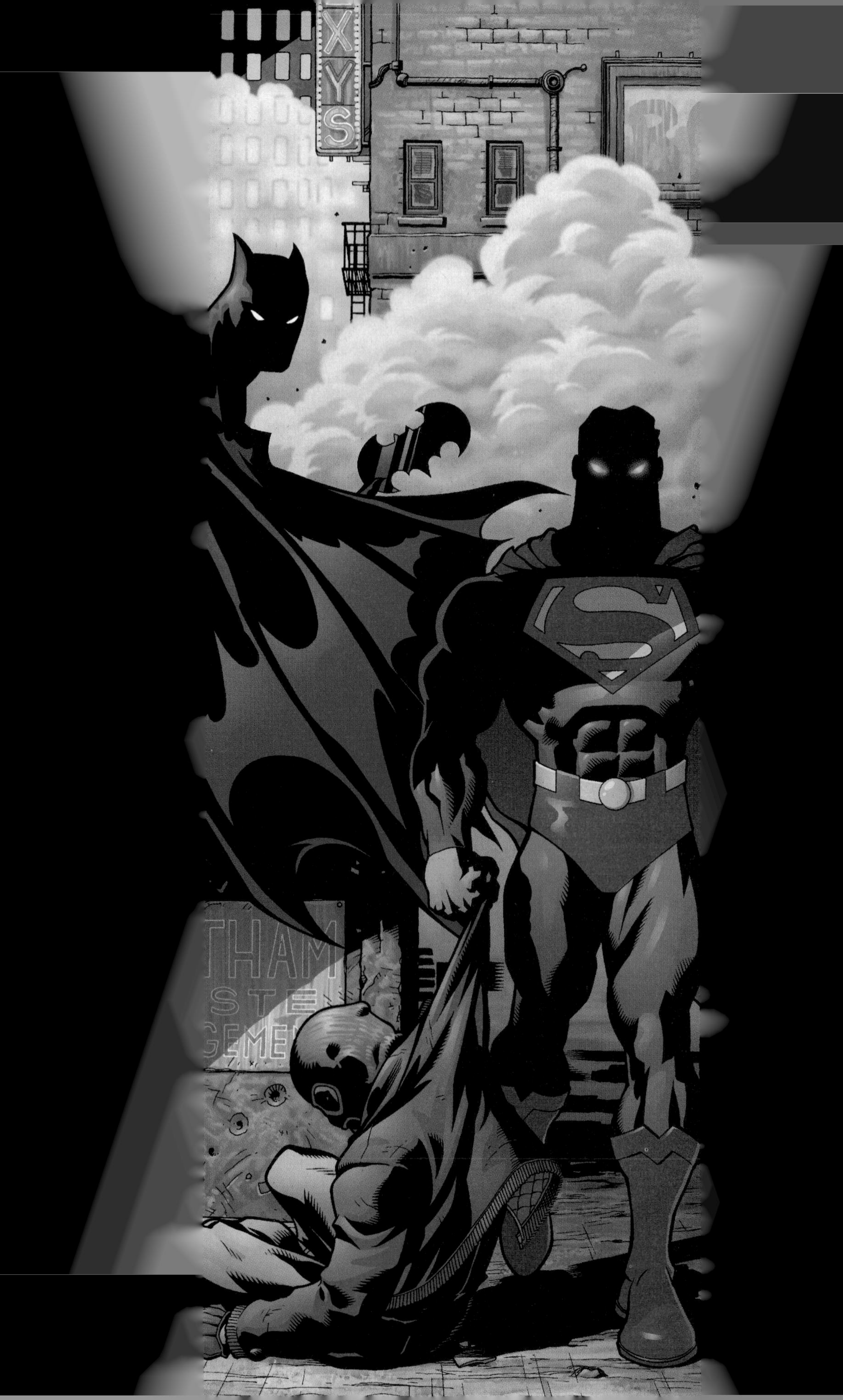

XYS
THAM
STE
GEMEN

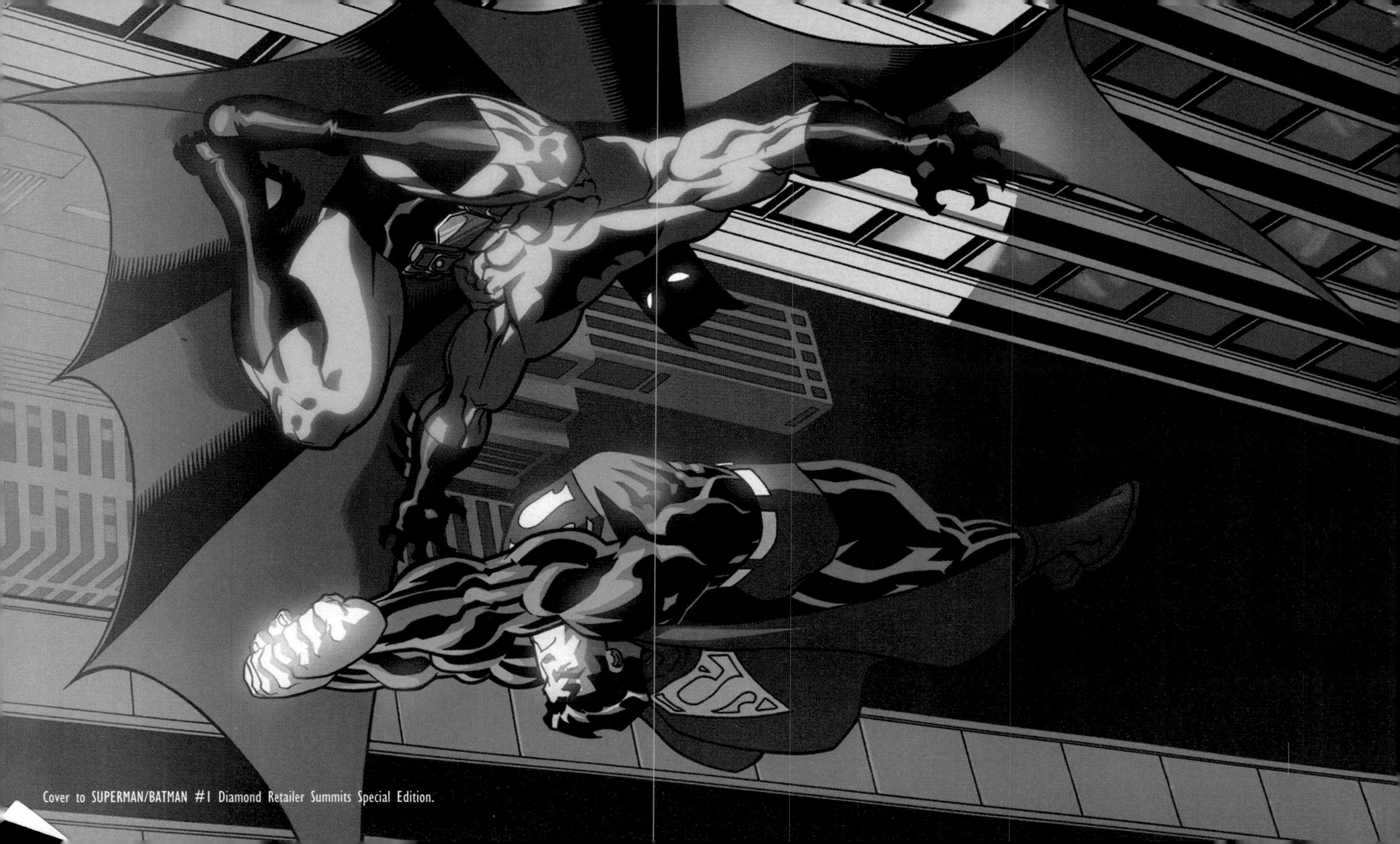

Cover to SUPERMAN/BATMAN #1 Diamond Retailer Summits Special Edition.

BIOGRAPHIES

JEPH LOEB is the author of BATMAN: THE LONG HALLOWEEN, BATMAN: DARK VICTORY, SUPERMAN FOR ALL SEASONS, CATWOMAN: WHEN IN ROME, CHALLENGERS OF THE UNKNOWN MUST DIE!, *Spider-Man: Blue, Daredevil: Yellow* and *Hulk: Gray* — all of which were collaborations with artist Tim Sale. He has also written SUPERMAN, THE WITCHING HOUR, *Cable, X-Man, X-Force,* and various other books. A writer/producer living in Los Angeles, his credits include *Teen Wolf, Commando* and *Smallville.*

ED McGUINNESS first gained the notice of comic-book fans with his work on *Deadpool* and *Vampirella.* His short run on WildStorm's MR. MAJESTIC landed him a gig on the monthly SUPERMAN title with Jeph Loeb, which led to the THUNDERCATS: RECLAIMING THUNDERA miniseries and arcs on SUPERMAN/BATMAN. He lives in Maine with his wife and four kids.

DEXTER VINES has been an inker in the comics industry for nearly a decade, having worked on numerous titles for various publishers, including *Uncanny X-Men, Weapon X* and *Wolverine* for Marvel Comics, *Meridian* for CrossGen Entertainment, and BATMAN: TENSES for DC.

DAVE STEWART began his career as an intern at Dark Horse Comics, and then quickly moved into coloring comics. His credits include DC: THE NEW FRONTIER, HUMAN TARGET: FINAL CUT, SUPERMAN/BATMAN/WONDER WOMAN: TRINITY, H-E-R-O, *Fray, Ultimate Fantastic Four, B.P.R.D.,* and *Hellboy: The Third Wish* (for which he won an Eisner and Harvey Award). He lives in Portland, Oregon.

RICHARD STARKINGS is best known as the creator of the Comicraft studio, purveyors of unique design and fine lettering — and a copious catalogue of comic-book fonts — since 1992. He is less well known as the creator and publisher of *Hip Flask* and his semi-autobiographical cartoon strip, *Hedge Backwards.*

TIM SALE is not only the artist for all the collaborations with Jeph Loeb listed above, but he has also worked on *Grendel, Wolverine/Gambit: Victims,* DEATHBLOW, BATMAN: LEGENDS OF THE DARK KNIGHT, and various other projects. He had the distinct honor of being the first creator chosen for the artist spotlight series SOLO.

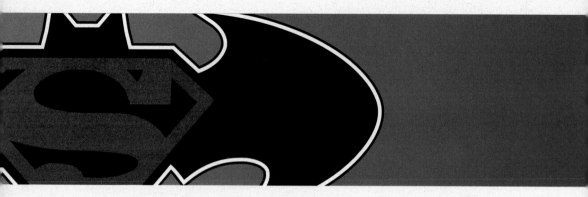

DAN DIDIO VP-Executive Editor EDDIE BERGANZA MATT IDELSON Editors-original series TOM PALMER, JR. Associate Editor-original series ANTON KAWASAKI Editor-collected edition
ROBBIN BROSTERMAN Senior Art Director PAUL LEVITZ President & Publisher GEORG BREWER VP-Design & DC Direct Creative RICHARD BRUNING Senior VP-Creative Director
PATRICK CALDON Senior VP-Finance & Operations CHRIS CARAMALIS VP-Finance TERRI CUNNINGHAM VP-Managing Editor STEPHANIE FIERMAN Senior VP-Sales & Marketing
ALISON GILL VP-Manufacturing RICH JOHNSON VP-Book Trade Sales HANK KANALZ VP-General Manager, WildStorm LILLIAN LASERSON Senior VP & General Counsel
JIM LEE Editorial Director-WildStorm PAULA LOWITT Senior VP-Business & Legal Affairs DAVID MCKILLIPS VP-Advertising & Custom Publishing JOHN NEE VP-Business Development
GREGORY NOVECK Senior VP-Creative Affairs CHERYL RUBIN Senior VP-Brand Management JEFF TROJAN VP-Business Development, DC Direct BOB WAYNE VP-Sales

SUPERMAN/BATMAN: PUBLIC ENEMIES

DC Comics, 1700 Broadway, New York, NY 10019. A Warner Bros. Entertainment Company. Printed in Canada. Fifth Printing. ISBN: 1-4012-0220-9. ISBN 13: 978-1-4012-0220-0.
Cover art by Ed McGuinness and Dexter Vines. All covers colored by Dave Stewart.